# HARD TIMES

THE GARLAND DICKENS BIBLIOGRAPHIES
(General Editor: Duane DeVries)
Vol. 3

GARLAND REFERENCE LIBRARY
OF THE HUMANITIES
Vol. 515

*The Garland*
*Dickens Bibliographies*

Duane DeVries
*General Editor*

*Our Mutual Friend*
compiled by Joel J. Brattin
and Bert G. Hornback

*David Copperfield*
compiled by Richard J. Dunn

*Hard Times*
compiled by Sylvia Manning

# HARD TIMES
## An Annotated Bibliography

Sylvia Manning

GARLAND PUBLISHING, INC. • NEW YORK & LONDON
1984

**Library of Congress Cataloging in Publication Data**

Manning, Sylvia Bank, 1943–
  Hard times.

  (The Garland Dickens bibliographies ; v. 3)
(Garland reference library of the humanities ; v. 515)
  Includes indexes.
  1. Dickens, Charles, 1812–1870.  Hard times—
Bibliography.  I. Title.  II. Series.  III. Series:
Garland reference library of the humanities ; v. 515.
Z8230.M36  1984  [PR4561]  016.823′8  84-45402
ISBN 0-8240-8895-6 (alk. paper)

Printed on acid-free, 250-year-life paper
Manufactured in the United States of America

# CONTENTS

Preface                                                             vii
Abbreviations                                                        xi
Introduction                                                       xiii
Acknowledgments                                                   xxiii

   I.   In Progress                                                   3
  II.   Commentary on the Text                                       7
 III.   Other Dickens Works Bearing on
        **Hard Times**                                               10
  IV.   Major Editions During Dickens's Lifetime                    13
   V.   Subsequent Editions Containing New Introductory
        or Textual Matter                                            16
  VI.   Adaptations for Stage, Screen, Radio, and
        Television
              Chronological Listing                                  22
              Commentary                                             26
 VII.   Parody; Musical Settings                                     31
VIII.   Illustrations                                                33
  IX.   Reviews                                                      37
   X.   Reception and Remarks by Dickens's
        Contemporaries                                               43
  XI.   Later Commentary and Criticism                               52
 XII.   Handbooks; Texts, Guides, and Commentary
        for Schools                                                 246
XIII.   Selected Bibliography                                       257

Index of Proper Names                                              263
Subject Index                                                      287

v

# PREFACE

There are certain hypotheses that one would think could be proved on a purely theoretical basis and remain thereafter invulnerable to empirical disproof. With such an assumption, I limited the range of this bibliography from the 1854 publication of **Hard Times** to the end of 1982 and imagined that the number of written works in English referring to **Hard Times** and published during that period would, by the laws of material things, be finite. On the basis of experience, I no longer believe that this is so. Although I have no hypothesis to account for the contrary state of affairs that appears to prevail, I am willing to venture no more than that I have tried to make this bibliography complete within the limits defined below, and that I am relatively certain that I have failed. The limits at least contain the possible scope of failure.

The first limit is a matter of language. This bibliography purports to list and describe only works published in English and mainly in Great Britain, the United States, and Canada, largely because a major bibliography of works on Dickens in other languages is in preparation under the editorship of Ada Nisbet, but also because reliable bibliographies in other languages can be prepared only by speakers of those languages working, usually, from within those countries. The latter condition holds for works published in English but in other countries. There are, however, exceptions to this limit. I have included a number of works in English published in countries such as India, Japan, and South Africa. I have also included several works in French, and a few in German. The decision to do so may have been influenced in some degree by the old graduate-school habit of expecting to read criticism in these languages. But there are better reasons too. The works in German included here are available in American university libraries and sometimes include abstracts in English. The works in French are mostly available, but even when they are more difficult to find they have a special relevance arising from the full penetration of English criticism of Dickens, including **Hard Times**, by French critics. One thinks immediately, of course, of Sylvere Monod, who is particularly important to **Hard Times** as the co-editor of the Norton Critical Edition, but students and colleagues of Monod have also made contributions that have entered the English critical dialogue, so that the latter is not complete without them. For **Hard Times**, the most recurrent figure is Anny Sadrin. It seemed foolish to include the works in English by these critics, but not the works in French. Finally, to find and read good essays and then set them aside was too hard.

The exclusion of works in other languages includes an exclusion of translations of the novel, and the latter has been absolute. I have included, however, two works that direct us to the major early criticism and translations in German (922) and Russian (920).

The second limit has been somewhat difficult to define, and inevitably certain decisions as to the application of my definition have been close to arbitrary. The bibliography lists not just books, chapters, essays, articles, and reviews devoted to **Hard Times**, but also short passages and paragraphs on **Hard Times**, and sometimes what are merely significant references to **Hard Times**. It excludes, however, what are merely insignificant references to **Hard Times**. That last boundary is worse than slippery. I have considered a reference insignificant when even the immediate point that is being made has to do with something other than **Hard Times** (for instance, that in **Great Expectations**, as in **Hard Times**, Dickens ...), or when a known fact is being stated briefly, with no particular point being made in regard to **Hard Times** (for instance, that while Dickens was in Boulogne in 1854, he completed **Hard Times**). On the other hand, however, a passing reference may be significant or not depending upon who made it. It is possible that one might regard the very fact that Freud said anything at all about **Hard Times** as more important than what he said. On such grounds, I have included very brief, and often not very illuminating, remarks by writers such as Henry James, Alain, Andre Maurois, Arnold Bennett, Sigmund Freud, and Sean O'Faolain, and by non-specialist critics such as Douglas Bush. Similarly, the reference to **Hard Times** by Octavia Hill is important mainly because it belies the generalization I make in the Introduction to this volume concerning the place of the novel in the years following Dickens's death.

The list of editions during Dickens's lifetime does not include the numerous re-issues of editions or editions of no particular interest. I have defined interest to mean anything published in 1854, anything authorized or revised or in any way supervised by Dickens, and anything including introductory material or illustrations. For a scholar seeking the kind of information as to popularity and profitability that a full list of reprints might offer, this list will not be adequate. Editions of interest only for their illustrations are not included in the lists of editions, lifetime or subsequent, but in the section on illustrations only. Collections of excerpts are not included. Abridged or simplified school editions are included only in the section on Handbooks and School Texts.

A major principle of this bibliography has been to see everything that I included. Where it has been impossible to do so, the entry is so noted. These exceptions cluster almost exclusively in the
section on adaptations for stage, film, and radio. When I have neither
seen the play nor read the text, I have indicated my source for the
listing. Furthermore, because texts are so difficult to come by for the
adaptations, I have treated reviews as commentary rather than simply
listing them as they are listed for critical works (see below), in consideration of the likelihood that these reviews will for many scholars
constitute the only access they will have to the originals.

Discussion of the illustrations of Dickens's works has so far
been confined to the original illustrators; **Hard Times** was published
without illustrations. The list of illustrations included here, ample but
surely not complete, may be of use to scholars who become interested in later illustrations, as acts of interpretation, aids to sales, or
whatever may fall between these poles. The illustrations are annotated lightly or not at all.

Ph.D. dissertations listed in the bibliography include those in
**Dissertation Abstracts** and **Dissertation Abstracts International** the
titles of which suggested relevance to **Hard Times**, dissertations from
Harvard University and the University of Chicago, to which I had direct
access, dissertations from other institutions that do not subscribe to
**DAI** but do lend their library copies on interlibrary loan, and published
dissertations. Omitted are dissertations from universities that neither
contribute to **DAI** nor offer dissertations on interlibrary loan, and to
which I could not travel. Dissertations that have reappeared as books
are usually listed, but the annotation merely refers the reader to the
book listing, even if there has been extensive revision. M.A. dissertations are omitted. Usually, annotation for dissertations is briefer and
more general than for published work.

The book reviews listed in the section on commentary and
criticism are only a sample, with the number of reviews offered
roughly following the significance of the book for **Hard Times** criticism, but only roughly. The section on bibliography does not include
the obvious, basic sources for Victorian fiction: **PMLA, VS, CBEL**, etc.

I have conceived the purpose of the annotations to be to provide in a very limited space as much information as possible about
the substance of the item. Occasionally I have remarked upon the
importance or later influence of a book or essay, and the cross-references provide similar indications to the significance of a work or to its
redundancy. Other forms of assessment, however, I have resisted, for
the most part, keeping in mind as rigorously as I could a distinction
between annotation and review that gives evaluation, judgment, praise,

and argument to the review, to the annotation mere synopsis and precis. At times, such restraint proved beyond my powers, and at those points the reader will find unmistakable snidenesses in tone, a more telling dead-pan summary, or even outright aspersion. In the very great majority of entries, I have left the reader to judge the worthwhileness of reading the work itself by what I have shown of it rather than said about it. This bibliography is not an appraisal of criticism of **Hard Times**, but a compendium; its virtues must lie in comprehensiveness and precision.

-------

The bibliography is divided into thirteen sections: (1) Letters, Number Plans, Manuscript, and Proofs; (2) Commentary on the Text; (3) Other Dickens Works bearing on **Hard Times**; (4) Major Editions during Dickens's Lifetime; (5) Subsequent Editions Containing New Introductory or Textual Material; (6) Adaptations for Stage, Screen, Radio, and Television; (7) Parody and Musical Settings; (8) Illustrations; (9) Reviews; (10) Reception and Remarks by Dickens's Contemporaries; (11) Later Commentary and Criticism; (12) Handbooks; Texts, Guides, and Commentary for Schools; and (13) Selected Bibliography. Sections (2), (3), (7), (8), (10), (11), (12), and (13) are arranged alphabetically, by author. Sections (1), (4), (5), and (9) are arranged chronologically. Section (6) is divided into a chronological arrangement of works followed by an alphabetical arrangement of commentary. The items are numbered consecutively across all thirteen sections. The distinction between "remarks by Dickens's contemporaries" and "later commentary" is based on date of publication: up to or after 1870, except for Forster's **Life**, which is counted as "contemporary." Dissertations are included in the same fashion as books and essays. Cross-references between items are indicated by item numbers in parentheses and attempt to trace major debates and to indicate direct responses, marked differences, or other curious relationships, but offer no substitute for the indexes of proper names and subjects.

-------

A final apology: this book has been set on a printing device that does not provide foreign accents; the accents are therefore, unfortunately, omitted.

# ABBREVIATIONS

| | |
|---|---|
| BBN | British Book News |
| BJRL | Bulletin of the John Rylands University Library |
| CE | College English |
| CEA | CEA Critic: An Official Journal of the College English Association |
| CL | Comparative Literature |
| CritQ | Critical Quarterly |
| DA | Dissertation Abstracts |
| DAI | Dissertation Abstracts International |
| DS | Dickens Studies |
| DSA | Dickens Studies Annual |
| DSN | Dickens Studies Newsletter |
| EA | Etudes Anglaises |
| E&S | Essays and Studies |
| EC | Essays in Criticism |
| EJ | English Journal |
| ELH | Journal of English Literary History |
| ELN | English Language Notes |
| ES | English Studies |
| JEGP | Journal of English and Germanic Philology |
| JNT | Journal of Narrative Technique |
| LJ | Library Journal |
| MLN | Modern Language Notes |
| MLQ | Modern Language Quarterly |
| MLR | Modern Language Review |
| N&Q | Notes and Queries |
| NewR | New Republic |
| NS | New Statesman |
| NYRB | New York Review of Books |
| ParR | Partisan Review |
| PMLA | PMLA: Publications of the Modern Language Association |
| PQ | Philological Quarterly |
| REL | Review of English Literature |
| RES | Review of English Studies |
| SEL | Studies in English Literature, 1500-1900 |
| SNNTS | Studies in the Novel, North Texas State University |
| SouthernR | Southern Review |

| | |
|---|---|
| TLS | [London] Times Literary Supplement |
| TSLL | Texas Studies in Language and Literature |
| UTQ | University of Toronto Quarterly |
| VN | Victorian Newsletter |
| VPN | Victorian Periodicals Newsletter |
| VQR | Virginia Quarterly Review |
| VS | Victorian Studies |
| YR | Yale Review |

# INTRODUCTION

The history of **Hard Times** criticism is a tale with a moral.

The story begins with the early reception. For this part, there are two variants: in one, the novel was immensely successful, in the other it was a failure from the start. The usual measure of success is the effect on the sales of **Household Words** once the novel had established itself there, which either doubled, if you take Forster's broad phrase (133), or quadrupled, if you follow Buckler's more precise accounting (234). For the argument for failure, the major evidence is the reviews, which found **Hard Times** lacking in humor, crudely plotted, crippled by caricatures, divided in interest, misguided in its satire, misinformed in its politics, and ignorant in its philosophy. (Usually no one critic found all these faults, but Mrs. Oliphant [122] and Edwin Whipple [155] came pretty close.) This hypothesis of failure is supported in some degree by Patten's report of the sales of the first volume edition (664), which by June 1855 were already behind back orders of the three preceding novels and even of **A Child's History of England**.

Early success or early failure, it seems certain that **Hard Times** barely participated in the popular revival of Dickens's work after his death. The critics of the late nineteenth and early twentieth centuries adopted a tactic of neglect, which by and large replaced the earlier attacks. David Masson may have pioneered this technique in his **British Novelists and Their Styles** (1859), where in a long section on Dickens and Thackeray he followed the fiction from **Dombey and Son** to **Little Dorrit** but scrupulously avoided **Hard Times**, even in a section on Novels of Purpose. R.A. Hammond, in **The Life and Writings of Charles Dickens: A Memorial Volume**, published in Toronto in 1871 (reprinted New York: Haskell, 1972), told his readers that "**Little Dorrit** followed **Bleak House**" (p. 286). Charles and Mary Cowden Clark's **Recollections of Writers** (New York: Scribners, 1878) referred to the publication of **Bleak House** and **Little Dorrit**, but omitted that of **Hard Times**. In 1881, **The Life of Charles Dickens** in Haughton's Popular Illustrated Biographies (London) listed **Hard Times** among the novels following **Dombey and Son**, but without comment. More remarkable in the same year was Albert Canning's **Philosophy of Charles Dickens** (London: Smith, Elder): this book had a chapter on each of **Sketches by Boz, Pickwick Papers, Oliver Twist, Nicholas Nickleby, The Old Curiosity Shop, Barnaby Rudge, Martin Chuzzlewit, A Christmas Carol, Dombey and Son, David Copperfield, Bleak House**, and **Edward Drood**; at the head of the **Drood** chapter, Canning mentioned **Little Dorrit, Our Mutual Friend, A Tale of Two Cities, Great Expectations**, and **The Uncommercial Traveller**, but apparently simply forgets **Hard Times**. Kitton did not forget **Hard Times** when he wrote **The Novels of Charles Dickens** (London: Elliot Stock, 1897), but deliberately relegated it to **The Minor Writings of Charles Dickens** (532). Similarly, John Eckel included **Hard Times** in his **First Editions of the Writings of Charles Dickens** (918) not in the first section, "The Important Novels," but in the second, "The Secondary Books," where it appears along with works such as **Sunday Under Three Heads**, the various **Sketches, American Notes**, the Christmas Stories, **Pictures from Italy, A Child's History of England**, and **The Uncommercial Traveller**.

Other notable exclusions were Percy Russell, **A Guide to British and American Novels** (London: Digby, Long, 1894), even in a section on "Novels of Business Life"; Edmund Gosse, **A Short History of Modern English Literature** (New York: Appleton, 1898); Robert Allbut, **Rambles in Dickens' Land** (London: Freemantle, 1899); William Frewen Lord, **The Mirror of the Century** (London: John Lane, The Bodley Head, 1906); William J. Long, **English Literature: A Text-Book for Schools** (London: Ginn, 1909); William Glyde Wilkins, **First and Early American Editions of the Works of Charles Dickens** (Cedar Rapids, Iowa: privately printed, 1910), which does include works such as **Memoirs of Joseph Grimaldi** and **Hunted Down**; T.H. Brown, **Charles Dickens, His Life and Work** (London, A.H. Stockwell, 1923); Sir Arthur Quiller-Couch, **Charles Dickens and Other Victorians** (Cambridge: Cambridge Univ. Press, 1925), except in a brief reference to its possibly having been influenced by Mrs. Gaskell's **Ruth**; and May L. Becker, **Introducing Charles Dickens** (New York: Dodd, Mead, 1940). Owen Ellison, in **Charles Dickens, Novelist** (London: Sisley's, 1908), mentioned **Hard Times** briefly in a notice of the Dickens family's summer holiday in Boulogne in 1854, but omitted it from the list of fourteen "Principal Novels" at the end of his text. Amy Steedman similarly omitted this novel from her list of works after **A Christmas Carol** in **Dickens For Boys and Girls** (London: T.C. & E.C. Jack, 1910). Francis H. Stoddard included in **The Evolution of The English Novel** (New York: Macmillan, 1900) a chapter on "The Novel of Purpose" that cited **Nickleby, Chuzzlewit**, and **Bleak House**, but not **Hard Times**. James C. Watt's **Great Novelists** (Edinburgh: MacNiven & Wallace, 1880) simply listed **Hard Times** as coming after (sic) **Little Dorrit**. William Lyon Phelps also ignored it in **The Advance of the English Novel** (New York: Dodd,

Mead, 1917), giving the honor of "poorest novel" to **Little Dorrit**, followed by **A Tale of Two Cities**. Even essays on Dickens and education could forget **Hard Times**: Mabel Ellery Adams's "Dickens's Influence on Education," **Dickensian**, 26 (1930), 177-81, is an effusion that mentions many children and all schools in Dickens, except those in **Hard Times**; and as late as 1952, Eleanor Graham left **Hard Times** entirely out of **The Story of Charles Dickens** (London: Methuen), not even mentioning it in the chapter on schools.

Perhaps the most charming piece of evidence of neglect comes from the one group that neglected nothing. In the early twenties, the Dickens Fellowship decided to adopt a procedure of examining closely a novel a year, taking the novels from last to first. By rotation, therefore, **Hard Times** became the Book for 1928, and Walter Dexter was moved to write in "When Found--" for the **Dickensian**, 23 (1927), 221: "According to the decision of the Conference--following the suggestion, adopted some years ago, to take the novels in the reverse order to that in which they were written, **Hard Times** becomes the book for the following season, 1928-29. It was urged, on the part of some delegates, that **Hard Times** should be missed, as it was 'uninteresting.' True, it has not the wide appeal of the others, but I feel confident, with a better knowledge of it, we shall find more in it than we anticipate."

Of course there were exceptions, most notably perhaps Ruskin (150) and Shaw (738), but the neglect was certainly pervasive enough to make Leavis's aura of discovery in his "Analytic Note" (553) not entirely factitious ("If there exists anywhere an appreciation, or even an acclaiming reference [to **Hard Times**], I have missed it.") And it is this essay, its authorial self-regard notwithstanding, that makes 1952 a "late" date for Eleanor Graham, or anyone, simply to forget **Hard Times** in a connection in which the novel is clearly germane. For 1947/48 marks as striking an about-face as the history of literary criticism may have to offer. With the publication of Leavis's "Analytic Note," first in **Scrutiny** in 1947 and then as an appendix to **The Great Tradition** in 1948, the fortunes of **Hard Times** are utterly changed. A critical beauty is born.

There remain, inevitably, perhaps also mercifully, some diehards, led by John Holloway (471), who insist that no clothing will render the emperor anything other than a fraud. On the other side, there are the Leavisite sycophants, whose essays begin with general remarks to the effect that Leavis's superb work has told us once and for all everything we need to know about **Hard Times** but that perhaps a small addition, a bit of polish, a footnote as it were, might be added--wherefore the following comments. But at the stronger center, a new branch of **Hard Times** criticism begins to grow. Rendered legitimate, taken seriously at last, the novel appears to offer an abundance of riches. Its place in the canon is no longer in doubt: it stands clearly where Lionel Stevenson put it, albeit without much admiration for it, in the middle of the trio of "Dark Novels" (774). And in the subsequent decades, the center of the dark sequence is a good position from which to gain attention. By 1972, one critic, Thomas J. Roberts (702), includes **Hard Times**, and of Dickens's works, only **Hard Times**, in the rank of **Hamlet, Tristam Shandy**, Wordsworth's Immortality Ode, **Modern Love**, and **Lady Chatterley's Lover**, as works that critics readily admit to be great.

Some readers still miss in **Hard Times**, dark novel or not, the quality of humor that seems fundamental to Dickensian "life." Others find the "blemish" of Stephen and the union more serious than Leavis allows, though still others are able to argue even this away, and only a few find it a canker that ruins the whole. Above all, no one ignores **Hard Times**. On the contrary, in addition to a healthy run of articles devoted to it and to its regular appearance in monographs on Dickens, **Hard Times** comes increasingly to enjoy the (often tacit) honor of being selected for discussion in a book that treats only one Dickens novel (Boulton [212], Goldknopf [426], Jameson [491], Lodge [576]). K.J. Fielding, Philip Collins, and Robin Gilmour present their illuminating research in historical matters relating to **Hard Times** without apology or explanation. Sylvere Monod, with charming and self-conscious candor, gradually decides that if in some sense **Hard Times** remains undickensian, it will still repay his remarkable effort, shared with George Ford, in preparing its Norton Critical Edition. No monograph on the work of Dickens or the later Dickens, brilliant or plodding, omits it. High school teachers find it among the most, or simply the most, teachable of Dickens's novels, and even of Victorian novels. **Hard Times** is examined in the context of novels of social purpose, of condition-of-England novels, of education, of industrialism, of imagination and reason, of serialization, of dramatic interpretation, of satire, of genres and mixed genres, of narrative structure, of verbal style, of patterns of imagery, of dialect, of Mrs. Gaskell, Wilkie Collins, and Conrad, of clowns, and more. In 1979, Peter Abbs suggests **Hard Times** as the novel to include in a short "contextual" course on industrial culture (**Reclamations: Essays on Culture, Mass-Culture, and the Curriculum**, London: Heinemann, 1979, p. 83). By 1972, Peter Brooker (223) selects it as the single work of fiction he uses, both playfully and seriously, to consider the likely future of post-structuralism in the English classroom (the ongoing interest of Marxist criticism in **Hard Times** seems to have been hardly significant in this choice).

**Hard Times** penetrates our literary vocabulary, so that its features can be used in shorthand. In the early period, only Gradgrind achieved this status. But in 1961 Louis Mumford could title chapter 15 of **The City in History** "Paleotechnic Paradise: Coketown," without explanation. In the **TLS** for 26 July 1974, a reviewer of Isobel Murray's edition of **The Picture of Dorian Gray** could write off-hand of "the conventions of reticence in the Victorian novel, from Louisa Gradgrind's phallic smokestacks to Dorothea's stroll through the art gallery" (that **Hard Times** is not yet **Middlemarch** is clear from the fact that Louisa needs identification by surname, but Dorothea does not). In 1957, concerned primarily with the image of the schoolteacher, Asher Tropp had warned that M'Choakumchild "should not be taken as a true picture of the college-trained teacher in this period" except in its indication of the teachers' "almost fierce desire to acquire knowledge" (809). But in 1964, also concerned primarily with schools, John R. Reed set M'Choakumchild in a tradition of literary criticism of education that has Orwell and Huxley as its twentieth-century end-points: "**Hard Times, Nicholas Nickleby,** and **David Copperfield** all include defenses of individuality against abusive authority, and, in this respect, resemble the criticism of twentieth-century writers." Another decade later, a much briefer reference to M'Choakumchild by E.G. West (837) indicates again how the Gradgrind/M'Choakumchild "School" has become an accepted archetype rather than a subject of dispute about journalistic accuracy.

What did Leavis do? Or is the "Leavis" more significant than the "do"? That the effect of his essay owed something to his personal influence is clear. Leavis declared that **Hard Times** was a moral fable and that a moral fable is a work in which "the intention is peculiarly insistent, so that the representative significance of everything in the fable--character, episode, and so on--is immediately apparent as we read." Hence we must see **Hard Times** as "a novel in which all the actions, incidents, and motives, which are grouped into a plot, are so fashioned that the story, as a whole, tends toward the accomplishment of some definite result." The latter quotation is not from Leavis or someone following Leavis on **Hard Times,** but from Francis Stoddard, noted above, who offered this definition of the "Novel of Purpose" (p. 153) and applied it not to **Hard Times** but to **Nicholas Nickleby, Martin Chuzzlewit,** and **Bleak House.** One may well doubt, however, whether even if Stoddard had liked Dickens in this mode (and he didn't) and had included **Hard Times** among the novels so described, his insight would have changed the critical fortunes of **Hard Times.** The first reviewers had made similar remarks on the style, but with the opposite valuation. For instance, in April 1855 **Blackwood's** described the story as like "an Eastern apologue" and stated that "fiction breaks down when it is bound within these certain limits, and compelled to prove and to substantiate a theory" (122). When Leavis turned the same generic redefinition to a celebration of this novel, people listened to him because Leavis was Leavis. And probably some people disagreed with him because Leavis was Leavis.

Something too was owing to the characteristics of style that made Leavis so powerful in the first place: displayed in full in his essay on **Hard Times** are the uncanny instinct for quotation, the brilliant close analysis of passages, the magisterial assertions of "genius," "serious," "poetic," "Laurentian." Most important, though, seems to have been the re-classification of genre, the assertion that the book is not a "novel" but a "moral fable." As a moral fable, the book could not be called to account for its relationship to its social and political environment, or for its failure to meet novelistic expectations. It is in the first regard that Leavis's fable differed from others'. If indeed no program like Mr. Gradgrind's educational system ever existed in England, as one contemporary reviewer asserted; if the portrayal of industrialism was critically dependent upon Dickens's vast ignorance of the North; if Dickens's fear of statistical surveys was reactionary and his attack on Parliamentary efforts at social legislation unfair; if Bounderby was an honest caricature and Slackbridge a disingenuous one; if Louisa's arraignment of her father was the worst of melodrama and Sissy's scolding of Harthouse yet more implausible--all these things, and others, need not matter, because this novel is different, different from other Dickens novels and different from most other novels generally (there has been some fruitful comparison with novels of related genres, such as the romance and the dystopia).

It was not merely that Leavis freed **Hard Times** from the constraints of conceptions of genre that may create arbitrary and detrimental boundaries to our range of literary appreciation. It was also, I think, that his trumpet sounded just as criticism was beginning to travel its long journey away from any history outside the realm of language and literature. **Hard Times** benefitted from the climate of the New Criticism because in that climate readers, or at least critics and teachers, were less concerned about the cavalier treatment of "social reality" in this novel that no research could fully gainsay. Probably it was the teachers, more than the critics, who by 1968 pushed the sales of **Hard Times** up to fourth among Dickens novels in the U.S. and third in England--see Ford (388). And it is plausible too that the popularity of **Hard Times** for school assignments was in part due simply to its relative brevity.

Leavis's limited entry into the circle of Dickens's admirers also coincided with certain changes in taste. It is curious that the one part of **Hard Times** that even Leavis could not swallow comfortably and that continues to distress the novel's most ardent defenders is the portrayal of Stephen and Rachael, a portrayal that to some of the early critics was the major, or only, strength of the story. Although Rachael has virtually no modern admirers, some degree of difference over Stephen persists. Robert Barnard (186) represents the more usual response in 1974: "The laboured allegory of his end in the 'Old Hell' shaft, squeezed so dry of all emotional impact by the dreary, obvious moralising as Stephen approaches the 'God of the poor,' is feeble beyond belief." In contrast, Geoffrey Thurley (803) writes two years later: "The alienation motif is beautifully consummated in Stephen's death: the accident by which he falls down a disused pit-shaft demonstrates the mastery Dickens had already achieved over the use of symbolic action." But these represent minor divisions (there are others) within a set of larger curves. Perhaps the most interesting is the way in which what the earlier critics saw as bareness or sparsity or cramping became control, freedom from redundancy, leanness in an age that shuns rotundity. The brevity that was a necessity in the face of students who resist reading was thus at the same time aesthetically preferred.

Short-run changes in political climate seem to have had less direct bearing on the fortunes of **Hard Times**, but one can trace a broad movement in its reception from the Left. Through its history this novel appears to have functioned as something of a piece of political litmus paper. For example, here are two writers treating **Hard Times** in the context of other social-reform novels of the period (by Mrs. Gaskell, Disraeli, Kingsley). Arthur Pollard (678), writing in 1961, says that all these novels are motivated by "an intense sympathy with suffering mankind and a strong desire for the amelioration of the human condition. The evil thing that separates, the baffling isolation of man from his fellow men, is what all these novels attack." Pollard represents what is essentially the majority view, his analysis of the novel explicitly follows Leavis. In contrast, P.J. Keating (515) argues that the industrial novelists could see the industrial worker only as "a class representative," and that the association of his jobs with "symbols of power and strength--the furnace, engine, and factory--added a further frightening element to his mass identity. It was his suffering to which novelists drew attention, but his potential power that was their true concern. The possibility that the workers might have ideas of their own about the uses to which this power could be put was discountenanced by the novelists." In this context, Dickens's treatment of the union appears typical, not singularly benighted. To some degree it is true that Keating's perspective is more typically post-mid-sixties (the book was published in 1971), and Pollard's truer to a fifties' liberalism, and other critics of the seventies have followed Keating's more radical line. But such antithetical interpretations coexist, albeit in varying ratios, throughout the last century and a quarter. With intellectual certainty and moral conviction, critics have praised the novel for its championship of the worker and decried its bias against the unions, have taken it for a stern warning against the menace of socialism and for an attack on bourgeois capitalism, and have celebrated its foresight in predicting the crippling of an economy through union power or the self-destruction of industrialism through greed. The significant trends are the changes in leftist evaluation, accompanied by the growing foothold of leftist criticism in the academy. Whereas Macaulay found "sullen socialism" in the novel and Ruskin and Shaw found social truth, Leavis had to apologize for--and then to skirt--the account of Slackbridge. Later leftist or liberal critics would amplify the apology, or refuse to render it. But these interpretive revisions of the politics of **Hard Times** track a different curve from that of its critical history. In the post-Leavisian heyday, political interpretation anywhere on the spectrum was less important than the issues of art, imagination, education, and love.

An Aesopian moral may be the most obvious act of interpretation performed upon a story. The story of **Hard Times** criticism is as indeterminate as one could desire. It may be read as an example of the larger volatility and the smaller self-contradictoriness of the critical enterprise. And a closer look at the early reviews and other contemporary comments may suggest that not only do we blandly, flatly, and unsystematically contradict each other, but in disconcerting degree we also frequently, and no doubt unconsciously, repeat the arguments of earlier generations, albeit translated into newer modes of discourse. On the other hand, our moral may have an utterly different tonality: we may turn it to a celebration of the openness and flexibility of the critical enterprise, or the powerfully heuristic ferment that can be started by one strong and radical mind.

Either way, the story also cautions us that it is not yet done. And certainly the time seems ripe for another major shift, though one not necessarily heralded as clearly as the first was. The development to watch, I think, will be how the new historicism reintegrates the questions that for Dickens's contemporaries were the ones that really mattered. Much or most of the detail needed has been forthcoming in the investigations by Baird, Bartrip, Brantlinger, Collins, Fielding, Gilmour and others concerned primarily with the specific tangents, such as the critics who have steadily undermined the facile equations of the Gradgrinds, father and daughter, with the Mills. In 1981, Igor Webb's ideological analysis in **From Custom to Capital** (832) brought fresh air to the crowded and stuffy room of the capital/labor issue, and for Nancy Armstrong (170), writing in 1982, the wider political context of the later nineteenth century was a principal focus. Lucien Pothet's archetypal study in 1979 (682) was delightfully new, but it seems nonetheless safe to say that the possibilities for study of **Hard Times** in purely literary and aesthetic dimensions, in the modes of the past forty-five years, have been exhausted. The historicism that preceded these modes, beginning as it did from simple assumptions of realism, was apparently helpless to assist appreciation or understanding of the novel. One might even argue that the early critics who liked the novel did so because the second term in their matrix of realism was not a perception of the "world" but a clearly held ideology--and indeed opposing critics said as much of Ruskin and Shaw. To put it crudely, Shaw did not find **Hard Times** great because it mirrors a hideous reality but because it says that reality is hideous. As both our understanding of that reality and our conception of how literature relates to it evolve, the challenge for criticism of **Hard Times** will be to join in a richer blend the two halves that its history has sundered.

# ACKNOWLEDGMENTS

This bibliography could not have been prepared without access to several libraries, to all of which I am grateful: Doheny Memorial Library at the University of Southern California; the University Research Library and the William Andrews Clark Memorial Library of the University of California, Los Angeles; the Henry E. Huntington Library, San Marino, California; the British Library, Bloomsbury; the library of the Victoria and Albert Museum, South Kensington; the library of the Dickens House, London; the Beinecke Library at Yale University; the Bodleian at Oxford; the Bibliotheque Nationale in Paris; the library of the University of Chicago. The inter-library loan staff at the University of Southern California were particularly helpful, and patient. I am also grateful to the University of Southern California for assistance through its Faculty Research and Innovation Fund, which made possible my work abroad. Tom King and Jack Roberson of USC's University Computing Center solved most of the unpredictable problems that arose during text and copy preparation. Les Perelman also helped with the quirks of the computer and he collected and reviewed all the Harvard University dissertations listed. Richard Dunn made dozens of decisions for his **David Copperfield: An Annotated Bibliography** that saved me all thought in like decisions for this book. Peter, Bruce, and Jason Manning offered steady moral support. Last and first, I wish to thank Jan Gorak, who spent three semesters as a research assistant in the first pass of collecting references; no one deserves more his present freedom of having launched his own career.

# HARD TIMES

An Annotated Bibliography

# I

# IN PROGRESS

## Dickens's Letters Concerning the Novel
## His Number Plans, Manuscript, and Proofs

1.  Dexter, Walter, ed. **The Letters of Charles Dickens.** 3 vols.
    Bloomsbury: Nonesuch, 1938. Vols. 2 and 3, passim.

    The powers of hindsight have found epistolary material rel-
    ovant to **Hard Times** as far back as 29 December 1838, when
    Dickens expressed to Edward Fitzgerald an intention to strike
    the "heaviest blow" in his power on behalf of the factory work-
    ers he had observed in Manchester. The letters that bear more
    certainly on this novel are in volume 2 of the sequence. On 27
    July 1853 Dickens wrote to W.H. Wills of his intention to write
    "Frauds on the Fairies" (see [14]), and on 18 September he sent
    a copy of the essay to Angela Burdett-Coutts; his immediate
    concern for "fancy" and children is clear. His favorable opinion
    of the working people in Birmingham is apparent in a letter to
    Miss Coutts written from Italy, 27 November 1853, and on 16
    January 1854 he reported to W.F. de Cerjat on the state of the
    Preston strike. Then on 20 January 1854 came the famous let-
    ter to Forster with its fourteen titles, three of which Dickens
    found very good, and his request that Forster pick his favorites
    (see Forster [133]). On the 23rd Dickens announced his new
    start to Miss Coutts (see Johnson [2]), and on the 29th the
    failure of his trip to Preston as quarry for the novel, to Forster.
    In February he complained to Forster, "The difficulty of the
    space is CRUSHING," and on the 20th he wrote to Mark Lemon
    for help with "slang terms among the tumbler and circus peo-
    ple." On 11 March he wrote at length to Peter Cunningham to
    insist that the location of the story was not Preston (see [131]).
    In a letter to Charles Knight, 17 March, he argued that a point
    he had "been working upon" in **Hard Times** was that the "Eng-
    lish are ... the hardest-worked people on whom the sun shines,"

and so should be allowed their "wretched intervals of pleasure."
A letter to Wills on 18 April suggested again Dickens's sense of
compression as he worked on this novel ("planning and planning ... out of materials for I don't know how long a story"). On
21 April he assured Mrs. Gaskell that he had "no intention of
striking" (see [135]). In June he suggested to Mark Lemon that
they go "to the public by the Thames where those performing
dogs go at night.... I may make something out of such an ex-
pedition ...." Letters from Boulogne later in the month and in
July suggest again the pressure of this novel, but on the 13th
he wrote to Carlyle requesting permission to dedicate it to him:
"It contains what I do devoutly hope will shake some people in
a terrible mistake of these days, when so presented. I know it
contains nothing in which you do not think with me ..." (this
letter appeared in the **Dickensian**, 12 [1916], 21). The next day
he expressed to Forster his hope that he had done "a good
thing with Stephen, taking his story as a whole," though the
effort for this novel has left him "three parts mad, and the
fourth delirious." Two days later he announced to Wills that he
had completed the novel that morning. Letters in the months
following spoke of his lassitude, or addressed business matters
such as advertising for the volume edition and relations between **Hard Times** and **North and South** in **Household Words**.
The lassitude is summed up most strongly in a letter to Mrs.
Richard Watson, 1 November: "Why I found myself so 'used up'
after Hard Times I scarcely know, perhaps because I intended
to do nothing in that way for a year, when the idea laid hold of
me by the throat in a very violent manner, and because the
compression and close condensation necessary for that disjointed form of publication gave me perpetual trouble. But I
really was tired."

In January 1855 Dickens wrote his letter of reassurance to
Charles Knight (144). There are not many later references. In
September 1866 he advised Charles Fechter that "When I did
Hard Times I called the scene Coketown. Everybody knew what
was meant, but every cotton-spinning town said it was the
other cotton-spinning town," and suggested similar discretion
to Fechter. On 29 March 1870, he quoted Mr. Sleary to Henry
Fielding Dickens.

Further letters with reference to **Hard Times** will be included in
the forthcoming Pilgrim edition. A letter to Wills, 25 January
1854, asked for help: "I want (for the story I am trying to ham-
mer out) the Education Board's series [?] of questions for the
examination of **teachers** in schools. Will you get it." (This letter is in the Huntington Library in San Marino, California.) And

to Henry Cole on 17 July 1854, Dickens explained: "I often say to Mr. Gradgrind that there is reason and good intention in much that he does--in fact, in all that he does--but that he over-does it. Perhaps by dint of his going his way and my going mine, we shall meet at last."

Many of these letters are most readily available in the Norton Critical Edition (45).

2.    Johnson, Edgar, ed.  **The Heart of Charles Dickens, as Revealed in His Letters to Angela Burdett-Coutts**. Boston: Little, Drown, 1952   xiv, 415 pp.  Also pub. as **Letters from Charles Dickens to Angela Burdett Coutts**. London: Jonathan Cape, 1953.

In his introduction to section III, "Vast Edges Drear (1854-1870)," Johnson says that "**Hard Times** unmasks the cold-hearted rationalizations of political economy and the greed that used economic 'laws' to justify a callous exploitation of the laboring classes." The letters include a number of references to the novel. On 23 January 1854 Dickens writes: "I have fallen to work again. My purpose is among the mighty secrets of the world at present; but there is such a fixed idea on the part of my printers and co-partners in Household Words, that a story by me, continued from week to week, would make some unheard-of effect with it, that I am going to write one. It will be as long as five Nos of Bleak House, and will be five months in progress. The first written page now stares at me from under this sheet of note paper. The main idea of it, is one on which you and I and Mrs Brown have often spoken; and I know it will interest you as a purpose." Johnson's footnote offers further details on the publication agreement and identifies the "purpose" as the long intended "heaviest blow" against industrialism and its exploitativeness. He comments on Dickens's fusion of this indictment with the portrayal of "utilitarian educational practice" to produce "a morality drama, piercing with prophetic denunciation to the very core of the laissez-faire view of human existence." On 11 July 1856 Dickens mentions "the Common Things" and Shuttleworth's preference for "knowledge of Watersheds and Pre Adamite vegetation," which Johnson relates to the satire on M'Choakumchild. Other references to **Hard Times** are of less interest. These letters are from the Pierpont Morgan Library, New York.

3.     Dickens, Charles. **Hard Times.** Bound manuscript and number
       plans. [1854]. In the Forster Collection at the Library of the
       Victoria and Albert Museum, London. Available on microfilm:
       **Manuscripts of the Works of Charles Dickens from the For-
       ster Collection in the Victoria and Albert Museum, London.,**
       London: Micro Methods, 1970. Reel 6.

       The "mems" or number plans are on six folded sheets,
       written on one side. The ms. itself is divided into five seg-
       ments: "No I" is 30 sheets, II is 32, III is 30, IV is 31, V and VI
       are 45. Most of the sheets are written on one side only, but
       occasionally there are a few lines on the verso. The numbers
       (I, II, etc.) are at the top of the first sheet and on the verso of
       the last sheet for each segment. Book I, chapter i is heavily
       corrected (see Tick [804]), but so are other passages.

4.     -------. **Hard Times.** Corrected proofs (1854). In the Forster
       Collection of the Library of the Victoria and Albert Museum,
       London. Available on microfilm: **Annotated Proofs of the
       Works of Charles Dickens from the Forster Collection in the
       Victoria and Albert Museum, London.** London: Micro Methods,
       1969. Reel 3.

       Appears to be comprised of two sets of proof sheets.
       Through chapter xxvi the proof is in single-column galley;
       starting at chapter xxvii it is double-column page proof; at
       chapter xxxi it reverts to the single-column galley. The dis-
       cussion of Rachael's little sister and its footnote reference to
       "Ground in the Mill" are still in this set. Louisa's tears "like the
       blessed rain" at the end of chapter xxix are marked for deletion.
       See Bartrip (6), Monod (10), and Woodings (11).

5.     -------. **Hard Times.** Page proofs. In the Dexter Collection
       of the British Library, London.

       Eleven leaves of page proofs.

## II

# COMMENTARY ON THE TEXT

### Scholarship Concerning Publication and
### Textual Matters

6.  Bartrip, Peter W.J. "**Household Words** and the Factory Accident Controversy." **Dickensian**, 75 (1979), 17-29.

    Elucidates the factory accident controversy in the context of Dickens's interest in factory legislation and especially in legislation concerning factory accidents. Bartrip reviews the manuscript and proof passage, later cancelled, containing Stephen's reference to the mangling of Rachael's sister in a machine, Rachael's reply ("Let such things be"), and Stephen's consequent promise. As to why Dickens cancelled the passage, Bartrip offers the speculation that perhaps Dickens "considered factual treatment of the accident problem to be preferable to a passing reference in a work of fiction." Compare Butwin (241), Monod (10), and Woodings (11).

7.  "Charles Dickens's Manuscripts." **Chambers's Journal**, 10 November 1877, pp. 710-12. Rpt. in **Eclectic Magazine**, January 1878, pp. 80-82. Also in **Potter's American Monthly**, 10 (1878), 156-58.

    Lists the manuscript of **Hard Times**; indicates that there were many alterations "where we are introduced to the gentleman who wants nothing but 'Facts,'" but that the erasures are too complete to be deciphered.

8.  Dexter, Walter. "The 'Library,' 'Peoples,' and 'Charles Dickens' Editions." **Dickensian**, 40 (1943), 186-87.

    Notes that the original volume edition of **Hard Times** cost five shillings. Describes briefly the two later collected editions, the "Library Edition" and the "Charles Dickens Edition," in which **Hard Times** appeared.

\*      Hill, T.W.

       See William Miller and T.W. Hill (9).


9.     Miller, William, and T.W. Hill.  "Charles Dickens's Manuscripts."
       **Dickensian**, 13 (1917), 181–85.

       Reports that **Hard Times** is the first manuscript written in
       the blue ink that Dickens used thereafter.


10.    Monod, Sylvere.  "Dickens at Work on the Text of **Hard Times**."
       **Dickensian**, 64 (1968), 86–99.

       Offers conclusions arrived at in the preparation of the text
       of **Hard Times** for the Norton Critical Edition (45) which would
       have been inappropriate to include in that volume. Monod sug-
       gests that since the space requirements for the weekly format
       were not as strict as they were for the monthly numbers,
       changes in the text would be more likely due to aesthetic or
       moral intention.  He explains why the extant proofs must be
       neither the first nor the last set and expounds upon various
       changes apparent in manuscript, proofs, and printed editions.
       The difficulty of Dickens's handwriting led to many printer's er-
       rors; Dickens usually corrected them, Monod points out, but of-
       ten did not refer to the manuscript, thus introducing changes.
       When Dickens failed to catch the error, it often persisted until
       1966.   Other errors were Dickens's own.   Monod notes that
       Dickens was excessively conscientious in the "thankless" efforts
       to perfect Sleary's lisp and Stephen's dialect and finds that
       Dickens's work on his own style shows many improvements in
       proof and in the first edition in volume form but few for the
       Charles Dickens edition.  Monod offers several examples of the
       various sorts of changes he describes, argues that the Charles
       Dickens edition should not be considered definitive, and exam-
       ines a series of improvements Dickens obviously made for ar-
       tistic purposes. He describes in detail the cancelled passage
       concerning Stephen's promise to Rachael and speculates on the
       reasons for its cancellation (compare Bartrip [6], Butwin [241],
       and Woodings [11]).


11.    Woodings, R.B.  "A Cancelled Passage in **Hard Times**." **Dicken-
       sian**, 60 (1964), 42–43.

Notes three sizeable changes between the published text and the proof-sheets. The first Woodings sees as probably an excision to avoid crude sentimentality (Louisa's tears upon Sissy's "O lay it here, my dear," III.i). The second is from chapter 10 of "Sowing." The third is the important passage of Stephen's promise to Rachael; Woodings speculates that it was cut either to avoid repetition with "Ground in the Mill" or to save space (compare Bartrip [6], Butwin [241], Monod [10].)

# III

## OTHER DICKENS WORKS
## BEARING ON HARD TIMES

12.  Dickens, Charles. **The Chimes.** London: Chapman & Hall, 1845.
175 pp.

Critics have seen Mr. Filer as a forerunner of Mr. Gradgrind.
The characters share a predilection for fact and figures, but the
latter is a far subtler and more complex portrait. See Hazama
(457) and Pendered (670).

13.  --------. "Full Report of the First Meeting of the Mudfog Association for the Advancement of Everything." **Bentley's Miscellany,** 2 (1837), 397-413. Rpt. in **Sketches by Boz.,** New Oxford Illustrated Dickens. London: Oxford Univ. Press, 1957.

"Section C. -- Statistics" shows an early combination of
satiric attacks on the uses of statistics and on education of
children that fails to recognize the place of fancy, which is
represented by fairy tales. Several members are said to have
"dwelt upon the immense and urgent necessity of storing the
minds of children with nothing but facts and figures."

14.  --------, ed. **Household Words. A Weekly Journal,** 6 (1852),
7 (1853), 8 (1853-54), 9 (1854), 11 (1855), 13 (1856), passim.

In some sense, all of **Household Words** bears upon **Hard
Times.** Listed here are articles that various commentators have
remarked as particularly relevant to issues raised in the novel.
They are arranged chronologically under three heads: Industrialism and Utilitarianism, Education and Art, and Divorce. Attri-
butions follow Anne Lohrli, **Household Words** (Toronto and
Buffalo: Univ. of Toronto Press, 1973).

(1) Industrialism and Utilitarianism. "In and Out of Jail," 7 (May
1853), 241-45, by Dickens, Henry Morley, and W.H. Wills, con-

tains an ironic reference to "The Gospel according to Cocker." "Locked Out," 8 (December 1853), 345-48, by James Lowe, describes Preston during the lock-out. The 'mob-orators" are said to exercise "pernicious sway" over the workers, and the ignorance in which labor is (unwisely) kept is deplored. Dickens's "On Strike," 8 (February 1854), 553-59, opens with the anti-unionist train companion "Mr. Snapper." The Delegates' meeting is described with high praise that includes the chairman's early silencing of "Gruffshaw," and the conclusion from it is that the workers' "mistake is generally an honest one." The essay affirms the unity of class interests and calls for mediation "Ground in the Mill," 9 (April 1854), 224-26, by Morley, discusses graphically factory accidents occuring to both adults and children because the Factory Act fencing requirements have been leniently interpreted to favor the mill-owners. Further articles on factory accidents, all by Morley and cited by Martineau (147), are "Fencing With Humanity," 11 (April 1855), 241-44; "Death's Cyphering Book," 11 (May 1855), 337-41; "Deadly Shafts," 11 (June 1855), 494-95; and "More Grist to the Mill," 11 (July 1855), 605-06. "Our Wicked Mis-Statements," 13 (January 1856), 13-19 (Morley, but see Stone [17]), is a reply to Harriet Martineau's pamphlet attack (147) on the veracity of these **Household Words** articles. "The Manchester Strike," 13 (February 1856), 63-66 (Morley), asserts the identity of class interests, argues that free competition is a good thing but does not work well in the labor market, and calls for greater understanding between master and men. Less directly relevant, but occasionally cited, are Dickens's "To Working Men," 10 (October 1854), 169-70, and Morley's "A Home Question," 10 (November 1854), 292-96. The first calls on working men to take the initiative in demanding decent housing; the middle class will then join them, and thus not only will Parliament be roused to action, but this united effort of the two classes will lead to better mutual understanding. The second continues this theme of public health.

(2) Education and Art. Morley's "A House Full of Horrors," 6 (December 1852), 265-70, is a lampoon of the "Correct Principles of Taste" advocated by the Department of Practical Art in Marlborough House (see Ames [165], Bell [195], and Fielding [376]). "Rational Schools," 6 (December 1852), 337-42, by Morley and Wills, offers a favorable account of the Birkbeck Schools, but ends with a note on the importance of also cultivating children's imaginative faculties and religious principles. "Frauds on the Fairies," 8 (October 1853), 97-100, is Dickens's attack on Cruikshank for moralizing fairy-tales, especially in "an utilitarian age."

(3) Divorce. A series of articles treat the issue of divorce, but unlike Stephen Blackpool's story, they approach the matter from the perspective of the maltreatment of wives and women's deprivation of civil rights. The first of these, which includes a lengthy exemplum about an abused wife, occurs in the same number as chapters ix-x of **Hard Times**, in which Stephen meets his wife. The articles are: "One of Our Legal Fictions," 9 (April 1854), 257-60 (Eliza Lynn); "A Legal Fiction," 11 (July 1855), 598-99 (Wills); "The Marriage Gaolers," 13 (July 1856), 583-85 (Eliza Lynn).

15.    -------. "Postscript." **Our Mutual Friend**. 2 vols. London: Chapman & Hall, 1865, II, 307-09.

In defense of his social criticism, Dickens includes the statement, "My friend Mr. Bounderby could never see any difference between leaving the Coketown 'hands' exactly as they were, and requiring them to be fed with turtle soup and venison out of gold spoons."

16.    Fielding, K.J., ed. **Speeches of Charles Dickens**. Oxford: Clarendon, 1960, pp. 166-68.

The speech "At a Reading of the **Carol**: Birmingham" includes a passage on education of the feelings very close in temper to the educational argument of **Hard Times**. The speech was delivered at the Birmingham Town Hall on 30 December 1853.

17.    Stone, Harry, ed. **Uncollected Writings from Household Words, 1850-1859**. 2 vols. Bloomington and London: Indiana Univ. Press, 1968, II, 485n and 556.

Stone attributes to Dickens a portion of "In and Out of Jail" (14 May 1853, Henry Morley and W.H. Wills) which includes the phrase "the gospel according to Cocker." In "Our Wicked Misstatements" (19 January 1856), written by Dickens with Henry Morley, Stone attributes to Dickens the passage including the sentence "We believe it was Mr. Bounderby who was always going to throw his property into the Atlantic, and we have heard of Miss Martineau's clients being indignant against Mr. Bounderby as a caricature. And yet this looks very like him."

# IV

## MAJOR EDITIONS DURING DICKENS'S LIFETIME

### (Chronological Listing)

18. Dickens, Charles. **Hard Times. Household Words. A Weekly Journal,** 9, nos. 210–229 (1 April 1854 – 12 August 1854).

    **Hard Times** was serialized from 1 April through 12 August 1854, the installment appearing as the leader for each issue. It was divided into 37 untitled chapters; there were no book divisions.

19. ———. "The Bully of Humility." In "Miscellaneous News," **Examiner,** 8 April 1854, p. 220.

    An excerpt of the first description of Bounderby, unremarked except for the citation of author and work. This is the selection that Thackeray first read (see [154]).

20. ———. **Hard Times. The Illustrated New York Journal,** 2 and 3 (1854).

    **Hard Times** was serialized beginning in May 1854 (vol. 2, 201–06) and continuing through September 1854.

21. ———. **Hard Times. For These Times.** London: Bradbury & Evans, 1854. viii, 352 pp.

    This first single-volume edition adds chapter titles and divides the novel into three books of sixteen, twelve, and nine chapters. The books are titled "Sowing," "Reaping," and "Garnering." In this edition, each book has its own title-page. On a separate page at the front, the work is inscribed to Thomas Carlyle.

22.      -------. **Hard Times.** Copyright Edition. Leipzig: Tauchnitz,
         1854. viii, 376 pp.

         This was volume 307 of the Tauchnitz "Collection of British
         Authors." The title-page includes the notice: "This Collection is
         published with copyright for Continental circulation, but all pur-
         chasers are earnestly requested not to introduce the volumes
         into England or into any British Colony." The edition is very
         like the Bradbury and Evans edition: divided into three titled
         books with separately numbered and titled chapters. It includes
         the dedication to Carlyle.

23.      -------. **Hard Times.** New York: Harper, 1854. 101 pp.

         An edition not authorized by Dickens. On the cover it is
         described as "Library of Select Novels, no. 192." It is printed in
         double columns, not divided into books, and without chapter ti-
         tles or dedication.

24.      -------. **Hard Times.** New York: T.L. McElrath, 1854. 108 pp.

         Another unauthorized edition. According to Podeschi (927),
         this edition derives from the typesetting for the periodical pub-
         lication of **Hard Times** in the American issue of **Household
         Words**, also published by T.L. McElrath (Podeschi, p. 135). The
         title-page bears the note: "From Dickens' 'Household Words.'"
         There are no book divisions or chapter titles.

25.      ------- **Barnaby Rudge and Hard Times.** Library Edition. 2
         vols. London: Chapman & Hall, 1858, II, 203-471. Reissued
         1862.

         Volume ten of the Library Edition. It contains volume two
         of **Barnaby Rudge**, pp. 1-201, and **Hard Times.** The book titles
         are not on separate pages but precede the first chapter title of
         each book. The 1862 printing includes four illustrations by F.
         Walker (112).

26.      -------. **Barnaby Rudge and Hard Times.** Diamond Edition.
         Boston: Ticknor & Fields, 1867, pp. 373-523.

         Volume ten of the edition, illustrated by S. Eytinge, Jr. (99).
         This is the first authorized American collection of Dickens's
         works.

27.    ───────.  **Hard Times and Pictures from Italy**. The Charles
Dickens Edition. London: Chapman & Hall, 1868, pp. 1-165.

An edition "theoretically at least" (Monod [45]) revised and
corrected by Dickens.  It introduced running headlines "almost
certainly composed by Dickens himself" (Monod) and omitted
the book titles and the dedication.  It includes the illustrations
by F. Walker (112).

# V

## SUBSEQUENT EDITIONS CONTAINING
## NEW INTRODUCTORY OR TEXTUAL MATTER

(Chronological Listing)

(Abridged school editions are included not
in this section but in section 12, below.)

28.  Dickens, Charles. **Barnaby Rudge and Hard Times**. 2 vols.
     The New Illustrated Library Edition. New York: Hurd & Hough-
     ton, 1876.

     Volumes eight and nine of the edition. The text is from the
     Library Edition. It is introduced by Edwin P. Whipple (155) and
     includes the illustrations by F. Walker (112) and one by F.O.C.
     Darley (98).

29.  --------. **Hard Times, Hunted Down, Holiday Romance, and
     George Silverman's Explanation**. The Gadshill Edition. Lon-
     don: Chapman & Hall; New York: Scribner's, 1897-99. xix, 444
     pp.

     Introduction and notes by Andrew Lang (547), with the il-
     lustrations by F. Walker (112).

30.  --------. **Hard Times for These Times**. The Temple Edition.
     London: J.M. Dent, 1899. xiv, 370 pp.

     Introduction by Walter Jerrold (497), colored frontispiece by
     M. Fisher (101).

31.  --------. **Bleak House and Hard Times**. The Autograph Edi-
     tion. London: Chapman & Hall, 1900, pp. 247-572.

Edited with an introduction by Richard Garnett (403). Includes the illustrations by F. Walker (112).

32.    -------. **Hard Times and Sketches by Boz.** The London Edition. Edinburgh:  T.C. & E.C. Jack, 1901-02.  xvi, 567 pp.

With editorial notes by Frederic Kitton (533).

33.    -------. **Christmas Books and Hard Times.** The Biographical
Edition. London: Chapman & Hall, 1903.  xxiv, 566 pp.

Introduction by Arthur Waugh (831), with the illustrations
by F. Walker (112).

34.    -------. **Great Expectations and Hard Times.** London and
New York: Macmillan, 1904.  xvii, 639 pp.

Introduction by Charles Dickens the Younger (339).

35.    ------- **Hard Times** Everyman edition. London: J.M. Dent.
1907.  xvi. 363 pp.  Reissued 1954, 1970; revised 1978.

Introduction by G. K. Chesterton (265).  The text is from the
Charles Dickens edition with running headlines by the Everyman
editor.  Reissued in 1954 and again in 1970 with an afterword
by Joanna M. Richardson (700); xiv, 272 pp.  Revised and reissued again in 1978 with a new introduction by Philip Collins
(294) and "some errors" in the 1907 text corrected.  The 1970
reissue is reviewed by Anne Smith, **DSN,** 4 (1973), 115-22.

36.    -------. **Hard Times and No Thoroughfare.** The Waverley
Edition. London: Waverley, 1912.  xvi, 312 pp.

Introduction by George Bernard Shaw (738) and illustrations
by Charles Pears (108).  Omits the dedication to Carlyle.

37.    -------. **Hard Times.** London: Readers Library, 1928.  250 pp.

The anonymous introduction offers some historical background and proclaims the novel "a political tract and a human
document of surpassing interest and value, and very obvious
present-day significance."

38.    -------.  **Hard Times.**  London and Glasgow: Collins, 1954.
       258 pp. Reissued 1973.

       Introduction by Frederick Brereton (218).

39.    -------.  **Hard Times for These Times.**  New Oxford Illustrated
       Dickens. London: Oxford Univ. Press, 1955. xviii, 299 pp.

       Introduction by Dingle Foot (386), with four illustrations by
       F. Walker and Maurice Greiffenhagen (112).

40.    -------.  **Hard Times for These Times.**  New York: Rinehart,
       1958. 274 pp.

       Introduction by William W. Watt (829). The text is from the
       Nonesuch edition. Review: Anne Smith, **DSN**, 4 (1973), 115-22.

*      -------.  **Hard Times.**  London: Heinemann, 1960.

       See below (878).

41.    -------.  **Hard Times.**  New York: Harper, 1960. xxi, 395 pp.

       Introduction by John H. Middendorf (624).

42.    -------.  **Hard Times for These Times.**  New York: New
       American Library, 1961. Rev. edn. 1980. 301 pp.

       Afterword by Charles Shapiro (736). The text is based on
       the 1854 volume edition with spelling and punctuation modern-
       ized and "obvious errors" silently corrected. The bibliography
       was revised for the 1980 edition. Review: Anne Smith, **DSN**, 4
       (1973), 115-22.

43.    -------.  **Hard Times.**  Bantam Classic.  New York: Bantam,
       1964. 373 pp.

       Edited and introduced by Robert Donald Spector (764). The
       text is based on the 1854 volume edition and amended by
       Spector for consistency of contemporary spelling and punctua-
       tion. Headings on the right-hand pages indicate the dates for

installments in **Household Words**. Part Two of the volume contains excerpts from the **Westminster Review**, October 1854 (120), Ruskin (150), Whipple (155), Fielding (375), Engel (367), Cockshut (284); from Dickens's letters and from **Household Words** ("On Strike," February 1854; "To Working Men," October 1854; "A Home Question," November 1854). There is also a selected bibliography.

44.    ‒‒‒‒‒‒. **Hard Times**. New York: Harper & Row, 1965.  xviii, 284 pp.

   Introduction by Walter Allen (162).

45.    ‒‒‒‒‒‒. **Hard Times**. Norton Critical Edition. New York: Norton, 1966. xiii, 377 pp.

   Edited and introduced by George Ford and Sylvere Monod (392). The text of this excellent edition was prepared from a comparative study of all surviving versions of the novel: manuscript, proofs, the text as published in **Household Words**, the text of the first single-volume edition in 1854, and the text of the Charles Dickens edition of 1868. Following the text of the novel, this edition prints Dickens's "Working Plans" (number plans or memorandums), the running headlines added to the Charles Dickens edition, and a collation of significant variants among the texts used. There follows a collection of extracts to provide "Backgrounds, Sources, and Contemporary Reactions." These include extracts from Dickens's letters; from the **Annual Register** and **The Times**; from **Household Words**; from Harriet Martineau's **The Factory Legislation** (147); from writings by J.M. M'Culloch; from Dickens's **Full Report of the First Meeting of the Mudfog Association** (13); from Darwin, Mill, Whipple (155), Taine (153), Ruskin (150), Shaw (738), F.R. Leavis (553), Monroe Engel (367), John Holloway (471), David M. Hirsch (467), Daniel P. Deneau (332), and Philip Collins (288). The edition concludes with a brief bibliography. Reviews: K.J. Fielding, **Dickensian**, 63 (1967), 149–52; Anne Smith, **DSN**, 4 (1973), 115–22.

46.    ‒‒‒‒‒‒. **Hard Times**. New York: Fawcett, 1966. 303 pp.

   Introduction by Raymond Williams (850). Review: Anne Smith, **DSN**, 4 (1973), 115–22.

47.      -------.  **Hard Times for These Times**. New York: Heritage,
         1966. xiv, 279 pp.

         Introduction by John T. Winterich (859) and illustrations by
         Charles Raymond (109).

48.      -------.  **Hard Times for These Times**. Harmondsworth: Pen-
         guin, 1969. 328 pp.

         Introduction by David Craig (308). The text is from the
         1854 volume edition but claims to emend Dickens's American
         spellings to British. It is followed by explanatory notes, pp.
         317-28. Review: Anne Smith, **DSN**, 4 (1973), 115-22.

49.      -------.  **Hard Times**. London: Longman, 1970. 389 pp.

         Heritage of Literature series. Commentary and notes by
         D.R. Elloway (365). The text is based on the 1854 single-vol-
         ume edition with "minor emendations." It is followed by "Ex-
         tracts from Dickens's Essays," Commentary, Notes, and Glossary
         of Lancashire Dialect Forms.

50.      -------.  **Hard Times for These Times**. Barre, Mass.: Imprint
         Society, 1972. xviii, 218 pp.

         Introduction by Monica Dickens (341) and illustrations by
         Richard Scollins (110). Ltd. edn. of 50 copies.

51.      -------.  **Hard Times**. London: Pan, 1977. 297 pp.

         Introduction, notes, and bibliography by George Levine
         (564). Although the Norton is the best text available, this edi-
         tion is valuable for the essay and editorial apparatus.

52.      -------.  **Hard Times for These Times**. St. Albans: Panther,
         1977. xiv, 303 pp.

         Introduction by Asa Briggs (219).

53.      -------.  **Hard Times**. With **Hunted Down, Holiday Romance,
         and George Silverman's Explanation**. Centennial Edition. Lon-
         don: Heron [?1978]. xv, 444 pp.

Reprints the introduction by Dingle Foot from the New Oxford Illustrated edition (386) and the Walker/Greiffenhagen illustrations (112).

# VI

## ADAPTATIONS FOR STAGE, SCREEN, RADIO, AND TELEVISION

### (Chronological Listing)

**Stage**

54.  Cooper, Frederick Fox. **Hard Times: a Domestic Drama**. London: C. Harris, 1854; also Henry Pownceby, 1854. 48 pp. Reissued in Dicks' Standard Plays, no. 785. London: John Dicks, 1886.

This production was first offered at the Strand on 14 August 1854, and then on 2-4 September 1854 at the Bower Saloon. It was revived at the Strand on 6 October 1854 and the Marylebone on 23 March 1858 (see Morley [82]). The story is revised in a number of ways, most notably in the happy ending in which Rachael is "given" in marriage to Stephen by Bounderby and Louisa goes home with Bounderby in reconciliation after she sees his generosity. Bounderby spreads bounty to all; Tom confesses, but only after he has returned the money. Reviews: **Athenaeum**, 19 August 1854 (83), **Illustrated London News**, 19 August 1854 (86); the anonymous **Charles Dickens, The Story of His Life** (141). See also Cooper (72), Fawcett (74), Fitz-Gerald (76), Morley (82), and Nation (59).

55.  Pitt, George Dibden. **Hard Times But Wait a Little Longer**. The Pavilion, London. September, 1854.

Listed in Allardyce Nicoll's "Hand-list of Plays Produced between 1850 and 1900," in **A History of Late Nineteenth Century Drama, 1850-1900** (Cambridge: Cambridge Univ. Press, 1946) as by Unknown Author; attributed to Pitt by Morley (82). The manuscript is in the Lord Chamberlain's collection in the British Library and is marked as received 2 September 1854 and license sent 4 September 1854. All the characters are coarsened and the play makes no effort to reproduce much beyond the names of the characters and the basic situation: Bounderby muses about selling Sissy, Gradgrind takes her in because he would like a free maid, Tom has his eye on her and attempts to have her kidnapped, Stephen rescues her; Jupe is a thief and he plots the robbery together with Mary Blackpool and Tom; and so on, without relief.

56.  Cowell, William. **Hard Times**. Boston Museum, Boston, Mass. 13 Nov. 1854.

The attribution is Morley (82), but compare Hudson (78). See also Lazenby. Text not available for examination.

57.  Robertson, T.W. **Household Words**. The Marylebone, London. 26 Nov. 1855.

Described by Morley (82) as a "small scale adaptation" of **Hard Times**. Not listed in Nicoll (see [55]). Text not available for examination.

58.  **Hard Times**. The Grecian, London. 20 Sept. 1866.

According to Morley (82), "would seem to come from Dickens." Listed in Nicoll (see [55]) as "Grec. 20/9/66." Text not available for examination.

59.  Nation, W.H.C. **Under the Earth; or, The Sons of Toil**. Dicks' British Drama. Vol. 6. London: John Dicks, 1871. Pp. 225–47.

Performed at Astley's, 22 April 1867. The attribution is Fitz-Gerald (76), followed by Morley (82). It is contested, however, by F.R. Cooper (72), who points out that except for the re-arrangement of some scenes and the addition of three new ones, this text is essentially the same as Fox Cooper's (54). The scenes are intended mainly to display characters, some based on **Hard Times** and some not. The play is called a "Romantic Drama" on the title page and is in four acts, with songs.

60.  [Hanworth, S.]. **Mr. Gradgrind's System**. Prince's Theatre, Llandudno. 3 July 1906.

See Fawcett (74), Fitz-Gerald (76), and Morley (82), who makes the attribution to Hanworth. Text not available for examination.

61.    Farrah, Mary. **The Model School, A Scene from** "**Hard Times.**" Part 7 of **Scenes from Dickens**. London: J. Curwen, [1909]. 7 pp.

       Extracts dialogue from the school-room scene. The characters are Gradgrind, Official Visitor, M'Choakumchild, Sissy, and Bitzer.

62.    Mason, Tom. **Hard Times**. St. John's Hall, Palmer's Green. 7 Feb. 1939.

       According to Morley (82), the last production of the Dickens Players. Text not available for examination.

63.    Simons, Victor. **Hard Times**. Birmingham. [1953].

       In "When Found ---," **Dickensian**, 50 (1954), 19, Leslie Staples mentions "a production of a dramatic adaptation ... by Mr. Victor Simons last year" by the Birmingham Branch of the Dickens Fellowship. Text not available for examination.

64.    Perrins, Tony. [**Hard Times.**] Victoria Theatre, Stoke-on-Trent. 1968.

       A musical version with music by Jeff Parton. See Bastable (70). Text not available for examination.

65.    Thomas, Hugh. The Playhouse, Oxford. November 1971. **Hard Times**.

       A musical version, Review: Michael Slater (85). A revised version was performed at the Belgrade Theatre, Coventry, November 1973. Review: **Dickensian**, 70 (1974), 52 (73). Text not available for examination.

66.    Jeffreys, Stephen. Various theaters in Cumbria. 16 June to 28 Aug. 1982. **Hard Times**.

Directed by Adrian Harris for the Pocket Theatre Cumbria. An adaptation very close to the original text, achieved in part by having various characters narrate portions to bridge drama- tized scenes, often keeping the language very close to Dick- ens's. One obvious interpolation is a lengthy speech by Ste- phen at the union meeting followed by a reply from a character named Mary Stokes who argues the other perspective. The ar- gument goes to Stokes, but the sympathy to Blackpool, with a resulting confusion of effect. Text not published.

## Film, Radio, and Television

67.  **Hard Times**. Great Britain: Trans-Atlantic, 1915.

Produced by Thomas Bentley, with Bransby Williams and Leon M. Lion. Silent, black and white, four reels. See Matz (81) and Zambrano (87). Print not available for examination.

68.  Hardwick, Mollie. ["Hard Times"]. [1966-67].

An announcement in the **Dickensian**, 62 (1966), 1/8, states that an eleven-part dramatization of the novel will be broadcast "commencing around Christmas time." Script not available for examination.

69.  **Hard Times**.  Boston: WNET and London: Granada Television, 1977. Available on 4 videocassettes (240 min.) from WNET/13 Media Services, New York; set includes **The World of Dickens's Hard Times: A Guide for the Viewer**, by George Ford and Ste- ven Marcus.

Adapted by Arthur Hopcraft, directed by John Irwin, de- signed by Roy Stonehouse. A four-part serialization. Cast in- cluded Alan Dobie as Blackpool, Barbara Ewing as Rachael, Jac- queline Tong as Louisa, and Patrick Allen as Gradgrind. Reviews: Anthony Burton, **Dickensian** (71); Michael Irwin, **TLS** (79); Michael Church, **Times** (London), 26 October 1977, p.9.

Commentary

70.    Bastable, Adolphus. "Our Theatres in the Sixties." **The Shavian**,
       3 (Winter 1968–69), 17–21.

       A review of the Perrins adaptation (64). Finds the version
       intelligent and sensitive, offering special praise for Bounderby
       and Louisa and the considerable avoidance of mawkishness in
       Stephen and Rachael.

71.    Burton, Anthony. "**Hard Times** on Television." **Dickensian**, 74
       (1978), 48–50.

       A review of the Granada television adaptation (69). Lists
       the major actors. Finds the production best in its making Ste-
       phen and Rachael credibly human, but generally finds it a "slow
       human drama" that perhaps should have been renamed "Louisa
       Gradgrind; or, the Awakened Heart." According to Burton, the
       satire is lost in this version.

72.    Cooper, F. Renad. **Nothing Extenuate: The Life of Frederick
       Fox Cooper**. London: Barrie & Rockliff, 1964, pp. 158–62,
       204–05, 246.

       Records the 14 August 1854 adapatation at the Strand (54),
       reproduces the design for Dicks' Standard Plays (1886) of **Hard
       Times** (54), and argues for the attribution of **Under the Earth**
       (59) to Cooper.

73.    "Dickens Entertains." **Dickensian**, 70 (1974), 52.

       An unsigned notice of the revised version of the Thomas
       adaptation (65). The reviewer comments that there "were many
       good and effective moments but the ending was still too
       abrupt and confusing."

74.    Fawcett, Frank D. **Dickens the Dramatist**. London: W.H. Allen,
       1953. P. 250.

       Lists the Cooper (54), Nation (59), and Llandudno (60) ad-
       aptations, but attributes only the Cooper. Fawcett indicates

that he is listing only the "most noteworthy" adaptations. He notices the "many liberties" taken by Cooper but argues that "in this case there was every excuse, for there is little light and shade in the story of soulless employers and downtrodden workpeople."

75.  Finlay, Ian F. "Dickens in the Cinema." **Dickensian**, 54 (1958), 106-09.

Erroneously notes that **Hard Times** has not been filmed. See Matz (81) and Zambrano (87).

76.  Fitz-Gerald, S.J. Adair. **Dickens and the Drama**. London: Chapman & Hall, 1910, pp. 256-61. Rpt. New York: Blom, 1971.

Lists the cast for the 14 August 1854 Strand production (54) and comments that Cooper's is "certainly ... a bad" version. He gives the cast list for **Under the Earth** at Astley's in 1867 (59) and attributes the adaptation to W.H.C. Nation. **Mr. Gradgrind's System** (60) is only mentioned.

*   Ford, George and Steven Marcus.

See (391).

77.  Fulkerson, Richard P. "The Dickens Novel on the Victorian Stage." **DAI**, 31 (1970), 3502A (Ohio State Univ., 1970). 378 pp.

Notes that **Hard Times** and **Little Dorrit** are the least popular sources for adaptations of Dickens.

78.  Hudson, Virginia O'Rear. "Charles Dickens and the American Theater." Ph.D. Dissertation. Univ. of Chicago, 1926. 356 pp.

Cites as the only record of an American production of **Hard Times** the production at the Boston Museum in the 1854-55 season (56), with William Warren as Bounderby. Hudson infers from other sources that the version used was Cooper's. Compare Lazenby (80) and Morley (82).

79.    Irwin, Michael.   "Granadaland's Coketown."   **TLS**, 4 November
       1977, p. 1295.

       A review of the Granada television production (69).  Judges
       the production to have dealt well with two major problems in
       the novel:  Dickens's failure to integrate successfully the two
       elements of Gradgrind and education on the one hand and Ste-
       phen and industrialism on the other and his achievement of
       satire at the expense of psychological probability.  But Irwin
       believes that the "town itself, and its industrial life, have been
       shown as briefly, and therefore perhaps as inadequately, as in
       the original."

80.    Lazenby, Walter Sylvester, Jr.   "Stage Versions of Dickens's
       Novels in America to 1900."  **DA**, 23 (1962), 2250  (Indiana Univ.,
       1962).  335 pp.

       Notes that **Hard Times** was one of the least popular of
       Dickens's novels for dramatization in Britain and the U.S., per-
       haps because of its "sullen socialism" or because "the charac-
       terization here was less striking, the humor less spirited, the
       action less engrossing."  The only American version was per-
       formed on 13 November 1854 at the Boston Museum, and it ran
       for almost two weeks.  The sub-title was "The Self-Made Man"
       and the role of Bounderby was played by William Warren.  Laz-
       enby offers a scene-by-scene summary based on the playbill.
       The production was revived in October 1866 at the same thea-
       ter.  Compare Hudson (78) and Morley (82).

81.    Matz, B.W.  "When Found--."  **Dickensian**, 11 (1915), 256.

       Remarks that in the Bentley film (67) "the book is followed
       very closely" and the " period costumes are accurate."  Matz
       judges the film to be "absolutely critic-proof."

82.    Morley, Malcolm.  "**Hard Times** on the Stage."  **Dickensian**, 50
       (1954), 69-73.

       Gives description and background for the Fox Cooper ad-
       aptations (54) at the Strand and at the Marylebone, the Pitt ad-
       aptation (55), the Robertson adaptation (57), the adaptation at
       the Grecian (58), the W.H.C. Nation adaptation (59), the Han-
       worth adaptation (60), and the Mason (62) and Cowell (56) ad-
       aptations.

83.    "Music and the Drama." **Athenaeum**, 19 August 1854, p. 1022.

    A generally favorable review of the Strand production (54). Finds that the story has made "a better drama than a tale; and, though the dialogue was in the main preserved, it told on the stage with more than ordinary effect." The sub-plot of Stephen was emphasized so that it "subdued, by contrast, the fanciful lesson and the ideal moral intended by the leading theme." The divorce issue aroused the greatest interest of the piece, moving the audience to "rather a strong demonstration."

84.    Pierce, Dorothy. "Special Bibliography: The Stage Versions of Dickens' Novels. Part III " **Bull. of Bibliography and Dramatic Index**, 16 (1936-37), 52-54.

    Lists only the Fox Cooper (54), W.H.C. Nation (59), and Llandudno (60) productions.

85.    S[later], M[ichael]. "Things Seen." **Dickensian**, 68 (1972), 50.

    A review of the Thomas adaptation (05). Finds it "rather a sudden pull-up" but still "a bold and innovative attempt to turn a nineteenth-century novel into a piece of modern theatre," preferable to Fox Cooper's version.

86.    "The Theatres." **Illustrated London News**, 25 (19 August 1854), 162.

    A review of the Strand production (54) that finds it much better than expected. "The theme of the fable is of some subtlety and the moral considerably refined in its tone and application," the reviewer states. "The insufficiency of utilitarianism for the adequate education of the human being is the leading doctrine of the novel, and the same great social lesson is prominently insisted on in the drama." The reviewer also notes the change to a happy ending.

87.    Zambrano, Ana Laura. **Dickens and Film**. New York: Gordon Press, 1977, p. 418.

    Lists the 1915 Bentley film (67).

88.      -------.  "Feature Motion Pictures Adapted from Dickens: A
Checklist – Part II."  **DSN**, 6 (1975), 9–13.

   Lists the 1915 Bentley film (67).

# VII

# PARODY; MUSICAL SETTINGS

89.    Bentzon, Jorgen. "Strenge tider." **Symphony No. 1.** Copenhagen: SBM, c. 1941–43.

     Listed in Gooch (92). A symphony for orchestra only. The score indicates that three movements, including the one entitled "Strenge tider," are "over motiver fra Ch. Dickens' voerker." Score not seen.

90.    [Brough, Robert B.]. "Hard Times. By Charles Dickens. Concluded as it ought to have been." **Diogenes,** 4 (1854), 70e–70g.

     The "revised ending" is the same as in Brough (91), below, except that in place of the footnote there is an introductory paragraph requesting the reader to forget or not to read the conclusion of **Hard Times,** as "Mr. Dickens was not himself when he wrote it." The death of Stephen was "a mistake," Bounderby could not have been given five years of prosperity, and so forth. The end of chapter 34 is therefore cancelled, Brough states, and chapters 35, 36, and 37 offered in its place, as Dickens would have written them had he been himself.

91.    B[rough, Robert B.]. "'Hard Times' by Charles Diggins." In **Our Miscellany.** Ed. Edmund H. Yates and Robert B. Brough. London and New York: Routledge, 1856, pp. 142–56.

     A footnote explains that the want of poetical justice in the original conclusion has led to the following revision of chapters 35 to 37. Bounderby is ground up in a melancholy-mad elephant. Rachael and Stephen marry. Gradgrind joins the Sleary troop, which goes to America and earns a fortune. Harthouse returns from Jerusalem and marries Louisa. Sissy marries Tom, Jr. The robbery is fixed on Mrs. Sparsit and Bitzer, who are transported. She amasses a fortune in a boarding-house, and so he murders her and is then executed. The irony of this rendition turns on the sentimentalism and absurdities in the plot

and repeatedly shows people to be selfish and corrupt. The final paragraph is: "And now, reader, let us love one another. If
you will, I will. I can't say fairer. And so, God bless us all."
See (90) above.

92.     Gooch, Bryan N.S., and David S. Thatcher. "Dickens, Charles
        John Huffam." **Musical Settings of Early and Mid-Victorian
        Literature: A Catalogue.** Garland Reference Library of the Hu-
        manities, 149. New York and London: Garland, 1979, pp.
        202-35.

              Lists three entries for **Hard Times**:    Bentzon (89), C.W.,
        "Hard Times Polka" (93), and Parton (64).


*       Parton, Jeff. **Hard Times**.

        See above (64).


*       Thatcher, David S.

        See Bryan N.S. Gooch and David S. Thatcher (92).


*       Thomas, Hugh. **Hard Times**.

        See above (65).


93.     W., C. "Hard Times Polka." Belfast: Hart & Churchill, n.d.  7 pp.

              Cited in Miller (925) under "Musical Works" and in Gooch
        (92). Not cited in T.W. Hill's "A Catalogue of the Miller Collec-
        tion of Dickens Music at the Dickens House," **Dickensian**, 37
        (1941), 48-54. Score not seen.

# VIII

## ILLUSTRATIONS

94.   Anderson, Scoular. Twelve illustrations for **Hard Times**. In the Collins abridged and simplified edition, 1979 (881).

95.   Bacon, H. "'Wondering again ' said Tom." Front plate to **Hard Times**. New Century Library. London: Thomas Nelson, 1901.

*   Clarke, Joseph Clayton.

     See Kyd (106).

96.   Cottam, Martin. Six illustrations for **Hard Times**. In the Alpha Classics edition, 1979 (880).

97.   Crane, Walter. "Dickens's Dogs; or, the Landseer of Fiction." **London Society**, 4 (1863), 48–61. Rpt. as "Charles Dickens' Dogs. With Illustrations by Walter Crane." **The London Home**, July 1895, pp. 79–86.

     These are six illustrations of dogs portrayed in Dickens's works. Merrylegs appears as a French poodle.

98.   Darley, F.O.C. Two illustrations for **Hard Times**. In **Hard Times for These Times**. New York: Sheldon, 1863. Also in the New Illustrated Library Edition, 1876 (28).

     The illustrations are "Stephen Blackpool" (seated on the bed, in despair, with Mrs. Blackpool reaching towards him) and "The Mouth of the Pit" from Book III, chapter viii.

99.   Eytinge, S[olomon], Jr. Six illustrations for **Hard Times**. In the Diamond Edition, 1867 (26).

The illustrations are (1) Thomas Gradgrind, (2) The Horse-Riding Party, (3) Mr. Bounderby and Mrs. Sparsit, (4) Stephen and Rachael, (5) Mr. Harthouse and Tom, and (6) Mrs. Bounderby and Sissy.

100.   Favorsky, V. "Three Woodcuts for **Hard Times** by Charles Dickens." **London Mercury**, 26 (July 1932), 197–99.

The three woodcuts are of Gradgrind at the school, Louisa and Tom visiting Stephen, and Louisa in a faint at Gradgrind's feet. Small emblems at the top and bottom embellish each one.

101.   Fisher, M. "Anxiety at the Pit's Mouth." Colored frontispiece to the Temple Edition, 1899 (30).

102.   Fraser, Claud Lovat. **Characters from Dickens**. London: T.C. & E. C. Jack, n.d. [1924].

These are eighteen character-studies for covers for Dickens novels, reed pen with washes of color. Mr. Bounderby appears on p. 57.

103.   French, H.   Eighteen illustrations for **Hard Times**.   In Lloyd's Sixpenny Dickens edition. London: Edward Lloyd, 1909–12.

*        Greiffenhagen, Maurice.

See F. Walker (112).

104.   Groome, W.H.C.   Seven illustrations for **Hard Times**.   In Collins's Illustrated Dickens edition. London and Glasgow:  1906.

105.   Houghton, Arthur Boyd.   One illustration for **Hard Times**.   In **Hard Times and Pictures from Italy**. London: Chapman & Hall, 1866.   Also in:   **Hard Times for These Times, Hunted Down, Holiday Romance, George Silverman's Explanation** (New York: Hearst's, [1868?]); **Hard Times and Other Stories**, the National edition (London: Chapman & Hall, 1907); **Hard Times and Great Expectations** (Bloomsbury: Nonesuch, 1937).

106.   Kyd. [Joseph Clarke Clayton]. "18 Original Character Illustra-
       tions to 'Hard Times.'" n.d. In the Gimbel Collection at Yale
       University; see Podeschi (927).

       The illustrations, including a title-page and a page listing
       the characters, are in pen and black ink and watercolor. The
       characters are Mr. Gradgrind, Young Mrs. Bounderby, Cissy
       [sic], Bitzer, Mrs. Sparsit, Josiah Bounderby, The Cub, Hon.
       Frederick, Mrs. Gradgrind, Cissy's Schoolmaster, Stephen Black-
       pool, Rachael, Stephen's Wife, Slackbridge, Mr. Sleary, Kidder-
       minster, E.W.B. Childers, Mrs. Bounderby Senr.

107.   Lamb, Lynton. Illustrations for **Hard Times**. In the Oxford Uni-
       versity Press abridged edition, 1959 (877).

108.   Pears, Charles. Four "Character Studies" for **Hard Times**. In
       the Waverley edition, 1912 (36).

       The characters are Mr. Gradgrind, Blackpool, Mrs. Bounder-
       by, and Tom Gradgrind the Younger.

109.   Raymond, Charles. Fifteen color plates; also black and white
       small chapter-head illustrations for **Hard Times for These
       Times**. In the Heritage edition, 1966 (47).

110.   Scollins, Richard. Twenty-one illustrations for **Hard Times for
       These Times**. In the Imprint Society edition, 1972 (50).

111.   Stacey, W.S. Eight illustrations for **Hard Times**. In **Hard Times
       and Master Humphrey's Clock**, London: Gresham, 1902.

       The illustrations are: "At the Edge of the Old Hell Shaft,"
       "Mr. Gradgrind is Shocked," "Stephen asks Mr. Bounderby's Ad-
       vice," "Mrs. Sparsit asks News of Bitzer," "Unexpected Visitors
       at Stephen's," "The Meeting in the Wood," "Louisa Startles her
       Father," and "The Ring of Sleary's Circus."

112.   Walker, Frederick.   Four illustrations for **Hard Times.**   In the
       1862 re-issue of the Library Edition (25).   Also in the Charles
       Dickens edition, 1868 (27), **Hard Times for these times, Hunted
       Down, Holiday Romance, George Silverman's Explanation**
       (New York: Hearst's [1868?]), the New Illustrated Library edition,
       1876 (28), the Gadshill edition, 1897–99 (29), the Autograph edi-
       tion, 1900 (31), **Hard Times and Reprinted Pieces** (the Authen-
       tic edition, London:  Chapman & Hall, and New York: Scribner's,
       1900–01), the Biographical edition, 1903 (33), **Hard Times and
       Other Stories,** (the National Edition, London: Chapman & Hall,
       1907), and **Hard Times and Great Expectations** (Bloomsbury:
       Nonesuch, 1937); with Maurice Greiffenhagen, in the New Ox-
       ford Illustrated Dickens edition 1955 (39) and the Heron edition,
       [?1978] (53).

       These four most commonly reprinted illustrations are "Ste-
       phen and Rachael in the Sick-room," "Mr. Harthouse Dining at
       the Bounderbys'," "Mr. Harthouse and Tom Gradgrind in the
       Garden," and "Stephen Blackpool Recovered from the Old Hell
       Shaft."

# IX

# REVIEWS

## (Chronological Listing)


113. "Our Library Table. **Hard Times For Theco Timoo**." **Alliehae-um**, 12 August 1854, p. 992.

Finds the "idea" of the novel good but not realized with Dickens's usual felicity: "In its essence, this is a poetical conception; and it required for its due exhibition an ideal framework. Mr. Dickens has been pleased to give it a prosaic framework and to people it with very repulsive and vulgar characters .... It has the beauties and the vices of his style." The reviewer does not comment on the theme of industrialism or on Stephen.


114. "**Hard Times -- for These Times**. By Charles Dickens." **The Epitomist**, [September 1854], pp. 202-04.

Finds the title puzzling because the novel shows little of poverty. The novel has two issues: "the Inaccessibility of Divorce for the poor, and the assumed solitary, tyrannous, and barren rule of Fact (signifying, as we suppose, the incarnation of Reason) in education, to the exclusion of fancy." The reviewer agrees that such divorce as is sanctioned by Scripture should be available equally to rich and poor. On education, he thinks that Dickens has created the dragon he slays--the issue of taste in chapter i and the portrait of Gradgrind discoursing on Fact are exaggerated, to the detriment of Dickens's argument for the (decidedly conceded) case of imagination. He criticizes gently the caricature of characters and their use as mouthpieces or subjection to the moral inculcated by the plot. He praises Dickens's description, humor, pathos, and the vividness of expressive detail, and sees the dialogue between Harthouse and Sissy as a "gem of its kind."

115.    [Forster, John]. "**Hard Times. For These Times.** By Charles
        Dickens." **Examiner,** 9 September 1854, pp. 568-69.

        Although this review is widely attributed to Forster, Fielding
        (378) argues that there is no evidence for this attribution and
        good reason against it. The review defends the book against
        charges that its social criticism, particularly in the matter of
        political economy, is inadequate, by arguing that such charges
        are inappropriate. A short work "clearly and powerfully written,
        full of incident and living interest" hasn't room for "a sufficient-
        ly full expression of opinion upon details." The story aims to
        touch the heart, not to argue, he asserts. Its principal message
        is that we must cultivate fancy. It shows a "singular closeness
        of purpose" and a remarkable "unsuperfluousness of ... details."

116.    "Lectures on Education, Delivered at the Royal Institution in
        May and June, 1854. 'Hard Times.' By Charles Dickens." **Gen-
        tleman's Magazine,** 42 (September 1854), 276-78.

        Offers a free paraphrase, accurate in the main, of Hodgson
        (138).

117.    "Hard Times." **British Quarterly Review,** 20 (October 1854),
        581-82.

        Summarizes the story briefly and judges that its faults "are
        the faults common to Mr. Dickens's authorship--the faults of
        one-sidedness and exaggeration." Bounderby, as a representa-
        tive of his class, is "falsehood and calumny." Gradgrind is sim-
        ilarly over-drawn. The reviewer takes Dickens to task for never
        showing religion as the basis of ideal character and only at-
        tacking false cant, thus in effect inculcating atheism.

118.    "Hard Times." **South London Athenaeum and Institution
        Magazine,** October 1854, pp. 115-19.

        Finds the book "thoroughly" disappointing because its
        themes--the Preston strike issues, utilitarianism, divorce--are
        imperfectly developed; perhaps there are too many for one
        book. Dickens has not done the service he usually does, but
        has gotten carried away in a "domestic tale," the reviewer
        points out. This novel "contains writing unsurpassed in el-
        egance of finish and poetical diction," but it is "ill-constructed."
        The tale of Stephen suffers least from the "merciless curtail-

ing," but Dickens has failed to lambaste the divorce laws as they deserve—perhaps he will yet do so, the reviewer suggests.

119.   [Simpson, Richard]. "Miscellaneous Literature." **Rambler**, n.s. 2 (October 1854), 361-62.

Summarizes the story and judges that "Here and there we meet with touches not unworthy of the inventor of 'Pickwick'; but, on the whole, the story is stale, flat, and unprofitable; a mere dull melodrama, in which character is caricature, sentiment tinsel, and moral (if any) unsound." Dickens should amuse and refrain from trying to instruct and to understand society, Simpson asserts. "The disease of Coketown will hardly be stayed by an abstinence from facts and figures; nor a healthy reaction insured by a course of cheap divorce and the poetry of nature." Dickens too suffers from "muddle."

120.   [Sinnett, Jane]. "Belles Lettres." **Westminster Review**, 62 o.s., 6 n.s. (October 1854), 602-22. (American edition, pp. 318-30.)

Criticizes the novel for having been diverted from the serious theme of the struggle in the north to the misbegotten theme of education: "we are not aware of such a system [as Gradgrind's] being in operation anywhere in England." The school system serves the imagination well, Sinnett concludes. This review suggests that the lower orders are adequately represented by Dickens's external methods, but that the more cultivated orders are more complex and hence more difficult to represent. Stephen, Rachael, Sissy, and Sleary are successful characterizations, but Bounderby and the Gradgrind family are preposterous. Dickens's strength is his style, but while the descriptions of Coketown are commendable, Mrs. Sparsit keeping her look-out is "intolerable **galimatias**."

121.   "Hard Times. By Charles Dickens." **Graham's Magazine** [a.k.a **Graham's Monthly Magazine of Literature, Art, and Fashion**], 45 (November 1854), 493.

Offers strong criticism of the novel that turns at the end to a sort of hollow praise: Dickens "evidently was tired himself of his materials, and huddled them up to a conclusion long before his original intention. There is more caricature, more repetition, more painful striving after effect, more dullness, and less geniality of sentiment and humor, in this novel than in any of his previous efforts. Yet it contains, with all its faults, enough genius to make a reputation, and it is calculated to impress the reader all the more with the author's great powers, when we consider that his failures would be another man's triumphs."

122. [Oliphant, Margaret]. "Charles Dickens." **Blackwood's Magazine**, 77 (April 1855), 451–66. Rpt. in **The Eclectic Magazine of Foreign Literature**, June 1855, pp. 200–14.

    Condemns the novel for its didacticism. It is a middle-class book in which we find "the petulant theory of a man in a world of his own making, where he has no fear of being contradicted .... We have seldom seen a more lamentable **non sequitur** than **Hard Times**." Oliphant criticizes the shift from the labor/capital question to the "lame and impotent conclusion" of the education theme. The redeeming features are Stephen and Rachael, the distinctness and identity of Louisa, the "perfect reality and truth" in Tom, the "clever outline" in Harthouse. Sissy is impossible, she asserts, but the circus people are doubtless "drawn to the life."

123. "Our Library Table. Mrs. Gaskell's **North and South**." **Manchester Weekly Advertiser**, 14 April 1855, p. 6.

    Argues that the serialization of **North and South** in **Household Words** "may retrieve" for the paper "some of the popularity which it lost, by being made the vehicle of that unjust and untrue caricature of manufacturing life, Dickens's 'Hard Times.'" This statement is curiously at odds with the sales figures for **Household Words** (see Buckler [234], Forster [133], and Patten [664]).

124. [Oliphant, Margaret]. "Modern Novelists – Great and Small." **Blackwood's Magazine**, 77 (May 1855), 554–68.

    **North and South** is briefly compared to **Hard Times**: "We are prepared in both for the discussion of an important social question; and in both, the story gradually slides off the public topic to pursue a course of its own."

125. W., A. "Factory Life--Its Novels and Its Facts." **The Christian Examiner**, 59 (November 1855), 354–79.

A review of **Hard Times** and **North and South**. A. W. concludes that **Hard Times** is "wholly successful" even though the field of factory life is new to Dickens and perhaps unsuited to his "light and jovial genius." **North and South**, however, comes out ahead in a comparison of the two novels, which is conducted mainly by juxtaposing pairs of characters and judging them (as people rather than as characterization). A.W. argues that both books are utterly fair in their presentation of the facts of industrial life.

126.   [Stephen, Fitzjames]. "The License of Modern Novelists." **The Edinburgh Review**, 106 (October 1857), 124-56.

This review of **Little Dorrit, It Is Never Too Late to Mend** (Reade), and Gaskell's **Life of Charlotte Bronte** includes a glancing allusion to **Hard Times**: "In every novel [Dickens] selects one or two of the popular cries of the day, to serve as seasoning to the dish which he sets before his readers. It may be the Poor Laws, or Imprisonment for debt, or the Court of Chancery, or the harshness of Mill-owners, or the stupidity of Parliament, or the inefficiency of Government, or the insolence of District Visitors ...."

127.   "The Works of Charles Dickens." **British Quarterly Review**, 35 (January 1862), 135-59.

Finds **Hard Times** "a strange disjointed kind of story"; accepts the criticism of Gradgrindian education but cannot see how that offered by the circus is sufficiently superior to render Sissy the heroine of the piece; is not surprised at the indignation that the description of Coketown has aroused in the north, and notes that its inhabitants are portrayed equally unattractively. The workers "do not awaken any great interest." The novel itself is a "muddle."

128.   "Modern Novelists: Charles Dickens." **Westminster Review**, 82, n.s. 26 (October 1864), 414-441. (American ed., pp. 194-206.) Rpt. in **The Eclectic Magazine of Foreign Literature**, January 1865, pp. 42-59.

A review of the Library Edition (1858-62). To show Dickens's decline from a purer humor to intrusive political and moral concerns and his lack of decorum in this regard, the reviewer compares two passages: Miss Monflathers accosting

Little Nell as a "wax-work child" and Mr. Gradgrind accosting Sissy in the matter of Facts. The latter strikes a false note, the reviewer believes, because the speaker is not a Miss Monflathers and the context is a professed treatise on education. The reader is struck by exaggeration where there should have been impartiality. Sleary on dogs is one of a number of instances that pay tribute to Dickens's powers of observation, the reviewer adds, and Sissy ranks with Pip as a great creation. Bounderby and Coketown, however, are social criticism that has come too late. The reviewer concludes that Dickens's tendency to over-emphasize feelings leads him to misjudge anything that appears hard, such as political economy; he resists the restraint of science.

# X

## RECEPTION AND REMARKS BY DICKENS'S CONTEMPORARIES

✦ Brachor, Peter Scholl

See below (213).

129. "Charles Dickens's Use of the Bible." **Temple Bar**, September 1869, pp. 225–34. Also in **Every Saturday: A Journal of Choice Reading, Selected from Foreign Current Literature**, 25 September 1869, and in **Appleton's Journal**, 16 and 23 October 1869.

   Asserts that Stephen's Star is "perhaps one of the most affecting references to the sacred narrative" in Dickens's work.

130. Clay, Walter Lowe. **The Prison Chaplain: A Memoir of the Reverend John Clay, Chaplain of the Preston Gaol.** Cambridge and London: Macmillan, 1861, p. 620.

   Quotes a letter to Miss Mary Carpenter, 25 August 1854: "I see that Dickens, in **Hard Times**, has a laugh at my 'tabular statements,' and also at my credulity. He is not the only man I have met who prefers to rely on his own theories and fancies rather than on well ascertained facts."

131. Cunningham, Peter. "Town and Table-Talk on Literature, Art, etc." **Illustrated London News**, 24 (4 March 1854), 194.

   Offers the following: "The title of Mr. Dickens's new work is 'Hard Times.' His recent inquiry into the Preston strike is said to have originated the title, and, in some respects, suggested the turn of the story." Dickens's dismay at this announcement is shown in a letter to Cunningham discussed at some length by Pope-Hennessy (681), Shusterman (743), and Wagenknecht (817).

\*        Dolby, George Charles.

         See below (344).


132.     "Eliza." "A Lady's Thoughts." "Correspondence." **The School
         and the Teacher**, 1 (June 1854), 115-16.

         The issue for May had printed the description of M'Choa-
         kumchild, without commentary, under the heading "Description
         of a Modern Trained and Certificated Schoolmaster" (p. 95).
         This letter to the editor, dated 1 May 1854, comments on that
         "quotation from Mr. Dickens: no doubt, it is very amusing, and I
         like to be amused, but I think it contains a **fallacy** .... I don't
         believe, Mr. M'Choakumchild would have taught a bit better, if
         he had known ever so much less. The truth is, that his great
         amount of knowledge might not make him 'apt to teach,' ... but,
         if he had this aptness, the more he knew, the better he would
         be able to teach ...."


133.     Forster, John. **The Life of Charles Dickens**. 3 vols. London:
         Chapman & Hall, 1872-74, III, 438-40. Republished frequently,
         including ed. J.W.T. Ley. London: Palmer, 1928, and ed. A.J.
         Hoppe. 2 vols. London: Dent, 1966.

         Cites a letter of 20 January 1854, in which Dickens sent
         him a list of fourteen titles with the instruction: "It seems to
         me that there are three very good ones among them. I should
         like to know whether you hit upon the same." The one title
         that they chose in common was **Hard Times**. In a footnote,
         Forster lists five further titles, without explanation. Forster also
         cites the letter concerning the "CRUSHING" want of space. He
         asserts that Dickens accomplished one intention perfectly,
         which was to improve the circulation of **Household Words**
         ("more than doubled"), and the other imperfectly, because the
         story is not among his best. The circus people and the
         Bounderby household are the strengths of the novel, the truths
         of which must be set against its faults of workmanship. For-
         ster demurs from Ruskin's high praise (150); cites Dickens's
         letter to Charles Knight (144) and the letter of 14 July 1854 on
         the completion of the novel; points to Taine's exaggerated
         praise (153). He denies the American rumor that Dickens went
         backstage at Astley's to gather material for the circus scenes
         but confirms that he did go to Preston, quoting the letter in
         which Dickens expresses his disappointment. On the matter of
         the circulation of **Household Words**, compare Buckler (234) and
         Patten (664).

134.   [Forsyth, William]. "Literary Style." **Fraser's Magazine**, 55
       (March 1857), 260-63. Rpt. in **Essays, Critical and Narrative**.
       London: Longmans, Green, 1874; also in Collins (293).

       A list of examples of Dickens's caricatures includes Grad-
       grind, who "is always practical, to a degree that ceases to be
       human."

135.   Gaskell, Elizabeth. **The Letters of Mrs. Gaskell**. Ed. J.A.V.
       Chapple and Arthur Pollard. Cambridge, Mass.: Harvard Univ.
       Press, 1967, pp. 279-81.

       Letter no. 191, to John Forster, 23 April 1854: "Oh! I wrote
       to Mr. Dickens, and he says he is not going to have a
       strike,--altogether his answer sets me at ease." The letter
       from Dickens is in **Letters**, 2, 554 (1).

136.   Gourdault, Jules. "Les Privileges et les pauvres gens dans les
       romans de Charles Dickens." **Revue des Cours Litteraires**, 2
       (1866), 333-41

       Praising Dickens as the English novelist of democracy and
       equality, selects two novels for lengthy comment: **Hard Times**
       and **Dombey and Son**. Gourdault sees **Hard Times** as the
       novel that demonstrates the two Englands, one of egoists
       (Gradgrind and Bounderby), the other of people of heart (Ste-
       phen and Rachael). Sissy and the circus do not figure in the
       scheme.

137.   Hill, Octavia. "Organized Work Among the Poor; Suggestions
       Founded on Four Years' Management of a London Court."
       **Macmillan's Magazine**, July 1869, pp. 219-26. Rpt. in **Homes
       of the London Poor**. London: Macmillan, 1875, 1883.

       In her argument that the "poor of London need joy and
       beauty in their lives," refers to **Hard Times** and especially Slea-
       ry's "'People mutht be amoothed, Thquire.'" On the tendency to
       overlook individual cases when dealing with large and complex
       problems, Hill remarks: "one is apt to forget Sissy Jupe's quick
       sympathetic perception that percentage signifies literally noth-
       ing to the friends of the special sufferer, who surely is not
       worth less than a sparrow."

138. Hodgson, W.B. "On the Importance of the Study of Economic Science as a Branch of Education for All Classes." In **Lectures on Education, Delivered at the Royal Institution of Great Britain.** London: John W. Parker, 1855, pp. 261-316.

Deplores Dickens's having lent his name to the discrediting of the science he advocates in this lecture. The misrepresentation is surely not willful, Hodgson asserts, but it is misrepresentation nonetheless. Dickens does not understand the science and mistakenly attributes various excesses to it, such as the discouraging of filial duty and marriage, the ability to see only statistical averages, and the destruction of the imagination. "By all means, let us have poetry," he concludes, "but first let us have our daily bread, even though man is not fed by that alone." This portion of the lecture is paraphrased in a report in **The Gentleman's Magazine** (116).

139. [Hoey, Mrs. Frances Cashel]. "The Life of Charles Dickens." **Temple Bar,** 38 (May 1873), 169-85. Rpt. in part in Collins (293).

A debunking review of Forster's **Life.** That Dickens was unfortunate when he talked of things he did not understand is apparent from, among other things, **Hard Times,** Hoey states.

140. [? -------]. "Two English Novelists: Dickens and Thackeray." **Dublin Review,** n.s. 16 (April 1871), 315-50. Rpt. in part in Collins (293).

Asserts that the political and social views of **Hard Times** are not "sufficiently sound or profound to merit the attention of educated minds, though they are striking and picturesque enough to interest the uneducated." The educational system that Dickens would substitute for Gradgrind's is little better than Gradgrind's, which is exaggerated "out of all practical utility as an example."

141. [Hotten, John C.]. **Charles Dickens. The Story of His Life.** London: John Camden Hotten, n.d. [1870], pp. 221-23. Also pub. New York: Harper, 1870. Rpt. Folcroft, Pa.: Folcroft, 1978.

The title-page of this book lists it as "By the Author of the 'Life of Thackeray'"--that is, John C. Hotten. The catalogue of the J.F. Dexter collection in the British Library attributes this work to H.T. Taverner and says that it is also attributed to Joseph Grego and to W.M. Thomas. The author states that **Hard Times** is the "least read and admired" of Dickens's books. The plot is "meagre and aimless," the characters are overdrawn. Charles Knight's plaint (144) and Dickens's reply, the Brough parody (91), and the Strand (54) and Astley's adaptations (59) are noted.

142.    Jacox, Francis. "Mr. Gradgrind: Typically Considered." **Bentley's Miscellany**, 60 (1866), 613-20.

This is an essay on education and the issue of fact versus fancy, with Gradgrind invoked at the beginning and in a few passing references in the body of the essay. The title and the references indicate the degree to which "Gradgrind" had become shorthand for an education confined to sheer fact, neglecting fancy.

143.    Jerrold, William Blanchard, ed. **The Best of All Good Company: A Day with Dickens, Scott, Lytton, Disraeli, Thackeray, Douglas Jerrold**. London: The Useful Knowledge Co., 1071, p. 25.

Asserts that **Hard Times** "is the poorest of all the great author's works."

*       Joubert, Andre.

See below (508).

144.    Knight, Charles. **Passages of a Working Life**. 3 vols. London: Bradbury & Evans, 1863-65, III, 187-88.

Before he published his **Knowledge Is Power** in 1854, Knight sent a copy to Dickens, thinking that "Although the general tendency of the writings of Mr. Dickens is to unite classes in feelings of a common brotherhood, I have sometimes thought he bore too hardly upon those who held that the great truths of political economy ... were not an insufficient foundation for the improvement of society." To Knight's fears that Dickens would find him in this book a "cold-hearted political economist" Dickens replied, "My satire is against those who see figures and averages, and nothing else .... Bah! what have you

to do with these!" Dickens's letter is included in **Letters**, 2, 620
(1). See Boulton (211).

145.    MacKenzie, R. Shelton.  **Life of Charles Dickens**.  Philadelphia:
        T.B. Peterson, 1870, p. 230.

        Selects a few characters for comment and praises the cir-
        cus scenes as equal to the theater scenes in **Nicholas Nickle-
        by**. MacKenzie quotes James T. Fields's assertion that Dickens
        went behind the scenes at Astley's to gather material for the
        horse-riding.

146.    Macaulay, Thomas B.  **Life and Letters of Lord Macaulay**.  2
        vols.  Ed. George O. Trevelyan.  New York: Harper, 1876, II, 320.
        Rpt. 2 vols. in one, New York:  Oxford Univ. Press, 1978.

        The journal entry for 12 August 1854 records Macaulay's
        reading of **Hard Times**: "One excessively touching, heart-
        breaking passage, and the rest sullen socialism." He adds that
        Dickens caricatures the evils he attacks, with little humor. Ma-
        caulay's phrase "sullen socialism" rapidly became a by-word of
        commentary on **Hard Times**.

147.    Martineau, Harriet.  **The Factory Controversy: A Warning
        Against Meddling Legislation**. Manchester: A. Ireland, 1855, p.
        36.

        Takes **Hard Times** as an adequate instance by itself of
        Dickens's failure in his mission to instruct his readers in
        **Household Words**. In response to the defense that the tale is
        fiction, Martineau suggests that it is in fact not likely to do
        great mischief because it is so far from life, so implausible.
        Thus in place of an "ideal creation," Dickens has nothing. He is
        nonetheless responsible for the even worse papers on the fac-
        tory controversy published in **Household Words**, she asserts,
        even if he did not write them.

148.    -------.  **Harriet Martineau's Autobiography**.  With memorials
        by M.W. Chapman.  3 vols.  Windemere (vols. 1 and 2), 1857
        and London (vol. 3), 1877; Boston: James Osgood, 1877.  II, 26,
        92. A new edition in 2 vols., London: Virago, 1983.

Vexed at Dickens's "vigorous erroneousness about matters of science," instances the controversies with employers in **Hard Times** and wishes that he would abstain from subjects for which knowledge is necessary. Martineau is equally dismayed at the novel and at the accounts in **Household Words** of the Preston strike and of the Factory and Wages controversy.

149. "Mr. Dickens's Last Novel." **Dublin University Magazine**, 58 (December 1861), 685-93. Rpt. in Collins (293). Bemoans the weakening powers of Dickens, remarking that "Doubtless there were some good souls who saw in 'Hard Times' and 'Little Dorrit' either the fitting outcome or the momentary eclipse of bygone triumphs won by the pen of 'Boz.'"

150. Ruskin, John. "Unto This Last." **Cornhill Magazine**, 2 (August 1860), 155-66. Issued in volume as **Unto This Last**. London: Smith, Elder, 1862. Section on **Hard Times** rpt. in the Norton edition (45) and in **The Dickens Critics**. Ed. George Ford and Lauriat Lane, Jr. Ithaca: Cornell Univ. Press, 1961.

Wishes that Dickens had limited his "brilliant exaggeration" when on such "a subject of high national importance" as in **Hard Times**. Ruskin finds that the work is diminished because Bounderby is "a dramatic monster" and Stephen "a dramatic perfection," but Dickens is "entirely right in his main drift" and **Hard Times** is of all his works "the greatest." Though much is "apparently unjust," "his view was the finally right one, grossly and sharply told." Ruskin's comments here have been of great comfort and use to defenders of **Hard Times**.

151. -------. **The Works of John Ruskin**. Ed. E.T. Cook and Alexander Wedderburn. 39 vols. London: G. Allen; New York: Longmans, Green, 1903-12, XXXVII, 7.

A letter to Charles Eliot Norton, 19 June 1870: "The literary loss [in Dickens's death] is infinite--the political one I care less for than you do. Dickens was a pure modernist--a leader of the steam-whistle party **par excellence** .... His hero is essentially the iron-master; in spite of **Hard Times**, he has advanced by his influence every principle that makes them harder ...." These remarks offer less comfort than the earlier ones in "Unto This Last" (150).

152. Stott, George. "Charles Dickens." **Contemporary Review**, 10
     (January 1869), 203-05. Rpt. in part in Collins (293).

     Argues that since Dickens is a man of genius, his faults
     need examining, and   goes on to examine   them at length.
     Wondering about how one could live in a world dominated by
     the likes of Tom Pinch and Esther Summerson, Stott concludes:
     "It would, indeed, require nothing short of that new birth into
     imbecility which Mr. Dickens is so fond of bestowing on his
     penitents, as Mr. Dombey and Mr. Gradgrind, to fit one for ad-
     mission into such a paradise of fools."

153. Taine, Hippolyte A.   "Charles Dickens, son talent et ses oeu-
     vres." **Revue des Deux Mondes**, 1 February 1856, pp. 618-47.
     Rpt. in **Histoire de la Litterature Anglaise**. 4 vols.   Paris: Ha-
     chette, 1864.   Trans. H. Van Laun as **History of English Litera-
     ture**. New York: John Wurtele Lovell, 1871.

     This very mixed evaluation of Dickens uses **Hard Times** for
     a number of examples, in itself something of note for the peri-
     od. The novel is "an abstract of all the rest." Stephen's dying
     speech is chosen to show how Dickens plays upon our sympa-
     thies, seeks out human miseries to envelop in despair. Bound-
     erby and Gradgrind are men who constitute a real class; their
     rigidity is not in the French character, Taine states. The por-
     trait of Harthouse is drawn with a sarcasm that Dickens always
     extends to his aristocrats.

154. Thackeray, William Makepeace. **The Letters and Private Papers
     of William Makepeace Thackeray**. Ed. Gordon N. Ray. 4 vols.
     Cambridge, Mass.: Harvard Univ. Press, 1946, III, 363.

     A letter to Percival Leigh, 12 April 1854, remarks upon an
     excerpt from **Hard Times** in the **Examiner** (19) representing a
     character like one he has drawn "in several varieties." Thack-
     eray still thinks he knows whose is the better English of the
     two, but wonders why no younger writer has yet knocked both
     of them off the stage. Ray suggests that the closest compan-
     ion portrait to Bounderby is old Osborne in **Vanity Fair**.

155.  Whipple,  Edwin  P.  "Dickens's  Hard  Times."  **The Atlantic
      Monthly**, 39 (March 1877), 353-58.  Rpt. in **Charles Dickens:
      The Man and His Work**.  2 vols.  Boston  and New York:
      Houghton Mifflin, 1912; rpt. New York: AMS, 1975.  First ap-
      peared as his "Introduction" to the New Illustrated Library edi-
      tion, 1876 (28), pp. ix–xix.

      Deplores Dickens's inability to generalize and the dominion
      of his benevolent sentiments, so that he attacked as untrue
      whatever seemed harsh.  "The time will come when it will be
      as intellectually discreditable for an educated person to engage
      in a crusade against the established laws of political economy
      as in a crusade against the established laws of the physical
      universe," Whipple states.  He compares the responses of Rus
      kin and Macaulay and remarks that neither sees how Dickens's
      power as a creator of character masks his weakness as a sati-
      rist.  Bounderby is humorous, but he is drawn externally, anti-
      pathy having superseded insight.  Whipple concedes some
      good incidents and descriptions in the novel, but finds the
      whole "ungenial and unpleasant."  Then he reverses direction,
      suggesting that if he forgets Adam Smith, Ricardo, and Mill and
      thinks of the book merely as the expression of "a humorous
      satirist profoundly disgusted with some prominent evils of his
      day," he can "warmly praise the book as one of the most per-
      fect of its kind."

# XI

# LATER COMMENTARY AND CRITICISM

156. Addison, William [Wilkinson]. **In the Steps of Charles Dickens**. London: Rich & Cowan, 1955, pp. 22, 191.

This book describes itself as a "topological approach" to Dickens. Addison notes that although the introduction of machinery was the most important development of his time, Dickens dealt with it only in **Hard Times**. He asserts that the novel is better than the critics have allowed. Mortimer Grimshaw, the strike leader, is both the Gruffshaw of "On Strike" and Slackbridge; Dickens denied the identification for fear of consequences. Coketown is not any one place in particular, but mostly Preston. On the identity of Slackbridge, compare Beer (193).

157. Adrian, Arthur A. "Dickens and Inverted Parenthood." **Dickensian**, 67 (1971), 3-11.

Argues in the closing paragraphs of the essay that despite the well-known concerns of Dickens for the state of English politics and his pessimism in that regard, we must remember as we assess the mood and even the social arguments of the later works, including **Hard Times**, Dickens's personal pain at the break-up of his family and his own childhood memories. The negligent father and the neglected child become the bungling politician and the neglected constituent.

158. -------. "Dickens and the Brick-and-Mortar Sects." **NCF**, 10 (1955), 188-201.

Includes the eighteen chapels of Coketown in a survey of Dickens's campaign against the Nonconformists.

159. Alain [Emile Chartier]. **En lisant Dickens**. Paris: Gallimard, 1945, pp. 130-35.

A laudatory exposition of "Les Temps difficiles." Alain sees the novel as based upon the tension between Coketown and Sleary's but coming to focus upon Louisa. He finds the study of Louisa of a power worthy of Shakespeare.

160. Alexander, Edward. "Disinterested Virtue: Dickens and Mill in Agreement." **Dickensian**, 65 (1969), 163–70.

Argues that Dickens and Mill were closer than either recognized, demonstrating their common attitudes on four fronts: aesthetic, educational, economic, and ethical. See also Arneson (171), Baker (180), Fielding (380), and Ryan (713).

161. Allen, Walter. **The English Novel: A Short Critical History**. London: Dutton, 1954, p. 188. Rpt. London: Phoenix, 1960.

Includes **Hard Times**, along with **Dombey and Son, Bleak House, Little Dorrit**, and **Great Expectations**, in a list of novels in which Dickens's "onslaught on the age is fundamental."

162. –––––––. "Introduction." **Hard Times**. In the Harper & Row edition, 1965 (44). pp. xlll–xviii.

Discusses the limitations of length, Leavis's perception of the novel as a moral fable (553) and its extensive effect in changing critical opinion, and the object of Dickens's satire as "the statistical conception of man," Carlyle's "cash nexus." Allen compares Louisa's crisis to Mill's, as described in his **Autobiography**, with the circus standing equivalent to Wordsworth. "The comedy is savagely and scornfully sardonic, to the virtual exclusion of the humor," Allen concludes; the weakest part of the novel is the presentation of the working classes, especially Stephen. Review: Anne Smith, **DSN**, 4 (1973), 115–22.

163. –––––––. **Six Great Novelists**. London: Hamish Hamilton, 1955, p. 122.

Makes essentially the same brief mention of **Hard Times** as in **The English Novel** (161).

164. Allott, Miriam. **Novelists on the Novel**. New York: Columbia Univ. Press, 1959; London: Routledge, 1962, pp. 26, 207.

Includes **Hard Times** among the novels of the 1840's that indicate the social concern of the nineteenth century. Allott finds the novel a novelist's moral fable, like **Jonathan Wild** and unlike **Rasselas**, the difference being that in the former human individuality takes precedence over abstract speculation.

165.    Ames, Winslow. **Prince Albert and Victorian Taste.** London: Chapman & Hall, 1967, pp. 84, 94.

Following K.J. Fielding's "Charles Dickens and the Department of Practical Art" (376), draws attention to Dickens's satire on Henry Cole, a central figure in the revolution of taste. Ames argues that Gradgrind's aesthetic preferences derive from the official and semi-official publications through which, by 1854, the "South Kensington team" of Victorian technologists had spread its doctrine. See also Bell (195).

166.    Andrews, Malcolm. "A Note on Serialisation." In **Reading the Victorian Novel: Detail into Form.** Ed. Ian Gregor. London: Vision, 1980, pp. 243–47.

Examines various aspects of serial publication and draws attention to the effect on contemporary readers' experience of contextual material in the magazines. **Hard Times** is the prime example. Andrews reviews the other material in the 1 April 1854 issue of **Household Words** to demonstrate the "sharp relief" created by the "familiar contextual material": writings "that emphasize colour, exoticism, sentimentality, jollity, and soft domesticity." Compare Butwin (241), Clark (279), and Fielding (381).

167.    Andrews, Michael. **Dickens on England and the English.** Sussex: Harvester; New York: Barnes & Noble, 1979, pp. 141–42, 156.

Draws attention to the similarity of the definitions of a horse in **Nicholas Nickleby**, chapter viii, and **Hard Times**, and compares Gradgrind to Dr. Blimber. Gradgrind, Blimber, and Squeers all fail to see the emotional needs of children.

168.    apRoberts, Ruth. **The Moral Trollope.** Athens: Ohio Univ. Press, 1971, p. 29. Also pub. as **Trollope, Artist and Moralist.** London: Chatto & Windus, 1971.

Offers Leavis's valuation of **Hard Times** (553) as an instance of the critical tendency to read novels in terms of politics and philosophy. Leavis therefore overlooks Dickens's "marvellous conjuring," apRoberts concludes.

169. Armstrong, Nancy. "Character and Closure in Selected Nineteenth Century Novels." **DAI**, 38 (1978), 6736A (Univ. of Wisconsin, Madison, 1977). 173 pp.

Uses a method derived from A.J. Greimas to study the development of character as it responds to changing social conditions. In the later Dickens we see "social atomization" in the wake of an automatically operating market. See below (169).

170. --------. "Dickens Between Two Disciplines: A Problem for Theories of Reading." **Semiotica**, 38 - 3/4 (1982), 243-75.

Chooses **Hard Times** as an instance to demonstrate the relationship between literary and historical interpretation, to "identify the procedures necessary for producing a plausible historical description of the novel, on the one hand, and a coherent literary interpretation on the other," and to show how each reading of the novel transforms the text. Armstrong takes Jameson (491) as the instance of a historian's reading. She argues that the novel was well received after 1870 but not in 1854 because the earlier historical moment did not match its thematic structure. For the example of a literary transformation, she works through V. Propp and Northrop Frye to a discussion of the conflict between romance and family romance in the novel. The argument is supported throughout with methodology derived from A.J. Greimas. Taking Leavis's word for it that his essay (553) established Dickens's artistic genius, Armstrong demonstrates the role of academic criticism in upholding certain cultural values of taste.

171. Arneson, Richard J. "Benthamite Utilitarianism and **Hard Times**." **Philosophy and Literature**, 2 (1978), 60-75.

Demonstrates affinities between Dickens's and Mill's criticism of Benthamism. Arneson argues that Blackpool's failure, his passivity, and the contrast between his treatment of Bounderby and the circus people's constitute a structural criticism of Christian resignation parallel to the argument against Utilitarian doctrine. He points out the linking of the recreation-

al and didactic aspects of fancy and the incestuousness of the
relationship between Tom and Louisa. See also Alexander (160),
Baker (180), Deneau (332), and Fielding (380).

*       Atkinson, F.G.

        See below (871).

172.    Augburn, Gerald Richard. "The Function of Death in the Novels
        of Charles Dickens." **DA**, 29 (1968), 2666A–67A (Columbia
        Univ., 1968). 286 pp.

        Death is seen as the antagonist in all the novels after
        **Pickwick**. In the later novels Dickens depicts a death–like so-
        ciety and attributes this condition to a particular human atti-
        tude. In **Hard Times**, Augburn concludes, the attitude is Philo-
        sophic Materialism.

173.    Axson, Stockton. "Dickens and Social Reform." **The Rice Insti-
        tute Pamphlet**, 3 (1916), 3–22.

        A broad discussion, referring only occasionally to particular
        novels: Axson mentions Dickens's assertion in **Hard Times** that
        Parliament must be reformed and notes Coketown's various
        societies for prevention and promotion, which seem only to
        prevent what should be promoted and promote what should be
        prevented.

174.    Axton, William. **Circle of Fire**. Lexington: Univ. of Kentucky
        Press, 1966, pp. 56, 102, 111, 153.

        **Hard Times** is mentioned only briefly. Axton offers Sleary's
        horse–riding as one example of Dickens's continuing theatrical
        and histrionic interests. He points to the similarity on the issue
        of factual education between **Hard Times** and the "Reports of
        the Mudfog Association" (13). He compares the melodramatic,
        stagey effect of Louisa's encounter with Gradgrind to the
        scenes between Edith Dombey and Carker and between Lady
        Dedlock and Esther. Reviews: T.J. Cribb, **RES**, 19(1968), 348–49;
        Lauriat Lane, Jr., **Dickens Studies**, 3 (1967), 170–75; Martin
        Meisel, **JEGP**, 67 (1968), 169–70; Katherine J. Worth, **VS**, 11
        (1968), 416–17.

175.    ———. "Dickens Now." In **The Victorian Experience: Novelists**. Ed. Richard A. Levine. Athens: Ohio Univ. Press, 1976, pp.
19–48.

    Examines Dickens's impact on "the generation of readers
who came to maturity by 1938," noting the absence of **Hard
Times, Bleak House, Great Expectations,** and **Our Mutual
Friend** from the high school curriculum of 1920–1950, and the
almost topical relevance for the twentieth century of much in
Dickens's "darker passages." Axton finds that Dickens's use of
incongruity and discontinuity creates, in both his light and his
dark comedy, a "haunting sense of the sinister or corrupt forces working within the familiar world."

176.    Aydelotte, William O. "The England of Marx and Mill as Reflect-
ed in Fiction." **Journal of Economic History**, Supp. 8 (1948),
42–58.

    Sets **Hard Times** in the context of the social novels of the
1840's, in particular those of Gaskell, Disraeli, and Kingsley.
Sissy's repudiation of utilitarianism is set alongside Sidonia,
Job's reply to Mr. Carson, and Kingsley's Tregaria. Aydelotte
similarly contextualizes the anti-unionism of the novel in the
essential conservatism of all these writers, although he shows
that Dickens was as likely to reverse their tendencies toward
nostalgia for the past and reliance upon the upper classes for
leadership. Aydelotte looks at Dickens's preoccupation with his
own position, his insecurity, and the growth of his sympathy
for the poor commensurately with his distance from them.

177.    Baily, F[rancis] E[vans]. "Charles Dickens (1812–1870)." In **Six
Great Victorian Novelists**. London: MacDonald, 1947, pp.
47–80.

    Describes the novel as "all about economic doctrines" and
revolving around "a place called Coketown."

178.    Baird, John D. "'Divorce and Matrimonial Causes': An Aspect of
**Hard Times**." **VS**, 20 (1977), 401–12.

    Sets the issue of divorce in the novel in the context of im-
mediate contemporary concerns, in particular the failed Divorce
and Matrimonial Causes Bill of June 1854 and the arguments on
this topic aired in **Household Words**. Baird's historical per-

spective offers a useful balance to the tendency of many critics to read the divorce theme entirely in terms of Dickens's own matrimonial discontent.   Louisa and Bounderby are seen as separated without the possibility of remarriage, and both Louisa and Stephen as victims of laws that are inhumane.

179.   Baker, Ernest.  **The Age of Dickens and Thackeray.**  Vol. 7 of **The History of the English Novel**.  London: Witherby, and New York: Barnes & Noble, 1936, pp. 297–99.

Calls the novel "pamphleteering literature" that fails because Dickens was not capable of such argument.  The book is "a tender-hearted and unreasoning **petitio principii**" that seeks to offset its lack of Dickensian warmth in the pure pathos of Rachael and Stephen and the glib play of the circus people.

180.   Baker, William J.  "Gradgrindery and the Education of John Stuart Mill: A Clarification."  **Western Humanities Review**, 24 (1970), 49–56.

Argues that Gradgrindian education parallels only a phantom of James Mill, a phantom invented by literary critics.  Mill's principles were in fact quite the opposite of what Dickens offers in Gradgrind, as Baker demonstrates by a close examination of J.S. Mill's **Autobiography**.  See also Alexander (160), Arneson (171), Fielding (380), and Ryan (713).

181.   –––––––.  "**Hard Times** and Orr's   **Circle of the Sciences**." **DSN**, 8 (1977), 78.

Finds in Gradgrind's speech to Tom and Louise in chapter iii, that "the circle of the sciences is open" to them, a likely reference to William Somerville Orr's **Orr's Circle of the Sciences; A Series of Treatises on the Principles of Science with Their Application to Practical Pursuits** (London: W.S. Orr, 1854).  The books in this series were published during the early stages of the writing of the novel; the first volumes dealt with mathematics.

182.   Banerjee, N.K.  "**Hard Times**: A Note on the Descriptive Titles of Its Books."  **Indian Journal of English Studies**, 13 (1972), 22–28.

Reads the novel in terms of the agricultural images of its three book-titles.

183.   Bank, Sylvia. "Dickens as Satirist." **DA**, 29 (1968), 559A (Yale Univ., 1967). 285 pp.

See Sylvia B. Manning, **Dickens As Satirist** (606).

184.   Barish, Jonas. **The Anti-Theatrical Prejudice**. Berkeley: Univ. of California Press, 1981, pp. 372–73.

Tracing the growth of a new tolerance and enthusiasm for the theater in the nineteenth century, offers Sleary's as an instance of the endorsement of theatricality. The horse-riding is a haven from the grim world of fact that by the end of the novel, in its rescue of Tom, triumphs even over the practicality of its philistine rival.

185.   Barlow, George. **The Genius of Dickens**. London: Henry J. Glaisher, 1909, p. 23. Rpt. New York: Haskell, 1975; Folcroft, Pa.: Folcrott, 1976.

Arguing that Dickens's portraits of women are more complex than has generally been recognized, offers Louisa, Sissy, and Rachael as three striking figures who show how Dickens's touch has grown "still surer" after **Bleak House**.

186.   Barnard, Robert. **Imagery and Theme in the Novels of Dickens**. Ph.D. dissertation. Univ. of Bergen, 1971. Bergen and Oslo: Universitetsforlaget; New York: Humanities Press, 1974, pp. 77–91.

Begins chapter 6, on **Hard Times**, by conceding the failure of the trade-union portion of the novel, but finds compensation in the success of the Hard Facts portion. Barnard traces images of the mechanical and mathematical and the countering images of fancy, religion, and love, concluding that the novel proclaims the ultimate victory of the fancy. Review: Barbara Hardy, **Dickensian**, 71 (1975), 113.

\*      Barnes, Catherine Weed.

See H. Snowden Ward and Catherine Weed Barnes (825).

187.    Barnes, Samuel G. "Dickens and Copperfield: The Hero as Man
        of Letters." In **The Classic British Novel**. Ed. Howard M. Har-
        per, Jr., and Charles Edge. Athens: Univ. of Georgia Press,
        1972, pp. 85-102.

        Sees **David Copperfield** as pivotal in Dickens's assimilation
        of Carlyle's philosophy, tracing it from the early effort in **The
        Chimes** to the "confident dedication" of **Hard Times**. Barnes
        speculates about a lack of enthusiasm in Carlyle's response to
        Dickens's letter asking permission to dedicate the novel to him.
        Compare Christian (269), Goldberg (421), and Oddie (644).

*       Bartrip, Peter W.J.

        See above (6).

188.    Basch, Francoise. **Relative Creatures: Victorian Women in
        Society and the Novel**. Trans. Anthony Rudolf. London: Allen
        Lane; New York: Schocken, 1974, passim. Rev. and enl. 2nd ed.,
        **Les Femmes victoriennes: Roman et societe**. Paris: Payot,
        1979.

        States that Louisa is an instance of the woman on the
        marriage-market and of the way in which the domestic burden
        is always and entirely woman's; Rachael and Sissy show wo-
        man's "proper mission"; Mrs. Sparsit is one of Dickens's anti-
        women; Louisa, like Lady Dedlock and Edith Dombey and as a
        woman "of industrial society as impure as the Newgate prosti-
        tute," is also a part of the critique of that society. Generally,
        Dickens does not fit well into the sociological vision of litera-
        ture espoused in this book, and his women are castigated as
        explaining "neither the particularity nor the complexity of hu-
        man beings, nor the specific problems of a particular condition
        or profession."

189.    Bayley, John. "Dickens and His Critics." **The Uses of Division:
        Unity and Disharmony in Literature**. London: Chatto & Win-
        dus; New York: Viking, 1976, pp. 90-103.

        Discusses F.R. Leavis's transformation of **Hard Times** (553)
        into "both Blakean and Jamesian social vision" and argues that
        although the novel suits Leavis's method it is "flashy," its social
        purpose dull and its imaginative organization consequently dull
        too. What is great in Dickens, Bayley concludes, is not social
        argument but vital writing.

190.    ------. "**Oliver Twist**: Things as They Really Are." In **Dickens and the Twentieth Century**. Ed. John Gross and Gabriel
Pearson. London: Routledge & Kegan Paul, 1962, pp. 49-64.

Finds Dickens's later symbolic technique close to Lawrence's, "purposeful and claustrophobic," constrained by authorial intention for meaning. "The Dickens of **Hard Times**,
whom Dr. Leavis admires, manipulates symbolic meaning in a
manner that reaches its apotheosis with Clifford Chatterley sit-
ting in his motor-chair," Bayley asserts.

191.    Deadlo, Gordon    "George Orwell and Charles Dickens: Moral
Critics of Society." **Journal of Historical Studies**, 2 (1969 70),
245-55.

Considers the intellectual relationship between Orwell and
Dickens. Both Orwell's socialism and Dickens's are a "non-i-
deological concern" for one's fellow-man, as shown in Sissy's
first principle of political economy. Dickens's satire on Benthamism in **Oliver Twist** and **Hard Times** can be compared to Orwell's criticism of the "smelly little orthodoxies" that threaten
human freedom.

192.    Beer, Gillian. "'Coming Wonders': Uses of the Theatre in the
Victorian Novel." In **English Drama; Forms and Development**:
**Essays in Honour of Muriel Clara Bradbrook**. Ed. Marie Axton
and Raymond Williams. Cambridge: Cambridge Univ. Press,
1977, pp. 164-85.

Looks at Sleary's horse-riding in light of the value Dickens
gives to theater, which arises from its "medley of noise, inven-
tiveness, formulaic happening, and high useless skill." The circus people are not actors, but performers, without illusions and
hard-working. In contrast, Bounderby invents a false fairy-tale
of his early struggles.

193.    Beer, M[ax]. **A History of British Socialism**. 2 vols. London:
G. Bell, 1929, II, 11, 175.

Claims that Slackbridge is "rather too much a caricature" of
Feargus O'Connor, an Irish leader of the Chartist movement.
Compare the arguments for Mortimer Grimshaw in Addison
(156).

194.    Belcher, Margaret E. "Bulwer's Mr. Bluff: A Suggestion for **Hard Times**." **Dickensian**, 78 (1982), 105–09.

        Speculates that the character of Mr. Bluff in Edward Lytton Bulwer's **England and the English** (1833) may have had influence both as a source for Mr. Gradgrind and on the use of the adjective "bluff" for Bounderby.

195.    Bell, Quentin. **The Schools of Design**. London: Routledge & Kegan Paul, 1963, pp. 212, 262.

        Endorses Fielding's identification of the third gentleman in chapter ii of **Hard Times** as Henry Cole (376). The Schools of Design served the interests of industry, and their system took over the art classes of the country. "The caricature in **Hard Times** was not so very remote from the truth," Bell concludes. "Written in 1854, it comes near to giving an exact account of the outcome of the great battle of the Schools of Design"--which Ruskin opposed, consistently and ineffectually. See also Ames (165).

196.    Benn, J. Miriam. "A Landscape with Figures: Characterization and Expression in **Hard Times**." **DSA**, 1 (1970), 168–82.

        Finds Dickens's solution to the problems created by the compression of this novel to be his near-allegorical use of metaphor to create character. According to Benn, the characters fail when they are subject to an unstable mixture of allegory and psychological realism: Gradgrind, for instance, goes from allegorical figure to a humanized father, and Louisa from a finely human character to a vehicle of heavy moralizing. Benn sees Bounderby and Bitzer, in contrast, as consistently allegorical and successful. Stephen, however, fails simply because of his rhetoric, because he carries too many underdeveloped themes, and because he is dull.

197.    Bennett, Arnold. **The Journals of Arnold Bennett**. Ed. Newman Flower. 3 vols. London: Cassell, 1932, I, 158.

        Recounts that Marcel Schwob (a general writer and bibliographer) called the opening of **Hard Times** "one of the finest things in English" and concludes, "Of course I disagreed."

198.  Bergmann, Helena. "**Hard Times** (1854)." **Between Obedience
      and Freedom: Woman's Role in the Mid-Nineteenth Century
      Industrial Novel**. Gothenburg Studies in English, 45. Goteborg:
      Acta Universitatis Gothoburgensis, 1979, pp. 40–44.

      Emphasizes Rachael, the representative of the working
      class, and Sissy, who moves from that class to the middle
      class. For Bergmann, both represent values critical of middle-
      class mores.

199.  Berman, Ronald. "Human Scale: A Note on **Hard Times**." **NCF**,
      22 (1067), 288–93

      Finds instead of the economic texture we see in Balzac a
      "persuasively tragic agon" in **Hard Times** between "the work of
      God and the work of Man." The thrust of the novel is allegori-
      cal and religious, but vague. Berman remarks upon and eluci-
      dates the allusive, indirect references to sexuality in the novel
      and the "symbolic zoology" that establishes a focus of "human
      scale" by which to measure the life-atrophying qualities of in-
      dustrialism. Against Coketown are set the human plenum of
      the circus and the apotheosis of Rachael by the power of love.

200.  Bernard, Catherine Adelaide. "Dickens and Dreams: A Study of
      the Dream Theories and Dream Fiction of Charles Dickens."
      **DAI**, 38 (1977), 2134A (New York Univ., 1977). 286 pp.

      In support of her argument that dream and nightmare of-
      fered Dickens increasing access to the inner life of his charac-
      ters, Bernard examines the "torturous night wanderings" of Jo-
      nas Chuzzlewit, Esther Summerson, and Stephen Blackpool.

201.  Bilan, R.P. **The Literary Criticism of F.R. Leavis**. Cambridge:
      Cambridge Univ. Press, 1979, passim.

      This is a study of Leavis, and although Leavis's essays on
      **Hard Times** recur in the discussion, they are discussed in rela-
      tion to Leavis rather than Dickens. Bilan does suggest that
      **Hard Times** is one of the few instances in which Leavis ap-
      pears more concerned with ethics than with art, noting Leavis's
      easy tolerance of the failure of Stephen Blackpool. He argues
      that Leavis makes **Hard Times** sound more successful than it
      is, but without discussing just how successful it really is. See
      Leavis (553).

202.  Bishop, Charles William. "Fire and Fancy: Dickens' Theories of
      Fiction." **DAI**, 31 (1970), 5351A (Duke Univ., 1970). 349 pp.

      Arguing that Dickens was more interested in artistic theory
      and in the imaginative nature of the artist than is generally
      supposed, instances Louisa's drawing of imaginative sustenance
      from the fire as a demonstration of the "almost magical power"
      Dickens associated with imagination.

203.  Blom, J.M. "The English 'Social-Problem' Novel: Fruitful Con-
      cept or Critical Evasion?" **ES**, 62 (1981), 120-27.

      Surveys the criticism of the "social-problem" subgenre
      from Cazamian (256) through Arnold Kettle (525), Raymond Wil-
      liams (849), John Lucas (585), and Sheila Smith (758), to argue
      that they are all guilty of a blurring of literary with social-his-
      torical issues that constitutes an evasion of literary judgment.
      The focus of this essay is upon the inferiority of the novels of
      Gaskell, Kingsley, Disraeli, and Reade, and **Hard Times** becomes
      the standard that the rest do not meet. **Hard Times** should be
      seen as art, Blom insists--and thus is Leavis (553) vindicated.

204.  Boarman, Joseph C., Martin Hollie Boarman, and James L. Harte.
      **Boz: An Intimate Biography of Charles Dickens**. Boston:
      Stratford, 1935, pp. 47, 157-59, 160-62.

      The first part of this book mentions **Hard Times** as a "sat-
      ire aimed at the factory system then prevailing." The second
      part, "Intimate Word-Sketches of Dickens' Important Charac-
      ters," by Martin Hollie Boarman, revised and edited by James L.
      Harte, includes a moralization upon men of Gradgrind's type
      and an indignant, also moralizing, sketch of Bounderby.

205.  Bodelsen, C.A. "The Physiognomy of the Name." **REL**, 2 (July
      1961), 39-48.

      Argues that Dickens relies increasingly upon the symbolic
      effects of names. Bodelsen classifies Bounderby and M'Choa-
      kumchild among the simple symbolic names, Slackbridge
      among the slightly more complicated, and Harthouse among
      the names with no particular relation to the character's per-
      sonality. Bodelsen finds Bitzer's name effective for its "sound
      symbolism."

206.  -------. "Some Aspects of Dickens' Symbolism." **ES**, 40
      (1959), 420-31.

      Refers briefly, in a discussion of clocks, to the "statistical
      clocks" of **Hard Times**.

207.  Boege, Fred W. "Point of View in Dickens." **PMLA**, 65 (1950),
      90-105.

      Defines Dickens as an "objective novelist," one who is su-
      preme in the external treatment of his characters and inade-
      quate in dealing with their inner lives, but whose interest in
      point of view is nonetheless worth examining.  Boege finds
      Dickens's method appropriate to novels in which the satire of
      an institution dominates ("materialistic economics" for **Hard
      Times**), but Dickens can also use it when dealing with the inner
      life.  Boege illustrates this with  Sydney Carton and Louisa
      Gradgrind.  Louisa is treated objectively only to the end of
      Book I.  Thereafter the enemy, sentimentalism, penetrates.  Her
      visit to her dying mother and her final visions do not tell us
      more about her.

208.  Bony, Alain. "Realite et imaginaire dans **Hard Times**." **EA**, 23
      (1970), 168-82.

      Locates the ultimate unsatisfactoriness of the novel in a
      conflict of genres.  Dickens begins a fairy tale on the theme of
      education and imagination: Louisa is the victim trapped by the
      ogres, Sissy the potential rescuer.  But then Dickens brings in
      the condition-of-England theme, which cannot bear the reduc-
      tive fairy-tale treatment and which is incompatible with the to-
      tality of fairy-tale resolutions.  So the downfall comes from the
      hubris of the ogres themselves, Bony concludes, and the fairy-
      tale solution is replaced by the parallelism of tragic destiny in
      Louisa and Stephen.  Their achievements are limited because
      Coketown, which is out of time and space, does not change.
      Because Dickens cannot choose between the adult realities of
      this theme and the fairy-tale imaginings of childhood, Bony as-
      serts, disequilibrium remains between the beginning and the
      ending of the novel.  For a reply to this essay, see Sheila Smith
      (756).

209.  Bornstein, George.  "Miscultivated Field and Corrupted Garden:
      Imagery in **Hard Times**." **NCF**, 26 (1971), 158-70.

Seeks to establish the "coherence of the book's imagery in terms of the central patterns of miscultivated field and corrupted garden." Bornstein argues that Dickens idealizes the middle way, the blend of pattern and spontaneity in the cultivated field or garden. Bornstein extracts these metaphors in three sections, corresponding to the levels on which the images function: the socioeconomic, the educational and personal, and the religious. The last section is particularly successful.

210.    Booth, Meyrick. **Charles Dickens und seine Werke in padago-gischer Beleuchtung**. Ph.D. Dissertation. Univ. of Jena [? 1909]. Zurich: Schulthess, 1909, passim.

Includes Gradgrind's in a survey of schools in Dickens's novels. The children of **Hard Times** are allocated a sub-chapter of summary and quotation.

211.    Boulton, J.T. "Charles Knight and Dickens: **Knowledge Is Power** and **Hard Times**." **Dickensian**, 50 (1954), 57-63.

Examines closely several aspects of Charles Knight's **Knowledge Is Power** (144) to show how far "it could have provided a focal point for the attack" on utilitarianism in **Hard Times**. Knight sets Dickens's differing opinions in happy relief.

212.    Boulton, Marjorie. **The Anatomy of the Novel**. London and Boston: Routledge & Kegan Paul, 1975, passim.

Chooses **Hard Times** as one of five novels for repeated reference, on the criteria that all five are great, short, simple, easy to find, and different from one another. The result is a large number of scattered references to **Hard Times**, but no sustained discussion of the novel. Bounderby's brazen doorplate is an example of a detail with significance, the novel itself is an example of the omniscient point of view, etc.

213.    Bracher, Peter Scholl. "Dickens and His American Readers: A Study of the American Reception, Reputation, and Popularity of Charles Dickens and His Novels During His Lifetime." **DAI**, 27 (1966), 1332A-33A (Univ. of Pennsylvania, 1966). xlix, 394 pp.

This study is a recovery of opinion and response, dividing the American reception of Dickens into three parts, the third of which is from **Bleak House** to Dickens's death. The sources are primarily contempory periodicals but include also letters, diaries, and journals. **Hard Times** is the only one of the novels after **Bleak House** not to be studied specifically, and perhaps in consequence there are only four references to it. We do learn, however, that along with **Barnaby Rudge, A Tale of Two Cities,** and **Martin Chuzzlewit**, it was the least successful of Dickens's novels in the United States.

214.     --------. "Muddle and Wonderful No-Meaning: Verbal Irresponsibility and Verbal Failures in **Hard Times**." **SNNTS**, 10 (1978), 305-19.

        Analyzes the novel in terms of failures of communication, dealing at once with rhetorical falsity (such as Slackbridge's rhetoric or Mrs. Sparsit's euphemisms), failures such as that between Louisa and her father, and misrepresentation (Bounderby's childhood). Coketown is revealed to be "a place of verbal surrealism."

215.     Brantlinger, Patrick. "The Case against Trade Unions in Early Victorian Fiction." **VS**, 13 (1969), 37-52.

        Extends House's discussion of the trade-union question (475) to show how Dickens's perspective was shared by the other novelists of the period who dealt with the issue. Brantlinger discusses Dickens's remarks on unionism and argues that the disparity between them and his remarks in **Hard Times** is not as great as it might first appear, since Dickens's attitude in "On Strike" is less than fully sympathetic. Brantlinger attributes what disparity there is to Dickens's symbolic purpose in the novel, which was to show that hard actions by masters produce hard actions by men. He notes that Dickens's supply-and-demand view of labor governed his belief in the futility of strikes and suggests that at least some of the "muddle" is in Dickens's thinking: he offers criticism of the unions and then puts it in the mouth of Bounderby, resulting in a curious mixture of prejudice and sympathy.

216.     --------. "Dickens and the Factories." **NCF**, 26 (1971), 270-85.

        Traces Dickens's views on industrialism through several works, arguing that the contradictions charted by Holloway (471), Gissing (418), Ruskin (150), and others are artistically significant. Dickens's most consistent social theory is of the limitations of social theories. At the end of this essay, Brantlinger focuses upon the first two paragraphs of chapter ii of **Hard Times**. He concludes that Dickens's lapses of logic are what make poetry possible. Compare Collins (289), Holloway (471), and Leavis (553).

217.    ———. **The Spirit of Reform: British Literature and Politics 1832–1867**. Cambridge, Mass.: Harvard Univ. Press, 1977, passim.

An important book for the study of **Hard Times**, though references to the novel are scattered. The book shows the growing conservatism of the period as radicalism gives way to progressivism and theories of progressive evolution. Brantlinger discusses Dickens's relation to Benthamism, the simultaneous view of the working classes as victims and as free agents, Daniel Doyce and Bounderby as poles of possibility rather than mutual contradictions, and the limitations of Dickens's concept of fancy as a form of romantic idealism. He argues that Dickens "senses the inadequacy of all remedies and theories, including his own, to cope with the situation." Compare Keating (515). Reviews: R. O'Kell, **VS**, 21 (1977), 504–06; Peter Stansky, **NCF**, 32 (1978), 473–76.

218.    Brereton, Frederick. "Introduction." In the Collins edition, 1954 (38), pp. 11–14. Reissued 1973.

Suggests that since Gradgrind's attitude prevailed in the 1850's, Dickens was courageous in his satire. Brereton finds Louisa's marrying for Tom's sake improbable, Gradgrind's character truer to life, and the novel imbalanced by the absence of a hero. He praises the love between Rachael and Stephen as having all the elements of classic tragedy and finds Stephen's "muddle" speech a proper reponse to Gradgrindian philosophy. In general, he takes the novel as a proposition towards the solution of social and industrial problems.

219.    Briggs, Asa. "Foreword." In the Panther edition, 1977 (52), pp. vii–xiv.

Interweaves various information on the background of the novel into a discussion of its themes. Briggs suggests that Sleary's moral is unimpressive if it is taken out of context: "It is

the Fancy in the fable as a whole and not a lesson deduced
from it which makes it possible to conceive of **Hard Times** as a
masterpiece."

220.   --------. **Victorian Cities**. London: Oldhams, 1963; New York:
       Harper & Row, 1965, 1970, pp. 100, 102, 103, 328.

       Various references to **Hard Times** include the statement
       that Coketown was really Oldham.

221.   Brook, George L. **Language of Dickens**. London: Andre
       Deutsch, 1970, passim.

       A description of language in Dickens, both narrative and
       descriptive language and the language of characters.  **Hard
       Times** is used for a variety of instances, with particular atten-
       tion to the contrast between the fine language Sleary employs
       for his advertisements and the slang spoken backstage.  There
       is also a lengthy analysis of Stephen and Rachael's dialect, with
       a vocabulary list and a list of twenty-two primary features of
       speech "which seem to be intended as regional."  Reviews:
       John Carey, **Listener**, 83 (1970), 724-25; John Holloway, **En-
       counter**, 34, vi (1970), 63-68; Norman Page, **Dickensian**, 66
       (1970), 250-51.

222.   Brooker, Arlin Thro.  "The Dickens Melodrama: Gentle Goodness
       and Passion in Dickens' Novels."  Ph.D. Dissertation.  Univ. of
       California, Berkeley, 1974.  257 pp.

       Examines the "stylistic and thematic discontinuities which
       Dickens introduces into his fiction" by supporting the "opposed
       actions of 'the Dickens melodrama:' a gentle goodness which ...
       is safe from emotional taint, and a strong emotion which ... is
       exempt from moral condemnation."  Brooker traces through
       three phases what he sees as Dickens's gradual reversal of his
       conscious attitudes towards these two melodramatic actions.
       In the third phase, he concentrates on **Bleak House** and **Hard
       Times**, in which he finds that Dickens "openly and impartially
       supports both gentle goodness and passion, insulating them
       from one another in opposed plots."

223.   Brooker, Peter.  "Post-structuralism, Reading, and the Crisis in
       English."  **Re-Reading English**.  Ed. Peter Widdowson.  London
       and New York: Methuen, 1982, pp. 61-76.

Uses Bitzer and Sissy in a playful opening that imagines a future essay topic on the relevance of post-structuralist theory to the teaching of English. Brooker describes Dickens at the time he wrote **Hard Times** as "inscribed ... in an ideological conjuncture whose main feature was the internal confrontation of middle-class romantic humanism and utilitarianism." At the end of this essay Brooker suggests that it would be possible to teach **Hard Times** "as historically produced and reproduced, in relation, say, to Carlyle, Ruskin, Leavis and its TV serialisation."

224.    Brown, Arthur Washburn. "Dickens' Props: An Analysis of Their Sexual Significance, with a Chapter of Death." **DA**, 28 (1967), 2236-37A (Columbia Univ., 1967). 239 pp.

        See Brown, below (225).

225.    --------. **Sexual Analysis of Charles Dickens' Props**. New York: Emerson, 1971, passim.

        Notes the curiously inverted relationship between Bounder-by and Dickens, with focus upon Bounderby's boast of having blacked boots. The method of this study is to take the props of the novels as Freud took the objects of dreams, but to relate them (usually) to the novel, not the dreamer/author. **Hard Times** is not analyzed at length, though some of its props come in as examples of various symbolic patterns (e.g., back-gammon, unlike cribbage, is not a precursor of sexuality, and Mrs. Sparsit plays backgammon with Bounderby; the "florid wooden legs" of the church in which Bounderby marries Louisa represent both his sexual excitement and his punishment for this January-and-May marriage; the downpour when Louisa elopes is related to the "fructifying copulation" represented by rainfall). Reviews: Martin Dodsworth, **Dickensian**, 68 (1972), 191-93; Susan Horton, **VS**, 16 (1972), 251-52; Lawrence Senelick, **DSN**, 4 (1973), 50-52.

226.    Brown, Ivor. "Dickens as Social Reformer." In **Charles Dickens 1812-1870**. Ed. E.W.F. Tomlin. New York: Simon & Schuster, 1969, pp. 141-67.

        Sees Dickens as caught between socialism and capitalism, distrusting state action on the one hand and repelled by ruthless methods on the other. Brown argues that Dickens saw both sides of the issue of unionism and spoke both, that in

**Hard Times** he did not manage to solve the problem of capitalism but did reach the complacent middle class, and that he shared some of Stephen's muddle in a novel in which the theme overwhelms the characters and the narrative gets bogged down.

227.    ———. **Dickens in His Time**. London and Edinburgh: Nelson, 1953, pp. 40-44.

Gently condemns Dickens for his failure to understand the positive aspects of trade unionism.    **Hard Times** is a failure, Brown asserts, and Dickens, knowing this too, was glad to be done with it.    Brown deals mainly with the economic theme, although he attributes the failure of the novel in part to the crowding of two main subjects into a short book.

228.    Brown, James M. **Dickens: Novelist in the Market-Place**. New York: Barnes & Noble; London and Basingstoke: Macmillan, 1982, passim.

Offers the trade union in **Hard Times** as an instance of class ideology mediating a presentation of social reality. Brown attacks critics who have failed to see the emblematic functions of imagery, arguing that literary works must be read as imaginative structures, not as documentaries of social facts.    **Hard Times** is offered as an example at various points in the argument, and in particular as an instance of people being reduced to machines.

229.    Brown, Robert Edwards. "Dickensian Allegory: The Dynamics of Abstraction." **DAI**, 40 (1980), 4049A (Univ. of Iowa, 1979). 488 pp.

Examines Dickens's fiction as allegory from **Oliver Twist** to **Our Mutual Friend**. Brown believes that with **Bleak House** and **Hard Times**, the allegory takes a "decidedly social turn."

230.    Browne, Gerald Duane. "The Significance of Time in the Novels of Charles Dickens." **DAI**, 31 (1971), 6541A-42A (Univ. of Wisconsin, 1971). 331 pp.

Suggests that the perception of time relates to a general sense of the world and of one's place in it.    In **Bleak House**,

**Hard Times, Little Dorrit**, and **A Tale of Two Cities**, "the most prominent feature is their presentation of time in relation to a divided sensibility, as manifested in the division between the individual self and the social self."

231.   Buchan, John.  **A History of English Literature**.  London: Thomas Nelson, 1923, pp. 491, 494.

Sees **Hard Times** as taking up Carlyle's cause against modern political economy and industrial progress.

232.   -------.  **A Shorter History of English Literature**.  Rev. and corrected by Majl Ewing.  New York: T. Nelson, 1937, pp. 362, 366.

Buchan's commentary on **Hard Times** is the same as in **A History of English Literature** (231), above.

233.   Buchen, Irving.  "**The Ordeal of Richard Feverel**:  Science Versus Nature."  **ELH**, 29 (1962), 47–66.

Sir Austin Feverel's system of education is contrasted briefly (twice) with Gradgrind's.

234.   Buckler, William E.  "Dickens's Success with **Household Words**."  **Dickensian**, 46 (1950), 197–203.

A table of the biannual profits of **Household Words** shows the sharp rise for the statement of 30 September 1854 and also the "Extra Payment" given Dickens for **Hard Times**.  On Forster's assertion that the circulation doubled with **Hard Times** (133), Buckler comments: "This is rather a misleading statement. In the first place, the circulation of the journal was almost at its lowest ebb in the half-year before the serialisation of **Hard Times** began.  If we consider this fact, plus the increased circulation necessary to return the profits in addition to the extra ... paid Dickens ..., we conclude that the circulation was increased by four or five times. It is, however, considerably less than double the other high-water marks in the circulation of the journal."

235.   Burton, H.M.  **Dickens and His Works**.  Methuen's Outline Series.  London: Methuen; New York: Roy, 1968.  91 pp.

Finds **Hard Times** of all Dickens's novels the one "written with the least enjoyment." Preston failed to offer the background Dickens expected; the characters are Londoners with Lancashire accents. Burton thinks little of the plot and deplores the lack of "a single comic character," but he praises the descriptions of Coketown. Review: Derek Brown, **Dickensian**, 65 (1969), 125–26.

236. Burton, Richard. **Charles Dickens**. Indianapolis: Bobbs Merrill, 1919, pp. 176–81, 271, 274.

Finds **Hard Times** secondary as a story and work of art, but important for its attack on the "old time method" of educa tion represented in Gradgrind. The themes of education and the condition-of-England are related because the young are the future citizens of the state.

237. Bush, Douglas. "A Note on Dickens' Humor." In **From Jane Austen to Joseph Conrad**. Ed. Robert C. Rathburn and Martin Steinmann, Jr. Minneapolis: Univ. of Minnesota Press, 1958, pp. 82–01.

Hopes that the new criticism on Dickens will not become too solemn: "People mutht be amuthed."

238. Butt, John. "Dickens's Notes for His Serial Parts." **Dickensian**, 45 (1949), 129–38.

Instances **Hard Times** in an argument that Dickens's number plans show not moments of creation but moments of translating ideas into practice. Notes the plotting of Harthouse's development in the first number plan.

239. -------. **Pope, Dickens and Others: Essays and Addresses**. Edinburgh: Edinburgh Univ. Press, 1969, pp. 159–60.

Suggests that the convention of dividing **Hard Times** into books and naming them may have come from Fielding and, more directly, from Thackeray's **Henry Esmond** (1852).

240. -------, and Kathleen Tillotson. "**Hard Times**: The Problems of a Weekly Serial." **Dickens at Work**. London: Methuen, 1957, pp. 201–21. The section on **Hard Times** rpt. in Gray (429).

Shows how Dickens continued to think in monthly numbers (five of them) as he worked in the less comfortable weekly format, dividing the monthly part into four. The essay uses the number plans to trace the development of the novel from the trial titles through the monthly and weekly segments, revealing lines of structure in the novel and Dickens's plans and hesitations as the novel progressed.

241.   Butwin, Joseph C.   "**Hard Times**: The News and the Novel." **NCF**, 32 (1977), 166–87.

Insists that **Hard Times** must be read within the context of its appearance as journalism, in **Household Words**. Butwin argues that this context encourages the reader to test the fiction in the real world and also allows the arguments of the novel to be completed in the accompanying journalistic essays; he instances the deletion of Stephen's reference to Rachael's sister having been killed by a machine and Morley's "Ground in the Mill." Compare Andrews (166), Clark (279), and Fielding (381) on serialization and Bartrip (6), Monod (10), and Woodings (11) on the cancelled passage.

242.   –––––––.   "The Paradox of the Clown in Dickens."   **DSA**, 5 (1976), 115–32.

The paradox examined in this essay is stated through Sleary's horse-riding: on the one hand, it embodies the values opposed to Coketown; on the other, it is marred by the image of Tom in blackface (also a clown), by Jupe's drinking, beating his dog, and abandoning Sissy, and by Sissy's choice of the outer world. Butwin traces this paradox from **Sketches by Boz** forward, finding the precariousness of the clown's life to be at root an economic fact. The difference between the gentle satire of the **Sketches** and the harshness of **Hard Times**, he finds, is that in the latter the circus in turn becomes the vehicle for satire of society. Our understanding of Sleary must include the realization that at the end the clown is an emblem of degradation, and Sissy and Rachael don't find the performance they watch very funny.

243.   Cahill, Patricia Ann Ellen.   "Beginning the World: Women and Society in the Novels of Dickens." **DAI**, 39 (1978), 1581A (Univ. of Massachusetts, 1978). 229 pp.

Argues that the development of Dickens's women characters shows the increasing wisdom and compassion of his maturity. Louisa is studied as one of the women who rebel against society and Sissy is included with Biddy and Lizzie Hexam in a trio of women who define themselves by their work and their personal integrity.

244. Calder, Jenni. **Women and Marriage in Victorian Fiction**. London: Thames & Hudson, 1976, pp. 70, 76–77, 83.

Finds that **Hard Times** fails to show the relationship "between work and living." Calder suggests that Louisa's domestic failure and flight are less interesting than Edith Dombey's because Dickens is "not very interested in women who are trapped by circumstances .... He is much better at women who are pursued by people."

245. Camerer, Rudi. **Die Schuldproblematik im Spatwerk von Charles Dickens**. Neue Studien Anglistik und Amerikanistik, 14. Bern, Frankfurt/Main, Las Vegas: Verlag Lang, 1978. English abstract in **English and American Studies in German. Summaries of Theses and Monographs**. Suppl. to **Anglia**. Tubingen: Max Niemeyer, 1979, pp. 74–75.

Examines the interrelatedness of individual guilt and guilt in the moral relationships between classes in Dickens's later novels. **Hard Times**, "a fundamental critique of civilization from a moral standpoint," is one of six novels studied in detail.

246. Cannon, Susan Faye. **Science in Culture: The Early Victorian Period**. New York: Science History; Folkestone: Dawson, 1978, pp. 20–23.

Sets Bitzer's definition of a horse and the "ologies" in the context of contemporary discussion of "good" and "bad" science, the latter being that of the classifiers, which was criticized by Wordsworth and Ruskin as well as by scientists of the day. Cannon demonstrates that Dickens's use of an astronomical simile for Gradgrind (book I, chapter xv) shows Dickens's assumption that what a true astronomer does is valid and his audience's agreement with that assumption.

247.  Carey, John. **The Violent Effigy**. London: Faber & Faber, 1973,
      passim. Published in the U.S. as **Here Comes Dickens**. New
      York: Schocken, 1974.

      Argues that we should look at the workings of Dickens's
      imagination and not his social criticism, if only because the
      latter is so weak and so inconsistent. Dickens was divided be-
      tween a side that loved order and cleanliness and one directly
      opposed; **Hard Times** was written by the side "which favours
      dirt, imagination, and circus performers." **Hard Times** recurs in
      Carey's discussion, offering instances for its various and pro-
      vocative theses. Particularly interesting is a discussion of Lou-
      isa as Dickens's first attempt to show the cohabitation of pas-
      sion and purity, a step Dickens never took any further. The
      concluding emphasis is on the importance of Dickens's humor.
      Reviews: William Axton, **JEGP**, 74 (1975), 251–54; K.J. Fielding,
      **RES**, 26 (1975), 235–37; R. Giddings, **DSN**, 6 (1975), 115–19; Mi-
      chael Goldberg, **NCF**, 29 (1974), 354–57; Barbara Hardy, **Dicken-
      sian**, 71 (1975), 49–51; Sylvere Monod, **EA**, 27 (1974), 236–37; S.
      Pickering, **MP**, 73 (1975), 205–07.

248.  Carlisle, Janice Margaret. "The Moral Imagination: Dickens,
      Thackeray, and George Eliot." **DAI**, 34 (1974), 6630A (Cornell
      Univ., 1973). 266 pp.

      See Carlisle, below (249).

249.  –––––––. **The Sense of an Audience: Dickens, Thackeray, and
      George Eliot at Mid-century**. Athens: Univ. of Georgia Press,
      1981; Brighton: Harvester. 1982. pp. 40–41. 98–99.

      Examines the effect of the artist's "sense of moral respon-
      sibility" on the "narrative form of his art." **Hard Times** shows
      Dickens trying to do the work of religion by "insisting on the
      traditional functions of the moral relevance of entertainment,
      Carlisle believes. The relationship between Sissy and the nar-
      rator shows an equation between her actions and the storytell-
      er's role, an equation that by **Little Dorrit** will be "a characters-
      tic feature" of Dickens's work. "By bringing the imagination
      into the realm of everyday experience," Carlisle states, "Sissy
      and the narrator avert the threat of dehumanization that con-
      temporary life poses and encourage the old virtues and senti-
      mental values embodied in the traditional nursery tale." Re-
      view: George Ford, **NCF**, 37 (1982), 214–20.

250. Carmichael, Thomas Arthur. "Self and Society: Marriage in the Novels of Charles Dickens." **DAI**, 38 (1977), 3511A-12A (Univ. of Illinois, Urbana-Champaign, 1977). 228 pp.

Argues that marriage becomes a significant part of Dickens's social criticism, more than just a critique of mercenary wedlock in **Dombey and Son** or of divorce laws in **Hard Times**.

251. Carnall, Geoffrey. "Dickens, Mrs. Gaskell, and the Preston Strike." **VS**, 8 (1964), 31-38.

Expands on K I Fielding's "The Battle for Preston" (373), examining the discrepancy between Dickens's article on Preston and the portrayal of the trade union in **Hard Times**. Carnall shows Mortimer Grimshaw's ideology to have belonged to an earlier period and argues that in ignoring George Cowell, a very different leader, Dickens ignored the capacity for enlightened self-government among the workers. Carnall suggests that as he worked out his plot Dickens fell prey to bourgeois prejudice, and contrasts Mrs. Gaskell's depiction of workers, though neither novelist is seen quite to have met the challenge of the workers' movements.

252. Carre, Jacques. "Le Proletariat industriel dans **Hard Times** de Dickens." In **Hommage a Georges Fourrier**. Centre de Recherches d'Histoire et Litterature. Paris: Univ. de Besancon, 1973, pp. 71-85.

Argues that Dickens overlooks the exploitation of labor by emphasizing martyrdom instead. Dickens makes Bounderby odious personally rather than in his role as exploiter. Thus Dickens forces the vital problems of the industrial proletariat out of the foreground. Coketown is a city wholly dedicated to work, it is uniform and it is a ghetto--but Dickens values it, Carre believes, as a source of solidarity, and so remains ambivalent about it. In requiring Stephen to reject the union if he is to remain true to himself, Dickens rejects all solutions that are not paternalistic. He looks at the human, not the economic, relations between employer and employed, and thus skirts the issues of working conditions and justice. He associates the union with subversion, and the dialect signifies the ontological impossibility of the proletariat's ever becoming master of its own destiny. He attacks utilitarianism as though it were the source of capitalism, rather than a later rationalization, and evades a true critique of social conditions when he places the good values in the circus, which is outside society.

253.    Carter, John Archer. "Dickens and Education: The Novelist as
        Reformer." **DA**, 17 (1956), 628–29 (Princeton Univ., 1956). 257
        pp.

        Surveys the schools in **Nicholas Nickleby, Dombey and
        Son, David Copperfield** and **Hard Times**, and concludes that
        Dickens's descriptions of conditions were based on fact.

254.    Cassid, Donna. "Dickens: A Feminist View." **Women**, 2 (1970),
        21–22.

        Demonstrates the usefulness of Dickens's work as quarry
        for evidence of the oppression of women. The instance from
        **Hard Times** is Louisa. Cassid believes that Dickens's "male
        chauvinism" intrudes as he implies that despite her intelligence
        Louisa is not a "true woman" because she will never know ro-
        mantic love. The mindless Sissy affords an unfavorable con-
        trast. The portrait of Mrs. Gradgrind is "satiric but accurate,"
        Cassid adds.

255.    Caudwell, Christopher [Christopher St. John Sprigg]. **Romance
        and Realism: A Study in English Bourgeois Literature**. Ed.
        Samuel Hynes. Princeton, N.J.: Princeton Univ. Press, 1970, p.
        69.

        Compares Gradgrind and Scrooge as characters of the
        bourgeois who are displacing the aristocracy of the eighteenth
        century. Caudwell finds Dickens weak in his portrayal of the
        proletariat; he is the novelist of the petty bourgeoisie.

256.    Cazamian, Louis Francois. **Le Roman social en Angleterre**.
        Ph.D. Dissertation. Univ. of Paris, 1903. Paris: Societe nouvelle
        de librairie et d'edition, 1904. Trans. Martin Fido as **The Social
        Novel in England 1830–1850**. London and Boston: Routledge &
        Kegan Paul, 1973, pp. 152, 159, 162–73, 299.

        Criticizes **Hard Times** for vague social thinking, lack of
        contact between author and subject, and the broader deficien-
        cies of Dickens's late style. Dickens's imagination is stifled by
        his outsider's view of industrialism. The "Christmas philosophy"
        is insufficient for the harsh economic conditions of industrial
        oppression, and Stephen is inadequately developed. Cazamian
        finds stylistic resemblances to Carlyle and sees Dickens as an
        intermediary figure in social thought between Carlyle and Rus-
        kin.

\*        -------.

See Emile Legouis and Louis Cazamian (558).

257.  Cecil, David.  **Early Victorian Novelists: Essays in Revaluation**.
London: Constable, 1934, p. 62. Rpt. 1966.

Commentary on **Hard Times** is limited to a remark upon its
"laissez-faire theory hostile to private charity," which is included in a series of objects against which was pitted Dickens's
natural kindness.

258.  Chadwick, Esther Alice (Mrs. Ellis H.).  **Mrs. Gaskell: Haunts,
Homes, and Stories**.  London: Pitman & Sons, 1913, p. 209.

Suggests that **Hard Times** may have prompted Mrs. Gaskell
to turn her thoughts again to the industrial north for her next
novel, **North and South**.

259.  Chancellor, Edwin Beresford.  **Dickens and His Times**.  London:
Richards, 1932, passim.  Rpt. Folcroft, Pa.: Folcroft, 1976; Norwood, Pa.: Norwood, 1977; Philadelphia: R. West, 1978.

Censures **Hard Times** for the excessive prominence of its
moral theme, while conceding that there were doubtless men
like Gradgrind and that the pictures of industrial life are true
and lifelike.

260.  Chapman, Raymond.  **The Victorian Debate: English Literature
and Society 1832-1901**.  London: Weidenfeld & Nicolson; New
York: Basic Books, 1968, pp. 118-21.

Points to the mounting acrimony in labor-capital relations
and argues that Dickens saw something of both sides of the
issue.  Chapman finds humor in the characterization of Bounderby and asserts that characters such as Bounderby, Stephen,
and Slackbridge must be seen as types.  He divides the novel
into the story of Stephen and the miseducation of Louisa and
Tom.  Review: Philip Collins, **Dickensian**, 65 (1969), 119-20.

261.  Charles, Edwin.  "Mrs. Sparsit's Staircase."  **Some Dickens Women**.  London: T. Werner Laurie, 1926, pp. 117-45.

This is a book of selections from Dickens's fiction with commentary and linking summaries. Charles suggests that the word "bounder" did not come into its present usage until nearly thirty years after **Hard Times** was written (compare Monica Dickens [341]). He tentatively attributes the gloom and restraint of style in the novel to Dickens's deep feeling for what he wrote and consequent despair.

262.    Cheek, Edwin Rives. "Dickens and Women's Lib: Pro and Con." **Victorians Institute Journal**, 1 (1972), 39–48.

Sees Louisa as a key figure in the development of Dickens's conception of the female temperament, "from prescriptive certainty in the early novels to uncertainty in the later novels." Cheek sums up Louisa as complex, individualized, imperfect, and prone to make wrong choices.

263.    –––––––. "Dickens's View of Women." **DA**, 28 (1968), 3633A–34A (Univ. of N. Carolina, 1967). 331 pp.

Examines Dickens's views of women as they develop and in relation to Victorian concepts of femininity. Cheek finds that from **Bleak House** to **Our Mutual Friend** Dickens increasingly emphasized "what seems natural to individual women, given their environment, temperament, and choices in life."

264.    Chesterton, G.K. **Charles Dickens**. New York: Dodd, Mead; London: Methuen, 1906, pp. 130, 161, 227, 229. Rpt. London: Burns & Oates. 1975. Rpt. as **The Last of the Great Men**, New York: Press of the Readers Club, 1942. Rpt. as **Charles Dickens**. Introduction by Steven Marcus. New York: Schocken, 1965. A section on **Hard Times** rpt. in Gray (429).

On Macaulay's "sullen socialism," states that "Dickens was never a Socialist any more than he was an Individualist; and whatever else he was, he certainly was not sullen." Chesterton finds **Hard Times** severe, but a great monument, a precursor of socialist philosophy.

265.    –––––––. "Introduction." **Hard Times**. In the Everyman edition, 1907 (35), pp. v–xi. Rpt. in **Appreciations and Criticisms of the Works of Charles Dickens**. London: Dent; New York: Dutton, 1911.

"Twenty times we have taken Dickens's hand and it has been sometimes hot with revelry and sometimes weak with weariness; but this time we start a little, for it is inhumanly cold; and then we realise that we have touched his gauntlet of steel," Chesterton states. He believes that this hardness arises from the political facts of the century, as Dickens kept his head and his "unspoilt" liberalism. Chesterton sketches the political climate and Dickens's resistance to it.

266.   --------. **The Victorian Age in Literature**. London: Williams & Norgate; New York: Henry Holt, 1913, pp. 122, 129. Rpt. London: Oxford Univ. Press, 1966.

Asserts that **Hard Times** reflects Dickens's perception of the country as "a dark place of divided ways and divided counsels." Chesterton finds that Dickens's views do not fit modern categories.

267.   Chevalley, Abel. "Dickens, Thackeray, and Their Contemporaries." In **The Modern English Novel**. Trans. Ben Ray Redman. New York: Alfred Knopf, 1925, pp. 30-38. Rpt. New York: Haskell, 1973.

Condemns the novels of the middle period; Dickens "comes to grief in **Hard Times**."

268.   Chew, Samuel C. **The Nineteenth Century and After, 1789-1939**. Vol. 4 of **A Literary History of England**, ed. Albert C. Baugh. New York: Appleton-Century-Crofts, 1948, pp. 1349-50.

Finds the artistic merit of the novel diminished by its bitter and prominent social purpose and argues that neither Bounderby nor Stephen are fair (representative) portraits. Nonetheless, Chew defends Dickens's right both to use the novel for social agitation and to decline offering practical remedies.

269.   Christian, Mildred G. "Carlyle's Influence upon the Social Theory of Dickens (Part Two)." **NCF**, 2 (June 1947), 11-26.

Asserts that **Hard Times** provides the most conclusive evidence for Carlyle's extensive influence upon Dickens in the later novels, citing in particular **Signs of the Times** and **Chartism**, and, as less important, **Characteristics** and **Latter-Day Pamphlets**. Christian offers no discussion of the differences between Dickens and Carlyle. Compare Barnes (187), Goldberg (421), and Oddie (644).

270.    Christie, Octavius F. **Dickens and His Age**. London: Cranton, 1939, pp. 61, 212. Rpt. New York: Phaeton, 1974.

Offers a variety of comments on **Hard Times** under a variety of heads, among them that Louisa is the only woman in Dickens who might have achieved "one intelligent remark on politics, or literature, or art, or the drama" and that M'Choakumchild, for all his rigidity, was an improvement over Mr. Wopsle's aunt. "It was Dickens's way to clamour for reforms," Christie states, "and then, when the reforms were effected, to caricature them and those who administered them."

271.    Churchill, R.C. "Charles Dickens." In **From Dickens to Hardy**. Ed. Boris Ford. Harmondsworth: Penguin, 1958. Rev. ed., London: Cassell, 1963, pp. 119–43.

Praises **Hard Times**'s adherence to its main theme; sees it as a masterpiece of a minor order, ignored until Leavis (553) established its artistic merit. Churchill finds the novel superb comedy, without melodrama or sentimentality, though he concedes failure in Blackpool, Rachael, and Slackbridge, attributable to Dickens's ignorance of the north of England.

272.    –––––––. "Dickens, Drama and Tradition." **Scrutiny**, 10 (1942), 358–75. Rpt. in **The Importance of Scrutiny**. Ed. Eric Bentley. New York: G.W. Stewart, 1948; New York: Gotham Library, 1964.

Finds **Hard Times** among the novels least marred by sentimentality. Churchill believes that its social reformism is of interest to both the historian and the scholar of literature, and shows that Dickens could be critical of his time.

273.    –––––––. **English Literature of the Nineteenth Century**. London: Univ. Tutorial Press, 1951, pp. 93, 96, 101.

Refers briefly to **Hard Times** as a masterpiece evidencing Dickens's ability to tackle serious social questions.

274.    --------. "Growing up with Dickens: 1923-1937." **DSN**, 9
        (1978), 97-100.

        Remarks, on the authority of personal acquaintance, that
        Leavis did not read **Hard Times** (or **Little Dorrit**) until "he was
        about fifty."

275.    --------. "The Monthly Dickens and the Weekly Dickens."
        **Contemporary Review**, 234 (1979), 97-101.

        Argues that the "weekly Dickens" was "the more planned,
        the less improviood," and instances **Hard Times** and its persis-
        tence in its main theme.

276.    Clark, Cumberland. **Dickens and Democracy, and Other Stud-
        ies**. London: Cecil Palmer, 1930, pp. 13, 38, 55, 57.

        Arguments for Dickens as a pioneer of democracy include
        references to and quotations from Blackpool, Gradgrind, M'Cho-
        akumchild, Sleary, Mrs Sparsit, and the Government Depart-
        ments of **Hard Times**.

277.    --------. **The Dogs in Dickens**. London: Chiswick, 1926, pp.
        47-51. Rpt. New York: Haskell, 1973.

        Merrylegs is instanced and described to show how Dickens
        could use canine instinct "to clear up a point respecting the
        fate of one of his characters."

278.    --------. **Shakespeare and Dickens**. London: Chiswick, 1918,
        p. 13. Rpt. New York: Haskell, 1973.

        Notes the theatrical quality of Sleary.

279.    Clark, Harold Frank, Jr. "Dickensian Journalism: A Study of
        **Household Words**." **DA**, 28 (1967), 1390A-91A (Columbia
        Univ., 1967). 392 pp.

        Finds that **Household Words** presents "a diluted Christian
        morality" with a childlike love and imagination at the heart.
        These are the qualities Sissy brings to **Hard Times**. The reform
        sought by **Household Words** is a spiritual reform in which love

and fancy predominate.   Compare Andrews (166), Butwin (241),
and Fielding (381).

280.   Clayborough, Arthur.   "Dickens: A Circle of Stage Fire."   **The
       Grotesque in English Literature.**   Oxford: Clarendon, 1965, pp.
       201-55.

       Defines the grotesque and the sentimental in Dickens as
       "the resolution of a conflict between Dickens's fundamentally
       practical and progressive temperament and the stubborn insis-
       tence of his religious sense on making its influence felt."   In
       **Hard Times** Gradgrindian philosophy is attacked "because of its
       social repercussions ... not because it is opposed to a tran-
       scendental reality, but because it prevents its victims from tak-
       ing a romantic view of the real, physical world."   Clayborough
       sees Sleary's horse-riding as a much more profound realization,
       offering at once "a symbol of the strangeness and richness of
       life and a solid and permanent reality."   Dickens always seeks
       to ornament things that are familiar.

281.   Clipper, Lawrence Jon.   "Crime and Criminals in the Novels of
       Charles Dickens."   **DA**, 24 (1963), 2474-75 (Univ. of N. Carolina,
       1963).   409 pp.

       In a discussion of crime and criminals in the novels, argues
       that Dickens has somewhat greater sympathy for criminals who
       are conditioned by their environment, though this liberal view
       never quite displaces the static view of criminals who are
       wholly irreclaimable.   Clipper places Tom Gradgrind among the
       former.

282.   Clutton-Brock, Arthur.   **Essays on Books.**   New York: Dutton,
       1920, p. 41.

       Suggests that along with a child's iconoclasm Dickens had
       a child's blindness: "He saw the Bumbles and the Gradgrinds
       making life unpleasant for the poor, just as stupid grown-ups
       had made life unpleasant for him when he was a child."

283.   Cockshut, A.O.J.   "**Edwin Drood**: Early and Late Dickens Recon-
       ciled."   In **Dickens and the Twentieth Century**.   Ed. John Gross
       and Gabriel Pearson.   London: Routledge & Kegan Paul, 1962,
       pp. 227-38.

Points out that Honeythunder is a "comedown from the brilliant portraits of Bounderby and Harthouse in **Hard Times**, each with his special, calculated and entirely credible type of hypocrisy lurking behind certain agreed social stereotypes."

284.    -------. **The Imagination of Charles Dickens**. New York: New York Univ. Press, 1962, passim. The section on **Hard Times** rpt. in Gray (429).

Passing references in the early chapters of the book include the remark that Bounderby "is rooted in his social context, a profound psychological study." The chapter on **Hard Times** (pp. 137-42) recognizes Leavis for bringing appropriate attention to the work and praises the contrast between Bounderby and Harthouse, but demurs from the assertion that the novel is a masterpiece. The bases for this opinion include the injudicious introduction of moral fable and fairy-tale elements, the weakness of Gradgrind and of Sleary (no Myshkin or Lear's Fool), the trade union scenes, the matrimonial parallels between Bounderby and Stephen, and the last chapter, which "could have been written by Gradgrind." The work is, however, one of great distinction, Cockshut concludes. Reviews: Steven Marcus, **New Statesman**, 62 (1961), 278-79; J. Hillis Miller, **VS**, 5 (1961), 174-76.

285.    -------. "Victorian Thought." In **The Victorians**. Ed. Arthur Pollard. London: Barrie & Jenkins, 1970, pp. 13-40.

In the course of a discussion of Mill and utilitarianism, asserts that **Hard Times** is not a fair book but that its critique of utilitarian ethics and of Manchester business theory is "brilliant and memorable."

286.    Coles, Nicholas Joe Howard  "The Making of a Monster: The Working Class in the Industrial Novels and Social Investigations of 1830-1855." **DAI**, 42 (1981), 222A (State Univ. of New York, Buffalo, 1981). 431 pp.

Examines the "shapes assumed by the working class in the consciousness of those writers" who attempted to understand the condition-of-England question. Dickens is included for **Hard Times**, in which he "finds no hope in a system which distorts all who are engaged in it"; but "in this bleak conclusion he himself distorts the agencies on which working people relied for hope."

287.    Collin, Dorothy W. "The Composition of Mrs. Gaskell's **North and South**." **BJRL**, 54 (1971), 67-93.

Speculates that Dickens's distress at the length of the installments of **North and South** for **Household Words** arose from his initial intention that they be about the same length as those of **Hard Times**. In fact, Collin points out, they were longer by about thirty-five percent.

288.    Collins, Philip. **Dickens and Education**. London: Macmillan; New York: St. Martin's, 1963, passim. The section on **Hard Times** rpt. in Gray (429).

The authoritative work on this subject, treats **Hard Times** principally in chapter 7 ("Good Intentions and Bad Results") but also in chapters 8 and 9. Collins compares M'Choakumchild to Blimber and Bradley Headstone ("a poor man's Blimber") and offers further parallels between Dombey and Gradgrind and between the two novels. In dissent from Leavis (553), he insists that for Dickens the "casual topicalities" were central to the firing of his imagination. He accuses Dickens of a degree of class prejudice in his view of the Queen's Scholars (whom M'-Choakumchild represents) and finds a similar "substantial accuracy, and ... lack of curiosity about causes" in Dickens's treatment of the object-lesson (the definition of a horse). On the Department of Practical Art, Collins follows Fielding (376), but more sternly, rebuking the inappropriateness of the satire to the theme and imagery of the book. He analyzes the "pastoral-primitivist belief" that governs the treatment of Sleary's horse-riding and fancy and treats briefly the relationship of **Hard Times** to the writings of Carlyle. Reviews: R.D. McMaster, **NCF**, 19 (1964), 306-08; Gilbert Thomas, **English**, 15 (1964), 64-65.

289.    –––––––. "Dickens and Industrialism." **SEL**, 20 (1980), 651-73.

Discusses issues of industrialism and fiction that bear upon **Hard Times**, stating that Dickens knew Birmingham better than Manchester, but neither well. On Dickens's social criticism, Collins follows the moderate evaluation of Brantlinger (216), avoiding the extremes of Leavis (553) and Holloway (471), pointing out that **Hard Times** "does not pretend to be a naturalistic study of provincial life" and noting its omission of many features common to the condition-of-England novels: child labor, unemployment, political violence, and industrial diseases.

290.    -------. "Dickens and the Popular Amusements." **Dickensian,**
        61 (1965), 7-19.

    Sleary's horse-riding is here considered in the context of
Dickens's other writings on popular amusements, which are
seen to arise from his natural effervescence, to turn deliberately to the low-brow, and to suffer an inability to conceive the
pleasures of solitude. The circus "palliates but does not modify
or, in any permanent way, enrich the quality of life in the industrial towns." Collins compares Dickens's inability to grant
lasting value to art to his idea of Christmas, with its lack of an
"urgent daily sense of Christianity."

291.    -------. "Dickens and the Trained Schoolmaster." **Univ. of
        Leeds Institute of Education Researches and Studies,** no. 22
        (1961), 43-55.

    Notes that the two schoolmasters who are the objects of
Dickens's attack on the state pupil-teacher system are M'Choakumchild and Headstone; the focus of this article is on Headstone.

292.    -------. "Dickens' Self-Estimate: Some New Evidence." In
        **Dickens the Craftsman.** Ed. Robert B. Partlow, Jr. Carbondale
        and Edwardsville: Southern Illinois Univ. Press; London: Feffer,
        1970, pp. 21-43.

    Suggests that Forster's reviews of Dickens's novels in **The
Examiner** can offer evidence for Dickens's self-estimation.
Collins notes the cool reception given **Hard Times** by Forster
and suggests that a full understanding of Dickens's intentions
in that novel might come from a perusal of **Household Words.**
Compare Fielding (378).

293.    -------. "**Hard Times** (1854)." In **Dickens: The Critical Herit-
        age.** Ed. Philip Collins. London: Routledge & Kegan Paul, 1971,
        pp. 300-21.

    Offers a rapid survey of criticism of **Hard Times,** with em-
phasis on the early tendency to ignore it or give it a very short
review. Collins notices that even Dickens seems to have forgotten it when he writes in the Preface to **Little Dorrit** of that
novel as the successor to **Bleak House.** The collection brings
together a number of pieces that may be difficult to locate:

[Forster], **The Examiner** (115); [Simpson], **Rambler** (119); [Sinnett], **Westminster Review** (120); part of Brough's "Hard Times (Refinished)" (91); Ruskin, "Unto This Last," **Cornhill Magazine** (150); part of Whipple, **Atlantic Monthly** (155). Elsewhere in the volume are references to **Hard Times** from Martineau (147); Taine (153); **Dublin University Magazine** (149); Ruskin's letter to Norton (151); **Dublin Review** (139); **Temple Bar** (140); [Forsyth], **Fraser's Magazine** (134); and Stott (152).

294.    ———. "Introduction." In the Everyman edition, 1978 (35), pp. v–xvii.

Offers a briefer version of the discussion of industrial fiction in "Dickens and Industrialism" (289) and reviews as well the issues of education and fancy, the Department of Practical Art, divorce, education and Miss Coutts, and industrialism and Carlyle. Collins comments on the spareness of the weekly format and on Dickens's heavy use of mouthpiece characters, the latter possibly a failure of judgment. The lisp and the dialect may have been meant to disguise Sleary's and Stephen's function as commentators. Collins cites the agreement of 28 December 1853 "to provide 'at his earliest convenience' and 'with a view to the enlargement of the circulation of **Household Words**' a story 'equal in length to five monthly numbers' of his usual twenty-number serials." (The agreement is in the Philip H. and A.S.W. Rosenbach Foundation Library, Philadelphia.) Collins concludes with the assertion that the novel is neither realistic nor meant to be.

295.    ———, ed. **The Public Readings**. Oxford: Clarendon, 1975, p. xix.

Notes that Dickens read the opening numbers of **Bleak House** and **Hard Times** to Angela Burdett-Coutts.

296.    ———. "Queen Mab's Chariot Among the Steam Engines: Dickens and 'Fancy.'" **ES**, 42 (1961), 78–90.

Elucidates the meanings that "fancy" and "imagination" held for Dickens, extending Cazamian's description of "la philosophie de Noel" (256). Collins quotes **Hard Times** often, "for it is Dickens's finest comment on this concept Fancy; the fable admirably defines and explores the issue." So does this essay.

297.    Colmer, John.   "The Victorian 'Condition of England' Novel."
        **Coleridge to Catch-22: Images of Society**. London: Macmillan;
        New York: St. Martin's, 1978, pp. 69-90.

        Finds **Hard Times** the best-known and most Carlylean of
        this genre but damaged by both Dickens's seriousness of pur-
        pose and the weekly serialization. In evaluating Dickens's criti-
        que of utilitarianism and of the circus alternative, Colmer steers
        between Leavis (553) and Holloway (471), finding the critique
        more successful than the plea for feeling and joy, and the cre-
        ation of monsters inconsistent with the argument that the true
        interests of monsters and victims are identical.

298.    Colwell, C. Carter.   **The Tradition of British Literature**.   New
        York: Putnam's, 1971, p. 325.

        **Hard Times** is mentioned briefly to show the image of
        Dickens as the social reformer "aghast at poverty and slum
        crime."

299.    Coolidge, Archibald C., Jr.   **Charles Dickens as a Serial Novel-
        ist**. Ames: Iowa State Univ. Press, 1967, passim.

        Coolidge cites **Hard Times** when the book or its characters
        figure as examples or instances in his various themes (stock
        characters, repeated devices of plot, use of symbols, etc.).
        There is no extended analysis of the novel, and what judgments
        are offered are usually quoted from Butt and Tillotson (240).
        Reviews: George Ford, **Novel**, 2 (1969), 184-85; Grahame Smith,
        **MLR**, 64 (1969), 409; J.A. Sutherland, **DS**, 4 (1968), 95-98.

300.    -------.   "'Great Expectations,' The Culmination of A Develop-
        ing Art." **Mississippi Quarterly**, 14 (1961), 190-96.

        Finds the focus on the theme of the education of the heart
        and on the idea of reform steadier in **Hard Times** than in
        **Dombey and Son**. The transitions and parallels suggested in
        the number plans, however (e.g., the parallel between Harthouse
        and Gradgrind), are not so thoroughly worked out in the novel
        itself, because this novel's interests are still diffused across a
        range of characters (in contrast to the interests of **Great Ex-
        pectations**).

301.    ———————. "Serialization in the Novels of Charles Dickens." **DA,**
        16 (1956), 2455 (Brown Univ., 1956). 486 pp.

        See Coolidge, Jr., above (299).

302.    Cooper, Lettice. **A Hand upon the Time: A Life of Charles
        Dickens.** New York: Pantheon, 1968, pp. 131–34.

        Written throughout in the simplest prose, this book renders
        a set of well received ideas for **Hard Times** concerning the trip
        to Preston, the shortness of the novel, and Dickens's desire to
        expose industrial conditions. One of the "main ideas" is that
        children need play and fun, the other concerns the relations of
        men and masters. Dickens was not sullen, Cooper asserts, but
        **Hard Times** is "mostly about sullen people, and it has none of
        the sparkle and color of his other novels." Cooper is remarka-
        bly free of Leavisian influence.

303.    Cooperman, Stanley. "Dickens and the Secular Blasphemy: So-
        cial Criticism in **Hard Times, Little Dorrit** and **Bleak House.**"
        **CE,** 22 (1960), 156–60.

        Following Taine (153), argues that Dickens takes up causes
        already well espoused by the middle class he represents. His
        ability to satirize the "painted verbalisms" of social pretension
        and at the same time turn out his own "no less rhetorical odes"
        is "a sort of emotional hypocrisy within uncompromising hon-
        esty, ... likely to confuse a modern reader when he realizes that
        Dickens was speaking for as well as to the middle class."
        Dickens's values are the values of property, Cooperman states;
        the circus in not a good in itself but a way of ensuring leisure
        necessary for the renewal of work.

304.    Coveney, Peter. "The Child in Dickens." **Poor Monkey: The
        Child in Literature.** London: Rockliff, 1957, pp. 71–119. Reis-
        sued as **The Image of Childhood.** Harmondsworth: Penguin,
        1967.

        Asserts that the study of **Hard Times** is valuable largely for
        its contextualization in a study of the child in adult literature
        from the late eighteenth century to the early twentieth. For
        Dickens, the child is "the symbol of sensitive feeling anywhere
        in a society maddened with the pursuit of material progress."
        Coveney believes that **Hard Times** is a great novel, and essen-

tially an educational drama (he mutes the theme of industrialism). Gradgrind and Sleary are seen to express the fundamental Dickensian antithesis "between the sensibilities of life and the sensibilities of death."

305. Cowden, David. "The Structure of Dickens's Novels." Ph.D. Dissertation. Harvard Univ., 1949. 416 pp.

Points to the effects on plotting and on the introduction of characters of Dickens's learning how to deal with shorter novels. Cowden argues that **Hard Times** focusses on the single theme of anti-utilitarianism.

306. Cox, C.B. "In Defense of Dickens." **E&S**, ser. 2, 11 (1958), 86-100.

Offers the "muddle" as an example of the experience of confusion that Dickens describes repeatedly.

307. Craig, David. "**Hard Times** and the Condition of England." **The Real Foundations: Literature and Social Change**. London: Chatto & Windus, 1973, pp. 109-31.

Essentially the same argument as in David Craig, "Introduction" to **Hard Times**. See below (308).

308. -------. "Introduction." In the Penguin edition, 1969 (48), pp. 11-36.

Sets the novel fully in historical circumstance, resisting any degree of metaphysical interpretation. Craig attributes to Dickens a high concern for the topicality of this novel, in both education and industrialism. He finds the novel weakened by a failure of realism in its presentation of the mass of people (Stephen in particular) but strong in its satire of the masters and of the conditions of their world. Reviews: K.J. Fielding, **Dickensian**, 65 (1969), 189-90; Anne Smith, **Dickensian**, 4 (1973), 115-22.

309. Crockett, Judith. "Theme and Metaphor in **Hard Times**." **Spectrum**, 6 (1962), 80-81.

Points to a number of metaphors and their relation to the theme; closes with the statement that "Dickens has reduced a continuum to its poles as he argues from partial truths."

310.   Cross, Wilbur L. **The Development of the English Novel.** New York: Macmillan, 1899, pp. 191, 272.

Asserts that even **Hard Times** is filled with material based on personal experience, but does not illustrate. Cross notes that the situation of Stephen is ripe for classic naturalist treatment, but that Dickens relieves the darkness with the light of "sublime suffering," which the naturalists regarded as sham.

311.   Crotch, W. Walter. **Charles Dickens: Social Reformer.** London: Chapman & Hall, 1913, passim.

The book  gathers together "the arguments  direct from Dickens" on society and politics. **Hard Times** is quoted in regard to education, on the Teetotal Society, on the "muddle," for the nasty human instances of Bitzer and Mrs. Sparsit, on the circuses and the failure of Gradgrind's system, and on Sleary's philosophy.

312.   ———. "Dickens as Educational Reformer: A Fragment." **Dickensian**, 12 (1916), 77–78.

Suggests that we look at **Hard Times** to understand the failure of modern education, for M'Choakumchild is only a faint exaggeration of those teachers who still today emphasize the memorization of facts.

313.   ———. "A Great Poet's Tribute." **Dickensian**, 9 (1913), 91.

On Swinburne on Dickens (788). Crotch cites Swinburne's appreciation of the construction of **A Tale of Two Cities**, "but **Hard Times** he found greater in moral and pathetic and humorous effect."

314.   ———. **The Secret of Dickens.** London: Chapman & Hall, 1919, passim. Rpt. New York: Haskell, 1972.

Finds **Hard Times** without blemishes in characterization, of social vision beyond that of Forster and other Victorians. It is "the greatest and most realistic attempt ever made to depict the conditions of life in a manufacturing town" and the turning-point to a revolutionary Dickens, but it fails to present "the highest intellectual outlook attainable" and leaves us without conviction of "first-hand contact with the life of the mill, the factory, or the mine."

315.   -------. **The Soul of Dickens**. London: Chapman & Hall, 1916, passim. Rpt. New York: Haskell, 1974.

Praises the characters of the novel as without failure, from Gradgrind to Bitzer; at another point excepts Bitzer as "unreal." Crotch sees a line of character from Harthourse to Carton and Wrayburn, and notes Dickens's fairness in allowing Harthouse to be a relief to Bounderby's hypocrisy. He quotes the novel at length.

316.   -----. **The Touchstone of Dickens**. London: Chapman & Hall, 1920, passim.

Asserts that in **Hard Times** Dickens destroyed the public esteem for the Factory System and that the novel's satire is still applicable to modern times.

317.   Crothers, Samuel McChord. "The Obviousness of Dickens." **The Century Magazine**, 83, n.s. 61 (1911–12), 560–74. Rpt. in **Humanly Speaking**. Boston and New York: Houghton Mifflin, 1912.

Concedes the obviousness of Dickens, but asserts imaginative genius notwithstanding. One instance of this obviousness is Mr. Gradgrind: we know all about him in the first chapter, Collins points out, and there is then no development of character possible.

318.   Cruse, Amy. **The Victorians and their Reading**. Boston and New York: Houghton Mifflin, 1935, pp. 147, 227, 229. Also pub. as **Victorians and Their Books**. London: Allen & Unwin, 1935.

Asserts that **Hard Times** is less an analysis of material conditions than a demonstration of the importance of imagination.

319.    Cunliffe, John W. **Leaders of the Victorian Revolution**. New York: Appleton-Century, 1934, pp. 22, 84. Rpt. New York: Russell & Russell, 1963.

Finds Dickens quite off course in his view of the north of England (compares him unfavorably to Mrs. Gaskell and the Brontes), but attributes the general failure of **Hard Times** to the problems of space.

320.    Cunningham, Valentine. **Everywhere Spoken Against: Dissent in the Victorian Novel**. Oxford: Clarendon, 1975, passim.

This book examines selected fictional accounts of Nonconformity, including that in **Hard Times**, within "real historical contexts." Stephen's star of Bethlehem is an instance offered of Dickens's sentimentalism, "based in or connected to no theological or experiential reference-point in the novels and hardly any outside them." Cunningham also mentions the eighteen chapels in Coketown in connection with Dickens's (immature) attack on Nonconformism. Review: James Kincaid, **DSN**, 8 (1977), 60-2.

321.    Daiches, David. **A Critical History of English Literature**. 2 vols. London: Secker & Warburg; New York: Ronald, 1960. 2nd ed., 1970. II, 1056.

Finds the novel too much of a simple fable, but praises its conflict of the imaginative and the mechanical; at its moments of high irony it reveals the tragic inadequacy of rational schematizations.

322.    Dark, Sidney. **Charles Dickens**. London & Edinburgh: T.C. & E.C. Jack, 1919, pp. 100-03. Rpt. Folcroft, Pa.: Folcroft, 1973; New York, Haskell, 1975.

Finds Bounderby "real" but Stephen "inhumanly good," and the novel not an "outstanding success." It is topical, Dark claims, with the moral that facts and figures must subserve Faith, Hope, and Charity. In trade unionism Dickens perceives "with a seer's insight the creation of a new tyranny."

323.    Darwin, Bernard. **Dickens**. London: Duckworth, 1933, p. 99. Rpt. New York: Haskell, 1973.

Briefly condemns the novel as "a bad shot." The circus is its one bright spot, and with the troupe's farewell to Sissy, the light fades from the book.

324. Davey, Samuel J. "Charles Dickens." **Darwin, Carlyle and Dickens, with Other Essays**. London: James Clarke, 1876, pp. 121-56. Rpt. New York: Haskell, 1971.

Asserts that **Great Expectations, Hard Times**, and **A Tale of Two Cities** are free of Dickens's prolixity and notable among his sketches and shorter stories.

325. Davis, Earle. "Dickens and Significant Tradition." **DSA**, 7 (1978), 49-67.

Traces Dickens's development as a critic of Victorian society. Davis finds **Hard Times** insufficient in narrative, weak in humor and melodrama. This novel has clarity of purpose, which appeals to critics such as Shaw and Leavis, he states, but it falters as art and story-telling.

326. -------. **The Flint and the Flame**. Columbia: Univ. of Missouri Press, 1963, passim. The section on **Hard Times** rpt. In Gray (429).

Contends that **Hard Times** is weaker than other novels of the "dark" period and the weakness is due to hurry and the cramping of the weekly format. The force of the novel comes from its purpose, which revolves three plot sequences around its thesis. But there is a want of humor, and the caricature often fails. The rhetoric is Carlylean, explaining rather than implying. Davis believes that critics who praise the novel out of their concern for the weaknesses of capitalism are special pleading, ignoring or diminishing Slackbridge, doing Dickens little good. Davis argues that Dickens is looking for cooperation between capital and labor, and suggests that Leavis's reasons for liking this novel (553) are better illustrated in other writers of the period. He also asserts that the circus people were suggested by similar scenes in Collins's **Hide and Seek**. Reviews: Archibald C. Coolidge, Jr. **MP**, 63 (1965), 84-87; W.J. Harvey, **N&Q**, n.s. 12 (1965), 77-78; Leslie L. Lewis, **ELN**, 3 (1965), 152-54; R.D. McMaster, **Dalhousie Review**, 45 (1965), 217-19; Michael Steig, **Literature and Psychology**, 15 (1965), 230-31.

327.    Davis, Nuell Pharr. **The Life of Wilkie Collins.** Urbana: Univ. of
        Illinois Press, 1956, p. 153.

        States that **Hard Times** is the first of Dickens's novels to
        show borrowing from Collins: Sissy and Sleary's horse-riding
        derive from the childhood of the heroine of **Hide and Seek.**

328.    Davis, Robert Con. "Revenge Against Time: The Father in Fic-
        tion." **DAI**, 40 (1979), 835A-36A   (Univ. of California, Davis,
        1979).  250 pp.

        **Hard Times** is one of four novels discussed at length in a
        historical survey of the presentation of the father in English
        fiction.  This section is followed by a theoretical discussion.

329.    Dean, F.R. "Dickens and Manchester." **Dickensian**, 34 (1938),
        111-18.

        Notes the setting of **Hard Times** in Lancashire. In Describ-
        ing Dickens's associations with Manchester in detail, Dean of-
        fers useful background to the novel.

330.    DeBacco, Ronald Eugene. "Dickens and the Mercantile Hero."
        **DAI**, 41 (1980), 1062A-63A (Indiana Univ. of Pennsylvania,
        1980).  262 pp.

        Traces Dickens's participation in the Victorian search for a
        mercantile hero who can reform industrial society, from **Nicho-
        las Nickleby** through the darkening vision of the later novels.
        By **Hard Times,** even the limited possibilities of Rouncewell in
        **Bleak House** are unavailable, DeBacco concludes.

331.    DeMille, Barbara Munn. "The Imperatives of the Imagination:
        Dickens, James, Conrad, and Wallace Stevens." **DAI**, 39 (1979),
        5522A-23A (State Univ. of New York, Buffalo, 1978). 198 pp.

        Examines both the demands made by the imagination and
        the imperative that the imagination be exercised.  DeMille ar-
        gues that Dickens finds imagination to be an imperative in a
        mechanistic society, but one that holds dangers of solipsism.

332.    Deneau, Daniel P. "The Brother-Sister Relationship in **Hard
        Times.**" **Dickensian**, 60 (1964), 173-77.

Argues that the dangers of the Gradgrindian system of education are shown not only in Tom's robbery and Louisa's marriage but in their relationship to each other: Tom is perverted to love of self, Louisa to sexual attraction to Tom. "Louisa reaches a point where her affection for Tom is not merely superlative sisterly affection," Deneau argues. He supports this contention by a close analysis of Louisa's attempt to confront Tom in his bedroom and remarks that Dickens's reticence was due to Victorian propriety. Compare Goldfarb (425).

333.    Dennis, Carl. "Dickens' Moral Vision." **TSLL**, 11 (1969), 1237-46.

Argues that Dickens's work explores the assumption that "the self is intrinsically moral ... and that to reject love is finally to reject life, to maim or kill part of the psyche." **Hard Times** is mentioned at a variety of points. It is the novel in which Dickens's "self-deficient child-quellers ... receive their fullest treatment" and in which the principle that love must arise from a free impulse of the heart and cannot be forced by an act of will becomes the central issue.

334.    Dent, Harold C. **The Life and Characters of Charles Dickens**. London: Joan Wheeler, 1933, p. 392.

Marvels at the success of **Hard Times** in stimulating the sales of **Household Words**, since it is such a weak and hardly Dickensian novel (except for Sleary's horse-riding), and speculates that perhaps Dickens's benevolence to the working men or his speeches in Birmingham and Bradford added readers of the "poorer classes." Gradgrind and Bounderby are "third-rate stagy villains played by a bad company."

335.    de Vooys, Sijna. **The Psychological Element in the English Sociological Novel of the Nineteenth Century**. Amsterdam: H.J. Paris, 1927, pp. 42-49.

Chooses **Hard Times** for discussion because it is the only novel in which Dickens offers "a picture of the workman at war with capital," but focusses the discussion on the story of Louisa, emphasizing her point of view and stating that the novel should not be forgotten if only for the sake of this character.

336.  Dexter, Walter.  "The Hard Times Country."  **The England of Dickens**.  London: Palmer; Philadelphia: Lippincott, 1925, pp. 242-64.

Chapter 11 is entitled "The Hard Times Country," but there is no extended discussion of the novel.  Coketown is situated in Lancashire, but is asserted definitely not to be Manchester. The chapter describes Dickens's visits to Manchester, Preston (including his readings there), Blackburn, and Liverpool.


\*          -------.

See also L.A. Kennethe (522).


337.  Dibelius, Wilhelm.  **Charles Dickens**.  Leipzig and Berlin: Teubner, 1916, pp. 225-26, 317-21.

Mentions **Hard Times** at various points, pointing out, for example, that Dickens's identification with Blackpool rather than Slackbridge is evidence of his failure to identify with the workers as a class and that Sissy shows an advance in realism over Little Nell.  Dibelius adds that the novel deals with three problems of modern industrialism: the ugliness; the creation of two new classes, worker and capitalist; the conflict between the two classes.  Dickens's advance is in his treatment of the first of these.


338.  Dicey, A.V.  **Lectures on the Relation Between Law and Public Opinion in England During the Nineteenth Century**.  London: Macmillan, 1905, pp. 418-22.

Notes the unsystematic nature of Dickens's thought and finds evidence for it in his shift of allegiance from Benthamite radicalism (in 1846 Dickens was the editor of the **Daily News**, "the organ of the Manchester school") to satire.  **Hard Times** is "a crude satire of what Dickens supposed to be the doctrines of the political economists."  This shift is the more impressive, Dicey feels, as it records, and perhaps anticipates, the similar change in public opinion and qualifies Dickens as a sensitive registrant of his age's moral temper.  Dicey notes another instance of lack of system in the novel's simultaneous calls for freedom in respect to divorce and restraint of economic individualism, two ideas that may be at odds in the matter of individual freedom.  Compare Engel (368), Goldberg (424), and Maine (601).

339. Dickens, Charles, the Younger. "Introduction." In the Macmillan edition, 1904 (34), pp. xiii–xvii.

Asserts that **Hard Times** found enemies because of its political stance, noting the Tory view of **Blackwood's Magazine** and citing other critics of like persuasion. This essay mentions the Fox Cooper adaptation and its production at the Strand and quotes from Dickens's letters concerning **Hard Times**.

340. Dickens Fellowship. **Dickens Criticism: Past, Present, and Future Directions; A Symposium, with George H. Ford, Edgar Johnson, J. Hillis Miller, Sylvere Monod, Noel C. Peyrouton.** At the 55th Annual Conference of the Dickens Fellowship, Northeastern Univ., Boston. Cambridge, Mass.: C[harles] D[ickens] R[eference] C[enter], 1962, pp. 12, 48.

In his opening address, Monod instances M'Choakumchild and Gradgrind as part of the evidence of Dickens's concern with a kind of truth that is not literal fact. In the discussion, Johnson offers Bounderby's false history as a form of the perverse fantasies through which the repressed imagination will return.

341. Dickens, Monica. "Introduction." In the Imprint Society edition, 1972 (50), pp. v–xiii.

Reviews briefly Dickens's concern with industrialism, starting with **The Old Curiosity Shop**; the conditions of publication of **Hard Times**; and the critical divergence on the novel. Coketown was modelled on Hanley, Staffordshire, Monica Dickens points out. She raises the issue of the success of the novel in terms of Dickens's striking his "heaviest blow," but dismisses these terms in favor of the power of the characters and the writing. She explores the differences between our taste and Dickens's in relation to our preferences for certain characters over others. She claims that the epithet "bounder" came into the language from Bounderby (compare Charles [261]).

342. Dickins, Louis G. "The Friendship of Dickens and Carlyle." **Dickensian**, 3 (1957), 98–106.

Reviews briefly the friendship and influence of Carlyle. **Hard Times**, Dickins asserts, is a novel in which Dickens developed a particularly Carlylean theme; "Mill's rootless Liberty as

well as Gradgrind's monstrous monism were now caught in the
deadly crossfire between Devonshire Terrace and Cheyne Row."

343.    Dilnot, Alan. "Dickens's Early Fiction and the Idea of Practical
        Utility." **Southern Review** (Adelaide), 8 (1975), 141–51.

        In response to Ford and Monod (392), Coveney (304), and
        Kincaid (528), argues that the early fiction should not be seen
        as anticipations of the later, and in particular that portions of
        **Oliver Twist, Nicholas Nickleby,** and **The Old Curiosity Shop**
        do not anticipate **Hard Times.** In passing, Dilnot notes the
        anti–middle–class bias of most twentieth–century literary criti-
        cism and he questions the premise that **Hard Times** is an at-
        tack on utilitarianism, but does not pursue that issue.

344.    Dolby, George Charles. **Charles Dickens As I Knew Him.** Lon-
        don: T. Fisher Unwin, 1885, p. 21. Rpt. New York: Haskell, 1970.

        In this story of the reading tours in England and America,
        one remark has particular relevance for **Hard Times.** Dolby re-
        cords that on 14 April 1866, the reading at Liverpool leaving
        them free for the evening, "Mr. Dickens's tastes being inclined
        to theatre or circus, we repaired to the circus; for, appreciative
        as he was of the actor's art, he had an immense admiration for
        the equestrian, and never failed to visit a circus whenever the
        chance presented itself."

345.    Donovan, Frank. **Dickens and Youth.** New York: Dodd, Mead,
        1968, pp. 152–59. Also published as **The Children of Charles
        Dickens.** London: Leslie Frewin, 1969.

        Calls **Hard Times** a crusade against the economic system
        of England with a focus upon the spiritual oppression of chil-
        dren. Donovan notes that M'Choakumchild presumably repre-
        sents the teachers of the recently established training colleges
        and that Dickens had previously criticized the absence of such
        training, but does not offer to account for the discrepancy.
        Compare Collins (288).

346.    Doran, W.J. "'Hard Times' and These Times." **Dickensian,** 15
        (1919), 199–200.

Finds the novel replete with "pungent thought" and recommends it be put in the hands of every British worker, apparently
hoping that Blackpool will offer an alternative model to the example of Russia.

347.    Drew, Philip. "Dickens." **The Meaning of Freedom**. Aberdeen:
        Aberdeen Univ. Press, 1982, pp. 294–310.

Asserts that Holloway's comment (471) that Dickens offers
no alternative to mercantilism is true but does not necessarily
affect the success of the book. Drew argues that **Hard Times**
fails, however, on its own terms. Two of the most striking
characters have nothing to do with the utilitarian theme
(Bounderby and Mrs. Sparsit). The promptings of the heart
seem difficult to distinguish from the various selfishnesses of
the characters who fail--Bounderby, Tom, Harthouse, Louisa.
Only Sissy's heart guides her rightly, and she has no relevance
to the industrial conflict. Thus Dickens's "presentation of a
complex moral situation" is weakened by "a failure to suggest a
solution to the problem of the authentication of values."

348.    Dudar, Eleanor Joan. "The Family in the Later Novels of Charles
        Dickens." **DAI**, 39 (1978), 1584A–85A (Univ. of Toronto, 1976).

Seeks recurrent patterns of familial relationships in the
novels from **Dombey and Son** to **Our Mutual Friend**. The
second chapter focusses upon Gradgrind and Louisa as one of
three pairs of fathers and daughters. Louisa and Tom are
studied in the chapter on siblings.

349.    Duncan, Robert W. "Types of Subjective Narration in the Novels
        of Dickens." **ELN**, 18 (1980), 36–46.

Traces the varieties of subjective narration in Dickens.
**Hard Times** is instanced for the indirectly recorded speech of
Bounderby's servant when Stephen comes to the door (I, xi:
"Mr. Bounderby was at lunch ..."): the compression of three
speakers in this speech allows it to reflect Bounderby's rude-
ness, Duncan indicates.

350.    Dunn, Richard J. "Carlyle and that **Hard Times** Dedication."
        **DSN**, 3 (1972), 60–61.

A response to Tarr's response (795) to Dunn's earlier article on the dedication (351). Dunn clarifies his point, which was not that there had been any rift but that the friendship of Dickens and Carlyle was "not oppressively close" during this period, perhaps thus enabling the novel's fusion of Dickensian "sentimental humanism with Carlylean critical insight."

351.    –––––––.  "Dickens, Carlyle, and the **Hard Times** Dedication."
**DSN**, 2 (1971), 90–92.

Argues that we may have overestimated the closeness of Carlyle to Dickens at the time the novel was written and that the dedication should be regarded as an example of Dickens's gratitude for a "general influence ... by then well asssimilated in his creative genius." See reply by Tarr (795) and response by Dunn (350).

352.    –––––––.  "Far, Far Better Things: Dickens' Later Endings."  **DSA**,
7 (1978), 221–36.

Argues that there is a distinct difference in the novels after **David Copperfield** between Dickens's treatments of his major and minor characters. The closing of **Hard Times** stresses the characters' abilities to see and foresee, rather than their specific fates. Clear-sightedness is correspondingly the key to the question of the novel's final paragraph on the responsibility to be accepted by artist and public, Dunn concludes.

353.    –––––––.  "Skimpole and Harthouse: The Dickens Character in
Transition."  **DS**, 1 (1965), 121–28.

Asserts that Skimpole and Harthouse show in part Dickens's progress "from stereotyped, poorly motivated, but amusing grotesques to more rounded characterizations of credible individuals who suffer from sociological and psychological distress." With Harthouse, for example, Dickens "attempts serious character analysis and ... no humor." Dunn compares Sarah Gamp and Micawber to these two.

354.    Dyson, A.E.  "**Hard Times**: The Robber Fancy."  **Dickensian**, 5
(1969), 67–79.  Rpt. as chapter 8 of **The Inimitable Dickens: A
Reading of the Novels**.  London:  Macmillan; New York: St.
Martin's, 1970.

Presents the novel as an analytical return to the nightmare
chapters of **The Old Curiosity Shop**, enhanced by a more
ruthless observation. It is lacking in poetry and resonance,
uniquely unDickensian, exhibiting extremes in both character
and society. Dyson adds that Coketown is a prison that holds
the reader too, whose hopes   for the story are repeatedly
thwarted. Sissy remains an irreducible element of good, but
the mood of the novel reflects deep inner sorrow.

355.    --------. **"The Old Curiosity Shop**: Innocence and Grotesque."
**CritQ**, 8 (1966), 111-130. Rpt. in **Dickens: Modern Judgments**.
Ed. A.E. Dyson. London: Macmillan, 1968.

References to **Hard Times** are to the constriction of space
in the weekly format, to its greater truthfulness about industrialism (compared to **The Old Curiosity Shop**), and to how the
didactic intention produced a novel that is powerful but "oddly
removed" from Dickens's usual strengths.

356.    --------, and Angus Wilson. "Charles Dickens." In **The English
Novel**. Ed. Cedric Watts. London: Sussex, 1976, pp. 53-75.

This dialogue includes various brief references to **Hard
Times**. **Hard Times**, says Dyson, is an attempt to show a
quintessence: the aridity of an entire society. But Dyson and
Wilson agree that if they had to give up a Dickens novel, they
would choose this one because so much of Dickens is missing
from it.

357.    Eagleton, Mary, and David Pierce. "Charles Dickens." **Attitudes
to Class in the English Novel from Walter Scott to David
Storey**. London: Thames & Hudson, 1979, pp. 41-47.

Distinguishes Dickens's contempt for the new hero of the
industrial age from Mrs. Gaskell's response, focussing upon the
monstrosity of Bounderby and seeing Bitzer as a sort of
"Frankenstein figure."

358.    Eagleton, Terence. "Ideology and Literary Form." **Criticism and
Ideology: A Study in Marxist Literary Theory**. London: NLB;
Atlantic Highlands: Humanities Press, 1976, pp. 102-61.

Argues that of all the major English writers of the nineteenth and twentieth centuries, Dickens is the "least contaminated by organicist ideologies." His "Romantic humanist critique of industrial capitalism" remains spontaneous, its character
seen in the "vulgar vitalism" of **Hard Times** and in the "Christmas spirit." The educational system in **Hard Times** is an instance of the "increasingly monolithic ideological apparatuses"
of modern capitalism, to which the "unified structures" of the
later novels allude, Eagleton argues.

359.     Easson, Angus. "Dialect in Dickens's **Hard Times**." **N&Q**, n.s.
         23 (1976), 412–13.

A reply to Norman Page (658). Easson argues that from
both internal and external evidence it is extremely unlikely that
Dickens used William Gaskell's **Two Lectures on the Lancashire Dialect** as a dialect source for **Hard Times**, but that it is
likely that he used one of Gaskell's sources, John Collier's **A
View of the Lancashire Dialect**, published in 1770 under the
pseudonym Tim Bobbin and in 1775 as part of Collier's **Miscellaneous Works**, a copy of which was in Dickens's library.

360.     -------. **Elizabeth Gaskell**. London: Routledge & Kegan Paul,
         1979, passim.

Finds going from Bounderby to Mr. Thornton of **North and
South** a move "from the grotesque to the naturalistic." Dickens's novel is often "angularly schematic," often confused, and
unsatisfying in its offering of Sleary's as its alternative to the
world of Coketown, but it is "yet one where the pressures of
institutions and the danger of the cash–nexus are clearly stated."

*        -------. **Hard Times: Critical Comment and Notes**.

See below (883).

361.     -------. "Introduction." **North and South**. By Elizabeth Gas-
         kell. London: Oxford Univ. Press, 1973, pp. ix–xviii.

Anticipates the comments in **Elizabeth Gaskell** (360).

362.   Edwards, Osman. **The Value of Dickens**. Hastings: F.J. Par-
       sons, 1912, pp. 18, 25.

       Argues that despite Dickens's efforts in **Hard Times** against
       the Manchester School and the "national dustmen" in Parlia-
       ment, he never succeeds in making politics a live issue in his
       novels. **Hard Times** is his single "political pamphlet," between
       the lines of which we should read Carlyle, Edwards claims.

363.   Eigner, Edwin M. **The Metaphysical Novel in England and
       America**. Berkeley: Univ. of California Press, 1978, passim.

       Analyzes the novels of Dickens, Bulwer, Melville, Hawt-
       horne, and Charlotte Bronte as oxymoronic blends of positivist
       observation and idealist point of view. This book offers the
       most provocative contribution to the genre-debate on **Hard
       Times**, though the novel is not given extended discussion. The
       mixed genre of the metaphysical novel troubled critics, who
       came to demand refinement in one direction or the other, Eig-
       ner states. In **Hard Times** Dickens emphasized his "long held
       conviction of the psychological necessity of fostering the im-
       agination." Though belief in experience does not make one a
       villain--Gradgrind is not--it does open the door to a Hart-
       house, a "Byronic Lucifer" who believes in nothing. Eigner says
       that the change in genre and vision, from naturalism to the
       metaphysical, is the plan and the point of the novel. Sissy is
       seen as a version of the "household Virgin, the hearthside Ma-
       donna," the one clear article of conventional religious faith in
       the metaphysical novel. The naturalism of Stephen's fate and
       his redemption through a star demonstrate the two-part vision
       of Dickens's imagination. Reviews: Robert Ballflower, **RES**, n.s.
       32 (1981), 342-44; A.M.C. Brown, **Dickensian**, 75 (1979), 106-07;
       Alan Burke, **DSN**, 10 (1979), 71-73; Richard Levine, **SNNTS**,
       11(1979), 119-20.

364.   Ellison, Eugenia Adams. "**Hard Times**: Victimized Childhood."
       **The Innocent Child in Dickens and Other Writers**. Burnet,
       Texas: Eakin Press, 1982, pp. 154-66.

       Summarizes the novel, with an emphasis on the theme of
       education. Ellison offers much quotation and some derivative
       critical commentary. The novel is seen as a melodrama with
       Louisa and Tom at the center, presenting the thesis that
       "healthful play and a 'useful' use of facts are vital if one is to
       lead a balanced existence."

365.  Elloway, D.R.  "Commentary."  In the Longman edition, 1970
      (49), pp. 315–56.

      "The Background" offers a great deal of information on po-
      litical economy, utilitarianism, and education.  "The Book" is
      fairly critical, finding the characters wanting in the rich human-
      ity we associate with Dickens, the treatment of the unions per-
      functory, the portrait of Blackpool marked with an "irritating
      submissiveness," the theme manipulating the characters, and
      the circus a dissolution into sentimentality.  Elloway reviews
      the emergence of symbolism in Sissy, Bitzer, and Coketown.
      He notes the confirmation of Dickens's insight into utilitarian
      education in the testimony of J.S. Mill (but compare Alexander
      [160], Arneson [171], Baker [180], and Fielding [380]).

366.  Elton, Oliver.  "Charles Dickens, Wilkie Collins, Charles Reade."
      **A Survey of English Literature, 1830–1880.**  2 vols.  London:
      Edwin Arnold, 1920, II, 195–230.  Rpt. Folcroft, Pa.: Folcroft,
      1977; New York: AMS, 1978.  Segment on Charles Dickens rpt.
      in **Dickens and Thackeray.**  London: Edwin Arnold, 1924.  Rpt.
      Folcroft, Pa.: Folcroft, 1969, 1971; New York: Haskell, 1970; Nor-
      wood, Pa.: Norwood, 1975; Philadelphia: R. West, 1976.

      States that **Hard Times** is pamphlet fiction, full of generous
      wrath but mechanical, and located in the North Country, which
      Dickens hardly knew.

367.  Engel, Monroe.  **The Maturity of Dickens.**  Cambridge, Mass.:
      Harvard Univ. Press, 1959, passim.

      Emphasizes the effects of constriction of space in this
      novel, its lack of density and poor measure of that imaginative
      recreation it champions.  Engel rejects the boosting of this
      novel at the expense of Dickens's other novels, in the manner
      of Leavis (553), and critical modernizing of it.  He suggests that
      the savagery of Dickens's attack on Gradgrind came from his
      eagerness to dissociate himself from the Benthamites and finds
      the defense of fantasy in the novel a good deal more satisfy-
      ing.  The deathbed scene of Mrs. Gradgrind is especially prai-
      seworthy, he states.  In general the novel's "figurative render-
      ings of experience" are more successful than its mechanical
      plot.  Reviews: John Butt, **RES**, n.s. 11 (1960), 440–43; Edgar
      Johnson, **NCF**, 14 (1959), 182–84; Ada Nisbet, **VS**, 3 (1960),
      311–13; N.C. Peyrouton, **Dickensian**, 55 (1959), 155–56.

368.    ------. "The Politics of Dickens' Novels." **PMLA**, 71 (1956),
        945-74.

        Offers important background to the novel. Engel's purpose
        is to clarify Dickens's political views by deriving them not ex-
        clusively from the novels but from his letters and all the essays
        in **Household Words, Household Narrative**, and **All the Year
        Around**, since he believes that the essays always reflected
        Dickens's views. He supports Dicey's argument (338) and
        Maine's (601) that Dickens was much indebted to Bentham and
        only clarified his differences from the Benthamites at about the
        time he wrote **Hard Times**. The essay of 2 February 1856, "The
        Manchester Strike," stands in contrast to the treatment of the
        trade union in the novel, he points out; the descriptions of
        Lancashire and Liverpool in **Household Words** and **All the Year
        Round** are "more factual accounts" than is Coketown.

369.    Evans, Mabel. "The Gradgrind Philosophy." **Dickensian**, 30
        (1934), 247-48.

        Argues that the novel is set in the difficult period of the
        transfer of work from the home to the factory and that in Dick-
        ens's concern for the suffering of people he fails to see the
        better future that lies beyond the hard times. Accordingly, Ev-
        ans defends Gradgrind for his extension of education to the
        people (he takes in Sissy as his own child) and speculates that
        the weakness of Mrs. Gradgrind is more likely blamable for
        Louisa's marriage to Bounderby than are the failures of Mr.
        Gradgrind. Gradgrind's tendency to over-value fact Evans sees
        as a tendency of his age.

370.    Fadiman, Clifton. "**Pickwick** and Dickens." **Party of One: The
        Selected Writings of Clifton Fadiman**. Cleveland and New
        York: World, 1955, pp. 203-50.

        Resists the "easy view" of Dickens as a revolutionary who
        couldn't quite make it to full love of the proletariat: **Hard Times**
        is full of sympathy for the oppressed worker, but hardly for the
        union. Its central theme is not political but poetical, Fadiman
        asserts, a plea not for the claims of the worker but for the
        claims of the imagination.

371.    Fawkner, Harald William. **Animation and Reification in Dick-
        ens's Vision of the Life-Denying Society**. Stockholm: Uppsala,
        1977, passim.

**Hard Times** is instanced at a number of points in this study of Dickens's use of animation and reification to describe and analyze man's imprisonment in a life-denying society. Fawkner notes Dickens's attack on both the factory system and education as manifestations of "scientific positivism" and argues that Dickens achieved a "profound critical understanding of ... modern capitalist society."

372.   Fido, Martin.   **Charles Dickens**.   Profiles in Literature Series. London: Routledge & Kegan Paul; New York: Humanities Press, 1968, pp. 9, 13, 76–79.

**Hard Times** is considered under the rubric of satire and caricatures that represent type or class.   According to Fido, Bounderby is one of those characters whose function includes criticism of his class or calling.   Both he and Mrs. Sparsit differ from the earlier grotesques in that greater attention is now focussed upon the masks of hypocrisy, less on the evil beneath. Unlike Quilp and Bumble, they are not obvious; they give themselves away only by the excess of their poses.   Review: R.L. Patten, **Dickensian**, 65 (1969), 124–25.

373.   Fielding, K.J.   "The Battle for Preston."   **Dickensian**, 50 (1954), 159–62.   Rpt. in Gray (429).

Points to the growth of strikes at the time and suggests the influence of the Preston strike on both Dickens and Mrs. Gaskell in their choice of subjects.   Fielding indicates that Dickens's views as presented in the novel need to be supplemented by the views expressed in **Household Words**, where he shares widely-held misgivings about the idleness enforced by strikes, protests the intransigence of the masters, and objects to the characterization of the mill-hands in the press.   Fielding notes that in the twentieth century critical dissatisfaction has shifted from Bounderby to Slackbridge.   He deduces that Slackbridge and Gruffshaw ("On Strike") both derive from Mortimer Grimshaw, a stump-orator described in **Eliza Cook's Journal**. He argues that Dickens was inaccurate in presenting Slackbridge as an outside agitator, thus turning his attention away from the local leaders.   Compare Carnall (251).

374.   -------.   **Charles Dickens**.   No. 37 of "Writers and their Work" series published for The British Council and The National Book League.   London: Longmans, Green, 1953, passim.   Rev. ed., 1960.

Mentions **Hard Times** to counter Chesterton's statement that any character from Dickens might appear in any Dickens novel and that Dickens never drew characters from life (Slackbridge), to underscore the relevance of biographical information to an understanding of the novels (letters, essays in **Household Words**), and to instance the relationship to the theme of education of the activities of the Board of Trade. Compare "Charles Dickens and the Department of Practical Art," below (376).

375.    -------.  **Charles Dickens: A Critical Introduction**. London, New York, Toronto: Longmans, 1958. 2nd ed., enlarged, 1964, pp. 158-69 and passim.

Finds **Hard Times** to have benefitted from the compression for weekly publication. Leavis's praise of the novel (553) was belated and more widely applicable to Dickens than he saw, but right in its definition of the moral fable, for the true subject of the novel is not the particular of industrial capitalism but all oppression of the human spirit. Dickens was not strong as an analyst of capitalism; he did not take sides between capital and labor, seeking instead conciliation, Fielding states. He also points out that the conditions in Coketown are closer to the engineering strike of 1852 than to the Preston dispute--the former was about the closed shop, the latter about pay.

376.    -------.  "Charles Dickens and the Department of Practical Art." **MLR**, 48 (1953), 270-77.

Notes the continuing specificity of Dickens's concerns about society. Fielding identifies the "third gentleman" of chapter ii of **Hard Times** as Henry Cole of the newly formed Department of Practical Art and offers a brief account of both. Dickens's chapter plans indicate his intention to satirize "Marlborough House Doctrine," which had been lampooned in **Household Words** by Henry Morley (4 December 1852). Fielding finds a possible source for Sissy's carpets with representations of flowers in the **First Report of the Department of Practical Art** (London, 1853). On the whole, the criticisms this novel makes are too veiled and too unfocussed, not consistent though effective, he claims. Dickens should not be seen as in the line of Ruskin or Morris. See also Ames (165) and Bell (195).

377.    ———. "Dickens and the Past: The Novelist of Memory." In **Experience in the Novel: Selected Papers from the English Institute.** Ed. Roy Harvey Pearce. New York and London: Columbia Univ. Press, 1968, pp. 107–31.

Finds that **Bleak House** and **Hard Times** show the benefits of the sense of time Dickens gained from his intense searching of his childhood in **David Copperfield.**

378.    ———. "Forster: Critic of Fiction." **Dickensian,** 70 (1974), 159–70.

Quotes Forster's comment that **Hard Times** was defective in workmanship and his demurral from Ruskin's praise of the novel, and compares these to the remarks in the **Examiner** review of "singular closeness of purpose" and the "remarkably close texture of the story," concluding that there is "nothing to show" that this reviewer was Forster. See (115) above. Compare Alec W. Brice, "Reviewers of Dickens in the **Examiner:** Fonblanque, Forster, Hunt, and Morley," **DSN,** 3 (1972), 68–80 on the general issue.

379.    ———. "Hard Times and Common Things." In **Imagined Worlds, Essays on Some English Novels and Novelists in Honour of John Butt.** Ed. Maynard Mack and Ian Gregor. London: Methuen, 1968, pp. 183–203.

Counters Holloway's attack on the novel (471) by demonstrating errors of fact in his attribution of essays in **Household Words** to Dickens, refuting his interpretation of Dickens's use of the Department of Practical Art, and criticizing his extension of the Charles Knight connection to the latter's **The Store of Knowledge.** Fielding proposes to demonstrate Dickens's thoughtfulness and experience in his subjects through the issue of education in **Hard Times,** which was influenced at least in part by Dickens's work and discussions with Miss Coutts. He reviews the "Common Things" movement in education and tentatively asserts its relationship to the novel: the "main idea" Dickens referred to in his letter to Miss Coutts was the idea of education. Gradgrind was not a caricature, at least in this matter.

380.    ———. "Mill and Gradgrind." **NCF,** 11 (1956), 148–51. Rpt. in part in Gray (429).

Pays tribute to Leavis's essay (553) but presents evidence to show that Gradgrind's educational system was not the system of James Mill, whose curriculum was far beyond fact-cramming. Dickens's satire was on a more widespread and harder philosophy, Fielding asserts. See also Alexander (160), Arneson (171), Baker (180), and Ryan (713).

381.    -------. "The Weekly Serialization of Dickens's Novels." **Dickensian**, 54 (1958), 134–41.

Reviews the monthly planning for **Hard Times** and the squeeze at the close. The proofs show a footnote to the chapter about the Old Hell Shaft directing the reader to a discussion of factory accidents in **Household Words**. This suggests, Fielding states, that Dickens "thought of **Hard Times** almost as a work of journalism itself." Compare Andrews (166), Butwin (241), and Clark (279).

382.    ------- and Anne Smith. "**Hard Times** and the Factory Controversy: Dickens vs. Harriet Martineau." **NCF**, 24 (1970), 404–27. Also in **Dickens: The Centennial Essays**. Ed. Ada Nisbet and Blake Nevius. Berkeley: Univ. of California Press, 1970, pp. 22–45.

Examines the break between Dickens and Martineau, pointing to astonishing factual errors in her account in the **Autobiography**, painting her as a combination of the worst of Bounderby, Gradgrind, and M'Choakumchild. The painful inadequacy of Blackpool should be understood in light of a crisis in Dickens's thinking: he was just emerging from the confinement which had limited "the imaginative understanding even of Dickens and certainly of most of his readers when faced with the results of the industrial revolution."

383.    Fisher, B.F., IV, and J. Turow. "Dickens and Fire Imagery." **Revue des Langues Vivantes**, 40 (1974), 359–70.

Examines the development of fire imagery from **Pickwick Papers** to **Edwin Drood**, arguing Dickens's increasing ability to control it for philosophic and artistic purposes. Although the opening paragraph lists **Hard Times** among the novels which contain prominent passages of fire imagery, the novel is not discussed in the body of the essay.

384.    Fitzgerald, Percy. **Memories of Charles Dickens**. Bristol: J.W.
        Arrowsmith; London: Simpkin, Marshall, 1913. Pp. 161, 163, 181.

        Dismisses the novel as ephemeral, amusing enough in its
        weekly issues, much less engaging in book form.

385.    Fleissner, Robert E. "'Ah, Humanity!': Dickens and Bartleby Re-
        visited." **Research Studies, Washington State University**, 50
        (1982), 106–09.

        Notes that Bartleby's name chimes with Bounderby's and
        that "a very real, human correlation exists between Melville's
        pathetic figure and Stephen Blackpool." Fleissner expounds the
        correlation, with interest not in influence but in the "common
        Humanitat."

386.    Foot, Dingle. "Introduction." In the New Oxford Illustrated
        Dickens edition, 1955 (39), pp. vii–xvi.

        Argues that all the characters except Bounderby and Mrs.
        Sparsit (who save the book) are puppets, because Dickens did
        not know Lancashire people. Foot discusses Dickens's snob-
        bery and argues that the book could have worked better had
        Stephen been active in the union and in consequence fired by
        Bounderby, but that Dickens's bias against trade unions pre-
        vented such a design. Dickens's solution, Christian charity, is
        banal, Foot asserts; the real solution in Dickens's novels is a
        fairy godfather with ample means. He adds that the failures in
        characterization arise from Dickens's love of melodrama, but
        that the book is redeemed by its description of Coketown. Re-
        view: Leslie Staples, **Dickensian**, 52 (1956), 44.

387.    Ford, George H. **Dickens and His Readers: Aspects of Novel-
        Criticism since 1836**. Princeton, N.J.: Princeton Univ. Press,
        1955, passim. Reissued New York: Norton, 1965. Rpt. New
        York: Gordian, 1974.

        An important interweaving of the criticism of **Hard Times**
        with that of the other novels. The negative response to this
        novel is set in the context of the surrounding novels, especially
        **Bleak House** and **Little Dorrit**. Reviews: Edgar Johnson, **VQR**,
        31 (1955), 644–48; Hudson Rogers, **EJ**, 44 (1955), 434; Franklin P.
        Rolfe, **NCF**, 10 (1955), 242–45.

388.  ———. "Dickens in the 1960s." **Dickensian**, 66 (1970), 163–82.

> Offers tables of sale of Dickens's works in 1968 showing that **Hard Times** was fourth in the U.S. (after **A Tale of Two Cities**, **Great Expectations**, and **Oliver Twist**), and third in England (after **David Copperfield** and **Great Expectations**). The table for U.S. sales is reprinted in Patten (664).

389.  ———. "Self-Help and the Helpless in **Bleak House**." In **From Jane Austen to Joseph Conrad**. Ed. Robert C. Rathburn and Martin Steinmann, Jr. Minneapolis: Univ. of Minnesota Press, 1958, pp. 92–105.

> States that the aspect of society represented by the Small-weeds, who have banished all levity and fancy, is given full-scale treatment in **Hard Times**.

390.  ———. "Stern Hebrews Who Laugh: Further Thoughts on Carlyle and Dickens." In **Carlyle Past and Present: A Collection of New Essays**. Ed. K.J. Fielding and Rodger L. Tarr. London: Vision; New York: Barnes & Noble, 1976, pp. 112–26.

> Concurs with Dunn (350) that we have no record of Carlyle's response to **Hard Times**, but quotes from a letter from Jane Carlyle a sentence with an intriguing exclamation point: "By the way, Dickens is going to dedicate Hard Times to Mr. C!"

391.  ———, and Steven Marcus. "Dickens's Uncanny 'Camera Eye.'" **New York Times**, 8 May 1977, sect. II, 29, 41.

> Derives from the television production of the novel (69), in which each segment held fifty-two minutes of story and eight minutes of discussion by Asa Briggs, George Ford, and Steven Marcus. Topics include Dickens's use of montage, the specificity of the Coketown setting, and Dickens's concern with gestures and visual effects, as bearing upon the adaptability for film of Dickens's novels, and especially of **Hard Times**.

392.  ———, and Sylvere Monod. "Introduction." In the Norton Critical Edition, 1966 (45), pp. vii–x.

Reviews the circumstances of writing and publication and, very briefly, the background of industrialism and education. The unhappy marriages in the novel are related to the unhappiness of Dickens's marriage at the time, the editors conclude. The text that follows is described briefly. See (45).

\*      Forster, John.

       See above (133).

393.   Fowler. Roger. **Linguistics and the Novel.** London: Methuen; Totowa, N.J.: Rowan & Littlefield, 1977, pp. 36, 38–39, 94–95.

       **Hard Times** occurs at a number of points among various examples. Fowler indicates, for instance that the houses of Bounderby and Gradgrind are "architectural diagrams of their semantic make-up," while Coketown expresses the drudgery of the workers. In one passage describing Bounderby, Fowler demonstrates how the external perspective leads to alienation from the observer/reader. He also points out that the series of images of balloons for Bounderby makes him a perplexing and intruding force that menaces our more human world.

\*      Freud, Sigmund.

       See Ernest Jones (506).

394.   Frewer, Louis B. "From Recent Books." **Dickensian.** 37 (1941), 113–16.

       Quotes four paragraphs from M. Beer, **A History of British Socialism,** which include reference to **Hard Times.** See Beer (193).

395.   Frye, Northrop. "Dickens and the Comedy of Humors." In **Experience in the Novel: Selected Papers from the English Institute.** Ed. Roy Harvey Pearce. New York and London: Columbia Univ. Press, 1968, pp. 49–81. Also in **The Stubborn Structure: Essays on Criticism and Society.** London: Methuen, 1970. Also in **The Victorian Novel: Modern Essays in Criticism.** Ed. Ian Watt. Oxford: Oxford Univ. Press, 1971. Also in **Literary Criticism: Idea and Act.** Ed. William K. Wimsatt. Berkeley and Los Angeles: Univ. of California Press, 1974.

Places Dickens within the New Comedy structure that sets in opposition two societies, the obstructing and the congenial. **Hard Times** is a dystopia, of the sort that threatens the writer himself as one who responds to fancy and fairy tale, Frye asserts. He also points out that the obstructing society is associated with utilitarian philosophy and a dangerously excessive trust in facts and statistics.

396. ———. **The Secular Scripture: A Study of the Structure of Romance.** Cambridge, Mass., and London: Harvard Univ. Press, 1976, p. 42.

In a discussion of prevailing notions of serious fiction, asserts that seriousness is found in the wisdom and insight a book brings to bear upon the world outside itself. Thus Dickens's obvious social concerns were what raised his status from that of a mere entertainer. In addition, Frye notes, a book as dull as **Hard Times** must have had some worthy nonliterary motive.

397. Furness, Edna L. "Portrait of the Dickensian Schoolteacher." **Educational Forum,** 33 (1969), 153-61.

Surveys Dickens's schoolteachers, their characters, the forces that act upon them, and their archetypal reach. In this context both Mr. Gradgrind and M'Choakumchild are presented.

398. Gadd, W. Lawrence. "Coketown." **Dickensian,** 6 (1940), 85-87.

Argues that Coketown is probably not Manchester, because Manchester was too big, too sophisticated, and too much a center for storage and distribution rather than production. Gadd suggests Blackburn or Rochdale as alternatives, but without certainty.

399. Gallagher, Catherine. "**Hard Times** and **North and South**: The Family and Society in Two Industrial Novels." **Arizona Quarterly,** 36 (1980), 70-96.

Finds the disappointing ending to **Hard Times** explicable as a consequence of Dickens's failure to integrate his dissimilar narrative and ideological structures. Gallagher argues that the family is related to society metaphorically; the social principle is social paternalism. Hence the parallel between the two main strands of the tale. The private solution, however, she points out, has no effect upon the social world, and the family retreats into itself. In contrast, she sees that the metonymic relationship of the family to society in **North and South** allows greater flexibility and allows the family to become a center of moral influence upon the social world around it.

400.   Ganz, Margaret. "The Vulnerable Ego: Dickens' Humor in Decline." **DSA**, 1 (1970), 23-40.

Argues the merits of the early Dickens against the solemn concerns of modern critics, and disparages the later. Ganz finds Mrs. Sparsit's forgetting Louisa's married name an outgrowth of failed invention, Bounderby poor compared to Mrs. Gamp, the circus poor compared to the Crummles troupe. The villains of this mischief were Dickens's concern with social issues and his preoccupation with plot and the serious delineation of character.

401.   Garis, Robert D. "**Hard Times**." **The Dickens Theatre**. Oxford: Clarendon, 1965, pp. 144-63.

Applies to **Hard Times** the book's program to restore the popular understanding of Dickens against the criticism that stresses symbolic significance. All of Dickens is a performance, Garis states, with the performer at the center. Garis notes a new economy in this novel, but underscores Ruskin's reservations concerning its theatricality. He argues that Leavis (553) over-valued the depth and imaginative range of the novel. What we see is "the theatrical virtuoso's ... execution of his powerfully simple refutation of the Utilitarian algebra." Thus the "Dickens problem" is apparent here: Dickens is not capable of "complete continuities." The performing voice remains at our ear, and it is separate from the awfulness of Coketown. Garis also offers a convincing analysis of Sissy contrary to Leavis's. Reviews: William Burgan, **VS**, 9 (1966), 208-10; George Ford, **DS**, 2 (1966), 96-101; Joan E. Hartman, **JEGP**, 65 (1966), 627-20; A.G. Hill, **CritQ**, 7 (1965), 379-80; Edgar Johnson, **NCF**, 20 (1966), 395-402; Martin Price, **YR**, 55 (1966), 290-96.

402.   Garland, Barbara Carolyn. "Comic Form in Nineteenth Century English Fiction." **DAI**, 33 (1973), 4412A (Indiana Univ., 1972). 331 pp.

Takes seven novels, including **Hard Times**, and describes the "variations on an idealized comic form," drawing upon the theories of Northrop Frye, Suzanne Langer, and Nelvin Vos.

403.     Garnett, Richard. "The Editor's Estimate" (Introduction). In the Autograph edition, 1900 (31), pp. 1–2 (preceding p. 247).

Considers **Hard Times** the "most mannered" of Dickens's novels. Its portraits are "spoiled by the laborious accumulation and relentless repetition of small details"; its satire is "misdirected." Garnett's only praise is for the exposure of the unfairness of the divorce laws

404.     ———, and Edmund Gosse. **English Literature: An Illustrated Record**. 4 vols. London: Heinemann; New York: Macmillan, 1903, IV, 238. New ed., Macmillan, 1935.

Finds **Hard Times** the "earliest flagging" of Dickens's power; it is a didactic satire on the Manchester school.

405.     Gattegno, Jean. **Dickens**. Paris: Seuil, 1975, passim..

Compares Coketown unfavorably with Dickens's London, sets Gradgrind's school in the context of other attacks on schooling as the wrenching of children into adulthood, and groups **Hard Times** with **Bleak House** and **Little Dorrit** as examinations of aspects of contemporary society united by the theme of machinery. Gattegno attributes the critical dislike of this novel to its form and its political stance, arguing that although the latter was not new, it was more dangerous in Dickens because of this wide popularity. In earlier Dickens novels there was always the philanthropist to reconcile the two classes, he states; here we have only Bounderby. Gattegno also argues that Slackbridge does not constitute Dickens's final word on the workers and urges us to look instead at Mrs. Sparsit's remarks in II,i, at Stephen's speech to Bounderby, and at Dickens's attack on the system of profit in II,i. Dickens's denunciation is not at all ambiguous, Gattegno asserts: the system is exploitation.

406.     ———, Isabelle Jan, and Anny Sadrin. "Le Dossier Dickens." **Romantisme**, 11 (34) (1981), 89–113.

A setting of Dickens within his times, includes Gradgrind's in a brief discussion of schools in the novels, as a place where the spirits of children are crushed.

407.    Gelfert, Hans-Dieter. **Die Symbolik im Romanwerk von Charles Dickens.** Stuttgart: Kohlhammer, 1974, passim.

Argues that Dickens looks at the social question only as it affects characters, so that, unlike Marx, who is interested in understanding the economic system that produces Coketown, Dickens finds only a muddle. Stephen's real problem is his wife more than his working conditions; he is concerned with the dehumanizing effects of the muddle, that is, with moral relations, Gelfert points out. He also indicates that Dickens seems to see the trade union as just another manifestation of Gradgrind/Bounderbyism. As the symbol of that system as it comes into being, Louisa is the central character of the book, the spiritual sacrifice, not unlike Edith Dombey. Gelfert remarks that this is a novel without a hero.

*       Gerber, Helmut E.

See below (886).

408.    Gerould, Gordon Hall. **The Patterns of English and American Fiction.** Boston: Little, Brown, 1942, pp. 261, 265, 272. Rpt. New York: Russell & Russell, 1966.

Sets fiction in intellectual history. **Hard Times**, like the rest of Dickens, Gerould points out, is untheoretical in its bent, concerned not with solutions to problems but with instances of individual suffering. Dickens is also not interested in the inner lives of his characters; with conversions such as Gradgrind's, we are attentive to the fact rather than the process by which it came about.

409.    Gerson, Stanley. "Name-creation in Dickens." **Moderna Sprak,** 69 (1975), 299-315.

Suggests that Stephen is meant to recall St. Stephen, the protomartyr. Childers "seems to be a memory" of the famous race-horse Flying Childers; he and Kidderminster also point to the message that children must be entertained. There is a "striking" similarity between "Sleary's" and "Astley's" (Astley's Circus). Surnames descriptive of persons include Bounderby (bounder), Slackbridge (unreliable), Harthouse (an ironically sentimental name), and Bitzer ("bits," the missing qualities of his character).

410.    ——————. **Sound and Symbol in the Dialogue of the Works of Charles Dickens.** Stockholm Studies in English, 16. Stockholm, Goteborg, Malmo: Almqvist & Wiksell, 1967, pp. xvii, 339–40.

Suggests that in **Nicholas Nickleby** and **Hard Times** Dickens may have borrowed accepted forms for Yorkshire and Lancashire dialect rather than creating them. For Blackpool Dickens uses only "the broadest effects possible" because for Dickens the message Stephen carries is a good deal more important than "the observance of linguistic details." Those forms Dickens does use are accurate and consistently applied, Gerson states. He disagrees explicitly with the criticism of the dialect in Langton (548) and Smith/Quirk (748).

411.    Gibson, Frank A. "Dogs in Dickens." **Dickensian**, 53 (1957), 145–52.

Merrylegs is included in this survey.

412.    Gibson, John W. "**Hard Times**, A Further Note." **DS**, 1 (1965), 90–101.

A rebuttal to Leavis (553) that demonstrates how unarguable both Leavis's and Gibson's positions are. Gibson finds the novel bland, lacking in honest conviction, lifeless. "The symbols are self-negating," he states; **Hard Times** shows us how good other Dickens novels are, **Bleak House** in particular. See also Sadock (714).

413.    Gifford, James Allen. "Symbolic Settings in the Novels of Charles Dickens." **DAI**, 38 (1977), 277A–78A (Univ. of California, Riverside, 1974). 236 pp.

Demonstrates how Dickens conveys his moral and social messages through symbolic settings, examining the thematic significance of the physical settings of several novels, including **Hard Times**.

414.    Gilmour, Robin. "Dickens and the Self-Help Idea." In **The Victorians and Social Protest: A Symposium**. Ed. John Butt and I. F. Clarke. Newton Abbot, Devon: David & Charles; Hamden, Conn.: Shoestring, 1973, pp. 71-101.

Examines the self-help idea and charts Dickens's allegiance to it. The "essential development" in Dickens's social thought is from "an eagerness to be identified with the established rather than the aspiring sections of the Victorian middle class" towards "an increasingly critical understanding of this class and of his relationship to it." **Hard Times**, according to Gilmour, records a "violent revulsion" from the self-made man and his social ambition. Social evils are no longer the legacy of the past but "the creation of the new men of mid-Victorian England--bankers, industrialists, trade unionists, utilitarians." The rejection of the self-help idea is not only a change in Dickens's social thought, Gilmour concludes, but a change in his attitude toward himself.

415.    -------. "The Gradgrind School: Political Economy in the Classroom." **VS**, 11 (1967), 207-24.

Takes issue with Holloway (471). Gilmour points out that Dickens's emphasis is not on the topical strike but on an attitude of mind. Specifically, Dickens attacks the Birkbeck Schools analyzed by Henry Morley in **Household Words** (25 December 1852). Comparison of the textbooks for these schools with the relevant passages in **Hard Times** reveals Dickens's accuracy, especially regarding the system of interrogation, Gilmour indicates. The circus represents a superior freedom, a much-needed free-play of imagination. Dickens attacked not the theorists like Mill but the popularizers who simplified the theories and in consequence made the lives of the workers harsher. Compare Sadrin (715).

416.    -------. **The Idea of the Gentleman in the Victorian Novel**. London: Allen & Unwin, 1981, p. 21.

Refers to Stephen Blackpool as an exemplar of the natural courtesy of the humble, set up in opposition to the Chesterfieldian idea of the gentleman, to which the Victorians responded harshly.

417.    -------. "Manchester Men and Their Books." **Dickensian**, 63 (1967), 21-24.

Explicates the tension between the "improving" aspects of education and the power of fables devoured by a people hungry for imaginative play. Gilmour shows that Dickens's reference to this issue in I, viii may have been stimulated by Henry Morley's "Manchester Men At Their Books," which appeared in **Household Words** for 17 December 1853, and that Dickens selected only one aspect of Morley's treatment for incorporation in his story, thus making his point more vivid. His public pronouncements show a greater balance between the two values, Gilmour states.

418.  Gissing, George. **Charles Dickens: A Critical Study**. London: Blackie & Son, 1898, pp. 54, 110, 193-94, 205-06. Rpt. St. Clair Shores, Mich.: Scholarly Press, 1972. A short passage rpt. in Gray (429).

Dismisses **Hard Times** as well-nigh and well forgotten, a book in which Dickens's humor failed him. More stringently, Gissing attacks Dickens for his failure to deal with the central issue of his time, the conflict between employer and worker. (Stephen suffers from the misery of a drunken wife, something that could happen to any man anywhere.) He also insists that Dickens could not deal with the articulate poor and was as far as any man who ever wrote from preaching true social equality.

419.  -------. "Mr. Swinburne on Dickens." **TLS**, 25 July 1902. Rpt. in **Gissing's Writings on Dickens**. Ed. Pierre Coustillas. London: Enitharmon, 1969, p. 219.

Reviews Swinburne's article on Dickens (788) and states that Swinburne was too kind in respect to **Hard Times**, a novel that deserves its comparative neglect.

420.  Gold, Joseph. "'Aw a Muddle': **Hard Times**." **Charles Dickens: Radical Moralist**. Minneapolis: Univ. of Minnesota Press, 1972, pp. 196-207.

Sees the novel as an attack on isms of all sorts, Dickens's nearest approach to the great dystopias. Gradgrind has a possibility of redemption because his various relationships with others keep a tenuous thread of sympathy unbroken, Gold states. Bounderby, on the other hand, shows a similar absolutism compounded in a myth of self-conception. The misalliance of Bounderby and Gradgrind leads to a loss of dignity to the individual (Stephen) and an incapacity for love. Set against this is the circus, with its interdependence, its interpenetrating boundaries, its capacity for love, Gold points out. He relates this novel more to the earlier work than to the psychological self-searching of the later, and argues that its controversial reception was due to its assaults on the social values of its audience. Compare Oddie (644). Reviews: Rachel Bennett, **RES**, 25 (1974), 371; Angus Easson, **Dickensian**, 69 (1973), 190–91; Stephen Gill, **N&Q**, 22 (1975), 471–72; Alexander Welsh, **YR**, 62 (1973), 281–87; George Worth, **CEA**, 73 (1974), 32–35.

421.   Goldberg, Michael. **Carlyle and Dickens**. Athens: Univ. of Georgia Press, 1972, pp. 78–99 and passim.

Argues that **Hard Times** shows Dickens's "widespread dependence on Carlyle's teaching to an extreme extent." Goldberg ties the opposition of fact and fancy to the utilitarian program with its rationalist heritage and the transcendental view of the Romantics. He suggests that Carlyle's "Signs of the Times" (**Edinburgh Review**, 1829) was virtually an "ideological prospectus to the novel." He also deals at length with the issue of education in the novel, showing the parallels to Carlyle. Compare Barnes (187), Christian (269), and Oddie (644). Reviews: Richard Dunn, **DSN**, 4 (1973), 72–76; K.J. Fielding, **Dickensian**, 69 (1973), 111–18; Sylvere Monod, **EA**, 26 (1973), 373–74; George Worth, **CEA**, 37 (1974), 32–35.

422.   -------. "The Dickens Debate: G.B.S. vs. G.K.C." **Shaw Review**, 20 (1977), 135–47.

Examines the contrast between "Chesterton's Dickens, the unrivalled comic genius, and Shaw's Dickens, the brilliant social critic." Mentions **Hard Times** passim.

423.   -------. "Dr. Pessimist Anticant and Mr. Popular Sentiment: The Influence of Carlyle on Dickens." **DA**, 28 (1966) 195A (Cornell Univ., 1966). 308 pp.

See Goldberg, above (421).

424.   -------. "From Bentham to Carlyle: Dickens' Political Development." **Journal of the History of Ideas**, 33 (1972), 61–76.

Traces the shift of Dickens's political allegiance from the teachings of Bentham to Carlyle, from the belief in social amelioration through the reform of particular institutions to a repudiation of Benthamism in **Hard Times**. Goldberg argues the closeness of Dickens's and Carlyle's views on parliament, democracy, emigration, hanging, philanthropy, slavery, leadership (cf. Stephen's speech on the need for leadership), and education. See also **Carlyle and Dickens** (421). Compare Dicey (338) and Maine (601).

425.   Goldfarb, Russell M. "Charles Dickens; Orphans, Incest, and Repression." **Sexual Repression and Victorian Literature**. Lewisburg: Bucknell Univ. Press, 1970, pp. 114-30.

Examines the bedroom scene between Tom and Louisa and chides Deneau (332) for not calling it "incest," implying that Deneau meant something less than incest. In fact, Deneau's essay seems merely periphrastic; Goldfarb adds only a note of greater insistence.

426.   Goldknopf, David. "The Morality of Hypocrisy: The Structure of **Hard Times**." **The Life of the Novel**. Chicago: Univ. of Chicago Press, 1972, pp. 143-58.

Concludes from an analysis of the "lines of rotational force" between Louisa, Gradgrind, Tom, and Bounderby that the plot of **Hard Times** is impressive. But although the miseducation of Louisa is the center of the novel, Dickens's analysis of Victorian education is callow and made from typically Victorian premises, Goldknopf states. He suggests that Gradgrind, unlike Dickens, was not a hypocrite and that the circus fails because Dickens is not really interested in it. It is degraded by the scene of Tom in blackface ("Dickens, like any successful social opportunist, ... could not forsee that some day Negroes would have their day too") and by Sleary's lisp, which is a sign of "dubious masculinity." (On the lisp, compare Naslund [640] and Page [656].) Goldknopf concludes that **Hard Times** brilliantly embodies the hypocritical zeitgeist. He also makes assertions others may have greater difficulty accepting, such as that Louisa allows herself to be destroyed in order to throw herself at her father's feet.

427.   Gomme, A.H. "Four Great Novels." **Dickens**. London: Evans, 1971, pp. 110-88.

Hard Times is selected along with Dombey and Son, Little Dorrit, and Great Expectations for detailed consideration. Gomme argues that this novel is not primarily "a piece of somewhat misdirected political satire" but a tragedy centered on Gradgrind and rendered in "a delicate and complex poetic language" that is evolving and dramatic. In explicating this poetic art, Gomme refers repeatedly to Leavis (553). He gives Sissy, Bitzer, Louisa, Tom, and Sleary their usual roles in this line of criticism, and finds Bounderby an "objectification of the logical conclusion" of Gradgrind's system. The novel is highly dramatized and brilliantly plotted, according to Gomme, but with serious flaws in the presentation of Slackbridge and unionism and in the sentimentalization of Stephen, which introduces a "cross-current" that Dickens cannot control.

428.    Gordon, Elizabeth H. The Naming of Characters in the Works of Charles Dickens. Univ. of Nebraska Studies in Language, Literature, and Criticism. Lincoln: Univ. of Nebraska Press, 1917, passim.

Sees Stephen as one of Dickens's characters "gifted with names figuratively descriptive." Bounderby and Mrs. Sparsit are examples of names that are a word descriptive of the character lengthened by a suffix. M'Choakumchild in clearly descriptive. Sleary is among the vaguely suggestive names, suggesting slush, sleazy, leer, blear, bleary. Gordon also states that "the names of Mrs. Pegler and James Harthouse appear to have been taken from life" (no further explanation).

429.    Gray, Paul E. "Introduction." Twentieth-Century Interpretations of Hard Times. Ed. Paul E. Gray. Englewood Cliffs, N.J.: Prentice-Hall, 1969, pp. 1–15.

Reviews the division in the criticism of Hard Times—the ideological arguments that have pervaded it in both the nineteenth and twentieth centuries—and locates the essential cause in a problem of genre. The novel exists on the borderline between fiction and non-fiction, sliding unpredictably between the one and the other. Gray also points out that Dickens attacks not institutions but the abuse of institutions, and Louisa's final position is really a modification of Gradgrind's; this middle-of-the-road stance has drawn fire from both sides. Gray points to contradictions in the novel: Bounderby is unchangeable, but the remedy is supposed to come from a change in the owners; humanity and charity are supposed to have the power to heal, but

Louisa's act of generosity to Stephen leads to his death. He argues that Dickens's understanding of industrialism, educational theory, or political economy is not germane to a critical evaluation of the novel, but does bring in J.M. M'Culloch (schoolmaster, clergyman, and author of popular textbooks who advocated teaching "facts" [1801-83]) in justification of M"Choakumchild.

430.    Green, Frank. **As Dickens Saw Them**. London: Arthur H. Stockwell, 1933, pp. 222-23.

The purpose of this book is to gather various characters by class and display them in so far as possible in Dickens's own words. M'Choakumchild is selected as perhaps the only type of schoolteacher that still exists, and the effects of teaching facts according to Gradgrind, as they are shown in the novel, are reviewed.

431.    Green, Robert. "**Hard Times**: The Style of a Sermon." **TSLL**, 11 (1970), 1375-96.

Analyzes characteristics of the narrative style of the novel: verbal and syntactic repetition, rhythm (as having signifying effect), and structural or extended metaphors. Green also points out that the use of noun series without verbs indicates the incompleteness of the Gradgrind ethos. The broken Gradgrind speaks in broken sentences. In contrast, the descriptive style for the circus is more relaxed. The latter description is of course repetitive as well, Green states, but this repetition is different because the lexical items have strong emotional connotations. He compares the style for similar features with short selections from Newman's sermons, to conclude that **Hard Times** was meant to be a moral sermon. He discovers Lodge (577) too late for consideration.

432.    Greenwood, Edward. **F.R. Leavis**. Harlow, Essex: Longman for the British Council, 1978, pp. 45-46.

On Leavis's claim in the preface to **Dickens the Novelist** (554) that Dickens had the capacity to read and understand Bentham, points out that there is no account of his having done so and notes the contempt of the Benthamite critics in the **Saturday Review** for Dickens's grasp of social matters. Leavis's claim might be modified to assert that Dickens grasped the underlying spirit of Benthamism, Greenwood concludes. Compare Dicey (338) and Engel (368).

433.   Groom, Bernard. **A Literary History of England**. London and New York: Longmans, Green, 1929, p. 338.

Considers all of Dickens's novels as fiction with a purpose and finds **Hard Times** a vigorous piece of social criticism, a grave study of the problems of capital and labor.

434.   Gross, John. "Dickens: Some Recent Approaches." In **Dickens and the Twentieth Century**. Ed. John Gross and Gabriel Pearson. London: Routledge and Kegan Paul, 1962, pp. ix–xvi.

Remarks that Sleary's circus is less a Lawrentian slice of life than an image of Dickens's own transformative, creative powers.

435.   Grubb, Gerald Giles. "Dickens' Pattern of Weekly Serialization." **ELH**, 9 (1942), 141–56.

Is primarily concerned with Dickens as editor, but notes his difficulty as a writer in following the weekly pattern accepted by himself and his staff.

436.   Grylls, David. "Jane Austen and Dickens." **Guardians and Angels: Parents and Children in Nineteenth-Century Literature**. London and Boston: Faber & Faber, 1978, pp. 111–52.

Finds the filial clash in **Hard Times** to be part of a wider indictment of a system, and calls Gradgrind's behavior "psychic cruelty." In Dickens, Grylls asserts, mistreatment of children is increasingly a matter of neglect rather than oppression: images of privation surround Tom, Louisa, and Bitzer.

437.   Guerard, Albert. **The Triumph of the Novel: Dickens, Dostoevsky, Faulkner**. New York: Oxford Univ. Press, 1976, pp. 4, 12, 14, 150.

Finds **Hard Times** a second-rate book and Leavis's praise of it perverse, for the novel rarely shows relaxed imaginative playfulness or high spirits. Reviews: Alan W. Friedman, **SNNTS**, 9 (1977), 232–33; Barbara Hardy, **Novel**, 11 (1977), 77–79.

*        Gummer, Ellis N.

         See below (922).

438.     Haberman, Melvyn. "The Courtship of the Void: The World of
         **Hard Times.**" In **The Worlds of Victorian Fiction.** Ed. Jerome
         H. Buckley. Cambridge, Mass.: Harvard Univ. Press, 1975, pp.
         37-55.

         Studies industrialism, education, and utilitarianism in the
         novel, mainly under the name of the last, which is a sort of in-
         dependent entity responsible for all the evils. Haberman shows
         that the circus is the humane and humanizing entity posed
         against it, which in its limited power can offer only escape, not
         deliverance.

439.     Haley, Bruce. **The Healthy Body and Victorian Culture.** Cam-
         bridge, Mass.: Harvard Univ. Press, 1978, p. 176.

         States that the Victorian notion of a single, fundamental
         requirement in the education of children is demonstrated in the
         first chapter of **Hard Times.**

440.     Halperin, John. "Dickens." **Egoism and Self-Discovery in the
         Victorian Novel.** New York: Burt Franklin, 1974, pp. 81-123.

         Groups **Hard Times** with **Little Dorrit, Great Expectations,**
         and **Our Mutual Friend** as novels in which the relationship be-
         tween the growth of capitalism and the decline of man is a
         theme, but the focus of Halperin's discussion is on **Dombey
         and Son, Great Expectations,** and **A Tale of Two Cities.**

441.     Harbage, Alfred B. **A Kind of Power: The Shakespeare-Dick-
         ens Analogy.** Philadelphia: American Philosophical Society,
         1975, passim.

         Mentions **Hard Times** in reference to Dickens's style and
         his poor comprehension of social institutions, but offers no ex-
         tended comment on the novel.

442.     Harder, Kelsie B. "Charles Dickens Names His Characters."
         **Names,** 7 (1959), 34-42.

Investigates patterns of names that reveal Dickens's attitudes. Harder includes Bounderby among the "high-sounding" names, M'Choakumchild among the terrorizing teachers, and both Gradgrind and Bounderby in a list of examples of names (there are six in the list) that survived even through the low ebb of Dickens's popularity.

443.    Hardwick, Michael, and Mollie Hardwick. **Dickens's England**. London: Dent; South Brunswick and New York: A.S. Barnes, 1970, pp. 115, 117, 150.

Finds that in **Hard Times** place has less personality than in any of Dickens's other novels. Coketown seems to be neither Manchester nor Preston, though the latter is more likely. The place is no more convincing than the dialect of Stephen.

444.    Hardy, Barbara. "The Change of Heart in Dickens' Novels." **VS**, 5 (1961-62), 49-67. Rpt. in **Dickens: A Collection of Critical Essays**. Ed. Martin Price. Englewood Cliffs, N.J.: Prentice-Hall, 1967.

Sets **Hard Times** within a pattern of moral conversion as theme and technical device that is traced through the novels. Gradgrind is converted by two images, his double and his opposite. The opposite is Sissy. The double is embodied in three characters: Tom Junior, Bitzer, and Louisa, though mostly Tom.

445.    -------. "Charles Dickens." **Tellers and Listeners: The Narrative Imagination**. London: Athlone, 1975, pp. 165-74.

Repeats material from "Dickens's Storytellers" (448).

446.    -------. **Charles Dickens: the Later Novels**. London: Longmans, 1968, passim.

States that Louisa and Edith Dombey display Dickens's insight into a more aggressive feminine sexuality, achieved even before he met Ellen Ternan. **Hard Times** is not as psychologically intense as the other later novels and it is weak in its treatment of the working-class characters and of industrial problems, but it does show a new kind of truthfulness about the social conditioning of character. Sissy is an improvement on Esther, Louisa on Edith Dombey, Harthouse on Carker, Hardy asserts. She believes that the novel lacks an adult paradigm for the life denied by Gradgrind, though we hardly notice the lack, and Louisa's inner life is implied rather than explored. Hardy praises the novel, however, for its subdued and reticent ending. Review: W.W. Robson, **Dickensian**, 65 (1969), 114–16.

447.    –––––––. "The Complexity of Dickens." In **Dickens 1970**. Ed. Michael Slater. London: Chapman & Hall; New York: Stein & Day, 1970, pp. 29–51.

Examines the complex relationship between Dickens's art and his humanity under three aspects, and **Hard Times** under the aspect of the social story in tension with the personal story. According to Hardy, the novel passes the tests of appropriate responsiveness in the ending (the only one in Dickens that allows peace, passion spent, and the end of disaster as a happy ending) and of responsiveness between the "central human case and the social indictment of the novel as a whole." Caricature in this novel, she states, is self-inflicted by the character, "a complex statement about education and ideology, and not a comic simplification."

448.    –––––––. "Dickens's Storytellers." **Dickensian**, 69 (1973), 71–78.

On the roles and functions of characters who tell stories. Hardy notes also the opposite, the occasional presence of the repressed story. One example of the latter is Louisa's inability to tell the story of her reluctance to marry Bounderby, because Gradgrind has repressed the story-telling of childhood. Thus she offers only "enigmatic statements, lyric rather than narrative." The change of heart in the story is shown, Hardy points out, through "a great release of story-telling."

449.    –––––––. **The Moral Art of Dickens**. New York: Oxford Univ. Press, 1970, passim.

The chapter entitled "The Change of Heart (1)" repeats "The Change of Heart in Dickens's Novels" (444). "The Change of Heart (2)" looks closely at Edith Dombey, Louisa, Estella, and Bella Wilfer. Louisa follows Edith's pattern, Hardy states, but she is not quite a coherent character, in part conditioned by her education, in part rejecting it. The characters in **Hard Times** shift "rather like characters in a Jacobean tragedy," but

Louisa is still sufficiently of one piece "to move and interest
us." Reviews: John Bayley, **NYRB**, 8 October 1970, p. 8; Stephen Gill, **N&Q**, 18 (1971), 425-26; Edgar Johnson, **NCF**, 26
(1971), 349-52; Lauriat Lane, Jr., **DSN**, 2 (1971), 47-49; Martin
Price, **YR**, 61 (1972), 271-79; Angus Wilson, **Dickensian**, 67
(1971), 45.

450.    Harris, Jack T. "The Factory Hand in the English Novel,
        1840-1855." **DA**, 28 (1967), 4176A (Univ. of Texas, 1967). 138
        pp.

        Traces the position of the character of the urban worker
        from that of central character in the 1840's to the periphery in
        the 1850's (**Hard Times** and **North and South**), when middle-
        class heroes return. According to Harris, Blackpool exists pri-
        marily as a foil for Bounderby, the indictment of whom is the
        focus of the novel. This change is connected to the collapse
        of Chartism in 1848.

451.    Harris, Stephen Leroy. "The Mask of Morality: A Study of the
        Unconscious Hypocrite in Representative Novels of Jane Aus-
        ten, Charles Dickens and George Eliot." **DA**, 25 (1964), 4699
        (Cornell Univ., 1964). 334 pp.

        Looks at the novelists' interest in morally defective but os-
        tensibly respectable characters who may cause more suffering
        than the criminal or calculating hypocrite. In **Oliver Twist**,
        **Dombey and Son**, **Bleak House**, **Hard Times**, **Little Dorrit**, and
        **Our Mutual Friend**, Dickens shows a world in which callous-
        ness and cruelty are fully compatible with respectability, Harris
        concludes.

452.    Harris, Wendell V. "Fiction and Metaphysics in the Nineteenth
        Century." **Mosaic**, 4, iii (1971), 53-65. Rpt. in **The Novel and
        Its Changing Form**. Ed. R.G. Collins. Winnipeg: Univ. of Mani-
        toba Press, 1972.

        Examines the "fictional results of empiricist, transcendental,
        and intentionally anti-philosophical orientations" in selected
        nineteenth-century English novelists to demonstrate the rela-
        tionship between metaphysical allegiances and technique and
        formal structure. For the third stance, Harris selects Dickens
        and **Hard Times**. Dickens opposes utilitarian philosophy as he
        understood it; he offers in its place not any sort of transcen-

dentalism but the idealized sentimentality embodied in Sleary's horse-riding, Harris asserts. He believes that Dickens's style reflects this neutrality, offering neither the abstractions of philosophy nor the transcendental flights of Carlyle. His animism suggests not a power beyond the visible world but the picturesque imagination in a wholly terrestrial world, "in which neither reason nor inspiration is as important as sympathy and benevolence."

453.  Harrison, Lewis. "Dickens's Shadow Show." **Dickensian**, 39 (1943), 187-91.

Believes that the novel's characters are ghosts of earlier personalities, but the novel is not a failure because it makes us realize the importance of our being interested in the dull and unattractive as well as in the attractive and brilliant. Harrison points out the importance of the brother/sister relationship for Dickens, in connection with Tom and Louisa.

*     Harte, James L.

See Joseph C. Boarman and James L. Harte (204).

454.  Harvey, William R. "Charles Dickens and the Byronic Hero." **NCF**, 24 (1969), 305-16.

Examines Dickens's use of the Byronic hero. Harvey points out that Harthouse combines this type with the dandy's cynical, sensual indifference and scorn.

455.  Hass, Robert. "Reason's Children: Economic Ideology and the Themes of Fiction, 1720-1880." **DAI**, 36 (1976), 8033A-34A (Stanford Univ., 1976). 385 pp.

Includes **Hard Times** and **Our Mutual Friend** in this study of economic and psychological themes related to the rise of capitalism. In particular, Hass looks at the effects upon private life of the new social doctrines and of an economic view of sexuality.

456.  Hayman, Ronald. **Leavis**. London: Heinemann; Totowa, N.J.: Rowan & Littlefield, 1976, passim.

Reviews Leavis's remarks on **Hard Times** (553), noting the adjustments Leavis made when the essay appeared in **Dickens the Novelist** (554).

457.    Hazama, Jiro.    "On **Hard Times** In Relation to **The Chimes**." **Research Reports of the Junior College of Engineering, Chiba University**, 7 (1968), 1–10.

Compares the relations between oppressors and oppressed in **Hard Times** and **The Chimes**, identifying Mr. Filer and Gradgrind and also Will Fern and Stephen as the major parallels of character.    Hazama finds parallels of theme in the warnings to society and the grievances against laws unfairly severe to the poor.    A major difference is the introduction in **Hard Times** of the notion of the tyranny of the unionized men against the individual, and this sombre note, like Stephen's final prayer, Hazama sees as consonant with  Dickens's more pessimistic view in the later work.

458.    Hazen, Lynn Shuford.    "Vessels  of  Salvation:  Fathers  and Daughters in Six Dickens Novels."  **DAI**, 39 (1978), 1587A–88A (Univ. of Wisconsin, 1978).  256 pp.

Argues that six of Dickens's novels concern relationships between selfish or inadequate fathers and selfless daughters that are essential in Dickens's development as a psychological moralist.    In this connection, Hazen examines Sissy and the Gradgrinds,  showing  that  Louisa's  paralysis  illustrates  Mill's criticism of Bentham as a philosopher of feeling.

459.    Hearn, Arthur S.    "Dickens Links with the Town of Reading." **Dickensian**, 19 (1923), 36–37.

Cites Charles Montague (635) for the identification of Sleary as Jack Clarke, a circus proprietor who was, like Sleary, on the asthmatic side.

460.    Heck, Edwin J.    "**Hard Times**: The Handwriting on the Factory Wall."  **EJ**, 61 (1972), 23–27.

Argues that **Hard Times** is relevant to us as it stands at the start of our world; summarizes the novel in its darkest terms ("a terrifying portrayal of institutions wielding dreadful power over individuals, of confusion and alienation ..."), so that the escape of some characters appears "an almost arbitrary act of will" on Dickens's part.

461.   Henderson, James P. "Charles Dickens's **Hard Times** and the Industrial Revolution." **Cresset**, 43 (1980), 13-17.

**Hard Times** is the occasion here for a review of the conditions of labor in the North of England at mid-century.

462.   Henkle, Roger B. **Comedy and Culture: England 1820-1900**. Princeton and Guildford: Princeton Univ. Press, 1080, pp. 155-56.

Studies the change in Victorian comedy towards a comedy of internalization, which takes place nowhere more strikingly than in the novels of Dickens. Henkle finds Sleary an "unpleasant" spokesman for comic flexibility and **Hard Times** ironic, or at least qualified, in its endorsement of comedy as a sustaining mode of dealing with experience because the circus is, after all, an illusion for chidren.

463.   Hibbert, Christopher. **The Making of Charles Dickens** London: Longmans, Green; New York: Harper & Row, 1967, passim.

Remarks the atmosphere of a Gothic fairy-tale in **Hard Times**, compares the Blimber and M'Choakumchild regimens, and notes the absence of the Cockney in Sissy's speech. Hibbert refers to Dickens's exhaustion upon completing the novel and quotes Shaw's praise of it (738).

464.   Hill, Nancy K. **A Reformer's Art: Dickens' Picturesque and Grotesque Imagery**. Athens: Ohio Univ. Press, 1981, pp. 110-23 and passim.

Argues that Dickens was concerned to effect change and to do so by altering our visual perceptions. In **Hard Times** the main concern is not the satire of particular institutions but "moral reform" of education and religion, Hill asserts. Hence the message remains as pertinent today as it was for Dickens's time. Hill identifies the unused churches of Coketown with the Commissioner's Churches built in the early nineteenth century to woo the masses back to the Established Church. Reviews:

Deirdre David, **VS**, 26 (1983), 93–96; M. Reynolds, **Dickensian**, 78 (1982), 170–72.

465.     ———. "Visual Art in the Imagery of Charles Dickens." **DAI**, 33 (1972), 2936A (Northwestern Univ., 1972). 236 pp.

See Hill, above (464).

466.     Hill, Thomas W. "Notes on **Hard Times**." **Dickensian**, 48 (1952), 134–41, 177–85.

A useful, mainly exegetical set of notes with chapter-by-chapter glosses.  Hill suggests Forster's low opinion of the novel as a possible cause of its neglect.

467.     Hirsch, David M. "**Hard Times** and F.R. Leavis." **Criticism**, 6 (1964), 1–16.

A violent rebuttal to Leavis's praise of the novel (553).  This essay and Holloway's (471) have become the major replies to Leavis.  Hirsch offers some stringent criticism of Leavis's rhetorical methods, along with a strong denunciation of the novel. Dickens's symbols represent rather than embody or encompass (in the manner of Jaspers); they are superficial and transparent. His characters are flat, and to use them to project a serious theme is to invite disaster.  Nor are they consistent: witness, Hirsch argues, the sudden flowering of rhetorical power in Sissy when this hitherto simple girl comes to expell Harthouse from Coketown.  To Gradgrind's fact-grubbing the novel offers, according to Hirsch, only "orgies of tears."  It is unfair to Dickens, he concludes, to make this dull and unsuccessful novel prominent, as Leavis has done.

*        Hirschfield, Claire.

See below (894).

468.     Hobsbaum, Philip A.  **A Reader's Guide to Charles Dickens**. London: Thames & Hudson, 1972, pp. 173–87.

Postulates that where Dickens fails it will be where a strand of a novel fails to work towards the total structure or theme. In **Hard Times** this failure comes in Stephen, whose martyrdom is a personal rather than social matter. Bounderby, on the other hand, Hobsbaum sees as at once a psychological portrait and capitalism personified. On the matter of the trade unions, Dickens "deliberately falsified"; Hobsbaum notes the similarity of Slackbridge's rhetoric to Chadband's. Hobsbaum believes that the circus fails as the pole to Coketown, never meeting its described meaning with adequate detail. Nonetheless, he feels, if the answers this novel offers are invalid, its questions are still with us, and the novel, for all its flaws, is a classic. Review: James Kincaid, **Dickensian**, 70 (1974), 57–59.

469.  Hodge, Jan Douglas.  "The Gospel Influence on Dickens's Art." **DAI**, 38 (1977), 805A–06A (Univ. of New Mexico, 1976). 475 pp.

Argues that the importance of the New Testament for Dickens has been overlooked and examines the novels for the use of the gospels as a basis for incident and technique. Hodge points out that in **Hard Times** Sissy is the exemplar of **caritas**, love and goodness, which prove stronger than the reality of the "hard facts."

470.  Holdsworth, William S. **Charles Dickens as a Legal Historian**. New Haven: Yale Univ. Press, 1928, p. 7. Rpt New York: Haskell, 1972.

Offers the anomalies of the divorce law as treated in **Hard Times** as one example of Dickens's emphasis on the human agents who administer a law rather than on the structure and organization of the laws.

471.  Holloway, John. "**Hard Times**: A History and a Criticism." In **Dickens and the Twentieth Century**. Ed. John Gross and Gabriel Pearson. London: Routledge & Kegan Paul, 1962, pp. 159–74.

An important counter-statement to Leavis's discussion of the novel (553). Holloway seeks "to trace the exact contour of significance which ran for Dickens himself ... through the material." He looks at J.M. McCulloch for "the world of naive but encyclopaedic fact against which Dickens was reacting" and at Charles Knight's **Store of Knowledge** (compare Boulton [211]). He argues that Dickens's satire was against the forces of enlightenment, "written from the standpoint of the mid-Victorian

middle-class Philistine," especially in regard to the Department
of Practical Art (compare Fielding [376]). Dickens's enthusiasm
for industrialism is the root of his falsification in regard to
Slackbridge. The Sleary troupe are "plain entertainers." The
only creed Dickens has to offer is that of "All work and no play
makes Jack a dull boy." Holloway notes the forced rhetoric and
banal imagery of Louisa's first confrontation with her father. In
praise of the novel he offers Harthouse's appearances and Mrs.
Sparsit's pursuit of Louisa (and her staircase), and suggests
that Dickens is at his best when he is not intent upon his moral
fable. Compare Brantlinger (216), Collins (289), Fielding (379),
and Gilmour (415).

472.    Hornback, Bert G. "**Hard Times** and **A Tale of Two Cities**: Two
        Late Fables." "**Noah's Arkitecture**": A Study of Dickens's My-
        thology. Athens: Ohio Univ. Press, 1972, pp. 111-24.

        The general thesis of this book is the inseparability of the
realistic and mythic elements in Dickens's novels. **Hard Times**
is a moral fable, Hornback states, a sermon with a central exemplum. The text of the sermon is, predictably, the "mad
world." Hornback sees in the description of Sleary evidence of
Dickens's doubt that the power of art could do or change anything. Love is the primary agent of salvation for Dickens,
Hornback concludes, and "art and the works of imagination ...
[are] intimately connected with the life of love." Reviews: Avrom Fleishman, **MLQ**, 34 (1973), 191-99; Joseph Gold, **DSN**, 4
(1973), 58-60; R.D. McMaster, **NCF**, 28 (1973), 107-11.

473.    -------. **The Hero of My Life**. Athens and London: Ohio Univ.
        Press, 1981, passim.

        Calls **Hard Times** a sermon characterized by heavy and
aggressive rhetoric.

474.    Horne, Lewis B. "Hope and Memory in **Hard Times**." **Dicken-
        sian**, 75 (1979), 167-74.

        Sees the relationships of the characters to time in parallel
to their relationships to fancy and fact. Sissy has a future,
Horne states; Louisa and Stephen are trapped in time, while
Bounderby and Harthouse misuse time.

475.   House, Humphrey. **The Dickens World**. London and New York:
       Oxford Univ. Press, 1941 (corrected 1942); 2nd edn., 1960, pp.
       203-11 and passim. The section on **Hard Times** rpt. in **Dick-
       ens: Modern Judgements**. Ed. A.E. Dyson. London: Macmillan,
       1968. Also in Gray (429).

       Finds the satire on Gradgrind objectionable because Grad-
       grind is the only Dickens character who is an "intellectual" of
       sorts, and unsuccessful because Dickens did not understand
       enough of any philosophy to mount a successful attack. Black-
       pool fails because Dickens refused to accept the "proper tragic
       solution." House brings more light to the issue of industrialism
       and trade unions than many discussions since (on either side),
       showing how Dickens shared contemporary fears and misconc-
       ceptions regarding trade unions. Yet he argues that Dickens's
       mixture of fascination with the powers of industrialism and re-
       vulsion at its impoverishment of human life creates the mood
       that make the book both unpopular and valuable. Compare
       Brantlinger (215).

476.   Houtchens, Lawrence Huston. "Carlyle's Influence on Dickens."
       Ph.D. Dissertation. Cornell Univ., 1929. 165 pp.

       Uses **Hard Times**, among other novels, as quarry for a less
       than trenchant analysis and comparison of Dickens's and Car-
       lyle's theories of education. In a chapter on style, Houtchens
       quotes various passages from **Hard Times** to illustrate similari-
       ties between stylistic characteristics of the two writers.

477.   Howard, David. "George Meredith: 'Delicate' and 'Epical' Fic-
       tion." In **Literature and Politics in the Nineteenth Century**.
       Ed. John Lucas. London: Methuen, 1971, pp. 131-72.

       Refers in passing to **Hard Times** as one among a number
       of examples of novels in which "the patronized dependent be-
       comes the saviour of the family" (in this instance, Sissy).

478.   Howells, William Dean. "Dickens's Later Heroines." **Harper's
       Bazaar**, 33 (1900), 1415-21. Rpt. in **Heroines of Fiction**. New
       York and London: Harper, 1901. Vol. 1, 148-60.

       Argues that Louisa is much more real than Lady Dedlock
       but that Dickens goes against probability in not having her el-
       ope with Harthouse. Howells finds the novel to have "a glut of

material" but nonetheless to have also "more affinity with the
actual world" than most of Dickens's novels. It displays Dickens's general heavy-handedness.

479.   Hudson, Samuel, Jr. "Victims or Parasites? Attitudes About the
       Poor in the Early Victorian Novel." **DAI**, 33 (1972), 2329A-30A
       (Wayne State Univ., 1972). 613 pp.

       Examines the presentation of the poor in seventeen novels
       published between 1832 and 1858, including **Hard Times**, find-
       ing in general that the approach was simplistic but the service
       to society "of the first order." In addition, Hudson remarks,
       Dickens and Mrs. Gaskell have literary value.

*      Hughes, Helen S.

       See Robert M. Lovett and Helen S. Hughes (581).

480.   Hughes, James Laughlin. **Dickens as an Educator**. New York:
       Appleton, 1901, passim. Rpt. New York: Haskell, 1971.

       The purpose of this book is to prove Dickens "the great
       apostle of the 'new education' ... and to bring into connected
       form ... the educational principles of one of the world's greatest
       educators." **Hard Times** is mentioned frequently, under heads
       such as "The overthrow of coercion," "Individuality," and "Free
       Childhood"; at points the novel is quoted amply.

481.   Hughes, William Richard. **A Week's Tramp in Dickens-Land**.
       London: Chapman & Hall, 1891, pp. 37, 414, 416.

       Does not deal with Coketown. **Hard Times** is mentioned as
       having been written at Tavistock House and as Dickens's first
       manuscript in blue ink.

482.   Hulin, Jean-Paul. "'Rus in Urbe': A Key to Victorian Anti-Urban-
       ism?" In **Victorian Writers and the City**. Ed. Jean Paul Hulin
       and Pierre Coustillas. Lille: Univ. de Lille III, 1979, pp. 11-40.

       Examines the theme of anti-urbanism in Victorian literature
       as it arises from the use of Nature as a conservative myth.
       The theme of **rus in urbe** consists in exploiting those natural

elements that have persisted in the city. Hulin illustrates this theme at length from Dickens and hypothesizes its gradual degradation in the later work. "More than anything," he concludes, "Coketown is the very symbol of the **urbs sine rure**, of the completely artificial city."

483. Humphrey, Harold E. "The Background of **Hard Times**." DA, 19 (1958), 318 (Columbia Univ., 1958). 474 pp.

Surveys the background on the issue of schools and education. On economics, Humphrey argues that Dickens was not unorthodox in any important way. The chief characters are seen as expressions of Dickens's moral intention in the novel. Humphrey gathers some representative criticism of the book and offers connections between its failure to accomplish Dickens's intention and its neglect.

484. Hunt, Peter R. "Chesterton and Dickens." Ph.D. Dissertation. Dalhousie Univ., 1980. 502 pp.

Summarizes Chesterton's comments on **Hard Times** (265) and points out that they are unique in their "neglect of Dickens' artistry." Hunt believes that Chesterton was carried away by the political issues: he also failed to comment in his **Hard Times** essay on the theme of education, on Sleary's, and on the book's comic satire.

485. Hurley, Edward. "A Missing Childhood in **Hard Times**." VN, 42 (1972), 11-16.

Sets out to uncover Stephen's childhood, through an analysis of his dream, interpreting it as a marriage to Rachael. Since Rachael is equivalent to his mother, the dream is a dream of incest, the ultimate sin, deserving the punishment meted out. Hurley argues that Stephen then "objectifies his fantasies and fears" by contriving his exile and death. With this reading, the novel is unified on the theme of "childhood's confrontation with adult reality," in which the sole victor is Sissy.

486. Ibe, Marcellinus Ukanwata. "The Educational Philosophy of Dickens." DAI, 37 (1977), 4207A (Univ. of Cincinnati, Ed.D., 1976). 250 pp.

Examines the educational ideas of Dickens in his novels and other writings. Ibe points out that **Hard Times** shows his disagreement with the utilitarians and his emphasis on imagination and the feelings.

487. Inglis, Fred. **An Essential Discipline: An Introduction to Literary Criticism.** London: Methuen, 1968, pp. 28–29.

Quotes the "Facts" passage to show Mr. Gradgrind as one who exhibits the "ruthless demand for functional information" characteristic of scientific rationalism.

488. Jackson, Holbrook. **Great English Novelists.** London: Grant Richards, 1908, p. 239. Rpt. Freeport, N.Y.: Books for Libraries, 1967.

A chronological account, describing **Hard Times** as Dickens's study of human conditions "under the heel" of modern capitalism.

489. Jackson, Thomas A. **Charles Dickens: The Progress of a Radical.** London: Lawrence & Wishart, 1937; New York: International Publishers, 1938, passim. Rpt. New York: Haskell, 1971.

Finds the novel characteristic of this period in Dickens's writing. Jackson offers several excerpts to demonstrate the closeness of Dickens's thinking to that of Marx and Engels. He notes the absence of "vivacious sparkle" and the utter mistake of the trade union, for which he blames the Tory press, the Whig politicians, and Carlyle. This novel stands to **Bleak House** and **Little Dorrit** as a furious raid to two systematic campaigns, Jackson states. Stephen's and Louisa's marriages illustrate Dickens's radical attitude towards the bourgeois family.

* Jain, S.P.

See R.P. Tewari and S.P. Jain (799).

490. James, Henry. **A Small Boy and Others.** New York: Scribner's, 1913; rpt. 1941, p. 119.

Mentions the "years in which the general contagious consciousness, and our own household response not least,
breathed heavily through Hard Times, Bleak House and Little
Dorrit."

491.  Jameson, Fredric. **The Prison-House of Language**. Princeton,
      N.J.: Princeton Univ. Press, 1972, pp. 167-68.

      **Hard Times** is used to illustrate A.J. Greimas's "semantic
      rectangle." The starting point is Fact, its negation is Imagina-
      tion, and the negation of negation, the denial of imagination,
      becomes theft, near adultory, and Ritzer. "Thus the absent
      fourth term comes to the center of the stage," Jameson states;
      "the plot is nothing but an attempt to give it imaginative being,
      to work through faulty solutions and unacceptable hypotheses
      until an adequate embodiment has been realized in terms of
      the narrative material .... With this discovery (Mr. Gradgrind's
      education, Louisa's belated experience of family love), the se-
      mantic rectangle is completed and the novel comes to an end."
      See also Armstrong (170).

*     Jan, Isabelle.

      See Jean Gattegno, Isabelle Jan, and Anny Sadrin (406).

492.  Janowitz, Katherine E.  "Inviolable Goodness: The Idyllic Mode
      in the Novels of Charles Dickens." **DAI**, 39 (1979), 6776A (Co-
      lumbia Univ., 1976). 167 pp.

      Traces images and themes of the idyllic in the novels after
      **Barnaby Rudge**. In the later works, according to Janowitz, the
      idyllic is seen increasingly in the aspect of human vision and
      creation rather than of natural order.

493.  Jansonius, Herman. "**Hard Times.**" **Some Aspects of Business
      Life in Early Victorian Fiction**. Ph.D. Dissertation. Univ. of
      Amsterdam, [1926?]. Purmerend: J. Muusses, 1926, pp. 48-53.

      Finds **Hard Times** a very qualified success. According to
      Jansonius, Gradgrind shows no advance over Filer, though
      eleven years had elapsed. He concludes that Dickens seems
      not to have studied political economy closely and not to have
      noted the altered conditions of the 1850's. Jansonius suggests

that his spending the evening in Preston at the theater rather than in the streets is an index of the failure of Dickens's visit; he remained ignorant of the North country. The use of caricature for Gradgrind and Bounderby has literary merit, Jansonius states, but tells us little about the conditions of trade and industry.

494.    Jarmuth, Sylvia L. "Dickens' Use of Women in His Novels." **DA**, 29 (1966), 568A-69A  (New York Univ., 1966). 234 pp.

   See Jarmuth, below (495).

495.    --------. **Dickens' Use of Women in His Novels**. New York: Excelsior, 1967, passim.

   Studies the use of women in Dickens's novels in clusters of novels that show his maturing artistic creativity. In **Bleak House**, **Hard Times**, and **Little Dorrit**, Jarmuth finds a new level of poetic symbolism; the women are vivid human beings and also symbolic representations of the evils of society.

496.    Jeans, Samuel. **Charles Dickens**. London: A. & C. Black, 1929, pp. 53-54.

   Cites Ruskin (150) but dissents from his opinion of **Hard Times**'s greatness. Jeans sees the novel as much more limited in appeal than most other Dickens novels, though Bounderby is a true character.

497.    Jerrold, Walter. "Bibliographical Note." In the Temple edition, 1899 (30), pp. xi-xiv.

   Recounts the history of the several titles for the novel; describes Dickens's correspondence with Charles Knight, his difficulty in writing, and his trip to Preston; quotes Ruskin (150).

498.    Johnson, Alan P. "**Hard Times**: 'Performance' or 'Poetry.'" **DS**, 5 (1969), 62-80.

   Traces a "complex and surprisingly consistent, coherent pattern" in the fire imagery as an index of Dickens's use of imagery in the novel. Johnson argues that Dickens often uses diverse images for a single situation, often gives various connotations to a single image, and may first elaborate, then neglect an image.

499. Johnson, E.D.H. **Charles Dickens: An Introduction to His Novels**. New York: Random House, 1969, passim.

This book is intended for the general reader who wishes background material. **Hard Times** is mentioned frequently, particularly in relation to social issues, and is grouped as a matter of course with the dark, later novels. Johnson speaks of Dickens's "persistent failure to do justice to the programs for reform supported by the Philosophical Radicals" and instances his satire on Bentham and the blue books.

500. Johnson, Edgar. **Charles Dickens: His Tragedy and Triumph**. 2 vols. New York: Simon & Schuster, 1952, II, 801–19 and passim. Abridged version: New York: Viking; London: Allen Lone, 1977; rpt. Harmondsworth and New York: Penguin, 1978. The criticism of **Hard Times** rpt. in Gray (429).

Sees **Hard Times** as the culmination of an orderly development of social criticism from **Dombey and Son** on, a "morality drama, stark, formalized, allegorical," in which the speech of the characters is not realistic but true to their inward nature. The only failures, according to Johnson, are Stephen and Slackbridge. The circus represents "the flowering of the humane imagination and the ennoblement of the heart" that are set against the cruel industrial scene. Reviews: John Butt, **NCF**, 8 (1953), 151–53; W.J. Carlton, **Dickensian**, 49 (1953), 53–58; Philip Collins, **TLS**, 21 April 1978, p. 446; Angus Easson, **Dickensian**, 75 (1979), 37–38; James Olney, **DSN**, 10 (1979), 23–27; Gordon N. Ray, **VQR**, 29 (1953), 297–302; Anthony West, **New Yorker**, 28 (1953), 81–88 (see [836]).

501. -------. "Dickens and Shaw: Critics of Society." **Virginia Quarterly Review**, 33 (1957), 66–79.

A description of Shaw's extensive knowledge of Dickens and some tracing of parallels in their writing, includes a number of references to **Hard Times**. Johnson suggests that the couching of Cashel Byron's music criticism in the jargon of prizefighting is anticipated in the commissioner of education in **Hard Times**.

502.    ———. "Dickens and the Spirit of the Age." **Bibliotheca Bucnellensis, 4** (1966), 1-13. Rpt. in **Victorian Essays: A Symposium**. Ed. Warren D. Anderson and Thomas Clareson. Kent, Ohio: Kent State Univ. Press, 1967.

Sees Coketown as Dickens's "'heaviest blow'" against the very essence of industrialism, the laissez-faire philosophy that offers freedom only to rapacity. Johnson remarks upon the contemporaries of Dickens whom one would have expected to sympathize, but who more often recoiled.

503.    ———. "Dickens's Anti-Chauvinism." In **Nineteenth Century Literary Perspectives (Essays in Honor of Lionel Stevenson)**. Ed. Clyde de L. Ryals. Durham, N.C.: Duke Univ. Press, 1974, pp. 201-210.

Includes **Hard Times** in the vision of urban, industrial evil that Johnson traces through Dickens's career, a campaign that he sees as beginning with **Oliver Twist**.

*       ———.

See Dickens Fellowship (340).

*       ———.

See below (875).

504.    Johnson, Wendell Stacy. "Introduction." **Charles Dickens: New Perspectives**. Ed. Wendell Stacy Johnson. Englewood Cliffs, N.J.: Prentice Hall, 1982, pp. 1-5.

Remarks that **Hard Times** "shows the range of possible relationships between parent and child and what each implies." In this novel the true social relations are family relations, and false family relations are social impositions, Johnson states.

*       Johnson, William C.

See below (898).

505.    Jones, Elizabeth Falk.   "Ends and Means of Fictions: **Hard Times**
        and **Mansfield Park**."   **DAI**, 39 (1979), 6776A–77A   (State Univ.
        of New York, Stony Brook, 1979).   216 pp.

        Following the critical approaches of R.S. Crane, Elder Olson,
        and Sheldon Sacks, argues the importance of recognizing the
        purpose of a work and distinguishing thus between mimetic
        and didactic works.   **Hard Times** is a true example of the latter,
        but **Mansfield Park** is not, Jones concludes.   **Hard Times** is an
        apologue, a fiction in service of a thesis.

506.    Jones, Ernest.   **The Life and Works of Sigmund Freud.**   Ed.
        Steven Marcus and Lionel Trilling.   New York: Basic, 1961, p.
        116.

        Cites Freud on **Hard Times** as "a cruel book that left him
        as if he had been rubbed all over by a harsh brush."

507.    Jones, Florence.   "Dickens and Langland in Adjudication upon
        Meed."   **VN**, 33 (1968), 53–56.

        Sees Langland and Dickens as collectivists concerned with
        the oppression of the poor.   Jones reads **Hard Times** as a
        morality structure: Mrs. Sparsit is Envy, Tom is Sloth, Harthouse
        is Lechery, Bounderby is Avarice and Pride.   She describes Ste-
        phen as sharing much with Piers Plowman and, from this base
        in **Hard Times**, rehearses **Piers Plowman** as Dickens might
        have reconstructed it.

508.    Joubert, Andre.   "Charles Dickens, sa vie et ses oeuvres."   **Le
        Correspondent**, 10 February 1872, pp. 520–38.   Also pub. sepa-
        rately, Paris: Charles Douniol, 1872.   23 pp.

        Prefers **Hard Times** to **Little Dorrit**, because it treats the
        questions of the day and its relevance continues.   Joubert
        praises Stephen, especially in contrast to the declamations of
        French socialist novelists.

509.    Joyce, Patrick.   **Work, Society and Politics: The Culture of the
        Factory in Later Victorian England.**   Brighton: Harvester, 1980,
        p. 148.

A historical study of the factory areas, particularly in the North. Joyce argues that at the time of **Hard Times**, Mrs. Gaskell's picture of industrial relations, especially in Thornton (**North and South**) was truer to actual conditions than Dickens's. Dickens conveyed "the older state of feeling" at a time of significant change.

510.    Jump, J.D. "Dickens and His Readers." **BJRL**, 54 (1972), 384–97.

Examines Dickens's relations with his public. Jump instances **Hard Times** for its "deservedly famous" opening and its use of repetition humorously elaborated (as in the description of Bounderby).

511.    Kaplan, Fred. **Dickens and Mesmerism: The Hidden Springs of Fiction**. Princeton, N.J.: Princeton Univ. Press, 1975, passim.

Several references to **Hard Times** include mention of Mr. Gradgrind's square forefinger as a product of Dickens's experience with the use of hands in mesmeric experiments; the mesmeric imagery of Stephen watching his wife as if under a spell; Louisa's illness as an instance of illness revealing the powers of mind. Kaplan ranges the characters of the novel along a spectrum of their ability to escape the egomania that blinds us to the future, from Bounderby at one extreme to Sissy at the other. Sissy's besting of Harthouse is an achievement of dominance through "plain faith," Kaplan states, while he sees the God of Love closest at the moment of Stephen's vision of the star. Reviews: Edwin Eigner, **MLR**, 73 (1978), 416–17; T.M. Parssinen, **VPN**, 11 (1978), 31–32.

512.    Karl, Frederick R. "Charles Dickens: The Victorian Quixote." **An Age of Fiction: The Nineteenth Century British Novel**. New York: Farrar, Straus & Giroux, 1964. Also published as **A Reader's Guide to the Nineteenth Century British Novel**. New York: Farrar, Straus, & Giroux, 1966, pp. 105–76.

Offers the usual background on Carlyle and Mill and analysis of the novel as homiletic. The social indictment is powerful even though the art may suffer from Dickens's exaggeration, Karl points out. The novel is tract or sermon-like, but the starting-point of Dickens's great works. Sissy pitted against industrialism and utilitarianism Karl sees as one of Dickens's several workings of the theme of innocence vs. experience.

513. Kauffman, Linda. "The Letter and the Spirit in **Hard Times** and **The Sound and the Fury**." **Mississippi Quarterly**, 34 (1981), 299-33.

Argues that both novels deal centrally with "the same fundamental polarities between head and heart, letter and spirit." The argument is based on comparisons of characters: Mrs. Compson with Mrs. Sparsit and Mrs. Gradgrind (Kauffman notes how in both novels spying is the main connection between people when emotions are suspect); the Compson with the Gradgrind children (Louisa and Caddy with with Jason, Quentin, and Tom); Mr. Compson with Mr. Gradgrind; Bounderby with Jason Compson; Cissy with Dilsey (as positive values); the circus troupers with the Negro parishioners.

514. --------. "Psychic Displacement and Adaptation in the Novels of Dickens and Faulkner." **DAI**, 39 (1978), 3573-74A (Univ. of California, Santa Barbara, 1978). 262 pp.

Examines the "similar mental, moral, and artistic temperaments" of Dickens and Faulkner, particularly as the similarities are manifest in their characters. See above (513).

515. Keating, P.J. **The Working Classes in Victorian Fiction**. London: Routledge & Kegan Paul, 1971, passim.

Although the main concern of this book is the presentation of the working classes in fiction after 1880, it offers valuable contextualization for **Hard Times**. Keating points to the virtual non-existence of working-class fiction in Victorian England in which the novelist is not committed to a class viewpoint. This didacticism hinders the author's powers of documentary. The industrial novels were written to address a social problem, and the characters were treated with a moral intensity designed to heighten the tragedy of their lives. Keating compares Rachael and Mrs. Plornish to demonstrate this solemnity. He also argues that the novelists could see the workers only as class representatives, and that their association with the powerful machines of industry rendered them all the more threatening. The novelists drew attention to the workers' suffering, but feared their power and failed entirely to see that they might have had their own ideas as to the uses of that power. Dickens's treatment of the unions in **Hard Times** is typical, not by any means singularly benighted, Keating points out; even Mrs. Gaskell attacks or undermines union efforts. Compare Brantlinger (217) and Pollard (678). Reviews: Michael Cooke, **YR**, 61 (1972), 433-41; Louis James, **DSN**, 4 (1973), 79-81; Joan Kirkby, **Southern R**, 5 (1972), 255-59; Jacob Korg, **NCF**, 27 (1972), 219; Sheila M. Smith, **RES**, 23 (1972), 374-76; Martha Vicinus, **VS**, 15 (1972), 504-06.

516.    Keim, Albert, and Louis Lumet. **Dickens**. Paris: Lafitte, 1913, pp. 105-07.

Finds Bounderby and Gradgrind impressive creations but showing less of Dickens's joviality, picturesqueness, and hilarity. Dickens is more serious in this novel and more given to judgment, Keim and Lumet state, noting how effect and detail are concentrated on the message and the consequent gravity of the novel.

\*       Kellogg, Robert.

See Robert Scholes and Robert Kellogg (728).

517.    Kelly, Thomas. "Character in Dickens' Late Novels." **MLQ**, 30 (1969), 386-401.

Defends Dickens's characterization in the late novels as wholly adequate, both in Jamesian terms and in opposition to them. **Hard Times** is offered in several instances: Stephen's dream (weak as allegory but incisive as a more abstract analysis of his situation); Bounderby's grand fiction, seen in relation to Mrs. Gamp's and Mr. Dorrit's; the use of fire imagery as symbol to develop Louisa's inner life; the use of disguise as an ironic device that reveals more than it conceals.

518.    Kelty, Jean McClure. "The Humanitarian Implications of Dickens' Creative Vision." **DAI**, 31 (1969), 2882A (Case Western Reserve Univ., 1969). 125 pp.

Examines Dickens's animal characters as they intensify and define the human characters around them and as Dickens uses them as symbols.

519.    Kennard, Jean E. "Emerson and Dickens: A Note on Conrad's **Victory**." **Conradiana**, 6 (1974), 215-19.

Suggests an allusion to **Hard Times** in Heyst's nickname "Hard Facts."

520.  Kennedy, Alan. "Agents and Patients in Dickens." **Meaning and Signs in Fiction**. London: Macmillan; New York: St. Martin's, 1979, pp. 70-104.

Points out that the reference to the blue books as the "stutterings" of Parliament is a metaphor that reminds us that social institutions are language. If all institutions are tainted by social corruption, then amelioration is not possible through them, Kennedy affirms; what is needed is a renewed language, but language too is social. It is this painful logic that makes Dickens's social criticism in **Hard Times** perplexing to many of his critics, Kennedy concludes. Review: David Lodge, **NS**, 98 (1979), 207.

521.  Kennedy, G.W. "Dickens's Endings." **SNNTS**, 6 (1974), 280-87.

**Hard Times** is offered as one of Dickens's experiments in finding ways to tell the conclusions to his characters' lives without the straightforward authorial jump into futurity. Kennedy concludes that Dickens's methods show progress in variety and subtlety.

522.  Kennethe, L.A. [Walter Dexter]. "Memorials of Friendship." **Dickensian**, 37 (1941), 89-98.

In reference to Dickens's dedications, notes the "severe and formal tone" of the dedication to Carlyle, "befitting the subject of the novel."

523.  Kent, William R.G. **Dickens and Religion**. London: Watts, 1930, passim.

A humorous attack on claims for Dickens as "deeply religious or or profoundly philosophical," mentions **Hard Times** briefly at several points in the argument.

524.  -------. "'Hard Times' from a Socialist Standpoint." **Dickensian**, 24 (1928), 293-96. Rpt. in **Der englische Soziale Roman im 19.Jahrhundert**. Ed. Konrad Gross. Wege der Forschung, 466. Darmstadt: Wissenschaftliche Buchgesellschaft, 1977.

Disagrees with Pugh's (688) declaration that Dickens was a socialist. Kent argues that one is a socialist or not on the basis of remedies prescribed, not diagnosis, and that Dickens "was singularly inept in his prescriptions." He suggests that the muddle in Stephen's head came from Dickens's, calls Stephen a male Mrs. Gummidge, and argues that fancy will not fill the workers' stomachs. Dickens, like Ruskin, was afraid to disturb the social structure, and "like most allegorists ... took pleasure in damning sins he had no mind to," Kent concludes. He ends with praise of Dickens for having "justified the title of his book."

See also "Letter to the Editor," **Dickensian**, 25 (1929), 76, for further remarks on Bounderby.

525.   Kettle, Arnold. "The Early Victorian Social-Problem Novel." In **From Dickens to Hardy**. Ed. Boris Ford. Vol. 6 of **The Pelican Guide to English Literature**. Harmondsworth: Penguin, 1958, pp. 169-87.

**Hard Times** is not a social problem novel in the way that **Sybil** or **North and South** are, Kettle states, but it shows preeminently how utilitarianism had become a primary target of the socially conscious novelists. The novel is outstanding in the "power and consistency of Dickens's vision."

526.   -------. **An Introduction to the English Novel**. 2 vols. London: Hutchinson Univ. Library, 1951, II, 11, 48. Rpt. New York: Harper & Row, 1960.

Includes **Hard Times** among various works in the tradition of the English moral fable. These works tend to be unduly rigid in pattern, more rigid than the pattern of life, Kettle believes. There is no further discussion of **Hard Times**.

527.   Killham, John. "The Use of 'Concreteness' as an Evaluative Term in F.R. Leavis's 'The Great Tradition.'" **British Journal of Aesthetics**, 5 (1965), 14-24.

**Hard Times** is referred to a number of times as Killham examines this "touchstone" term of Leavis's to conclude that it can register the sense of excellent representation but cannot refer to a particular feature of a work.

528.  Kincaid, James R.  "Laughter and Pathos: **The Old Curiosity Shop**." In **Dickens the Craftsman**. Ed. Robert B. Partlow, Jr. Carbondale and Edwardsville: Southern Illinois Univ. Press; London: Feffer, 1970, pp. 65-94.

Sees Mrs. Jarley's "inventive genius" as a foreshadowing of Sleary's circus.

529.  Kingsmill, Hugh  [Hugh Kingsmill Lunn].  **The Sentimental Journey, A Life of Charles Dickens**.  New York: William Morrow, 1935, passim.  Rpt. Folcroft, Pa.: Folcroft, 1978.

Attacks Dickens generally for espousing only causes that already had the weight of popular opinion behind them.  **Hard Times** is one example, Kingsmill indicates; its reforming capacity has been overestimated by Shaw and Chesterton, as witnessed by its effect upon the circulation of **Household Words**. Kingsmill points out inconsistencies between Dickens's attitudes in and outside the novel.  He argues that in **Hard Times** Dickens imitates Carlyle, softening the portrait of the workers, caricaturing the union men and the manufacturers.  Kingsmill suggests that Georgina Hogarth was the model for Rachael and that Dickens's own guilt is charged into the character of the vulgar, grasping Bounderby, thus making the novel a revelation of Dickens's own unhappiness, particularly in his marriage.

530.  Kitton, Frederic G.  **Charles Dickens: His Life, Writings and Personality**.  London and Edinburgh: T.C. & E.C. Jack, 1902, pp. 228-31.

Notes the several titles considered for the novel and Forster's and Dickens's selection of one in common.  Kitton identifies Coketown as Manchester.  He also cites Dickens's letters, Mrs. Oliphant (122), and Ruskin (150), and refers to the novel as Dickens's "'socialistic romance' (as it has been termed)."

531.  -------.  **The Dickens Country**.  London: A. & C. Black, 1905, pp. 71, 132-36.  Rpt. Folcroft. Pa.: Folcroft, 1979.

States that Manchester is the model for Coketown; at Preston Dickens found only "'a nasty place.'"  Kitton quotes at length the description of Coketown.

532.    ───────.  **The Minor Writings of Charles Dickens**: **A Bibliography and Sketch**. London: Elliot Stock, 1900, pp. 28–33. Rpt.
New York: Haskell, 1970; New York: AMS, 1975.

In the companion volume, **The Novels of Charles Dickens**
(1897), **Hard Times** was omitted. Here it is included following
**Sketches by Boz**, **American Notes**, and **Pictures from Italy**
and before the Christmas books. The commentary is the same
as in **Charles Dickens**, above (530).

533.    ───────.  "Notes." In the London edition, 1901–02 (32), pp. ix–x.

Reproduces the information from Forster (133) concerning
the circumstances of publication, the titles, and the crush of
space; quotes Taine (153); offers a very brief look at the plot
and characters; and mentions the 1867 drama "Under the Earth"
(59).

534.    Klingopulos, G.D.  "Notes on the Victorian Scene." In **From
Dickens to Hardy**. Ed. Boris Ford. Vol 6 of **The Pelican Guide
to English Literature**. Harmondsworth: Penguin, 1958, pp.
11–56.

A section of this essay deals with "Utilitarianism: the
meaning of Plugson, Gradgrind, Bounderby, and Bulstrode."
Klingopulos argues that by setting his opening in a school
Dickens makes it possible to go beyond the economics of utilitarianism to its psychological and educational ideas. We cannot simply dismiss Dickens as a bad economist, he states; "We
do not go to Dickens for a careful appraisal of the influence
and achievements of the utilitarians, but to make connexion
with the living spirit." On the trade unions, however, Klingopulos believes that Dickens made a mistake.

535.    Knight, Everett.  "The Case of Dickens." **A Theory of the Classical Novel**. London: Routledge & Kegan Paul, 1970, pp.
106–42.

Knight's book is a radical leftist reading of the novel from
the end of the picaresque novel to Kafka, and very full of its
radicalness. **Hard Times** figures in a series of brief references
as evidence, mainly, of Dickens's failure to deal with the problem of the poor and reality. Knight notes Orwell's remark on
Stephen as the only worker in Dickens and adds that of the fif-

teen to twenty books of criticism he has read, only Orwell's (650) is worthwhile. He believes that for Dickens reform means efficiency, but the evil Dickens sets out to attack in **Hard Times** cannot be cured by efficiency. Knight finds that the circus people are typical nineteenth-century nostalgia for a return to nature. He compares Dickens's failure to Faulkner's: Stephen is a worker "infected with middle-class morality"; Faulkner's Negro heroes are "white men with a few drops of Negro blood." Despite its smugness, Knight's work is stimulating. Its main thesis is to connect the bourgeois novel with the issue of identity, which is individual, and its aim seems to be to turn our perceptions to the group; somehow, such a change, Knight believes, will eliminate classism and racism. Reviews: Arnold Kettle, **RES**, 22 (1971), 520-22; B. Knapp, **LJ**, 95 (1970), 2479.

536.    Knoepflmacher, U.C. **George Eliot's Early Novels: The Limits of Realism**. Berkeley and Los Angeles: Univ. of California Press, 1968, p. 196.

        Compares Mr. Deane of **The Mill on the Floss** with Dickens's Gradgrind and Podsnap (**Our Mutual Friend**).

537.    Kogan, Bernard. "Narrative Technique in the Later Novels of Charles Dickens." Ph.D. Dissertation. Univ. of Chicago, 1953. viii, 367 pp.

        Examines the validity of dividing Dickens's technical development into pre-**Bleak House** and post-**Bleak House** periods. With **Hard Times**, Kogan reviews briefly the critical history of the novel, summarizes the plot to show the "real unity of action" and of place, and reviews the novel's objects of social criticism. He concludes that Dickens's "customary careful balance of humor, pathos, melodrama, and thought has been upset here, and not unwittingly"--in favor of thought. But the spareness he sees as a harbinger of style to come.

538.    Kotzin, Michael. "Dickens and the Fairy Tale." **DAI**, 30 (1968), 328A (Univ. of Minnesota, 1968). 210 pp.

        See Kotzin, below (539).

539.    -------. **Dickens and the Fairy Tale**. Bowling Green, Ohio: Bowling Green Univ. Press, 1972, passim.

Sets the circus and the allusions to fairy tale in **Hard Times** in the wider context of this theme in Dickens. Kotzin notes in particular "Little Children," an article by Sala that had appeared in November 1853. The circus and fairy tales are sources of joy; they battle for individual and national salvation, Kotzin points out. He remarks the fairy-tale use of animism in the description of Coketown and the themes of the Babes in the Wood and the slaughter of the innocents. Blackpool he sees as an overgrown child. Reviews: R.D. McMaster, **NCF**, 28 (1973), 107–11; Harry Stone, **Dickensian**, 69 (1973), 121–23.

540.    Kovacevic, Ivanka. **Fact into Fiction**. Leicester: Leicester Univ. Press; Belgrade: Faculty of Philology, Univ. of Belgrade, 1975, pp. 70, 92, 109–28.

Argues that Bounderby exposes the gospel of self-help through satirical portraiture and Dickens debunks the educational principles of the utilitarians, but that in the main both Dickens and Martineau fail to render their beliefs "in a logical manner" through the fictions they invent for this very purpose. Kovacevic shows failures of realism in Stephen and contradictions in Dickens's consideration of the political and economic issues. She complains of a lack of detail on the conditions of poverty and their effects. For example, she points out that Dickens does not consider the personal risk to himself and his family that Slackbridge runs. The root of this failure is Dickens's purpose: he "stooped to preaching the dogma of 'identical interests'" and so came to the same conclusions as Martineau. Because he "could not undertake" the logical "frontal attack on the social system," his emotions are stifled and his style is consequently "selfconscious," Kovacevic claims.

541.    –––––––. "Summary: The Proletarian Fiction of the Industrial Revolution." **Romanopisac i Cartizam**. Belgrade: Univ. of Belgrade, 1968, pp. 167–92.

Sees two themes, only, in **Hard Times**: criticism of the Manchester School and condemnation of the trade unions for their tyranny over the workers. In consequence, Dickens fails as a proletarian novelist, Kovacevic states; he relied on feeling instead of reason, thus displaying a satiric anger that is incompatible with the recommendation of "humility to the oppressed and compassion to the privileged." Kovacevic attributes the paucity of Dickens's writing on industrialism and the tension of **Hard Times** to Dickens's ambivalence: his feelings are divided between sympathy for the workers and fear lest they should rebel.

542.   Kreutz, Irving W. "Sly of Manner, Sharp of Tooth: A Study of Dickens's Villains." **NCF**, 21 (1968), 331–48.

In an aside, mentions Harthouse along with Steerforth and Wrayburn as a trio "who deserve a closer look." They are "charming, they are bored, and while they may not intend harm to others, they hardly intend to do good .... It is as if they really don't want to be cads, but can't figure out how not to be." Compare Moers (630).

543.   Kucich, John. **Excess and Restraint in the Novels of Charles Dickens.** Athens: Univ. of Georgia Press, 1981, passim.

Mentions **Hard Times** a number of times, but it is not one of the novels selected for primary study of how "Dickens tries to violate the world of common sense to stage liberating encounters with the freedom represented by death." These encounters, Kucich points out, "take place in a way that legitimates the expenditure [i.e., "the temporal experience of timeless release from discontinuity"] within a more conservative framework of values." Reviews: Larry Clipper, **Arnoldian**, 10 (1982), 76–79; Peter K. Garrett, **Novel**, 16 (1983), 181–84.

544.   Laird, John. "Philosophy in the Works of Dickens." **Philosophical Incursions into English Literature**. Cambridge: Cambridge Univ. Press, 1946, pp. 136–60.

Believes that the attacks on Bentham, including that in **Hard Times**, constitute one of only two instances of "academic moralism" in Dickens.

545.   Lamb, Cedric. "Love and Self-Interest in Dickens' Novels." **Paunch**, 33 (1968), 32–47.

Demonstrates in **Hard Times** and **Our Mutual Friend** Dickens's presentation of the wholly commercial society and his failure to offer real alternatives: the love relationships are merely manifestations of that same commercialism. The circus is a symbol and Sissy a child, Lamb states; Rachael is too idealized, a madonna; Louisa appears incapable of love except, in her narcissistic way, for Tom. Lamb's analysis of society is far from subtle.

546.    Lambert, Mark. **Dickens and the Suspended Quotation**. New Haven: Yale Univ. Press, 1981, pp. 68, 120–28, 133.

Uses the opening of **Hard Times** to examine the effect of reading late Dickens as his audience read him, with the early Dickens in immediate recollection. Lambert argues that the change in temperature Chesterton asserts (the gauntlet of steel [265]) arises from the withdrawal of the cicerone, the guiding, suspending, authorial voice. He takes issue with Lodge (577) as he finds essential to the reading experience Dickens's violation of his readers' conditioned response. He offers a similar stylistic analysis of Rachael and Stephen by the bedside of Stephen's wife and shows how this scene might have been written by the early Dickens. Reviews: C.C. Barfoot, **ES**, 63 (1982), 544–45; Deirdre David, **VS**, 26 (1982), 93–96; David Karlin, **TLS**, 17 July 1981, p. 808; Sylvere Monod, **MLR**, 78 (1983), 64–66; Susan Shatto, **DSN**, 13 (1982), 85–89; George J. Worth, **JEGP**, 82 (1983), 134–46.

547.    Lang, Andrew. "Introduction." In the Gadshill edition, 1897–99 (29), pp. v–xiii.

Sees the novel mainly as an attack on Dickens's "lifelong enemies, 'honorable members' of the High Court of Parliament." Political economy is rather badly treated in the novel, Lang asserts, since it is only a set of laws and the fault lies in the mere existence of trade--but Dickens would not go this logical length. Bounderby is "very close to actual fact," Stephen "more idealised," Lang asserts. He finds the theatrical defects of the book conspicuous, especially in Louisa, but also in Harthouse. But the "muddle" of industrial society, he feels, is still with us.

548.    Langton, Robert. **The Childhood and Youth of Charles Dickens**. Manchester: by the author, 1883. Rev. and enl. edn., London: Hutchinson, 1891, 1912, pp. 79, 208.

Notes Bounderby's reference to the label on blacking bottles as an allusion to Dickens's experience in the blacking warehouse. Langton points out that the inscription on the sign of the Pegasus Arms, where Sleary's circus has put up, "Good malt makes good beer [etc.]," was taken from a sign at the

Malt Shovel, at the foot of Chatham Hill. Coketown is Manchester, or some other Lancashire town. The dialect spoken by Stephen is "very far from being correct" (compare Gerson [410] and Smith/Quirk [748]).

549.  Lansbury, Coral. **Elizabeth Gaskell: The Novel of Social Crisis.** London: Paul Elek, 1975, pp. 44, 68, 95–6.

Suggests that the relationship of Jemima and her father in **Ruth** inspired Dickens in his delineation of Gradgrind and Louisa. The difference between the two novelists is the difference between allegories that change the world's image of itself and reality transcribed into literal forms, Lansbury states, concluding that "When Dickens borrowed from Elizabeth Gaskell, as he did in **Hard Times**, reality was changed into parable."

550.  Larson, Janet Karsten. "Identity's Fictions: Naming and Renaming in **Hard Times**." **DSN**, 10 (1979), 14–19.

Modifies Rounds (710) to reveal "a more fully ironic dimension" to the naming and re-naming of characters in the novel. Abusers of language, who re-name others as objects, are themselves objectified and dehumanized, Larson states. She points out the abstract nature of Gradgrind's Facts, the fictiveness of Bounderby's, and the abstraction and fictiveness of Mrs. Sparsit's.

551.  Lary, N.M. **Dostoevsky and Dickens: A Study of Literary Influence.** London and Boston: Routledge & Kegan Paul, 1973, p. 6.

In place of Edmund Wilson's suggestion of Jonas Chuzzlewit as a precursor of Raskolnikov, offers **Hard Times**, because of the importance of utilitarian motives to Raskolnikov. Lary asserts that in both **Hard Times** and **Crime and Punishment** we find a sister who wishes to sacrifice herself for the sake of her brother and to marry a new-made man who spouts the economic slogans of the age; both brothers commit a crime that is implicit in the prevailing ideology.

552.  Leacock, Stephen. **Charles Dickens: His Life and Work.** London: Peter Davies, 1933; New York: Doubleday, 1934, pp. 154, 169–72.

Condemns **Hard Times** thoroughly as interesting only in its colossal failure. Leacock states that much of the novel is mere trash, and the character names that survive, Gradgrind and Bounderly (sic), survive as good names, not because of the characters. He believes that none of the excuses usually offered will explain Dickens's production of such a bad novel; he had been flattered too much and so attempted things he did not understand.

553.   Leavis, F.R.   "The Novel as Dramatic Poem (1): **Hard Times.**" **Scrutiny**, 14 (1947), 185–203. Rpt. as chapter 5, "**Hard Times**: An Analytic Note." In **The Great Tradition**. London: Chatto & Windus, 1948; rpt. Harmondsworth: Penguin, 1962.

Absolutely the most significant piece of criticism of **Hard Times**, for decades following the near-inevitable starting or ending point for all further criticism. The novel is praised extensively as the great exception to the general unsatisfactoriness of Dickens's work. Leavis sees it as a "moral fable" in which "the creative exuberance is controlled by a profound inspiration." Dickens is "for once possessed by a comprehensive vision, one in which the inhumanities of Victorian civilization are seen as fostered and sanctioned by a hard philosophy, the aggressive formulation of an inhumane spirit." Leavis examines closely the contrast of Sissy and Bitzer to argue that "the symbolic intention emerges out of metaphor and the vivid evocation of the concrete." Sissy and the circus represent vitality. Leavis concedes Dickens's failure to understand the trade unions and parliament and to portray Stephen convincingly, but essentially the essay is a paean that uses deft and lengthy quotation to argue that "by texture, imaginative mode, symbolic method, and the resulting concentration, **Hard Times** affects us as belonging with formally poetic works." Compare Bayley (189), Bilan (201), Collins (288), Garis (401), Gibson (412), Holloway (471), Sadock (714), and Waldock (818). For reviews, see (554).

554.   ------, and Q.D. Leavis.   "**Hard Times**: The World of Bentham." **Dickens the Novelist**. London: Chatto & Windus; New York: Pantheon, 1970. pp. 187–212.

This is essentially the essay in **Scrutiny** and **The Great Tradition** (553), revised to remove the latter's limitation of its praise to **Hard Times** at the expense of other Dickens novels. In addition, a note is added to refute Holloway (471). Reviews:

John Carey, **Listener**, 84 (1970), 591–92; George Ford, **NCF**, 26 (1971), 95–113; Barbara Hardy, **NS**, 80 (1970), 456–57; Marvin Mudrick, **Hudson Review**, 24 (1971), 346–54; W.W. Robson, **Dickensian**, 67 (1971), 99–104; Ian Watt, **Listener**, 85 (1971), 298, 300–01. The review by Ford pays considerable attention to the changing valuation of **Hard Times** from exception to one instance among many in the Dickens canon.

555.   Leech, Geoffrey N., and Michael H. Short. **Style in Fiction: A Linguistic Introduction to Fictional Prose**. London and New York: Longman, 1981, passim.

The purpose of the book is to demonstrate the usefulness of examining the language of a literary text as a means to a fuller understanding of the writer's achievement. **Hard Times** is used to illustrate points concerning idiolect, speech as an index of character, and the names by which people are addressed.

556.   Leffman, Henry. **About Dickens**. Philadelphia: By the author, 1908, pp. 26, 37, 44, 46–47.

Discusses briefly Merrylegs and Sleary's dog and horses in connection with the animals in Dickens. Suggests that the novel will repay study "as an exposition of some of Dickens' opinions on economic questions."

557.   –––––––. "Charles Dickens as a Native-Faker." **Dickensian**, 5 (1909), 213–16.

See above (556).

558.   Legouis, Emile, and Louis Cazamian. "Dickens." **Histoire de la litterature anglaise**. Paris: Hachette, 1924. Trans. W.D. MacInnes and the author as **A History of English Literature**. 2 vols. New York: Macmillan, 1926–27. Rev. and reset as one vol., New York: Macmillan, 1929; London: Dent, 1933, pp. 1129–37. Rpt. London: Dent, 1957.

In **Hard Times**, as in **Barnaby Rudge** and **A Tale of Two Cities**, a too rigid intention controls the work. The result is an effect of strain, according to the authors. The claim that **Hard Times** is a "purely social" novel, and that Dickens knows little or nothing of the real life of the working classes in the midlands and the north (he is the novelist of the lower middle classes).

559.    Leimberg, Ingeborg. "**Hard Times**: Zeitbezug und Uberzeitliche Bedeutung." **Germanisch-Romanische Monatsschrift**, 52 (1971), 269-96. Rpt. in **Der englische soziale Roman im 19.Jahrhundert**. Ed. Konrad Gross. Wege der Forschung, 466. Darmstadt: Wissenschaftliche Buchgesellschaft, 1977.

Takes the elements of parable in the novel as the basis of a discussion of the generic question of whether this novel is an allegory or a **roman a these**. Leimberg pays close attention to the descriptions of Coketown and to the book and chapter titles.

560.    Lemonnier, Leon. **Dickens**. Paris: Albin Michel, 1946, passim.

Notes the influence of Carlyle in **Hard Times**. Lemonnier suggests that the failure of the visit to Preston was due to the nature of Dickens's imagination, which did not work from direct documentation or objective observation. He relates the title and the nightmare quality of the novel to Dickens's personal life at the time, associating both Rachael and Mrs. Sparsit with Georgina (one the idealized version and the other the traits in Georgina, especially jealousy, that occasionally irritated Dickens). Lemonnier also associates the circus troupe with Dickens's amateur company of actors. Gradgrind is the father Dickens did not want to be and the plea for fancy is a defense of his own childhood reading. Lemmonier concludes that **Hard Times** was one of the most anguishing (**angoissants**) of Dickens's novels, as witnessed in his exhaustion when it was done.

561.    Lerner, Laurence. "The Bourgeois Imagination: Literature and Class Prejudice in Mid-19th-Century England." In **Literature and Western Civilization**. Ed. David Daiches and Anthony Thorlby. Vol. 5 of **The Modern World II: Realities**. London: Aldus, 1972, pp. 203-28. Rpt. in Lerner's **The Literary Imagination: Essays on Literature and Society**. Brighton: Harvester; Totowa, N.J.: Barnes & Noble, 1982.

Discusses **Hard Times** among the "mixed cases" of success and failure in the Victorians' attempts at understanding the working classes via the imagination. Lerner states that the two who were really undermining the system that Dickens attacked

were Gradgrind and Slackbridge. Gradgrind, says Dickens, was
proving that the Good Samaritan was a Bad Economist, but the
factory-owners had nothing to fear from the Good Samaritan
because charity supports the system. It was not fair of Dickens
to ally Gradgrind and Bounderby, Lerner insists. The portrait of
Slackbridge as a union organizer was a "calumny"--and Dickens
knew it, as is apparent from "On Strike." The whole episode of
Slackbridge and Stephen Lerner finds implausible: "Dickens be-
trayed the truth and made a mess of his novel." Yet the social
point of the novel is that all is a "muddle." Lerner explains the
anomaly: "When industrialism is an independent force, a ray of
light in the fog, an invention defying the Circumlocution Office,
[Dickens] is all for it; but when industrialism has become the
Establishment [as in Coketown], fear and hatred are the only
possible reaction." Thus we get the odd combination of the
attack, the radical response to authority that Dickens always
has, and the calumny and unfairness, which show Dickens as
the leader of the steam-whistle party.

562.     -------. "An Essay on **Dombey and Son**." In **The Victorians**.
         Ed. Laurence Lerner  New York; Holmes & Meier, 1978, pp.
         195-208.

         Argues that despite **Hard Times** Dickens was of the
         steam-whistle party.

563.     -------, and Barry Supple. "Novelists and Social Change." In
         **The English Novel**. Ed. Cedric Watts. London: Sussex, 1976,
         pp. 31-52.

         Supple dismisses **Hard Times** as not largely about the fac-
         tory but "insofar as it's about an economic problem, about the
         urban society as a whole."

564.     Levine, George. "Introduction." In the Pan edition, 1977 (51),
         pp. 13-23.

         Discusses the austerity created by the weekly format and
         the unfavorable reception of the novel. A society committed to
         the ideology attacked did not see the ambivalence of the at-
         tack, which leads to some of the simplifications in the novel,
         Levine points out, adding: "Dickens was beginning to articulate
         a newly disenchanted vision, and was struggling to reconcile
         the disenchantment to his earlier joyous exuberance and faith

in the great potentiality of his class." Levine offers a detailed discussion of Bounderby as "a kind of surrogate Dickens" and claims that he is the figure "in whom the richest and most complicated aspects of the novel are focussed." He argues that Dickens's failure to work out his themes fully is visible in Slackbridge and the union issue and in the education theme. Sissy is a weak character, but Louisa anticipates some of Dickens's finest later achievements. The novel as a whole Levine finds interesting as "the battleground on which Dicknes was beginning to fight out his own ambivalences about himself, his class and his society."

565.    --------. The Realistic Imagination: English Fiction from Frankenstein to Lady Chatterley. Chicago and London: Univ. of Chicago Press, 1981, passim.

        Considers Hard Times the most allegorical handling of the conflict between "life" and utilitarianism. References to the novel are brief.

566.    Levine, Richard A. "Dickens, the Two Nations, and Individual Possibility." SNNTS, 1 (1969), 157–80.

        Proposes to examine "Dickens' method of treating the two nations, then discuss his reading of the individual's possibilities of accommodation within an environment so constructed, and, finally, comment on the 'reliability' of the novelist's views." Levine offers extended analysis of Dombey and Son, Little Dorrit, and Great Expectations, but not of Hard Times, though it is mentioned frequently.

567.    Levy, Herman Mittle. "Dickens and the Novel in Parts." DA, 26 (1965), 6024A (Univ. of Florida, 1965). 199 pp.

        Hard Times and Great Expectations are treated together as weeklies, in the context of this study of the effects of serial publication in Dickens's work.

568.    Ley, J.W.T. "The Apostle of Christmas." Dickensian, 2 (1906) 324–326.

        Remarks that Ruskin was "wide of the mark" when he called Hard Times Dickens's best book (150).

569.    ------. "The Case of 'Hard Times.'"  **Dickensian**, 24 (1928),
        257-61.

     Suggests that Ruskin (150) and  Shaw (738) liked **Hard
Times** because both saw it as a social tract.  Ley believes that
it lacks "characterisation and humour," but can be considered
great as an earnest contribution to social literature.  Dickens
created the humanitarian atmosphere necessary to the solution
of economic problems, Ley adds; "We listened to him just in
time.  In 1917, in Eastern Europe, the Great Bear awoke."

570.    ------. "Dickens and Carlyle."  **Dickensian**, 12 (1916), 313-16.

     Traces the friendship between Carlyle and Dickens, a tri-
umph for Dickens because Carlyle was generally not charmed
by fictions.  Ley asserts that **Hard Times** reveals Carlyle's influence "in every chapter."

571.    ------. **The Dickens Circle: a Narrative of the Novelist's
Friendships**  New York: Dutton, 1919, pp. 196, 206.  Rpt. New
York: Haskell, 1972.

     Cites Dickens's letter to Fitzgerald on his "heaviest blow,"
which was not delivered until **Hard Times**.  The novel was
largely influenced by Carlyle, Ley states, but Dickens was first
roused by Lord Shaftesbury's activities.  The background for the
novel is Manchester.

572.    Lightwood, James T.  **Dickens and Music**.  London: Charles H.
Kelly, 1912, pp. 56, 59.  Rpt. New York: Haskell, 1970.

     "The boom of the bell is associated with many of the vil-
lains of the novels ....  Blackpool and Carker hear the accusing
bells when in the midst of planning their evil deeds" (sic), insists Lightwood.  He also notes the image of the tambourine as
simile for Bounderby's hat and of a colossal strip of music paper for the electric wires against the evening sky, and remarks
M'Choakumchild's preparation to teach, among many other
things, vocal music.

*      Lincks, J.F.

     See below (899).

573.    Lindsay, Jack.   **Charles Dickens: A Biographical and Critical Study.**  London: Andrew Dakers, 1950, pp. 310-13 and passim. Rpt. New York: Kraus, 1970.

Finds the novel a sketch, the material intractable for Dickens.  Lindsay believes that Dickens wanted the workers to unite, but feared the consquences of such solidarity.  The circus is the one point in the novel of real Dickensian symbolism, but Dickens never goes fully to the heart of his theme, Lindsay states.  He suggests a relationship between the ending of the novel--Rachael and Stephen united in Dickens's brother/sister myth--and "A Tale of the Forest of Dean" in **Household Words**, 9 August 1851.  Reviews: Lionel Stevenson, **MLN**, 66 (1951), 416-17; G.G. Grubb, **NCF**, 5 (1951), 317-24.

574.    Linehan, Thomas M.   "Rhetorical Technique and Moral Purpose in Dickens's **Hard Times**."  **UTQ**, 47 (1977), 22-36.

Seeks to unify the novel through Dickens's moral purpose to persuade his audience of the disastrousness of a social organization based on pure fact.  Dickens believes that nothing good can come of this situation, including good unions, and he discredits the system with single-minded energy.  For Linehan the novel makes its argument through a variety of cases: Gradgrind, Tom, Bounderby, the denial of fancy, the circus, Stephen.  The denial of fancy he also sees as a denial of religious impulses, and Stephen's "rugged fancy" as the source of religious emotions that bind men together.  The circus is a world of perpetual childhood, but Stephen's ordeal offers the sharpest contrast to the values of Coketown.

575.    -------.   "Social Criticism and Fictional Form In Three Dickens Novels."  Ph.D. Dissertation.  Univ. of Chicago, 1974.  388 pp.

Is concerned with the relationship between journalism and fiction, "between the immediate social end of a magazine article and the artistic end of a narrative work of fiction."  With **Hard Times**, Linehan concludes with a study of the critical disagreement regarding the relation of satire in the novel to real institutions, arguing for neither univocal correspondence nor dismissal of the social and historical features as incidental background, but a complex movement between these two poles.  Linehan's detailed discussion of the novel itself is presented in a revised version in "Rhetorical Technique and Moral Purpose in Dickens's **Hard Times**" (574).

576.   Lodge, David.   "How Successful Is **Hard Times?**"   **Working With Structuralism**.   Boston, London, and Henley: Routledge & Kegan Paul, 1981, pp. 37–45.

Sees rhe novel as a "moralised theatricality" of rapid tempo and without a character whose perspective dominates--without, that is, a hero or heroine.   Its distinctive quality is that of the pantomime, Lodge holds, and Dickens's bold if less than wholly successful experiment was to treat the "condition of England" question in that spirit.   The effect is comparable to Brecht's alienation effect, "to defamiliarise not merely the subject-matter of the story, so that we perceive it freshly, but also the method of presentation itself, so that ... we are compelled to recognize its artificiality and to consider its ideological implications."

577.   -------.   "The Rhetoric of **Hard Times**."   **The Language of Fiction**.   London: Routledge & Kegan Paul, 1966, pp. 145–63. Rpt. 1979.   Rpt. in **Dickens: Hard Times, Great Expectations, and Our Mutual Friend: A Casebook**.   Ed.   Norman Page. London: Macmillan, 1979; also in Gray (429).

An important essay arguing that the polemical effectiveness of **Hard Times** must be accounted for in terms of its rhetoric, though at one point allowing that behind successful rhetoric must lie successful conception.   Lodge examines the first chapter closely to demonstrate its success as rhetoric, insisting that its historical accuracy is beside the point.   He treats the relationship between character and appearance and Dickens's use of keywords.   Gradgrind is a success, but Slackbridge and the Whelp are failures and Dickens's presentation of Fancy is merely bread and circuses.   Lodge examines in detail the use of fairy-tale elements and argues that they succeed when they are used ironically but fail when they are meant to suggest a means of redemption.   What **Hard Times** shows is that society must change, but Dickens's characters cannot change.   Reviews: W.J. Harvey, **EC**, 17 (1967), 231–37; Laurence Lerner, **RES**, 18 (1967), 356–58; Ronald Paulson, **JEGP**, 66 (1967), 245–49.

578.   Lopez, Toni Ann.   "The Victorian Novel: A Perceptual-Conceptual Compromise."   **DAI**, 38 (1977), 2812A   (Florida State Univ., 1977).   244 pp.

Uses F.S.C. Northrop's description of contemporary chaos to examine four mid-century Victorian novels, including **Hard Times.**

579.  Lougy, Robert E. "Dickens' **Hard Times**: The Romance as Radical Literature." **DSA**, 2 (1972), 237-54.

Draws on Northrop Frye, Sigmund Freud, Dickens's "Frauds on the Fairies," Percy Bysshe Shelley, and Herbert Marcuse in an argument that the novel presents "a world of romance gone mad." The explanation is thematic, Lougy asserts: the novel is not about the conflict between capital and labor but about the battle "between Eros and Thanatos," and thus must be read psychologically, not socially. Hence Stephen is incapable of effecting significant change. Bounderby Lougy sees as an "antiartist," Dickens's "modern figure of death," and the circus people as artists asserting themselves against a world that is dominated by "reason and the reality principle."

580.  Love, Theresa R. **Dickens and the Seven Deadly Sins.** Danville, Illinois: Interstate Printers & Publishers, 1979, passim.

Argues that Dickens always traces social and personal evils back to one of the seven deadly sins. The movement from Coketown to the Gradgrind family is a typical structure, from society to the individual. Love compares briefly the Dombey and Gradgrind children as victims of paternal mania.

581.  Lovett, Robert M., and Helen S. Hughes. **The History of the Novel in England.** Boston and New York: Houghton Mifflin, 1932, pp. 226, 228, 247.

Considers **Hard Times** Dickens's most serious social novel and compares it with Reade's **Put Youself in His Place** (1870) for their similar treatment of the unions.

582.  Lucas, Audrey. "Some Dickens Women." **Yale Review**, n.s. 29 (1940), 706-28.

Offers Louisa as an example of the punishment accorded the very occasional appearance of shaded virtue (that is, neither black nor white).

583.  Lucas, John.  **Charles Dickens: The Melancholy Man**.  London:
      Methuen, 1970.  2nd ed. pub. as **The Melancholy Man: A Study
      of Dickens's Novels**.  Brighton: Harvester; Totowa, New Jersey:
      Barnes & Noble, 1980, pp. 242, 253–55, 276.

      This book generally in praise of Dickens finds **Hard Times**
      unsuccessful because of its "bleakly deterministic view." Lucas
      agrees with Leavis (553) that it has a "peculiarly insistent moral
      intention" but does not find that description honorific; the book
      is thin and reductive.  **Little Dorrit** is the great answer to **Hard
      Times**, he believes, and the differing opinions expressed in
      **Household Words** show that Dickens really knew better.  Re-
      views: K.J. Fielding, **Dickensian**, 67 (1971), 115–16; Margaret
      Ganz, **VS**, 15 (1971), 234–36; Stephen Wall, **EO**, 21 (1971),
      261–80.

584.  –––––––.  "Dickens and **Dombey and Son**: Past and Present
      Imperfect." In **Tradition and Tolerance in Nineteenth-Century
      Fiction**.  Ed. David Howard, John Lucas, and John Goode.  Lon-
      don: Routledge & Kegan Paul; New York: Barnes & Noble, 1966,
      pp. 99–140.

      Argues that in **Hard Times** Dickens creates an entirely es-
      capist world, putting into Sleary's all the qualities he believes
      can no longer exist in our world.  Lucas finds this the most
      pessimistic of Dickens's novels, representing an imaginative
      breakdown.  The circus is the end of the line that begins with
      the Wooden Midshipman and reveals the dichotomous terms in
      which Dickens had come to think of England and its values, he
      sates.  Review: Jerome Meckier, **DS**, 5 (1969), 97–103.

585.  –––––––.  "Mrs. Gaskell and Brotherhood." In **Tradition and
      Tolerance in Nineteenth-Century Fiction**.  Ed. David Howard,
      John Lucas, and John Goode.  London: Routledge & Kegan Paul;
      New York: Barnes & Noble, 1966, pp. 141–205.

      Treats **Hard Times** extensively, but largely as a foil to
      **North and South**.  The novel is attacked on essentially the
      same grounds as in **The Melancholy Man** (583).  Lucas finds it
      "a compilation of cliches based on an external and distanced
      acquaintance" with the North.  He demands "demonstration" for
      the "assertions" Dickens makes and berates the pessimism,
      which he labels cynicism, of the novel.  He uses Holloway (471),
      Williams (849), Orwell (650), and the **Wesminster Review** (120)
      to dispute Leavis's claims for the novel (553), calling Dickens's

protest "journalistic," "shoddy rhetoric," and hasty improvisation; it lacks hard thought and is simple denunciation. Lucas attacks Dickens's "predetermined hostility" to Coketown with equal hostility and argues that the connection Dickens forges between Bounderby and Gradgrind and the degradations of industrialism are specious. Ruskin liked the novel because Sleary's is "dangerously close" to his own escapism, Lucas points out. Dickens was led into absurdity because he was so deeply shocked at the North; he saw masses not as individuals and he created a highly deterministic view of character that he could not hold. Review: Jerome Meckier, **DS**, 5 (1969), 97–103.

*       Lumet, Louis.

        See Albert Keim and Louis Lumet (516).

586.    Lundgren, Bruce Raymond. "Dickens and the Rhetoric of Romance." **DAI**, 33 (1971), 728A–29A (Univ. of Western Ontario, 1971).

        Examines the effects of the Victorian controversy over the merits of realism and romance in relation to three novels of Dickens's middle period, including **Hard Times**. Lundgren pays particular attention to the means by which Dickens adapts the romance to accommodate the realism increasingly demanded by his readers and critics.

*       Lunn, Hugh Kingsmill.

        See Kingsmill, Hugh (529).

587.    Lupton, Edward B. **Dickens the Immortal**. Kansas City: Alfred Fowler, 1923, pp. 17–18. Rpt. Folcroft, Pa.: Folcroft, 1976; Norwood, Pa.: Norwood, 1977.

        Considers **Hard Times** a failure as a novel but a great success as didactic literature. Lupton remarks the influence of Carlyle.

588.    McCarthy, Mary. **Ideas and the Novel**. New York and London: Harcourt Brace Jovanovich, 1980, pp. 114–18.

Takes **Hard Times** as a significant exception to the general barrenness in nineteenth-century English fiction of ideas. Gradgrind and Bounderby are men of fixed ideas and global expectations, McCarthy asserts, and the novel shows that the two upholders of social order are as mad as the terrorists of **The Possessed**. But as it treats facts for its own purpose, McCarthy adds, the book has one foot in Gradgrind's camp.

589.   McCormick, I.C.   "A Defense for 'Hard Times.'" **Dickensian**, 12 (1916), 89–91; also **The Living Age**, 290 (1916), 690–92.

Defends the novel against general critical dislike on the grounds that it arouses the best emotions. It has plenty of plot, McCormick asserts. Rachael is the Ideal Woman, Blackpool a true type of the artisan of the time. The other characters too are perfect in their own ways; the novel is above all a novel with several purposes.

590.   McCormick, John.  **Catastrophe and Imagination: An Interpretation of the Recent English and American Novel.**  London: Longmans, Green, 1957, p. 45.

Attacks Leavis's use of the term "poetic" to describe the novel (553) as a term used "whenever he wishes to praise without qualification, a vicious habit which ... displays as basic a confusion about the differences between the novel and the poem on the part of the critic as on the part of delinquent authors." A general distaste for Dickens, who is seen as capable of fleeting genius as a stylist, governs this criticism.

591.   McGillis, Roderick F.   "Plum Pies and Factories: Cross Connections in **Hard Times**." **DSN**, 11 (1980), 102–07.

"Dickens's ironic use of fairy tale and nursery rhyme points out the pessimism of **Hard Times** but, paradoxically, the **fact** of fairy tale and nursery rhyme points out the imaginative power and resilience of the human mind," McGillis states. He analyzes the use of fairy tale at length, arguing that the novel is "about language as much as anything else" and its theme a confrontation of languages.

592.   McKenzie, Charles H.  **The Religious Sentiments of Charles Dickens**. London: Walter Scott, 1884, passim. Rpt. New York: Haskell, 1973.

Identifies the religious sentiments of this novel along with those of the rest of the canon.

593.  McKenzie, Gordon. "Dickens and Daumier." In B.H. Bronson, **et al**. **Studies in the Comic**. Univ. of California Publications in English, 8, 2. Berkeley and Los Angeles: Univ. of California Press, 1941, pp. 273-98. Rpt. Darby, Pa.: Arden, 1978.

Finds in **Hard Times** the exception to the general rule in Dickens that what stands out is the particular scene or character: "there is extensive development of character which necessitates a long, slow movement." Later McKenzie compares this novel to Swift's **A Modest Proposal** and the fourth book of **Gulliver's Travels** for its intense mixture of laughter and anger, and he compares the method of comic treatment for a very serious theme to Daumier's satire.

594.  MacKenzie, Norman, and Jeanne MacKenzie. **Dickens, a Life**. New York: Oxford Univ. Press, 1979, pp. 262-66 and passim.

Summarizes the plot and the circumstances surrounding the publication of **Hard Times**. Reviews: Sylvere Monod, **EA**, 33 (1980), 472-73; Andrew Sanders, **Dickensian**, 76 (1980), 44-45; Michael Slater, **VS**, 23 (1980), 520-22; Harry Stone, **NCF**, 34 (1980), 438-44.

595.  McMaster, R.D. "'Society (Whatever that was)': Dickens and Society as an Abstraction." **EA**, 23 (1970), 125-35.

Sees Dickens's sympathies as divided between rebellion and a reactionary love of law and order. In **Hard Times**, Dickens "directly attacks the operation of abstractions in Society" and their tendency to dominate over natural feelings, McMaster states. He finds the farcical presentation of the conflict between understanding and intuition to make what Leavis sees as Lawrentian (553) somewhat superficial. He compares Dickens with Dostoevsky, mostly unfavorably, though he finds them equal in the effective portrayal of the inner stresses of our civilization. He disagrees with Johnson (500) on the matter of Dickens's continuing hope in the regeneration of society through individual change of heart, finding too strong the power of Dickens's depiction of muddle, vice, and obfuscation.

596. McMurtry, Jo. **Victorian Life and Victorian Fiction: A Companion for the American Reader.** Hamden, Conn.: Archon, 1979, passim.

Includes **Hard Times** in a list of novels that "are exceptional in that each focuses almost exclusively on the working-class characters" and refers to the novel under various headings (Mrs. Sparsit, the school, the train, the phrase "sent to Coventry"). The novel is a quarry, not a subject, for this book.

597. McNulty, J.H. "Dickens--All the Year Round." **Dickensian,** 37 (1941), 99–103.

On the seasonal charms of Dickens's books. **Hard Times** is for January, between the festivities of Christmas and the promise of Spring, McNulty asserts. He notes the unpopularity of the novel and Ruskin's contrary view (150) and agrees that a system of education that turned children into "examination-passing machines" would be a national calamity.

598. McVeagh, John. "From Industrialism to Big Business, 1830-1900." **Tradefull Merchants: The Portrayal of the Capitalist in Literature.** London: Routledge & Kegan Paul, 1981, pp. 128-59.

Argues that by the addition of Gradgrind, the "theorist of selfishness," and Bounderby, "its practical example," Dickens extends the criticism he began with Dombey. Bounderby is savagely worse than Dombey, McVeagh states, but the precise type favored by the new creed and practice.

599. Macey, Samuel L. **Clocks and the Cosmos: Time in Western Life and Thought.** Hamden, Conn.: Archon, 1980, pp. 93, 191.

Two brief references to **Hard Times** note the simile of the Dutch clock and Tom Gradgrind's snoring (in the context of Dickens's people seeming to be like clocks), and the "deadly statistical clock" of the mechanical Coketown values opposed to Sissy and the circus people.

600. Magnuson, Gordon Arnold. "Narrator Voice and Moral Vision in Six Novels of Charles Dickens." **DAI,** 40 (1979), 1483A-84A (Univ. of Arkansas, 1979). 402 pp.

Includes **Hard Times** among the six novels selected. This study focusses on three narrator voices, the editorial, the ironic, and the public, and the narrator's spatial, temporal, and moral relations to the characters.

601.   Maine, Sir Henry James Sumner. **Popular Government.** London: John Murray, 1885. 2nd ed. London: John Murray; New York: Holt, 1886, p. 153.

In the course of a discussion of how political theories may survive their impracticability, offers as an example the degree to which Dickens is indebted to Bentham in his hardly ever having written a novel without attacking an abuse. There is no direct reference here to **Hard Times**, but Maine's comment has inspired later critics to think twice about the easy identification of Gradgrindism with Benthamism. Compare Dicey (338), Engel (368), and Goldberg (424).

602.   Manheim, Leonard F. "The Dickens Pattern – A Study in Psychoanalytic Criticism." **Microfilm Abstracts**, 10 (1950), 4, 218–19 (Columbia Univ., 1950). 386 pp.

An early psychoanalytic study of the novels, chronologically arranged.

603.   Mankowitz, Wolf. **Dickens of London**. New York: Macmillan, 1976, pp. 77, 178, 180.

Notes Dickens's early visit to Lancashire and his inspiration to strike the "heaviest blow" in his power, and his later visit to Preston specifically for **Hard Times**. Yet the book is not strongly marked as documentary, offering more an analysis of industrialism than an experience of it. Reviews: Philip Collins, **Dickensian**, 73 (1977), 114–16; R. Giddings, **DSN**, 8 (1977), 81–84; Branwen Bailey Pratt, **NCF**, 33 (1978), 262–68.

604.   Manning, John. "Charles Dickens and the Glasgow System." **School and Society**, 83 (1956), 202–06.

Identifies the "Glasgow system" in Dickens's letter to Angela Burdett Coutts, 16 September 1843, as referring to the teacher-training school of David Stow, in Glasgow. Stow's manual, Manning points out, deplores a number of practices specifically attacked or contrasted in Dickens's work, including rote memorization (Bitzer's definition of a horse) and fact-cramming (M'Choakumchild). Manning states that M'Choakumchild shows what Dickens thought of the very different English system of teacher-training.

605.   -------. **Dickens on Education**. Toronto: Univ. of Toronto Press, 1959, passim.

Offers much background material against which to view the issue of education as presented in **Hard Times**. Manning finds Dickens unfair and not very funny in his depiction of M'Choakumchild's training, and compares it to the actual training of the time. Review: P.A.W. Collins, **RES**, n.s. 12 (1961), 312–14.

606.   Manning, Sylvia B. "**Hard Times**." **Dickens As Satirist**. New Haven: Yale Univ. Press, 1971, pp. 132–54.

Attempts to move the novel away from the immediate concerns of unions, education, and so forth towards a reading of it as "satiric vision." Thus **Hard Times** becomes "moral satire" concerned with the oppositions between mechanical rigidity and vital fluidity, scientific learning and intuitive knowledge, self-propelling masculine aggressiveness and nurturing feminine receptivity. Reviews: Duane DeVries, **DSN**, 2 (1971), 51–53; Lauriat Lane, Jr., **SNNTS**, 5 (1973), 125–38; Martin Price, **YR**, 61 (1972), 271–79; G.B. Tennyson, **NCF**, 27 (1972), 371.

607.   Marcus, Steven. **Dickens: From Pickwick to Dombey**. London: Chatto & Windus; New York: Basic Books, 1965, pp. 9, 14.

Remarks that the later work of Dickens, including **Hard Times**, elicits from the reader the kind of uneasy, equivocal response we give to **The Wasteland** or **The Possessed**.

608.   -------. **Engels, Manchester, and the Working Class**. New York: Random House, 1974, passim.

Praises Dickens's rendering of Coketown/Manchester and offers an interesting analysis of Dickens's description of Manchester in 1838.

\*       ———————.

See George Ford and Steven Marcus (391).

609.   Marriott, Sir John.   **English History in English Fiction.**   New
       York: Dutton, 1941; London: Blackie, 1944, pp. 262–63.

       Considers **Hard Times** a popularization of Carlyle's attack
       on the Manchester school.   Gradgrind is a caricature, Marriott
       asserts, but as there is no smoke without fire, so the caricature
       must hold a substratum of truth.

610.   Marshall, Percy.   **Masters of the English Novel.**   London: Den-
       nis Dobson, 1962, pp. 115, 127.

       Sees Dickens as a novelist of changing social conditions
       and includes Gradgrind in a list of characters who show Dick-
       ens's hatred of the governing class, a hatred arising from his
       experience in the law courts.

611.   Marshall, William H.   **The World of the Victorian Novel.**   Lon-
       don: Thomas Yoseloff; South Brunswick and New York: Barnes,
       1967, pp. 82, 211, 471.

       Emphasizes the mythic rather than the social life of the
       Victorian novel and so argues that **Hard Times** is primarily
       concerned with man isolated in a world of increasing ugliness
       and diminishing meaning.   The novel demonstrates the failure
       of modern man to achieve identity in economic terms, Marshall
       states; in this regard, he compares Dombey and Gradgrind.

\*       Martin, Robert Bernard.

       See Thomas Marc Parrott and Robert Bernard Martin (663).

612.   Marzials, Frank T.   **Life of Charles Dickens.**   London: Walter
       Scott, 1887, pp. 126–29.   Rpt. in **Studies in Dickens.**   Ed. Ma-
       belle S. C. Smith.   Chatauqua, New York: Chatauqua Press, 1960;
       Folcroft, Pa.: Folcroft, 1973.

       Sees **Hard Times** as intended to popularize certain ideas:
       that men are not calculating machines, that human relations

cannot be established purely on the basis of supply and demand, that Parliament is contemptible. The story is exaggerated, Marzials states, and therefore flawed. Between Macaulay's "sullen socialism" (145) and Ruskin's "entirely right in main drift and purpose" (150), Marzials chooses "entirely right in feeling," warning that novelists, not being philosophers, cannot grapple with "complex social and political problems" and give us "right conclusions" to them.

613.   Matz, B.W. "Dickens, Carlyle, and 'Hard Times.'" **Dickensian**, 20 (1924), 32-33.

Reproduces the letter to Carlyle requesting permission to dedicate **Hard Times** to him and asserts Carlyle's influence on the novels. Matz remarks that the price of the book was five shillings, the lowest price at which any of Dickens's novels had been issued so far.

614.   ------ **Dickensian Inns and Taverns**. London: Palmer, 1922, pp. 175-77.

Because Coketown is a composite (with a great deal of Preston), it is difficult to identify any locations. The inscription at the Pegasus's Arms, however, Matz points out, tallies with that on the inn-sign of the Malt Shovel, which once stood at the foot of Chatham hill.

615.   Maurois, Andre. **Un Essai sur Dickens**. Paris: B. Grasset, 1927. Also pub. as "Dickens." **Etudes anglaises**. Paris: B. Grasset, 1928, pp. 13-168. Trans. as **Dickens** by Hamish Miles. London: Bodley Head, 1934, pp. 6, 72.

Describes the dialogue between Stephen and Bounderby as utterly unbelievable, but offers the scene concerning wallpaper and carpets as an example of high realism and finds the scene of Louisa and Tom peeking at the circus to be one of fine symbolism.

616.   Meakin, David. **Man and Work: Literature and Culture in Industrial Society**. New York: Holmes & Meier, 1976, pp. 24-25.

Explores visions of alienation that offer an imaginative response to industrialism that Marx's analysis missed; Coketown is one.

617.   Meckier, Jerome. "Dickens and **King Lear**: A Myth for Victorian
       England." **South Atlantic Quarterly**, 71 (1972), 75-90.

       Argues that Dickens's use of the Lear story adds support to
       a Laurentian reading of the novel. Meckier states that Sissy's
       malapropisms are allied to the punning wit of the Fool. The
       scene between Louisa and her father, with the rainstorm out-
       side, is as close as Dickens can come to the storm on the
       heath and Shakespeare's vision of the close association of po-
       litical, philosophical, and natural orders. But, Meckier believes,
       Dickens needs two Cordelias: Louisa to undergo paternal rejec-
       tion and, because Louisa is too much a product of her father's
       system to save him from it, Sissy to act as the redeemer. The
       novel shows Lawrence's dread of the effects of business and
       industry upon our values and personalities.

618.   --------. "Dickens and the Dystopian Novel: From **Hard Times**
       to **Lady Chatterley**." In **The Novel and its Changing Form**.
       Ed. R.G. Collins. Winnipeg: Univ. of Manitoba Press, 1972, pp.
       51-58.

       Considers **Hard Times** a "seminal dystopia" that "isolated
       the Industrial Revolution as **the** central trauma for modern dys-
       topian thought." Meckier offers a particularly interesting com-
       parison of the opening scenes of **Hard Times** and **Brave New
       World**. Dickens, he points out, indicts a Victorian preference
       for the practical over the imaginative or theoretical and a will-
       ingness to see human nature bent to accomodate the practical.

619.   --------. **Hard Times**: A Seminal Distopia" (sic). **South Cen-
       tral Bulletin**, 30 (1970), 112.

       Abstract. States that **Hard Times** is a dystopia "that pro-
       tests against the lifestyle it fears will result from the Industrial
       Revolution .... Wells, Huxley, Lawrence hold the key" to this
       novel since they all "borrowed from it, in spirit and in specifics,
       to fashion their own nightmare visions of the future. Compare
       "Dickens and the Dystopian Novel: from **Hard Times** to **Lady
       Chatterley**" (618).

620.   Meers, Geneva Mae. "Victorian Schoolteachers in Fiction." **DA**,
       13 (1953), 1196-97 (Northwestern Univ., 1953). 346 pp.

A comparison of fictional treatment of Victorian schoolteachers with accounts of actual teachers of the time, covering
ninety-five novels and seventeen short stories, including **Hard
Times**.

621.  Meier, Stefanie. **Animation and Mechanization in the Novels
      of Charles Dickens**. Bern: Francke, 1982, pp. 137-48.

      An utterly derivative reading of the novel, finds that **Hard
      Times** "probably contains the most lucid expression of the in-
      terdependence between" the three qualities of charity, animistic
      creativity, and poetic potential. This view leads to the standard
      opposition of Sissy to Gradgind, utilitarianism, and Bitzer.
      Sleary's represents art, Sissy is a source of poetic energy. The
      important quality of childlikeness is seen in all of Sleary's peo-
      ple.

622.  Melada, Ivan. **The Captain of Industry in English Fiction
      1821-1871**. Albuquerque: Univ. of New Mexico Press, 1970, pp.
      110-17, 140, 144.

      Seeks to trace the changing image of the industrialist in
      novels written between 1821 and 1871, from the perspective of
      social history.  Melada finds in Bounderby a satire upon the
      simplistic laissez-faire assumptions of the captains of industry
      and upon the myth of the self-made man.  He concludes that
      Dickens's picture is distorted and exaggerated but, as Ruskin
      pointed out (150), true.  In novels after 1850, except for **Hard
      Times**, the industrialist is depicted with a degree of sympa-
      thetic realism.  Review: K.J. Fielding, **NCF**, 26 (1972), 485-86.

623.  Michasiw, Barbara Lorene.  "The Heroines of Charles Dickens:
      Their Meaning and Function."  **DAI**, 37 (1977), 6505A (Univ. of
      Toronto, 1974).

      Explores the theme of love and affection as developed
      through the heroines.  Sissy shows the link between the ca-
      pacity for love and affection and the creative imagination, Mi-
      chasiw states.  She also points out that Louisa's feminine affin-
      ity for the affectional life has been nearly destroyed by her
      education.  Although the consequences of suppressing the im-
      agination are evident in Coketown, Michasiw concludes, Dickens
      did not examine the dark side of the active imagination until he
      came to Pip.

624.    Middendorf, John H. "Introduction." In the Harper edition, 1960
        (41), pp. v–xx.

        Reviews the divided reception and critical history of the
        novel, Dickens's work up to **Hard Times**, and the circumstances
        of publication for this novel. Middendorf acknowledges faults
        in the work--the unmasking of Bounderby, Tom's escape, Ste-
        phen's patience, Slackbridge--but finds them more than offset
        by the consistency of tone, the coherence of structure, and the
        overriding moral purpose. He sees the novel as moral allegory,
        pitting "uncontrolled egoism" and "intellect in its more analytic,
        least appealing form" against love and imagination. The novel
        demonstrates Dickens's faith in the indestructibility of the vir-
        tues represented in Sissy.

625.    Middlebro', Thomas Galbraith. "The Treatment of Industrialism
        in the Later Novels of Charles Dickens." **DAI**, 34 (1973),
        735A–36A (McGill Univ., 1972).

        Examines the paradoxical implications of the new industrial
        values as shown in the later novels. In **Hard Times**, Middlebro'
        concludes, Dickens looks at irresponsible industrial power and
        its utilitarian apologists who suppress men's capacities for loy-
        alty, love, and imagination.

626.    Miller, J. Hillis. **Charles Dickens: The World of His Novels.**
        Cambridge, Mass.: Harvard Univ. Press, 1959, pp. 226–27, 332.
        A segment on **Hard Times** rpt. in Gray (429).

        Sees **Hard Times** in terms of the opposition between or-
        ganization based on love (the circus) and a civilization in which
        everything has its price. **Hard Times** is not one of the six
        novels treated at length in this book.

627.    Mills, Nicolaus C. "Romance and Society: A Re-Examination of
        Nineteenth Century American and British Fiction." **DA**, 28
        (1967), 687A–88A (Brown Univ., 1966). 247 pp.

        Pairs twelve novels, including **Hard Times** and **The Blithe-
        dale Romance**, in order to compare American and British fic-
        tion. Mills emphasizes textual analysis, arguing that "the pri-
        mary difference betwen American and British fiction can be
        observed in structural terms."

628. Miyazaki, Koichi. **A Study of Two of Dickens's Late Novels.**
      Tokyo: Seijo Univ., 1971, pp. 34-47. The chapter on **Hard
      Times** rpt. in his **The Inner Structure of Charles Dickens's
      Later Novels.** Tokyo: Sanseido, 1974 also published as **The In-
      ner Construction of Dickens's Later Novels,** no place or date
      of publication.

      Argues that in **Hard Times** the elements of allegory and
      realism exist side by side without integration. Miyazaki praises
      the realism of the early presentation but finds most of the res-
      olution--Gradgrind's conversion, Louisa's outburst, Sissy rout-
      ing Harthouse--to be fairy-tale or simply not credible.

629. Miyoshi, Masao. **The Divided Self.** New York: New York Univ.
      Press; London: Univ. of London Press, 1969, pp. 268, 270.

      The "double plot" of **Hard Times,** the Gradgrind and Ra-
      chael/Stephen stories that rarely come in contact, is seen as an
      instance of the structural features that exhibit the divided self
      of Dickens's imagination. Miyoshi compares Steerforth and
      Harthouse as Gothic villains accomplished in the science of
      deportment.

630. Moers, Ellen. "Dickens." **The Dandy: Brummel to Beerbohm**
      New York: Viking, 1960, pp. 215-50.

      Includes Harthouse among the "grey men" of Dickens's lat-
      er novels, figures who fill Dickens first with aversion but last
      with "a guilty sympathy" and who include Carstone, Skimpole,
      Gowan, Carton, Pip, Wrayburn, and Lightwood. They represent
      for Moers attitudes "above, beyond, and inimical to those of the
      middle class." Harthouse, she states, adds to the qualities he
      shares with Carstone and Skimpole "a thoroughgoing dandyism
      of dress and manner." He is heartless, a devil, a bad influence
      on Tom, and a near-seducer--but Dickens is "relatively lenient"
      with him because Harthouse "despises the new bourgeoisie as
      much as Dickens" does and so is "on his author's side." The
      final presentation of him adds to the pathos already established
      "a lyrical quality reflecting Dickens's guarded sympathy."

631.  Monod, Sylvere. "Deux diversions: roman social et roman his-
      torique." **Dickens romancier: Etude sur la creation litteraire
      dans les romans de Charles Dickens**. Paris: Hachette, 1953,
      pp. 412–41. Trans. and rev. as "Two Interludes: Social and His-
      torical Novels." **Dickens the Novelist**. Norman: Univ. of Okla-
      homa Press, 1968, pp. 440–71. Section on **Hard Times** rpt. as
      "Dickens as Social Novelist" in Gray (429).

      Considers **Hard Times** and **A Tale of Two Cities** undicken-
      sian novels by virtue of their weekly format, length, and Carly-
      lean influence. Monod notes how the mems for **Hard Times**
      show Dickens still to be thinking in terms of the monthly num-
      ber. For Monod **Hard Times** has two theses: divorce, and the
      oppression of the poor, the latter obscured and confused by
      Dickens's desire to attack the political economists. The social
      thought is not coherent and lacks a constructive side, he
      states, but the sentiment is strong. Monod also faults the por-
      trait of Slackbridge, and the presentation of Stephen and Ra-
      chael for its solemnity and pathos. This novel is lacking in hu-
      mor, he adds; stylistically, it shows an intensification of
      Dickens's use of repetition and alliteration and a loss of verve
      in description.

632.  ———————. "**Hard Times**, an Undickensian Novel?" In **Studies in
      the Later Dickens**. Ed. Jean-Claude Amalric. Montpellier: Univ.
      Paul Valery, 1973, pp. 71–92.

      Reviews the critical history of **Hard Times**, from the early
      favorable public reception and unfavorable critical reception
      through the growing hostility or neglect until Leavis's revolu-
      tionary essay (553), and sets his own writing on the novel in
      this context. Monod finds **Hard Times** still undickensian in re-
      gard to its weekly format, brevity, focus on the social theme,
      and relative diminution of humor, but also characteristic in its
      humor, psychological acumen, pathos, and mastery of its medi-
      um. He suggests that the long failure of the novel to gain rec-
      ognition was caused by its high degree of stylization and the
      weakness of its philosophy. The description of social evil he
      finds "on the whole wonderfully accurate" but the suggested
      remedies "on the whole  deplorably vague and inadequate."
      Nonetheless, he concludes, the book is a landmark in the evo-
      lution of Dickens's stylistic artistry.

633.  ———————. "1900–1920. The Age of Chesterton." **Dickensian**, 66
      (1970), 101–20.

Cites Shaw's introduction to **Hard Times** (738), offering some lively disagreement and also some endorsement.

634.    ———————. "Preface." **Les Temps difficiles**. Trans. Jacques Papy. Paris: Le club francais du livre, 1960. [Pages not numbered.]

Reviews the circumstances of publication, discusses the weakness in social argument and the want of humor in the portrayal of Stephen and Rachael, and concludes that the novel nonetheless displays the particularly Dickensian qualities that grace all his work.

\*        ———————.

See Dickens Fellowship (340).

\*        ———————.

See George Ford and Sylvere Monod (392).

635.    Montague, Charles W. **Recollections of an Equestrian Manager**. London and Edinburgh: W. & R. Chambers, 1881, pp. 90–91.

States that the original of Sleary was "old Jack Clarke, a notability in his way as a circus proprietor," asthmatic and with almost a lisp like Sleary's.

636.    Moses, Belle. **Charles Dickens and His Girl Heroines**. New York and London: Appleton, 1911, pp. 260–61.

Sees **Hard Times** as grave, serious, tragic, short, powerful enough to be a masterpiece. Moses compares Louisa and Sissy, who represent a contrast between fact and emotion. Neither jingles housekeeping keys, as Esther does in **Bleak House**, though Sissy does become the capable housekeeper of the Gradgrind establishment.

637.    Muller, Charles H. "Dickens's 'Hard Times': The Gradgrind Educational System, Coketown, and the Circus." **Crux**, 9 (1975), 45–48, 52.

Describes what Muller sees as the three main themes of the novel: Gradgrind's educational system, the hard-fact philosophy (which emerges as Coketown), and the circus.

638.    Murry, John Middleton. **Pencillings**. New York: Thomas Seltzer, 1925, p. 39.

Finds **Hard Times** the only work of Dickens that we might wish to reject.

639.    Nadel, Ira Bruce. "'The Mansion of Bliss,' or the Place of Play in Victorian Life and Literature." **Children's Literature**, 10 (1982), 18-36.

Surveys the changing attitude toward play in Victorian life and literature. For Nadel **Hard Times** presents "most forcefully" the "reaction against the rule-making and rationalist appropriation of play" in "an insistence on the value of imagination and creativity." Sleary's "People mutht be amuthed" is, he states, "a view the Victorians gradually, if grudgingly, accepted."

640.    Naslund, Sena Jeter. "Mr. Sleary's Lisp: A Note on **Hard Times**." **DSN**, 12 (1981), 42-46.

Argues that Sleary's lisp and his wandering eye are "emblematic of his spiritual achievement," which is to combine head and heart, a feat no other character in **Hard Times** can match. To read the lisp we must "act" Sleary--we must, momentarily, be him, join him imaginatively. Naslund also notes several puns afforded by the lisp and expatiates on Sleary's role at the center of the "ring of fancy." Compare Goldknopf (426) and Page (659).

641.    Nelson, Harland S. **Charles Dickens**. Boston: Twayne, 1981, passim.

**Hard Times** is mentioned frequently, but is not subject to extended discussion. Nelson notes in particular Coketown's exhibition of straight lines (as opposed to the curves of nature) and the opposition between system and imagination with Sissy as the center.

642.    --------. "Staggs's Gardens: The Railway through Dickens' World." **DSA**, 3 (1974), 41-53.

Coketown presents the most direct challenge to the pleni-tude and variety Dickens values increasingly. Thus Nelson compares Stone Lodge with Staggs's Gardens: Coketown's op-pressive triumph of calculating industry is the destination of the social transformation being wrought by the railroad in **Dombey and Son**. Nelson also compares Sissy and Paul at length. He contrasts the city in Dickens's early work with the city in this later work, a sad monotony of roaring streets from which people seek the shelter of private happiness.

643.    Newman, S.J. **Dickens at Play**. New York: St. Martin's, 1981, pp. 2, 56-7, 73.

This book traces the development of Dickens's imagination from **Sketches by Boz** to **Martin Chuzzlewit**, to "set against Coleridgean, Arnoldian, Jamesian and Leavisite principles ... the value of an art which is discrete, creative, irresponsible and young." Newman finds that in her staircase metaphor Mrs. Sparsit "is embodying Dickens's cruel pleasure in his melodra-matic imagination--a pleasure that notably conflicts with the ostensible purpose of extolling life-enhancing creativity over death-dealing materialism."

644.    Oddie, William. "**Hard Times**." **Dickens and Carlyle: The Question of Influence**. London: Centenary, 1972, pp. 41-60 and passim.

Argues that **Hard Times** may be less Carlylean than Dick-ens thought it was but that it is still Dickens's most Carlylean work. Oddie finds the influence "formative and not merely ac-cidental" and having to do with "the profundity of vision, and the 'insistence' ... that informs the whole novel." He asserts the influence of Teufelsdrockh's education on the theme of educa-tion in **Hard Times** and points out that Harthouse, Bounderby, and Gradgrind constitute a Carlylean demonology of Dilettante, Mammonism, and Logic-Chopper rationalism. Stephen's desire to be free of his wife reflects Dickens's. Compare Barnes (187), Christian (269), and Goldberg (421). Reviews: K.J. Fielding, **Dickensian**, 69 (1973), 111-18; Michael Slater, **VS**, 17 (1975), 328-30; G.B. Tennyson, **DSN**, 5 (1974), 24-28.

645.  O'Faolain, Sean. "Dickens and Thackeray." In **The English Novelists: A Survey of the Novel by Twenty Contemporary Novelists.** Ed. Derek Verschoyle. New York: Harcourt, Brace, 1936, pp. 148–59. Rpt. Folcroft, Pa.: Folcroft, 1970.

Praises Dickens when he was free in his wildly romantic imagination, but condemns the conventional thought and morality of the serious efforts. As the novelist of bourgeois thought, O'Faolain states, Dickens "became the creature of his times––**Hard Times.**"

646.  O'Flinn, Paul. "Hands, Knees and a Book by Dickens." **Them and Us in Literature.** London: Pluto, 1975, pp. 60–66.

Sees **Hard Times** as an instance of literature recording the efforts of employers to produce Wombles ("tame, hard working and only half human" beings). Stephen is one of the first anti-heroes: "a brief, shabby, confused life and a violent, accidental death, a man robbed of his birthright but unable to name the thief." O'Flinn then moves to the subject of this essay (which is sub-titled "or, Remember You're a Womble"), a light and witty Marxist analysis that sees us today as mouths (consumers), just as Stephen was a hand; so long as there is no whole being, O'Flinn concludes, the world is safe for the capitalist.

647.  Olsen, Stein Haugom. "Literature and Truth." **The Structure of Literary Understanding.** Cambridge: Cambridge Univ. Press, 1978, pp. 46–81.

In the context of an examination of the view that literature provides a special type of truth, examines the truth-claims made by criticism and instances Leavis on **Hard Times** (553). Olsen distinguishes here between truth claimed about the work and truth claimed about the world as well, showing that the first may be argued but the second is merely offered.

648.  O'Mealy, Joseph Howard. "Charles Dickens' Sense of His Past." **DAI**, 36 (1976), 6118A (Stanford Univ., 1975). 278 pp.

Asserts that **Hard Times** is one of the novels after **David Copperfield** that show Dickens's more pessimistic understanding of the past and of the need to connect the past and present.

649.    Organ, Dennis.   "Compression and Explosion: Pattern in **Hard Times**."   **RE: Artes Liberales**, 8 (1981), 29–37.   Also, earlier abstract in **South Central Bulletin**, 36 (1976), 94.

Notes the images of compression and explosion that contribute to the unity of the novel and express the violence of repressed emotion and imagination.   Organ states that Dickens may have been wise not to have answered the social questions posed by the novel, since they are difficult and enduring.

650    Orwell, George.   "Charles Dickens."   **Inside the Whale**.   London: Gollancz, 1940.   Rpt. in **Dickens, Dali, and Others** in **Studies in Popular Culture**.   New York: Reynal & Hitchcock, 1946; rpt. New York: Harcourt Brace Jovanovich, 1970.   Rpt. in **Collected Essays, Journalism and Letters**.   Ed. Sonia Orwell and Ian Angus.   4 vols.   New York: Harcourt, Brace & World, 1968, I, 413–60.   A section on **Hard Times** rpt. in Gray (429).

Criticizes Dickens's criticism of society as exclusively moral and insists that there is nothing socialistic about it, that in fact its tendency "is to be pro-capitalist, because the whole moral is that capitalists ought to be kind, not that workers ought to be rebellious."   If Bounderby and Gradgrind were better men, Orwell points out, the system would work well enough.   This view implies the "Good Rich Man," he states, though in the novels of the fifties he has either disappeared or "dwindled ... to a **rentier**" as Dickens seems to have grasped "the helplessness of well-meaning individuals in a corrupt society."

651.    –––––––.   "A Hundred Up."   **The Observer**, 13 Feburary 1944.   Rpt. in **Collected Essays, Journalism and Letters**.   Ed. Sonia Orwell and Ian Angus.   4 vols.   New York: Harcourt, Brace & World, 1968, III, 93–95.

On **Martin Chuzzlewit**, concludes that "in spite of its frequent flashes of genius, it is difficult to feel that by following up this vein in himself Dickens could have given us anything to compensate for the loss of **Hard Times** and **Great Expectations**."

652.    Osborne, Esther Euraleen.   "Charles Dickens and the Middle Classes."   **DAI**, 31 (1970), 6563A–64A (Howard Univ., 1970).   81 pp.

Sees Dickens as developing from attacks on specific abuses to broader social observation. Thus, for Osborne, **Hard Times** continues to trace the anatomy of Dickens's social milieu under changing conditions, showing his increasing observation of the life of the Victorian middle class.

653.   Ousby, Ian. "Figurative Language in **Hard Times**." **Durham Univ. Journal**, 74, n.s. 43 (1981), 103–09.

Argues that figurative language used properly, by the narrator, illuminates reality through the exercise of fantasy, but used improperly, by Bounderby and other believers in fact, is deformed and debased. The language of the novel mocks and discredits the Utilitarians' philosophy of life, Ousby states. He analyses the effect of a large number of the novel's images, proper and improper.

654.   Packe, M. St. John. **The Life of John Stuart Mill**. London: Secker & Warburg, 1954, pp. 310–11.

Remarks on Dickens's mauling of Mill's **Principles of Political Economy** in **Hard Times**.

655.   Page, John T. "Charles Dickens: Collected Annotations on His Life and Writings." **East London Advertiser and Tower Hamlets Independent**, 12 March 1910. (This article is collected in the B.W. Matz scrapbook collection at the Dickens House, London; there are no page numbers.)

Quotes the "well reasoned" review in the **Athenaeum** (113), Dickens's letter to Charles Knight (144), and Ruskin on **Hard Times** (150).

656.   Page, Norman. "Dickensian Elements in **Victory**." **Conradiana**, 5,i (1973), 37–42.

Suggests the influence of **Hard Times** on Conrad's **Victory**--in Heyst and "Hard Facts" and in the mental feebleness of Mrs. Schomberg and of Mrs. Gradgrind. Conrad's major debt to Dickens in this novel, however, is to **Dombey and Son**, Page asserts.

657.    -------. "Forms of Address in Dickens." **Dickensian**, 67
        (1971), 16-20.

        Argues that Sissy offers a series of examples of the way
        linguistic behavior relates to social position.  Louisa is "Miss
        Louisa" to her, Page asserts, but she is "Sissy" to Louisa.  She
        is "my girl" to the belligerent Bounderby but "Jupe" to the
        gentler Gradgrind.  To Sleary she is "Thethelia," an address at
        once comical and courteous.

658.    -------. "'Ruth' and 'Hard Times': A Dickens Source." **N&Q**,
        216 (1971), 413.

        Finds the influence of Elizabeth Gaskell's **Ruth** in the simi-
        larities of Gradgrind to Bradshaw and in the dialect speech of
        Sally, and remarks the influence of the Rev. William Gaskell's
        **Lectures of the Lancashire Dialect**, published in 1854.  See
        Easson (359) for a reply to the latter assertion.

659.    -------. **Speech in the English Novel**. London: Longman,
        1973, passim.

        Examines **Hard Times** for its use of dialect and other lin-
        guistic markers.  Page points out that Sleary's marked lisp an-
        noys us because it slows us down and forces us to listen to
        Sleary even when we are reading silently.  It could have been
        indicated with less interference as "he lisped." (Compare Nas-
        lund [640].)  Stephen's dialect indicates both integrity and
        class, Page asserts.  He demonstrates the degree to which
        Dickens varies the extent of dialect indications both within any
        given speech and from one scene to another, depending upon
        dramatic purpose.  As with other character markers, he points
        out, there is often more dialect at the beginning of a chapter
        than later.  The manuscripts and proofs show Dickens's uncer-
        tainty with the dialect; Page contrasts Mrs. Gaskell's greater fa-
        miliarity.  He notes Dickens's request to Mark Lemon for circus
        language as a way in which an author can deal with his own
        lack of information.  Reviews: R. Coppieters, **ES**, 55 (1974),
        580-82; D. Hewitt, **RES**, 26 (1973), 249-50.

660.    Palmer, William J. "**Hard Times**: A Dickens Fable of Personal
        Salvation." **Dalhousie Review**, 52 (1972), 67-77.

Follows motifs of shipwreck, play of light, dark cavern and yawning abyss, inner light (of salvation), and fire to show that the images define the action, theme, and world of the novel, creating "the most satisfying" of Dickens's "fables of personal salvation." The novel is "Dickens's most powerful and realistic statement that man by redeeming himself can redeem the whole ugly world that he has selfishly built." Thus Gradgrind's conversion "gives expression to that single moral truth that social salvation depends upon the ability of individual men to redeem themselves."

661.    Panitz, Esther. "Fagin and Philistinism." **The Alien in Their Midst: Images of Jews in English Literature.** Rutherford, N.J.: Fairleigh Dickinson Univ. Press; London and Toronto: Associated Univ. Presses, 1981, pp. 103-26.

Sees Bounderby's marriage as an "unholy alliance between money-bound capitalism and the utilitarian philosophy," cementing Bounderby and Gradgrind but shattered by Harthouse, who has "a bit of the Jew about him," according to Panitz. Thus Dickens aligns "the aristocratic or upper middle class ... with those who are deep in fraudulent financial activities, presumably indulged in by Jews, together with like-minded, vulgar Bounderbys and myopic Gradgrinds." Panitz suggests that Harthouse is a caricature of Disraeli, with a touch of Tancred in his travels to Jerusalem.

662.    Parnell, Nancy Stewart. "Schools in the Novels of Charles Dickens." **Dickensian,** 25 (1929), 108-10.

Traces the "cry" of children in Dickens's novels. Parnell finds Gradgrind's perhaps the most interesting day-school in Dickens and stresses its relevance for the present day.

663.    Parrott, Thomas Marc, and Robert Bernard Martin. "Dickens." **A Companion to Victorian Literature.** New York: Scribner's, 1955, pp. 178-85. Rpt. Clifton, N.J.: Kelley, 1974.

Describes **Hard Times** as an earnest attack on the vulgarity and materialism of the rising middle class and Bounderby as a caricature in Dickens's liveliest style.

664.    Patten, Robert L. **Charles Dickens and His Publishers.** Oxford: Clarendon, 1978, passim.

Reviews with care the circumstances of publication of **Hard Times** in relation to the sales of **Household Words**, the sales of the volume edition in 1854 (5,616 copies) and their profitability, and the sales thereafter. Patten notes that in June 1855 back numbers of **Bleak House, David Copperfield, Dombey and Son**, and even **A Child's History of England**, outsold the volume edition. He tabulates the sales and profits of **Hard Times** from 1854 to 1866 and reprints the table from Ford (388) of sales in the U.S. for 1968. He also offers accounts of Dickens's transactions with Hachette and Tauchnitz. Reviews: Philip Collins, **NCF**, 34 (1980), 444–48; Angus Easson, **Dickensian**, 76 (1980), 165–66; Donald Gray, **VS**, 23 (1980), 416–18; Sylvere Monod, **EA**, 33 (1980), 223–24; Harvey P. Sucksmith, **JEGP**, 79 (1980), 136–39; James Sutherland, **BBN**, April 1979, p. 356, Deborah Thomas, **SNNTS**, 14 (1982), 126–28.

665. Payne, Clyde Ladell, Jr. "Dickens and Mammon: Character Corruption in the Novels." **DA**, 27 (1966) 2134A (Stanford Univ., 1966). 304 pp.

States that in the later novels money and change in character become increasingly related. Payne traces the theme of the sympathetic character who is corrupted by money and property, which is clearly present in **Bleak House, Hard Times**, and **Little Dorrit**.

666. Peacock, W.F. "Charles Dickens's Nomenclature." **Belgravia**, 20 (1873), 267–76.

Bounderby's is a name with vowels which are "capacious mouthfuls, significant of personal arrogance, mental obtuseness, ultra pomposity." "Slackbridge" comes from the Lancashire dialect use of "jaw" or "slack" for excessive loquacity and the "bridge" from Coketown to "the high ground of success." "Gradgrind" is among the names made up of "Gr" plus a hard or hissing consonant to denote cruelty, greed, or a half-savage state. Merrylegs's name is indicative of his calling, and M'Choakumchild's is associated with his. "Blackpool" identifies a location, which is "a disused pit near Walton-le-Dale" (Coketown is Preston).

667. Pearson, Ann Bowling. "Setting in the Works of Charles Dickens." **DAI**, 32 (1971), 3323A–24A (Auburn Univ., 1971). 236 pp.

Examines Dickens's use of setting to create atmosphere, foreshadow events, reveal character, and attack a multiplicity of social injustices, particularly in the "dark novels" of his maturity.

668.    Pearson, Hesketh. **Charles Dickens: His Character, Comedy and Career.** New York: Harper, 1949, pp. 93, 203–05, 285.

Counters Macaulay's remark (145) with the assertion that Dickens was instead "individualistic, humanistic, anti-bureaucratic, anti-socialistic." His main thrust in **Hard Times** was against the bureaucratic mentality that substituted scientific accuracy for imaginative reality, Pearson states. He points to the current tendencies in education and social life that have solidified what Dickens saw. He also suggests that the inhibited space that confined this novel dispelled the special Dickensian essence.

669.    Pechey, R.F. "Dickensian Nomenclature." **Dickensian,** 52 (1956), 180–82.

Points out Dickens's extensive use of the Bible for Christian names (Rachael, Josiah, Thomas, Stephen). Among the characters whose names are "delightfully incongruous" with their prototypes is Bounderby (the pious King Josiah). Pechey finds a happy congruity in Rachael and in Stephen.

670.    Pendered, Mary L. "Dickens the Rebel." **Dickensian,** 9 (1933), 101–09.

Looks at Dickens's concern with social ills, especially those which are still not completely redressed. **Hard Times**, while not one of his best novels, abounds in instances of his mordant satire, Pendered points out. She links it to the theme of retributive justice in **A Tale of Two Cities** and to **The Chimes**.

671.    Perkins, Donald. **Charles Dickens: A New Perspective.** Edinburgh: Floris, 1982, passim.

Finds the real religious sense of Dickens to be a vision of the human soul "in its search for freedom, security and identity." For Perkins, **Hard Times** is a novel of middle age, facing the materialistic tendency to value life quantitatively. Gradgind's "school of facts" is not quite like any school but shows "the general conception of education in the Dickens age; as it is, indeed, today."

672. Petersen, Barry Thorvald. "No Shadow of Another Parting: Dickens' Concept of the Family." **DAI**, 41 (1980), 264A-65A (Indiana Univ., 1980). 377 pp.

Examines the centrality of the concept of the family as an ethical philosophy in a number of Dickens's works, including **Hard Times**. Petersen relates that centrality to Dickens's childhood experience.

673. Petlewski, Paul John. "Order to Disorder: A Study of Four Novels by Charles Dickens." **DAI**, 34 (1974), 7201A (Univ. of Florida, 1973). 168 pp.

Examines the shift from Dickens's sense of the universe as providential and harmonious to his predominantly modern conception of the world. Petlewski asserts that the worlds of **Hard Times, A Tale of Two Cities**, and **The Mystery of Edwin Drood** exhibit an increasing entropy. He finds that **Hard Times** shows a world in which "a genuine but latent disorder is barely contained by the imposition of a mechanical order." Petlewski also looks at the ways in which Dickens's characters attempt to adjust to their worlds.

* Pierce, David.

See Mary Eagleton and David Pierce (357).

674. Pinion, F.B. **A Bronte Companion**. London: Macmillan, 1975, p. 128.

Compares Bronte's treatment of capital-labor relations in **Shirley** with Dickens's in **Hard Times**, remarking that Bronte speaks reasonably from the workers' point of view through William Farren as Dickens did through Stephen Blackpool.

675. -------. **A D.H. Lawrence Companion**. London: Macmillan, 1978; New York: Barnes & Noble, 1979, p. 162.

Suspects the influence of **Hard Times** in Ursula's experience in a Board of Education school in **The Rainbow**.

676.   Pocock, D.C.D. **The Novelist and the North**. Univ. of Durham,
       Dept. of Geography, Occasional Pubs., n.s. 12. Durham: Univ. of
       Durham, Dept. of Geography, 1978, p. 32.

       Argues that literature can be a vital source for the geogra-
       pher studying the "man-environment relationship" and mentions
       **Hard Times** in regard to the chimneys and smoke of Coketown.

677.   Pollard, Arthur. **Mrs. Gaskell: Novelist and Biographer**. Man-
       chester: Manchester Univ. Press, 1965, pp. 35, 62, 99.

       Suggests that **Mary Barton** may have had some part in
       Dickens's decision to write **Hard Times**, a similar work, and that
       Bradshaw, in **Ruth**, represents Mrs. Gaskell's nearest approach
       to a character like Gradgrind.

678.   –––––––. "'Sooty Manchester' and the Social-Reform Novel
       1845-55: An Examination of **Sybil**, **Mary Barton**, **North and
       South**, and **Hard Times**." **British Journal of Industrial Medi-
       cine**, 18 (1961), 85-92.

       Compares the four novels on various matters: trade unions,
       the portrayal of the masters, local description, etc. Pollard ar-
       gues that they all issue from an intense sympathy with the
       suffering of mankind and a strong desire to ameliorate the hu-
       man condition.   On the other hand, Pollard notes Dickens's
       phrase, "inhabited by people equally like one another" in the
       description of Coketown, as an indicator of Dickens's distance
       from his subject.   With Leavis's explanation that the novel is a
       fable (553), he turns to Dickens's methods.   "The evil thing that
       separates, the baffling isolation of man from his fellow men, is
       what all these novels attack," Pollard concludes.   Compare
       Keating (515).

679.   Pook, John. "Allegory and Thematic Imagery in **Dombey and
       Son** and **Hard Times**." **Anglo-Welsh Review**, 20 (1971),
       101-08.

       Argues that both novels use allegory as a structural device.
       Pook states that **Hard Times**, though less complex than **Dom-**

**bey and Son**, is yet not purely allegorical and is enlivened by psychological depth. But he finds that both novels are poor in their presentation of the relations between the individual and society and of "ordinary people" who are not partly archetypes. He also points out that Dickens is inconsistent on the trade unions.

680. Pope, Norris. **Dickens and Charity**. New York: Columbia Univ. Press, 1978, passim.

Remarks on **Hard Times** principally in relation to the Sunday question, noting Ookotown's eighteen chapels and the chaos that ensues when the emotional instincts are starved and the lower orders treated as an abstraction. Reviews: Asa Briggs, **Encounter**, 53 (1979), 70-77; Edgar Johnson, **NYRB**, 22 March 1979, p. 24; A.S. Watts, **Dickensian**, 75 (1979), 111-13; Judith Wilt, **Criticism**, 21 (1979), 273-76.

681. Pope-Hennessy, Una. **Charles Dickens, 1812-70**. London: Chatto & Windus, 1945, pp. 142, 340, 345-49. Rpt. Harmondsworth: Pelican, 1970.

Notes the influence on Dickens's social theory of both Carlyle and Henry Layard; remarks Dickens's annoyance at Peter Cunningham for having led the public to see **Hard Times** as dealing specifically with Preston (131), which Dickens had found dull; and describes Dickens's worrying away at the novel and at England's social problems.

682. Pothet, Lucien. **Mythe et tradition populaire dans l'imaginaire dickensien**. Paris: Lettres Modernes, 1979, passim.

**Hard Times** enters at a variety of points in this study arranged by archetypal patterns and relations. For example, Pothet connects Sleary's association with horses, and his opposition to the commercial vanguard represented in Bounderby and Gradgrind and associated with the railway, to Dickens's nostalgia for coaching and the larger matter of nostalgia for a grander past. Gradgrind is associated also with earth and stone, and so opposed to Sissy's light and sun; these images indicate that the conflict is cosmic, between earth and sky, its proper terms. As an instance of how the symbolism of natural phenomena is more evident when something is unrealistic, Pothet points out that Stephen could not have watched any

star except the North Star for two nights--but the star of hope
and redemption, like the star of Christmas, is not subject to ordinary laws. Pothet includes the rainstorm in which Mrs. Sparsit pursues Louisa in his exposition of the association of rain
with illicit sexuality, and Merrylegs and Sleary's dog and horse
in the tradition of animals that help heroes. Harthouse is a
devil in pleasing shape, Coketown an instance of the city as
hell. Sleary's fixed eye is related to the myth of the Cyclops
and the all-seeing, as Sleary is a sort of sage. Bitzer's light,
cold eye is an antitype to the eye of fire; divine intervention is
suggested by the role of animals in foiling him. The oedipal
conflict of the Gradgrind family is marked as Mrs. Gradgrind
disappears and at the end Mr. Gradgrind and Louisa are aligned
against Tom.

683.    Pratt, Branwen Elizabeth Bailey. "Dickens and Love: The Other
        as the Self in the Works of Charles Dickens." **DAI**, 33 (1973),
        4430A (Stanford Univ., 1972). 278 pp.

        Compares the earlier with the later works of Dickens, argu-
        ing a progressive change in Dickens's attitudes toward the im-
        portance of spiritual as opposed to material good.

684.    Preston, Edward A. "The Theme of Escape in the Novels of
        Charles Dickens." **DAI**, 41 (1980), 1616A (Univ. of N. Carolina at
        Chapel Hill, 1980). 287 pp.

        Studies Dickens's growth as a novelist in terms of the
        theme of escape, from **Pickwick Papers** to **Our Mutual Friend**.

685.    Priestley, J.B. **Charles Dickens: A Pictorial Biography**. Lon-
        don: Thames & Hudson, 1961, pp. 84-86. Also pub. as **Charles
        Dickens and His World**. New York: Viking, 1969. Rpt. New
        York: Scribner's; London: Thames & Hudson, 1978.

        Suggests Henry Layard's influence on Dickens's social
        thought and Dickens's lack of enthusiasm in writing **Hard
        Times**. Priestley states that the novel has never been liked ex-
        cept by the ideologically like-minded (like Shaw) and finds it
        unconvincing and unattractive, lacking Dickens's customary
        pungency as a social critic.

686.    -------. **Victoria's Heyday**. London: Heinemann, 1972, pp.
        167-68.

Against the opinion of "one Cambridge pundit" (see Leavis [553]), states that **Hard Times** is the novel of Dickens the least worth reading. It is propaganda, a failure as fiction. Priestley offers the strain of ungestated and weekly publication as the cause, combined with Dickens's ignorance of industrial England.

687. Procter, William C. **Christian Teaching in the Novels of Charles Dickens.** London: H.R. Allenson, 1930, passim.

Lists four explicit, specimen references to the bible in **Hard Times**, without comment.

688. Pugh, Edwin. "**Hard Times.**" **Charles Dickens, The Apostle of the People.** London: New Age, 1908, pp. 191-207. Rpt. New York: Haskell, 1971; New York: AMS, 1975.

Argues that Dickens would have been a socialist had he lived "today," and that he was one without knowing it--though he was also middle-class. Pugh finds **Hard Times** austere and lacking in Dickens's special combination of humor and pathos, with Stephen a failure and the characterization of Slackbridge unfair, but defends Bounderby against Ruskin (150) and calls the book his second favorite because it exposes important truths. For a reply, see Kent (524).

689. Quiller-Couch, Sir Arthur. **Charles Dickens and Other Victorians.** Cambridge: Cambridge Univ. Press, 1925, pp. 211-12.

Although **Hard Times** is not discussed in any of the four essays on Dickens in this volume, it is mentioned in the essay on Mrs. Gaskell as having possibly been influenced by **Ruth.**

690. Quirk, Eugene Francis. "Dickens' Men of Law: Dickens' Changing Vision of English Legal Practice." **DAI**, 34 (1973), 738A (Univ. of Illinois, Champaign-Urbana, 1972). 220 pp.

**Hard Times** and **Little Dorrit** "present Dickens' impression of a rapacious social system enriching the few at the cost of the many. Quirk adds that the law "plays a limited role here, but it always serves the ends of established wealth and power."

691.    Quirk, Randolph D.    **Charles Dickens and Appropriate Lan-**
        **guage**.  Durham: Univ. of Durham Press, 1959, pp. 17, 20, 23.
        Rpt. Folcroft, Pa.: Folcroft, 1974; Norwood, Pa.: Norwood, 1976;
        Philadelphia: R. West, 1977.

        Argues that the language of calculation and materialism is
        seen not only in the characters who are criticized but in those
        who enjoy the author's sanction.    It is also used in Dickens's
        first number plan.  Sleary and Mrs. Gradgrind emerge "solely as
        a particular kind of linguistic behavior."    The use of phonetic
        spelling to mark dialect, Quirk states, is exceptionally pro-
        nounced in Stephen's speech.

692.    –––––––.  "Charles Dickens, Linguist."    **The Linguist and the**
        **English Language**.  London: Edwin Arnold; New York: St. Mar-
        tin's, 1974, pp. 1–36.

        Examines Dickens's language for individualization, for typi-
        fication, structurally, and experimentally.    Quirk lists the circus
        jargon in **Hard Times** as one example of typification.  He notes
        that Blackpool serves as a reminder that Dickens could use a
        complicated and markedly non–standard linguistic system not
        only for comic characters but with high seriousness.    As in
        **Dickens and Appropriate Language** (691), Quirk finds that in
        **Hard Times** the "mathematical materialism ... deeply affects
        language and imagery: even the syntax takes up calculating
        postures."

*       –––––––.

        See A.H. Smith and Randolph Quirk (748).

693.    Raleigh, John H.  "The Novel and the City: England and America
        in the Nineteenth Century."  **VS**, 11 (1968), 291–328.

        Coketown is among the eight geographical centers that
        Raleigh locates in Dickens's work.    The essay concentrates,
        however, on Dickens's London.

694.    Rance, Nicholas.    **The Historical Novel and Popular Politics in**
        **Nineteenth–Century England**.  London: Vision, 1975, p. 136.

Hard Times and Felix Holt are both novels perplexed with fear of organized labor, attacking statistics and distorting the utilitarian ethic. Rance states that the circus is like Froude's paradise of the unconditioned will.

695.  Rantavaara, Irma. **Dickens in the Light of English Criticism.** Helsinki: Annales Academiae Scientiarum Fennicae, 1944, pp. 112–13, 154–80. Rpt. Folcroft, Pa.: Folcroft, 1971; Norwood, Pa.: Norwood, 1976; Philadelphia: R. West, 1977.

Looks at the publication of the novel and the responses of Macaulay (145), Ruskin (150), and the reviewers. Rantavaara discusses the responses to the social issues and concludes that the novel has become antiquated, not in its theme but in the way that the theme is handled: instead of offering a picture of the workers' struggle, the novel becomes a "dissertation on education."

696.  Rathburn, Robert Charles. "Dickens' Periodical Essays and Their Relationships to the Novels." **DA**, 17 (1957), 2002 (Univ. of Minnesota, 1957). 635 pp.

Concerns the historical, thematic, and stylistic relationships between Dickens's periodical essays and his novels; includes the theme of education.

697.  Ray, Laura Krugman. "The Child in the Novels of Charles Dickens." **DAI**, 32 (1971), 7001A (Yale Univ., 1971). 293 pp.

Argues that in the middle period of his career, Dickens "elaborated a system of child psychology in which emotional deprivations are more significant than psychological needs; and neglected children, instead of dying like Nell, lose their childhood to become precocious adults of great moral strength."

698.  Reed, John P. **Old School Ties: The Public Schools in British Literature.** Syracuse, N.Y.: Syracuse Univ. Press, 1964, pp. 22–23.

Sets M'Choakumchild in a tradition of literary criticism of education that has Orwell and Huxley as its twentieth-century end-points. Compare Tropp (809) and West (837).

699.    Reed, John R.  **Victorian  Conventions**.  Athens: Ohio Univ.
        Press, 1975, pp. 21, 92.

        As an instance of the secularized typology that persists
        into the nineteenth century, offers the parallel between Stephen
        in **Hard Times** and the story of Jacob, Leah, and Rachael.  In a
        discussion of the commercialization of the Samaritan figure in
        Victorian literature, Reed remarks Dickens's quip in **Hard Times**
        that the Good Samaritan was a poor economist (II, 12).

700.    Richardson, Joanna M.  "Afterword."  In the Everyman edition,
        1954, 1970 (35), pp. 269-72.

        Discusses the several proposed titles and the letters con-
        cerning **Hard Times** and surveys briefly the responses of con-
        temporary critics.  Review: Anne Smith, **DSN**, 4 (1973), 115-22.

701.    Roberts, David.  "Paternalism and Rebellion in the Early Victori-
        an Novel."  **Paternalism in Early Victorian England**.  New
        Brunswick, N.J.: Rutgers Univ. Press; London: Croom Helm, 1979,
        pp. 85-101.

        Remarks that Stephen's complaint that the factory owners
        are "not drawn nigh to folks wi' kindness and patience and
        cheery ways" is one of Dickens's most paternalistic statements,
        but argues that Dickens was not a paternalist because of his
        rebellious nature.  The latter is seen everywhere in his novels,
        Roberts says; one instance is Louisa's rebellion against both
        husband and father.  For Roberts, Dickens's novels moved from
        paternalism    toward humanitarianism,  from deference   toward
        rebellion.

702.    Roberts, Thomas J.  **When Is Something Fiction**?  Carbondale
        and Edwardsville: Southern Illinois Univ. Press, 1972, p. 40.

        Lists **Hard Times**, along with **Hamlet, Tristram Shandy,
        Modern Love, Lady Chatterley's Lover**, and the Intimations Ode
        as works that "critics are willing to admit are great."

703.    Robertson, P.J.M.  **The Leavises on Fiction: An Historic Part-
        nership**.  New York: St. Martin's; London: Macmillan, 1981, pas-
        sim.

Claims that Leavis's essay on **Hard Times** (553) was a landmark in his criticism, especially in relation to the definitions of "relevant" and "significance." Robertson shows the influence of Q.D. Leavis on F.R. in relation to **Hard Times**.

704.    Robison, Rosalee Irene. "Innocence in the Novels of Charles Dickens." **DA**, 30 (1969), 4424A (Univ. of Toronto, 1969).

An examination of the importance of the conception of innocence in Dickens's novels, includes detailed analysis of all the novels except **Master Humphrey's Clock**. Robison looks to Dickens's "creation of a dichotomy between mind and heart and his insistence upon the primacy of the feelings," among other themes.

705.    Rodd, Walter B. "Stephen Blackpool's Prayer." **Dickensian**, 6 (1910), 186–87.

Notes the similarity between Stephen's dying prayer and the final stanza of a poem by Thomas Bracken, "Not Understood."

706.    Roe, Frank G. "Surnames in Dickens." **Dickensian**, 31 (1935), 83–90.

Presents a number of surnames in Dickens that were actual names. Roe notes that Dickens often humorously changes a vowel or initial consonant of a familiar form, and instances Powler (Sowler). He has not found Harthouse, but thinks Blackpool probable in Lancashire. Jupe and Bitzer appear to have been actual names, and Sleary reminds us, Roe says, that Kipling's Sleary was not the first of that name.

707.    Romanofsky, Barbara Ruth. "A Study of Child Rearing Practices in the Middle Novels of Charles Dickens." **DAI**, 38 (1978), 4853A (City Univ. of New York, 1977). 474 pp.

Notes that **Hard Times** is the only novel in which the central children are reared in a carefully planned (but spiritually crippling) system devised by their natural father. Romanofsky concludes that Dickens sees affection as the one absolute necessity for a child.

708.   Rooke, Eleanor. "Fathers and Sons in Dickens." **E&S**, series 2,
       4 (1951), 53-69.

       Dickens's unsatisfactory relationships with his own father
       and with his sons made him unable to give life to the father
       and son theme in his books, except very occasionally. In **Hard
       Times**, "as we should expect," Rooke states, "the father much
       prefers the daughter .... Dickens alters his usual pattern, in
       making Mr. Gradgrind interfere actively with the daughter's life
       and not with the son's."

709.   Rosenberg, Edgar. "The Shaw/Dickens File: 1885 to 1950. Two
       Checklists." **Shaw Review**, 20 (1977), 148-70, and 21 (1982),
       2-19. "The Shaw/Dickens File: 1914 to 1950. An Annotated
       Checklist (Concluded). Addenda: 1885 to 1919." **Shaw**, 2
       (1982), 101-45.

       A checklist of Shaw's allusions to Dickens, first in canonical
       sequence of Shaw's writings, then in canonical sequence of the
       Dickens corpus, prefaced by a discussion of Shaw and Dickens
       and of what the allusions show. **Hard Times** and Shaw's pre-
       face (738) are mentioned passim. Several of the brief allusions
       listed are not comments on the novel but infiltrations of the
       novel and its characters into Shaw's language.

710.   Rounds, Stephen R. "Naming People: Dickens's Technique in
       **Hard Times**." **DSN**, 8 (1977), 36-40.

       Argues that characters in **Hard Times** "gain and confirm
       power by possessing strong, firmly-held, well-known names.
       Second, characters can dominate others by assigning reductive
       names to them." Rounds discusses Gradgrind, Bounderby, Mrs.
       Sparsit, Hands, girl number 20, Cecilia vs. Sissy, "the whelp,"
       and various mis-namings. Weak people accept names given
       them, he states. Compare Larson (550).

711.   Routh, Harold Victor. **Money, Morals and Manners as Re-
       vealed in Modern Literature**. London: Ivor Nicholson & Wat-
       son, 1935, pp. 54-56.

       Believes that Dickens's desire for realism in **Hard Times**
       has quelled his characteristic flashes of genius. The appeal to
       the heart is weak, Routh points out, and Stephen's "muddle" is
       a failure to indicate specific abuses in an intelligible diagnosis.

But though he is unconvincingly righteous, Routh adds, Stephen epitomizes the humanitarian causes at issue.


712.    Russell, Frances Theresa. **Satire in the Victorian Novel**. New York: Macmillan, 1920, pp. 138, 198, 218.

Finds little mirth in the industrial satire of **Hard Times**.


713.    Ryan, Alan. "Mill and Dickens." **J.S. Mill**. London and Boston: Routledge & Kegan Paul, 1974, pp. 23-26.

Attacks with vehemence Leavis's contention (553) that **Hard Times** was a critique of utilitarianism and a successful one. Ryan argues that Gradgrind's education was not like James Mill's (the latter had a penchant for theory, not fact). Any subject can be appropriated for misuse, and Dickens does not show us in the novel that economics is more likely to be abused than, say, Christianity (Ryan suggests that it is not). Ryan shows a hearty dislike of this novel and its tendency "to social and political schizophrenia." Compare Alexander (160), Arneson (171), Baker (180), and Fielding (380).


714.    Sadock, Geoffrey Johnson. "Dickens and Dr. Leavis: A Critical Commentary on **Hard Times**." **DSA**, (1972), 208-16.

Attacks the "arbitrary choice and historical inaccuracy" in Leavis's inclusion of **Hard Times** in **The Great Tradition** (553). Sadock agrees with Leavis on the conflict in the novel between reason and sensibility or imagination and on Sissy as a symbol of natural virtue, but balks at raising her to an informing literary principle or the embodiment of a potent moral resurgency. He argues that the moral center of the novel is Stephen, who represents the vague religious longing that Dickens sets against the industrial spirit. Sadock elucidates the image of the circus-ring and argues that the theme of the book is "the breakdown of interpersonal communications under the strain of laissez-faire industrialism." He also refutes Gibson (412).


715.    Sadrin, Anny. "The Perversion of Desire: a Study of Irony as a Structural Element in **Hard Times**." In **Studies in the Later Dickens**. Ed. Jean-Claude Amalric. Montpellier: Univ. Paul Valery, 1973, pp. 93-110.

Analyzes various forms of "need, needful, want, missed, fancy, craving" as variations on the theme of desire that controls the book. Dickens brings out the truth that the significant opposition is not, as Gradgrind thinks, between facts and fancy, Sadrin states, but between good fancy and the "maimed or distorted remains of the not-killed robber Fancy."

716.    ------. "A Plea for Gradgrind." **Yearbook of English Studies**, 3 (1973), 196-205.

States that had Dickens been more consistent, Tom Gradgrind would have become an anarchist and the novel would have been truly seditious. Instead, it returns to the safety of traditional morality. Sadrin argues that the moral fable does "not altogether tie up with" the narrative. In the latter, Gradgrind soon disappears as Dickens finds in Bounderby, the bank, and money the true objects of his attack. In these regards, Gradgrind is blameless, Sadrin asserts, and therefore the punishment visited upon him is too harsh. She sees Gradgrind as a product of the utilitarian spirit, not its creator. Sadrin also challenges Gilmour (415) on the matter of the Birkbeck schools.

717.    ------. "La Ville dans **Hard Times**." In **La Raison et l'imaginaire**. Societe des Anglicistes de l'Enseignement Superieur, Actes du Congres de Rennes, 1970. **EA**, 45 (Paris: Didier, [?1973]), 151-62.

States that Coketown is neither Oldham nor Preston nor any real city but exists outside time and space, blasphemous in its idolization of property. It has contaminated the country, which can therefore offer no escape, Sadrin states. She sees Gradgrind as a product of Coketown, not Coketown of Gradgrind, and Bounderby as a victim of triangulated desire. Sadrin traces the images of people looking in and out of windows and argues that the denouement of the novel backs away from its revolutionary promise (Tom should have been a rebel hero).

*       ------.

See Jean Gattegno, Isabelle Jan, and Anny Sadrin (406).

718.    Saintsbury, George. "Charles Dickens." **Corrected Impres-
sions: Essays on Victorian Writers**. London: Heinemann, 1895,
pp. 117–37. Rpt. Freeport, N.Y.: Books for Libraries, 1972; Folcroft, Pa.: Folcroft, 1974.

Criticizes the absence of "a sense of limit" in **Hard Times**,
but states that he has come to think better of the novel than
he did at first.

719.    ———. "Dickens." In **Cambridge History of English Literature**. Ed. A.W. Ward and A.R. Waller. 14 vols. Cambridge:
Cambridge Univ. Press, 1916, XIII, 303–39.

Though the novel has been praised for the Sleary group
and the pathos of Stephen and Rachael and though he believes
that Louisa has more reality than any girl before Estella,
Saintsbury still ranks **Hard Times** among the lowest of Dickens's novels, finding its good things "buried in such a mass of
exaggeration and false drawing that one struggles with the
book as with a bad dream." He suggests that its popularlity
with foreign critics may have come from its unity of plot and
action and from its unfavorable portrayal of England, "rather
consistent with the continental view of us."

720.    ———. **A History of Nineteenth-Century Literature**. New
York: Macmillan, 1896, p. 150. Rpt. 1904.

Asserts that in **Bleak House, Hard Times**, and **Little Dorrit**,
the mania of purpose and the blemish of mechanical manne-
rism have increased significantly.

721.    Sampson, George. **The Concise Cambridge History of English
Literature**. Cambridge: Cambridge Univ. Press; New York:
Macmillan, 1941. 2nd ed., 1961; 3rd ed., 1970, p. 775.

This book is based on the fourteen-volume Cambridge history, and echoes Saintsbury's judgments of **Hard Times** (719).

722.    Sanders, Andrew. **The Victorian Historical Novel 1840–1880**.
London and Basingstoke: Macmillan, 1978; New York: St. Martin's, 1979, p. 87.

Dickens was ignorant of his subject in **Hard Times**, as he was in **A Tale of Two Cities**, but in both powerful images emerge as Dickens's exaggeration creates force, allowing the works to convey "a far deeper understanding of an underlying human dilemma than we might at first have supposed."

723.   Sanders, George DeWitt. **Elizabeth Gaskell**. New Haven: Yale Univ. Press, for Cornell Univ.; London: Humphrey Milford, Oxford Univ. Press, 1929, p. 25.

States that Dickens owed to Mrs. Gaskell the inspiration for **Hard Times** as she was the only novelist who had treated the problem of the two nations.

724.   Sawchuck, Mariette Timmins. "The Pilgrimage of Charles Dickens: A Study of Dickens' Evolving Vision of the Relationship between Conduct and Fate." **DAI**, 35 (1975), 7878A-79A (Stanford Univ., 1975). 410 pp.

Studies the changes in Dickens's moral vision during his creative life. In **Bleak House, Hard Times**, and **Little Dorrit**, Sawchuck states, he shows the effects of the social environment upon the fate of characters.

725.   Schachterle, Lance Edward. "Charles Dickens and the Techniques of the Serial Novel." **DAI**, 31 (1970), 5424A (Univ. of Pennsylvania, 1970). 236 pp.

Studies Dickens's use and expansion of the techniques of his predecessors in the serial novel, with some attention to the special qualities of the weekly serial.

726.   Schelly, Judith May. "A Like Unlike: Brother and Sister in the Works of Wordsworth, Byron, George Eliot, Emily Bronte, and Dickens." **DAI**, 42 (1981), 205A (Univ. of California, Berkeley, 1980). 246 pp.

**Hard Times** is among a number of works in which Victorian writers are seen to explore the impact of change on the brother and sister relationship as the siblings mature.

727.   Schilling, Bernard N. **Human Dignity and the Great Victorians**. New York: Columbia Univ. Press, 1946, p. 230.

Recommends **Hard Times** for its humanitarian impulses and as Dickens's only attempt to deal directly with the problems of the factory-worker.

728.  Scholes, Robert, and Robert Kellogg. **The Nature of Narrative**. New York: Oxford Univ. Press, 1966, p. 113.

Offers **Hard Times** as one example of the tendency of satire to shift toward mimesis.

729.  Schramm, David Eugene. "Theme and Action in the Novels of Charles Dickens: A Developmental Study." **DAI**, 32 (1971), 2103A (Washington Univ., 1971). 221 pp.

Challenges the belief that action is the weakest element in Dickens's novels through a study of action, in the broadest sense, across the canon, demonstrating increasing complexity of social and psychological insight. The treatment includes **Hard Times**.

730.  Schwarzbach, F.S. "**Hard Times**: The Industrial City." **Dickens and the City**. London: Athlone, 1979, pp. 143-50.

Emphasizes the similarities between Coketown and the London of **Bleak House**, arguing that Coketown represents an effort by Dickens to generalize his characterization of the urban environment. Schwarzbach also compares the pattern of stunted growth imagery in the two novels. He suggests that **Hard Times** looks forward to **Little Dorrit** in its identification of people with their habitations and in the theme of the failure of the will. Reviews: Bernard Bergonzi, **Encounter**, 53 (1979), 67-72; Avrom Fleishman, **NCF**, 35 (1980), 105; Ruth Glancy, **BBN**, July 1979, pp. 606-07; Sylvere Monod, **EA**, 33 (1980), 878; Robert Patten, **Dickensian**, 76 (1980), 168-70.

731.  Scudder, Vida D. **Social Ideals in English Letters**. Boston and New York: Houghton, Mifflin, 1898. Enl. ed. 1923, pp. 126, 134, 186, 250-51.

Sees **Hard Times** as significant in containing one of the early appearances in literature of the trade unions, but poor in its understanding of them. Stephen and Rachael are weak figures, Scudder points out; Dickens did not understand that the great future rested with the productive classes. The hint of wider compassion in Louisa's encounter with Stephen is a small start beyond Dickens's usual conception of femininity, Scudder adds. What success he achieves with Stephen comes from intuition rather than knowledge.

732.    Sedgely, Anne. "**Hard Times**: Facts or Fantasy?" **Critical Review**, 6 (1973), 116–32.

Argues against Leavis (553) that **Hard Times** is hardly an analysis of industrialism or utilitarianism; that Gradgrind is inconsistently and uncertainly conceived in the early parts of the book, and not well differentiated from Bounderby, as he will be later; that the relationship between utilitarianism and capitalism is explored neither analytically nor dramatically (what Bounderby does he does mainly because he is Bounderby); and that Dickens hardly seems aware of his portrayal of Louisa as almost forcing Gradgrind to push her to the marriage, because Dickens's attention is focussed on Gradgrind. Sedgely shows the contradiction as Gradgrind accepts responsibility for Louisa's fall but not for Tom's. Stephen is a mixture of middle-class morals with working-class problems and a "heavy dullness of mind peculiar to himself." The life of the novel is in the "comic bits," when the prose is energized by imaginative release, supremely in Mrs. Sparsit's pursuit of Louisa. In fact, Sedgely concludes, the novel is about "people watching, calculating, waiting for the opportunity to reach out and overwhelm anyone who is suddenly in a position of weakness."

733.    Seehase, Georg. "Hard Times." **Charles Dickens, zu einer Besonderheit seines Realismus**. Halle (Saale): Niemeyer, 1961, pp. 92–109.

A study of the relationship between Dickens's caricature and his realism, argues that **Hard Times** is true despite caricature because caricature portrays essence and the book is true to the class confrontation between capital and proletariat. Review: George Worth, **JEGP**, 62 (1963), 405–07.

734.    Seiple, Jo Ann Massie. "Charles Dickens and the Self-Denying Woman." **DAI**, 40 (1980), 4061A (East Texas State Univ., 1979). 162 pp.

Argues against the "prevailing" view of the Dickensian heroine through a detailed analysis of Esther Summerson, Louisa Gradgrind, and Lizzie Hexam. Seiple asserts that Louisa forfeits her own identity in accepting the life offered her; her rebellion against it is Dickens's first explicit rejection of the feminine ideal.

735. ‒‒‒‒‒‒‒. "Implications of the Disguise: A Psychological Analysis of Charles Dickens's **Hard Times**." **Publications of the Arkansas Philological Association**, 4 (1978), 45-51. Abstract in **PAPA**, 4 (1977), 13.

Focusses on Louisa, whose unmarried, childless future is asserted to be not an unhappy ending, but the beginning "of her development into a whole person." Seiple does not exactly demonstrate this assertion; she traces Louisa's development in basic Freudian terminology from her childhood to the vision of her future relations with the people around her.

736. Shapiro, Charles. "Afterword." In the New American Library edition, 1961 (42), pp. 293-97.

Focusses on the continuing relevance of the fable and asserts the artistic excellence of the work. Review: Anne Smith, **DSN**, 4 (1973), 115-22.

737. Sharma, Basudeo. "Schools and Schoolmasters in Dickens." **Indian Journal of English Studies**, n.s. 1 (1980), 107-15. Rpt. as "The Little Labouring Hind: Charles Dickens (1812-70)." In **The Victorian Novel: Problems and Portraits of the Child** New Delhi: Arnold-Heinemann; Atlantic Highlands, N.J.: Humanities Press, 1982.

Includes Gradgrind's school in a list of a dozen "very conspicuous" schools in Dickens's novels, which are reviewed chronologically. Gradgrind's is "a typical Benthamite school." Mr. Gradgrind "stands for utilitarianism, Mr. Choakumchild [sic] for diabolic knowledge, Sleary ... for love, and Sissy for 'wisdom of babes and sucklings.' The fate of its pupils symbolises the futility of the utilitarian philosophy."

738.    Shaw, George Bernard. "Introduction." In the Waverley edition,
        1912 (36), pp. v–xvi. Rpt. in **Bernard Shaw's Nondramatic Lit-
        erary Criticism**. Ed. Stanley Weintraub. Lincoln, Neb.: Univ. of
        Nebraska Press, 1972; also in **The Dickens Critics**. Ed. George
        H. Ford and Lauriat Lane, Jr. Ithaca: Cornell Univ. Press, 1961;
        Westport, Conn.: Greenwood, 1972; also in **Dickens: Hard
        Times, Great Expectations, and Our Mutual Friend: A Case-
        book**. Ed. Norman Page. London: Macmillan, 1979.

        This famous essay asserts that in **Hard Times** Dickens de-
        clares "that it is not our disorder but our order that is horrible."
        The novel is less pleasurable than the earlier novels because
        the evils it depicts are real threats to us, Shaw states. Dickens
        now "casts off ... all restraint on his wild sense of humor" and
        "begins at last to exercise quite recklessly his power of pre-
        senting a character to you in the most fantastic and outra-
        geous terms, putting into its mouth ... hardly one word which
        could conceivably be uttered by any sane human being, and yet
        leaving you with an unmistakeable and exactly truthful portrait
        of a character that you know and recognize at once as not only
        real but typical." Shaw does find some failure in Sissy's lan-
        guage to Harthouse, in Slackbridge ("a figment of the middle-
        class imagination"), and in the behavior of the workmen toward
        Stephen. Dickens's anti–unionism he calls the idealized
        Toryism of Ruskin and Carlyle. As a final note, Shaw remarks
        that "in this book Dickens proclaims that marriages are not
        made in heaven, and that those which are not confirmed there,
        should be dissolved." For commentary on this introduction, see
        Monod (633).

739.    –––––––. "On Dickens." **Dickensian**, 10 (1914), 150–51.

        The editor of the manuscript newspaper of the Sheffield
        Branch of the Dickens Fellowship wrote to Shaw to ask if he
        was a Dickensian. This letter is Shaw's reply. It includes ref-
        erence to his preface to **Hard Times** and his assertion that this
        novel marks a turning-point in Dickens's development from
        satirist and reformer to prophet and from humor that was riot-
        ous and extravagant to humor that was "utterly reckless when
        he realised that humanity is so grotesque that it cannot be
        caricatured."

740.    Sheff, Pamela H. "The Allegorical Vision: A Study of Charles
        Dickens' Late Novels as Allegories." Ph.D. Dissertation. Harvard
        Univ., 1975. 187 pp.

Compares the "more compressed allegories," including **Hard Times**, to the "digressive, labyrinthine" structure of the later works; explores symbolic conflicts and motifs.

741.  Shelden, Michael Carl. "The Appointed Time: Dickens and the Free Trade Millenium." **DAI**, 40 (1980), 4062A (Indiana Univ., 1979). 199 pp.

Argues that Dickens participated much more fully than is generally recognized in the belief in a free-trade millenium. Thus **Hard Times** does not reject the ideal of progress through industrialization, Shelden points out, but rather criticizes those industrialists who were undermining the dream of the free-trade millenium by exploiting the system for selfish ends.

742.  Shelston, Alan. "Dickens." In **The Victorians**. Ed. Arthur Pollard. London: Barrie & Jenkins, 1970, pp. 74-106.

Finds **Hard Times** weak. The attack on utilitarianism is lucid and forceful, Shelston concedes, but the characterization is often unsubtle and the irony labored. The culprit is the restriction of space, he asserts, because amplitude is fundamental to Dickens's art.

*    Short, Michael H.

See Geoffrey N. Leech and Michael H. Short (555).

743.  Shusterman, David. "Peter Cunningham, Friend of Dickens." **Dickensian**, 3 (1957), 20-35.

Surveys the relationship between Dickens and Cunningham, including their contretemps when Cunningham announced in the **Illustrated London News** (131) that the story of **Hard Times** was suggested by the Preston strike. Shusterman points out that in his reply to Cunningham Dickens was deceptive, since he claimed that the title was weeks old and that several chapters of the story were written before he went to Preston, claims that Dickens's correspondence with others disproves. Shusterman refuses to speculate on the reasons for Dickens's deceptiveness. Compare Wagenknecht (817).

744.    Simpson, David. "Charles Dickens: 'Nothing But Figure.'" **Fetis-
        hism and Imagination**: Dickens, Melville, Conrad. Baltimore
        and London: Johns Hopkins Univ. Press, 1982, pp. 39–68.

        Presents Dickens as "a critic of the fetishized imagination"
        and offers **Hard Times** as an instance at various points in this
        analysis of the "fetishized representations" in Dickens's work.
        Simpson sees the world view of this novel as among Dickens's
        "most uncompromising and successfully consolidated." In
        Coketown, metaphoric activity is a threat to the fetish of "fact,"
        upon which a society is founded.

745.    Skilton, David. **The English Novel: Defoe to the Victorians.**
        London: David & Charles; New York: Barnes & Noble, 1977, pp.
        114, 125, 133–34.

        Finds **Hard Times** exceptional in the context of Dickens's
        major works and in comparison to other industrial novels of the
        time. Characterized by a lack of realistic description and con-
        crete detail, it is a fable, a brilliant satire and a sentimental vi-
        sion of the clash between utilitarian ideology and common
        warmth and humanity, Skilton asserts. Stephen is hopelessly
        obtuse and both his problems and his quietist solution render
        him atypical. The circus is worked too hard in the novel, Skil-
        ton believes, and reveals anxieties Dickens could not reconcile.

746.    Slater, Judith Fairbank. "The Development of Impressionistic
        Technique in the Novels of Dickens." **DAI**, 32 (1971), 400A–01A
        (Ohio State Univ., 1970). 270 pp.

        Analyzes in detail the uses of impressionism in the sym-
        bolic structures of the later novels. The impressionistic devel-
        opment in **Hard Times** and **A Tale of Two Cities** is one of
        counterpoint, Slater concludes.

747.    Sloane, David E.E. "Phrenology in **Hard Times**: A Source for
        Bitzer." **DSN**, 5 (1974), 9–12.

        Argues that the specific source for Bitzer is George Parker
        Bidder (1806–78), "the Calculating Boy," a parliamentary adviser
        in the fifties who in his youth gave public demonstrations of
        his talent for arithmetic and who figures largely as a subject in
        the science of phrenology.

748. Smith, A.H., and Randolph Quirk. "Some Problems of Verbal Communication." **Transactions of the Yorkshire Dialect Society**, Part 54, Vol. 9 (1955), 10-20.

In this paper on the vast differences between spoken and written usage and the consequent problems of written presentations of speech, **Hard Times** is instanced to discuss the compounded difficulties of a writer who tries to present dialect speech. Compare Gerson (410) and Langton (548).

749. Smith, Anne. "**Hard Times** and **The Times** Newspaper." **Dickensian**, 69 (1973), 153-62.

Attempts to show how Leavis's approach fails to do justice to Dickens's sense of the complexity of the social issues he treats in this novel. Smith notes Dickens's reliance on newspaper reports, especially **The Times**, and argues from these reports the appropriateness of many details in the novel that have been criticized. She points out that on a matter such as the issue of the trade union, Dickens's is a widely held position.

750. ――― ―――. "The Martyrdom of Stephen in **Hard Times**." **JNT**, 2 (1972), 159-70.

Argues that Stephen is not as perfect as the critics complain of his being, and that in fact Dickens originally intended him to be very imperfect, but allowed himself to slip into patronizing benevolence. Smith attempts to demonstrate Stephen's remaining defects through a detailed criticism: Stephen is almost as dumb as Toots; Stephen's willingness to break his marriage vow is inconsistent with his refusal to break his promise to Rachael; Stephen is too deferential to Bounderby, is too morally dependent on Rachael (in the matter of poisoning his wife), is self-pitying, is immoral for considering living with Rachael outside marriage; Stephen should set Rachael free to lead a better life. Smith speculates that Bounderby and Slackbridge at the bargaining table would be more successful than Stephen and Gradgrind.

* ―――――.

See K.J. Fielding and Anne Smith (382).

751.    Smith, David. "**Mary Barton** and **Hard Times**: Their Social In-
        sights." **Mosaic**, 5 (1972), 97-112.

        Finds Dickens freer of the dominant ideology than Gaskell.
        Dickens was blind to the unions, but a visionary in regard to
        education, Smith states. He sees **Hard Times** as a moral fable
        or allegory that offers an essential vision of a dehumanized so-
        ciety, not a realistic account. The satire is directed against or-
        ganizations that enforce conformity and treat people as mas-
        ses. The circus represents a direct challenge to the ethos of
        Coketown and enables Dickens to strike at the root of the in-
        dustrial myth. He understands, and rejects, political economy,
        Smith concludes.

752.    Smith, Frank. "Perverted Balance: Expressive Form  in **Hard
        Times**." **DSA**, 6 (1977), 102-18.

        Argues that **Hard Times** is a novel "of perverted balance.
        Within the almost perfectly balanced gross structure Dickens
        has created a complement of grotesquely balanced minor forms
        ... a world in which everything has been so carefully arranged
        in such an evil way that time must prove the balance false and
        reconstruct a true stability." Smith illustrates this thesis
        through the pattern of perverted balances between pairs of
        characters (male and female) held in balance by the "extremes
        of the characters involved": Sissy/Bitzer, Stephen/his wife,
        Gradgrind/Mrs. Gradgrind, Tom/Louisa, Mrs. Sparsit/Bounderby.
        He argues that nature restores a healthy balance through the
        agency of the circus. Compare Stewart (776).

753.    Smith, George W. "Dickens and Periodical Publication." Ph.D.
        Dissertation. Harvard Univ., 1958. 399 pp.

        Points out how the number plans show Dickens to have
        thought of **Hard Times** in terms of his twenty-part monthly
        structures and argues that the differences between this novel
        and the others is only in scale. See Butt and Tillotson (240)
        and Monod (631).

754.    Smith, Grahame. **Dickens, Money and Society**. Berkeley and
        Los Angeles: Univ. of California Press, 1968, pp. 198, 199-200.

        **Hard Times** is not examined at length in this book, but is
        offered as an example of Dickens's ability to combine the "sug-

gestive directness" of symbol with "a sensuous exactness that prevents any limiting schematization of the richness of life" (in particular, in the interview between Louisa and Mr. Gradgrind). The novel is seen as an attack on the "moral arithmeticians" who believe themselves to have probed the human personality.

755.   Smith, Sheila M.  "Blue Books and Victorian Novelists."  **RES**, series 2, 21 (1970), 23-40.

Dickens appears mainly as a foil to Kingsley and Disraeli in this discussion of their use of Blue Books.  Smith points out that Dickens characterized Gradgrind's Blue Books unfairly; they explored social problems, but did not settle them.  Dickens's reaction to statistics was emotional and imaginative, she adds.

756.   -------.  "Dickens in France."  **Dickensian**, 67 (1971), 51-52.

A response to Bony (208), arguing that the apparent conflict between fairy-tale and social realism may arise from Dickens's misconception of fairy-tales, which are full of social significance.  The relationship of Coketown to its inhabitants is allied to the grotesqueness of the story of Beauty and the Beast.  Smith does not address Bony's structural argument.

757.   -------.  **The Other Nation.  The Poor in English Novels of the 1840s and 1850s.**  Oxford: Clarendon; New York: Oxford Univ. Press, 1980, pp. 77-83 and passim.

Relates Dickens's description of industrial scenes in **Hard Times** and **The Old Curiosity Shop** to the picturesque and to the pictorial tradition stemming from the medieval Hell-mouth. Smith compares the image of Coketown in I, v, "unnatural red and black like the painted face of a savage" to the prejudice apparent in the essay "The Noble Savage" in **Household Words** (7 [1853], 337-39), here attributed to Dickens, and suggests that the similar associations in the novel distance the people of Coketown.  She finds the crudity of Dickens's reaction to the industrial towns evident in his repetition, in **The Old Curiosity Shop, Bleak House**, and **Hard Times**, of the three facts of smoke, flame, and sounding machinery.  The lack of humor surrounding Stephen makes him solemn but not serious, and implies condescension rather than understanding, she states. Bounderby, in contrast, has a powerful essence arising from the intensity of ironic description.

758.    ————. "Truth and Propaganda in the Victorian Social
        Problem Novel." **Renaissance and Modern Studies**, 8 (1964),
        75-91.

        Examines "the kind of literature which is produced by the
        novelist concerned with social problems, and ... the degree of
        success which he achieves in creating an imaginative entity
        from the observed facts which distress or horrify him." Smith
        asserts that "paradoxically, Dickens's imaginative reconstruction
        of life in Coketown is more compelling than Mrs. Gaskell's
        faithful observation of Manchester"; though his notion of unions
        is old-fashioned and of utilitarianism crude, Coketown is "an
        enduring image of a fact of [Dickens's] time." Hence Smith
        concludes that a novel "may have its own authenticity without
        being factually accurate."

759.    Smithers, David Waldron. **Dickens's Doctors**. Oxford: Perga-
        mon, 1979, pp. xiii, 7.

        Notes that Mrs. Gradgrind's "protective symptoms" (against
        her husband) are described by Dickens with "miraculous in-
        sight."

760.    Solomon, Pearl Chesler. **Dickens and Melville in Their Time**.
        New York and London: Columbia Univ. Press, 1975, pp. 96-7.

        Remarks that Bounderby is Dickens's argument that there is
        no such creature as the self-made man. According to Solo-
        mon, in Mrs. Pegler's story Dickens is emphasizing, as Samuel
        Smiles emphasized, parental influence and hard work. Solomon
        also asserts that in **Hard Times** Dickens was indicting the
        heartless dealings of the British economic system with its la-
        borers. Review: C.C. Barfoot, **ES**, 58 (1977), 542-43.

761.    Sonstroem, David. "Fettered Fancy in **Hard Times**." **PMLA**, 84
        (1969), 520-29.

        Argues in mediation between Leavis (553) and Holloway
        (471), Hirsch (467), and other dissenters that **Hard Times** is "a
        truly impressive achievement of meaningful symbolic structur-
        ing, but weak dramatically, because the personalities of certain
        characters do not support their full symbolic charge." The
        novel holds two concepts of Fancy for Sonstroem. The first,
        imaginative play, is represented exclusively in the narrator; the

second, fellow feeling, is represented in various characters. The two may stand in contradiction, as when the narrator betrays his utter want of sympathy for certain characters (Bitzer, Stephen's wife, the Whelp, Slackbridge, Mrs. Sparsit, Bounderby, Mrs. Gradgrind until her death), or when the virtuous characters such as Sissy are utterly devoid of imaginative play. Imagination is also conceived as a buffer for the innocent against reality, a notion that shows Dickens at cross-purposes, caught between the idea of the heart going out to others and the idea of insulated, self-protecting innocence. Sonstroem examines in detail the images of bridges between fact and fancy that Dickens offers. But Dickens fails, he concludes, "because the forces of Fancy are so confused, there is no clear, attractive alternative to the Facts of Gradgrindism." On the narrative style, compare Stewart (776).

762.   Spanberg, Sven-Johan. "Education and Moral Insight in Dickens, Mrs. Gaskell, and Meredith." **Studia Neophilologica**, 48 (1976), 76–89.

Looks at the "pattern of events, situations, and character types" that dramatizes the subject of education in **Ruth**, **Hard Times**, and **The Ordeal of Richard Feverel** to show that this ostensible theme "functions primarily as a vehicle for other concerns" for human relationships and values. Spanberg states that the values, shared by the three novelists, are the championship of the pure in heart and simple in spirit against the self-aggrandizing oppressors.

763.   Speare, Morris Edward. **The Political Novel: Its Development in England and America**. New York: Oxford Univ. Press, 1924, p. 29.

Places **Hard Times** in a line, from Bunyan and Crusoe, of novels of purpose marked by strong moral emphasis, didacticism, and a spirit of reform.

764.   Spector, Robert Donald. "Introduction." In the Bantam edition, 1964 (43), pp. 3–15.

The first parts of this introduction deal with Dickens biographically and in relation to the novel. The third part is on **Hard Times**. Spector cites, with assent, Leavis (553), Orwell (650), and Watt (829), in praise of this "grim, purposive morality drama." He sees it as showing Dickens's condemnation of the exploitation of labor and as supporting unionism but not the opportunism of Slackbridge. But the central issue of the novel is "the materialistic values that crush the imaginative spirit in men's lives." The figure of Gradgrind and the effect of his teaching, Spector argues, "control all the other elements of the story."

765.   Spilka, Mark. **Dickens and Kafka: A Mutual Interpretation**. Bloomington: Indiana Univ. Press, 1963, pp. 73, 85, 156, 244.

For Dickens and Kafka, disruption on the personal and so-cial levels is theme and technique. Spilka compares Kafka's Uncle Jacob in **America** to Bounderby, offers Sleary as evi-dence of Dickens's sympathetic response to the squalid, and cites the utilitarian blight in **Hard Times** as one example of Dickens's social prisons.

*       Sprigg, Christopher St. John.

See Christopher Caudwell (255).

766.   Stang, Richard. **The Theory of the Novel in England, 1850-1870**. New York: Columbia Univ. Press; London: Rout-ledge & Kegan Paul, 1959, pp. 23-24, 28, 71.

Takes Leavis (553) to task for describing the seriousness of **Hard Times** as exceptional in Dickens's work, and cites the let-ters. **Household Words**, and **All the Year Round**. Stang com-pares Gradgrind's position on facts with a notion suggested in a statement in **All the Year Round** (Vol. 18, p. 120) that facts must be conceived in relation to the larger principles of which they are examples. He suggests that the hostile review in **Blackwood's Magazine** (122) was due not to the fact that the novel espoused a theory but to the fact that it espoused a theory uncongenial to the reviewer. Reviews: G. Armour Craig, **VS**, 4 (1960), 173-75; V.S. Pritchett, **NS**, 58 (1959), 851-52; Irene Simon, **MP**, 58 (1961), 62; Kathleen Tillotson, **RES**, n.s. 12 (1961), 95-98; Donald T. Torchiana, **CE**, 22 (1960), 60, and **NCF**, 14 (1960), 372.

*       Stapleton, Peter T.

See below (907).

767.   Stark, Myra Carol. "The Home Department: The Uses of Chil-
       dren in the Novels of Charles Dickens." **DAI**, 31 (1970), 6073A
       (New York Univ., 1970). 251 pp.

       Analyzes the characters, relationships, and functions of
       children in Dickens's novels. The child is a moral touchstone
       of man and society, a symbol of "life's primal goodness and in-
       nocence," Stark concludes.

768.   Stein, Sondra Gayle. "**Woman and Her Master**: The Feminine
       Ideal as Social Myth in the Novels of Charles Dickens, William
       Thackeray, and Charlotte Dronto." **DAI**, 37 (1977), 5149A
       (Washington Univ., 1976). 269 pp.

       Includes a discussion of the debate on divorce leading up
       to the Matrimonial Divorce Bill of 1857.

769.   Steiner, George. **Language and Silence**: **Essays on Language,
       Literature and the Inhuman**. New York: Athenaeum, 1967, pp.
       235, 332.

       In a discussion of Leavis, suggests that his preference for
       **Hard Times** over Dickens's much greater achievements, such as
       **Bleak House** or **Great Expectations**, shows Leavis's preference
       for Jamesian "awareness" over a Dickensian "seriousness of
       committed feeling." In a discussion of Lukacs's definition of
       the illusion of realism, Steiner offers the fallacy of facts as ex-
       hibited by Gradgrind.

770.   Steinmann, Martin, Jr. "The Old Novel and the New." In **From
       Jane Austen to Joseph Conrad**. Ed. Robert C. Rathburn and
       Martin Steinmann, Jr. Minneapolis: Univ. of Minnesota Press,
       1958, pp. 286–306.

       **Hard Times** is one example offered of the "novel of social
       purpose" which "usually demands large blocks of exposition."
       M'Choakumchild is included in a list of characters with allegori-
       cal names.

771.   Stern, J.P. **On Realism**. London and Boston: Routledge & Ke-
       gan Paul, 1973, pp. 5, 94.

Dickens's exposition of injustice and heartlessness in **Hard Times** is seen as part of his realistic presentation of England, constituting a greater interest in social institutions than simply to expose them. Critical emphasis on symbols and image clusters, Stern points out, has obscured our notice of how prominently institutions stand in the foreground of Dickens's novels (for **Hard Times**, the institution is the industrial North).

772.    Stevens, James S. "Dickens's Use of the English Bible." **Dickensian**, 21 (1925), 32-34, 93-95, 152-57, 214-18.

        Lists four biblical allusions in **Hard Times**.

773.    ———. **Quotations and References in Charles Dickens**. Boston: Christopher, 1929, pp. 54-55.

        For **Hard Times** lists nine references to the Bible, four to nursery rhymes, and others to Goldsmith ("The Deserted Village"), the classics (Brutus and the Spartan mothers), common proverbs, and **Robinson Crusoe**.

774.    Stevenson, Lionel. "Dickens's Dark Novels, 1851-1857." **Sewanee Review**, 51 (1943), 398-409.

        This famous essay defines the "dark novels," **Bleak House**, **Hard Times**, and **Little Dorrit**, by their "atmosphere of bitterness and frustration," the absence of farce, the "self-consciously elaborate and rhetorical style," the complicated plots, the offering of higher social strata in realistic detail, and the penetration of the story by the purpose of social criticism. Stevenson looks at Dickens's concerns with social issues, his literary competition, and his personal crises of the period. He suggests that **Hard Times**, a "sociological treatise on industrial conflict and capitalistic greed," was Dickens's answer to challenges from Gaskell and Kingsley. The conflict is presented so boldly, Stevenson asserts, that "the story has a machine-made effect, totally devoid of those inconsistent human traits that give verisimilitude to even the most exaggerated characters and episodes in all [Dickens's] other books."

775.    ———. **The English Novel: A Panorama**. Boston: Houghton Mifflin; London: Constable, 1960, pp. 311-12. Rpt. Westport, Conn.: Greenwood, 1978. Section on **Hard Times** rpt. in Gray (429).

Argues that **Hard Times** is weak because the characters do not come alive--they were invented to demonstrate a theory. Dickens's research for this novel (the request for the reports of the Board of Education, his visit to Preston) shows an "unwonted caution," Stevenson states. He adds that the scorn for the utilitarians comes "straight from Carlyle."

776.    Stewart, Garrett.  **Dickens and the Trials of Imagination.** Cambridge, Mass.: Harvard Univ. Press, 1974, passim.

Argues that in **Hard Times**, "the most explicit, the most harrowing picture of the Victorian assault against imagination," the style figures the subject; there is less play of mind over language, and instead we find "relentless argument" and a "punctual and peremptory" antithetical structure. (Compare Frank Smith [552].) To the argument that the style of the narrator offers the countering energy and play (no critics are cited specifically), Stewart instances the image of the fairy-palaces, which is ironic, "a trenchant parody of the whole romantic sensibility as it becomes an aestheticizing indifference to human pain." He suggests that Louisa has raised fire-gazing, her escape, "to a visionary power." On the narrative style, compare Sonstroem (761). Reviews: K.J. Fielding, **RES**, 28 (1977), 102-03; Sylvere Monod, **EA**, 30 (1977), 105-06; C.I. Schuster, **PQ**, 55 (1976), 142-44; Alexander Welsh, **Novel**, 10 (1978), 79-84.

777.    -------.  "The Trials of Imagination: Style in Dickens." **DAI**, 32 (1971), 7008A  (Yale Univ., 1971.)

See Stewart, above (776).

778.    Stoehr, Taylor.  **Dickens: The Dreamer's Stance.** Ithaca: Cornell Univ. Press, 1965, passim.

Compares Dickens's literary manner to Freud's notion of dream-work and analyzes the last six novels as though they were dreams. Stoehr remarks that despite the tightness of space, Dickens continued his use of the double plot in **Hard Times**, a structure that "keeps the sexual and the social problems from intermingling"; the "guilt and punishment are ... displaced and not clearly related to their psychological sources." Stoehr believes that the novel avoids the class confrontations necessary to "final integration." Some headway in bringing the two stories together is made in the connection between Tom

and Stephen through the robbery. Tom and Stephen are
doubles, Stoehr states, with the bad side of the proletarian image displaced to Tom. This accounts for the "intensity of dis-
gust" in the description of Tom in blackface. Between them,
Stoehr concludes, Tom and Stephen express Dickens's conflict
between moral revulsion from the imprisoning society and
moral revulsion against those who break its laws. Reviews: T.J.
Cribb, **RES**, 17 (1966), 331–39; K.J. Fielding, **Dickensian**, 62
(1966), 22–24; Barbara Hardy, **MLQ**, 27 (1966), 230–33; Martin
Price, **YR**, 55 (1966), 290–96; Lawrence Senelick, **DS**, 2 (1966),
152–55; Alexander Welsh, **VS**, 9 (1966), 207–08.

779.    Stone, Donald David. **Novelists in a Changing World**. Cam-
        bridge, Mass.: Harvard Univ. Press, 1972, pp. 305, 307.

        Notes that in Mr. Vetch of **The Princess** James echoes
        Stephen Blackpool, but argues that "James's easy helplessness
        is in contrast to Dickens' anguished resignation." In compari-
        son to Dickens's warning to cultivate the fancy and the affec-
        tions in the poor, Stone concludes, James was a good deal less
        liberal.

780.    ———. **The Romantic Impulse in Victorian Fiction**. Cam-
        bridge, Mass.: Harvard Univ. Press, 1980, passim.

        Traces Dickens's divided loyalty, and pronounced antipathy,
        to both Byron and Wordsworth, his extremes of Romantic will-
        fulness and Romantic quiescence. For Stone **Hard Times** offers
        the basic Dickensian Romantic solution: the genii of Fancy win
        out against the ogres of Fact. But this notion is reduced to its
        "barest bones," he states, and the novel suffers by its card-
        board characters and fairy-tale logic. The loss of Louisa's tra-
        gic potential Stone finds unforgivable. The instinct that leads
        to truth of feeling is shown in a dog, not by the domestic circle
        of the previous novels. Stone suggests a relationship between
        **The Ordeal of Richard Feverel** and **Hard Times** in Mrs. Berry
        and Sissy Jupe, and Richard and Louisa. Reviews: A. Duck-
        worth, **NCF**, 36 (1982), 475–82; Karl Kroeber, **ELN**, 19 (1981),
        156–58; James Maddox, **Novel**, 15 (1982), 263–66; Sylvere Mon-
        od, **EA**, 35 (1982), 339–41; Stuart Sperry, **VS**, 25 (1982), 252–54.

*       Stones, Sandi Brinkman.

        See below (908).

781.  Straus, Ralph.  **Charles Dickens: A Biography from New Sources.**  New York: Cosmopolitan Book, 1928, passim.  Also published as **Charles Dickens: A Portrait in Pencil.**  London: Gollancz, 1928.  Also **A Portrait of Dickens.**  London: Dent, 1938.

   Suggests that **Hard Times** taxed Dickens in the extreme and that after this "socialistic romance" Dickens was perpetually unsatisfied with his "old routine."

782.  ———.  "Household Words: Bleak House: Hard Times."  **Dickens: the Man and the Book.**  London: Nelson, 1936, pp. 133–62.

   This is an anthology of brief excerpts with running commentary.  For **Hard Times** there is commentary, but no excerpt.  The novel is criticized in the usual ways, for overstatement and exaggeration, harsh satire, too hurried an examination of the industry of the North.  Straus finds the story of Rachael and Stephen "tenderly told" and remarks the "whimsical fun" of Sleary's.  He hints at a relationship between the lack of grace in this work and the state of Dickens's marriage when he wrote it.

783.  Stumpf, Willy.  "Der Dickenssche Roman **Hard Times:** seine Entsehung und seine Tendenzen."  Ph.D. Dissertation.  Univ. of Greifswald, 1911.  114 pp.

   Considers the social and literary history that shaped the evolution of the book and studies its social and educational argument.

784.  Sucksmith, Harvey Peter.  **The Narrative Art of Charles Dickens: The Rhetoric of Sympathy and Irony in his Novels.**  Oxford: Clarendon, 1970, passim.

   **Hard Times** is discussed at a variety of points in this comprehensive study of Dickens's theory and practice of fiction.  One issue is the use of a character as model for the reader in the induction of sympathy, a technique that has its costs.  Another important aspect is the "rhetoric of irony," which, like that of sympathy, is analyzed in detail that includes close examination of the revisions of the first and second descriptions of Coketown.  Sucksmith relates the differences between sympathy and irony to the clash of intellect and affection, and examines the latter in **Hard Times**. He finds Carlyle's influence important and concludes that the "idea of repression, boldly worked out in terms of a human life, is presented in its most complete and convincing form in **Hard Times**, which contains the fullest exposition of Dickens's general view of human psychology." He argues also that the title-list shows Dickens clarifying his original idea. Reviews: K.J. Fielding, **VS**, 14 (1970), 211–12; Sylvere Monod, **EA**, 21 (1971), 102–04; Richard Stang, **DSN**, 1,iii (1970), 5–7; Michael Steig, **Criticism**, 13 (1971), 319–20; Patricia Thomson, **RES**, 22 (1971), 509–12; Stephen Wall, **EC**, 21(1971), 261–80.

785.    Sullivan, Mary Rose. "Black and White Characters in **Hard Times**." **VN**, 38 (1970), 5–10.

In complement to Leavis (553), analyzes the black/white imagery of the novel in a Lawrentian polarity of black as life and vitality and white as the opposite, with considerable discussion of the significance of the will to life and some elaborate argument to fit all the imagery into the categories posited.

786.    Supple, Barry. "Material Development: The Condition of England, 1830–1860." In **The Victorians**. Ed. Laurence Lerner. New York: Holmes & Meier, 1978, pp. 49–69.

Refers Dickens's use of the pistons of the steam engines in striking the key-note for Coketown to the fact that the steam engine was perhaps the most striking example of the new industrial technology of the period.

*       ———.

See Laurence Lerner and Barry Supple (563).

787.    Sussman, Herbert L. "The Industrial Novel and the Machine: Charles Dickens." **Victorians and the Machine: The Literary Response to Technology**. Cambridge, Mass.: Harvard Univ. Press, 1968, pp. 41–75 and passim.

In this examination of the ambivalent Victorian attitude toward the machine, Dickens emerges as the only writer of fiction who could use machine technology as vehicle rather than

tenor. In **Hard Times** industrial reality has become the whole
of England and so the machine is synecdochally related to the
condition of England, moral and psychological as well as tech-
nological and economic, Sussman asserts. He points out that
the work is grim because Dickens was not interested in the in-
tricacies of industrial technology, and pessmistic because of his
convictions about industrialism. Dickens, unlike most of his
contemporaries, sees the emotional effects of machine-tending,
according to Sussman, although he does not see the moral effects (Stephen and Rachael are unimpaired in this regard, despite their labor). The circus is not a "serious alternative" because Dickens will not renounce the economic system that the
technology supported. Reviews: Richard Altick, **JEGP**, 68 (1969),
192–94; Vineta Colby, **MP**, 67 (1969), 100–02; Karl Kroeber, **VS**,
12 (1969), 480–81.

788.    Swinburne, Algernon Charles. "Charles Dickens." **Quarterly
        Review**, 196 (July, 1902), 20–39. Rpt. in **Charles Dickens**. Lon-
        don: Chatto & Windus, 1913; rpt. Folcroft, Pa.: Folcroft, 1977.
        Also in **The Complete Works of Algernon Charles Swinburne**,
        Ed. Edmund Gosse and T.J. Wise. London: Heinemann; New
        York: Gabriel Wells, 1926, pp. 57–88.

        Describes **A Tale of Two Cities** and **Hard Times** as "the
        two shorter novels which would suffice to preserve for ever the
        fame of Dickens," preferring the latter as "greater in moral and
        pathetic and humorous effect." In opposition to Ruskin (150),
        Swinburne finds Stephen, though a beautiful character study,
        too overdone for anything except a martyrology and Bounderby
        "only too lamentably truer and nearer to the unlovely side of
        life." He recognizes weakness in the satire of "society" in
        Dickens, but reminds us that Mrs. Sparsit is "as typical and im-
        mortal as any figure of Moliere's." See Gissing's reply (419).

789.    ------- **The Swinburne Letters**. Ed. Cecil Y. Lang. 6 vols.
        New Haven: Yale Univ. Press, 1959–62, II, 29–30.

        In a letter to Emilie Venturi, 28 September 1869, Swinburne
        writes, "I beg to inform you that I, like Mr. Sparsit, am a Powler,
        and also associated with the Scadgers family. I.e. the late Duke
        of Northumberland was my great uncle."

790.    Symons, Julian. **Charles Dickens**. London: Arthur Barker, 1951,
        pp. 37, 43, 55–56, 58–59. Rpt. New York: Haskell, 1974.

Suggests that there is an undertow of personal resentment in Dickens's later novels, arising from a sense of having lost a struggle with society. As an example, Symons argues that behind Dickens's dislike for the trade unions is a dislike for the mob, from which he had escaped, or emerged. In **Hard Times** Dickens fails to offer any examination of the morality of the Coketown civilization, because he would not attack the achievements that were the props of bourgeois power, Symons states. He suggests a time lag in Dickens's social criticism (compare House [475]) and remarks that Bounderby-baiting was more to Dickens's taste than sustained social criticism. He does allow that in his railroad scenes Dickens combined machinery and emotion to good dramatic effect. Review: T. Hill, **Dickensian**, 48 (1952), 13-14.

791.    Szirotny, J.S. "A Classical Reference in 'Hard Times' and 'Middlemarch.'" **N&Q**, 213 (1968), 421-22.

In reference to Dickens's "wipe out all their tears with one dirty sponge" (I,15), cites Cassandra's last words in Aeschylus's **Agamemnon**, "a sponge moistened in gall, And wipes each beauteous character away." The Gad's Hill library contained a copy of Robert Potter's translation of the play, Szirotny points out, and Potter's introduction cites the image as one of the finest any poet ever conceived. Szirotny suggests that the allusion reveals a more intimate knowledge of the classics than Dickens is usually credited with.

792.    Tanabe, Masami. "A Study on [sic] **Hard Times** --As an Example of the Collapse of a Novel." **The Hiroshima University Studies, Literature Department (Hiroshima daigaku bungakubu kiyo)**, 29, no. 2 (1970), 125-42. English synopsis in "Abstracts," p. 7.

Finds more pessimism or despair than irony in the novel. Dickens's artistic ambition creates a diabolical world for Bounderby and Gradgrind that is apart from the ordinary human world.

793.    Taplin, Kim. **The English Path**. Ipswich: Boydell, 1979, pp. 37-38.

Asserts that Dickens offers the "most extreme expression" of the attitude towards the countryside "as an escape, a rest-ing-place, a paradise." One example Taplin gives is Sissy and Rachael's Sunday walk: the link with death is realized when they come to the Old Hell Shaft.

794.   Tarantelli, Carole Beebe. "The Working Class in the 'Social Problem' Novel: 1830-1855." **DAI**, 36 (1975), 2857A-58A (Brandeis Univ., 1975). 222 pp.

Investigates the image of the working class in five novels. Chapter 6 is devoted to **Hard Times**, with emphasis on Stephen and his passivity, on Slackbridge, and on the dichotomy between moral goodness and action.

795.   Tarr, Rodger L. "Carlyle and the Problem of the **Hard Times** Dedication." **DSN**, 3 (1972), 25-27.

Quarrels with the interpretation of evidence and the conclusion in Dunn (351), insisting that one cannot infer "either a philosophical or a personal rift between Dickens and Carlyle."

796.   -------. "Carlyle's Influence upon the Mid-Victorian Social Novels of Gaskell, Kingsley, and Dickens." **DA**, 29 (1968), 2285A (Univ. of S. Carolina, 1968). 186 pp.

Asserts and examines the "profound impact" of Carlyle's precepts upon **Hard Times** (among other novels).

797.   Tassone, Frank Allen. "Charles Dickens: His Ideas about Education and Their Implication for the Educational Administrator." **DAI**, 43 (1982), 1383A (Columbia Univ. Teachers College, 1982). 109 pp.

**Hard Times** is one of five novels of chief concern in this examination of Dickens's ideas on education and how they can be applied today. Tassone notes the continuing relevance of the issue of fact and fancy.

798.   Tewari, R.P. "Dickens and Democracy." **Agra University Journal of Research (Letters)**, 24 (1976), 21-27.

Demonstrates Dickens's contempt for politicians, referring to **Hard Times**, among other novels, for its comments on Parliament and on Gradgrind as M.P.

799.    --------, and S.P. Jain. "Dickens and the Law." **Agra Universi-**
        **ty Journal of Research (Letters)**, 21 (1973), 41–45.

        Presents Dickens's criticism of the law, with emphasis on
        **Bleak House** and **Great Expectations**, but with a glance at the
        divorce law as treated in **Hard Times**, noting the relation of di-
        vorce to money.

800.    Theimer, Robert Hugo. "Fairy Tale and the Triumph of the Ideal
        in Three Novels by Charles Dickens." **DAI**, 30 (1969), 1185A
        (Stanford Univ., 1969). 197 pp.

        Examines the pattern of fairy-tale action in **Hard Times,**
        **The Old Curiosity Shop**, and **Our Mutual Friend**. The fairy-
        tale presents a sense of the fabulous that is juxtaposed with
        the world of fact, an opposition central to these three novels.

801.    Thomas, L.H.C. "Otto Ludwig and Charles Dickens: A German
        Reading of **Great Expectations** and Other novels." **Hermathe-**
        **na**, 111 (1971), 35–50.

        Reports Ludwig's notes on **Hard Times** as full of "harsh
        criticism." Ludwig concludes that "Dickens exposes injustice, ...
        but in such a way that he forfeits the sympathy of the reader,
        who loses that sense of cosiness towards which the author
        seems to be steering him." Ludwig finds that "Dickens sides
        with the workers yet portrays the employers more truthfully:
        thus he gives a discordant impression and alienates the read-
        er's sympathy for the cause he champions."

802.    Thompson, A. Hamilton. **A History of English Literature**. Lon-
        don: John Murray, 1901, pp. 664, 665, 667.

        This chronological survey finds **Hard Times** a powerful and
        tragic story dealing with social problems, though Thompson
        mistakenly believes that is was written for Dickens's **All the**
        **Year Round**.

803.    Thurley, Geoffrey. "**Hard Times**." **The Dickens Myth: Its Gen-**
        **esis and Structure**. New York: St, Martin's; London: Routledge
        & Kegan Paul; St. Lucia, Queensland: Univ. of Queensland Press,
        1976, pp. 203–24.

A revaluation of Dickens that promises not to make him Jamesian after all, sees Dickens as the great novelist of bourgeois snobbishness, a class phenomenon that Americans cannot understand. **Hard Times** is "externally conceived," Thurley states, that is, it is about something rather than being a vehicle for the author's self-projection. Thurley investigates the issue of mode (the parable in contrast to the "private" action of the novel). The essential terms are life, energy, and freedom (Sissy, the circus), opposed to fact, cold, bourgeois restraint, and material advancement. The novel is great as a piece of social, political, and moral prophecy, Thurley concludes, even in its insight into the "trade union mentality." Reviews: C.C. Barfoot, **ES**, 58 (1977), 542; Richard Dunn, **Review**, 1 (1979), 91–104; Robin Gilmour, **Dickensian**, 73 (1977), 116–17; Sylvere Monod, **EA**, 30 (1980), 498–99.

804. Tick, Stanley. "**Hard Times**, Page One: An Analysis." **VN**, 46 (1974), 20–22.

Argues that the first chapter functions as a sort of preface and that the metaphors **are** the meaning, Dickens's attack on Fact. Tick notes that the MS of this page is highly worked and concludes with the suggestion that Dickens "got this opening page too right; composing the remainder of the novel became far too easy."

*        Tillotson, Kathleen.

See John Butt and Kathleen Tillotson (240).

805. Timmerman, John Hager. "Feet of Clay: Concepts of Heroism in the Works of Carlyle, Dickens, Browning, Kierkegaard, and Nietzsche." **DAI**, 34 (1974), 5933A (Ohio Univ., 1973). 356 pp.

In looking at Dickens, focusses on the attack on social institutions for hypocrisy and the stifling of imagination, and on the social-outcast children who offer creative vision and compassion.

806. Tindall, William York. **The Literary Symbol.** New York: Columbia Univ. Press, 1955, p. 44.

Offers the sequence on Facts in the first chapter of **Hard Times** as an index of the belligerence of the party of fact in the world of divided reality inherited by the nineteenth century.

807.   Torgovnick, Marianna.  **Closure in the Novel**.  Princeton, N.J.: Princeton Univ. Press, 1981, p. 49.

Argues in regard to **Bleak House** that the tendency to conclude with the private withdrawal from the social world is made problematic by Dickens's having shown how "twisted social values impede and distort private life," and offers the Gradgrind family as an example.

808.   Trilling, Lionel.  **The Liberal Imagination**.  New York: Viking, 1950; London: Secker & Warburg, 1951, p. 12.  Rpt. New York: Harcourt Brace Jovanovich, 1978.

Suggests that **Hard Times** shows us that the principles of J.S. Mill's upbringing were not exclusive to him and that they nearly destroyed him, as they did destroy Louisa Gradgrind. Compare Alexander (160), Arneson (171), Baker (180), Fielding (380), and Ryan (713).

809.   Tropp, Asher.  **The School Teachers: the Growth of the Teaching Profession in England and Wales from 1800 to the Present Day**.  London: Heinemann, 1957, p. 24.

States that Dickens's characterization of M'Choakumchild should not be taken as a true reflection of the college-trained teachers of the period, except as it indicates their "almost fierce desire to acquire knowledge." Compare Reed (698) and West (837).

*       Turow, J.

See B.F. Fisher, IV, and J. Turow (383).

810.   Ueki, Kensuke.  "Charles Dickens; **Hard Times**--His Creative Power and Social Criticism."  **The Hiroshima University Studies, Literature Department (Hiroshima daigaku bungakubu kiyo)**, 33 (1974), 300-28.  English synopsis in "Abstracts," pp. 16-17.

Examines the influence of Carlyle, the style of **Hard Times**, and the rhetorical imbalance between the world of Gradgrind and the circus world of fancy, an imbalance tentatively attributed to Dickens's own realization of the inadequacy of the image of the circus to cope with the "muddle."

811. Van Ghent, Dorothy. "The Dickens World." **Sewanee Review**, 58 (1950), 419–38. Rpt. in **The Dickens Critics**. Ed. George H. Ford and Lauriat Lane, Jr. Ithaca, New York: Cornell Univ. Press, 1961.

This important essay defines the "principle of relationship between things and people in the novels of Dickens" as a "transformation of attributes" in which things imitate the human and humans imitate the inhuman. **Hard Times** recurs in the development of this thesis: Lady Scadgers' leg, the Coketown "hands" and streets, and Stephen's near hallucination as he walks home.

812. Van Hall, Sharon K. "The Foe in the Mirror: The Self-Destructive Characters in Charles Dickens' Novels." **DAI**, 36 (1975), 2860A (Univ. of Illinois, Champaign-Urbana, 1975). 183 pp.

Includes James Harthouse among the self destructive characters analyzed.

813. Van Heyningen, C. "Aspects of Dickens." **Theoria**, 42 (1974), 65–77.

Deals with four aspects of Dickens's work: landscape, women characters, madness, and crowds. In regard to women characters, Van Heyningen uses the instance of Stephen and his wife in **Hard Times** as evidence of how "entirely realistic" Dickens became toward marriage.

814. Vincent, John. "Literary Victorians." **Listener**, 22 March 1973, pp. 384–86.

A curious passing reference in a nasty review of George Watson's **The English Ideology**: "There is history, and there is Eng Lit history. The latter genre, to which this book belongs, exists in a world all its own. Its professors have clear ideas ... that ... have been reached without any process of study known to historians and they have all passed through a traumatic experience on reading that implausible melodrama, **Hard Times**."

815.  Vogel, Jane. **Allegory in Dickens**. University: Univ. of Alabama Press, 1977, passim.

Transforms Dickens into an allegorist of the New Testament, and thus includes **Hard Times** at various points. The title is tied to "Old Time," and thus the initials O.T. and the passion for retribution. Sissy, Tom, and Louisa represent the soul-fettering education that clips the wings of figurative imagination. Much is made of Stephen stoned by the law, stoning and Hard, Stone Lodge, and Gradgrind/grindstone. Reviews: A.O.J. Cockshut, **TLS**, 17 March 1978, p. 308; Richard Dunn, **Review**, 1 (1979), 91–104; D.A. Miller, **VS**, 22 (1979), 473–74; Branwen Bailey Pratt, **NCF**, 33 (1978), 262–68; A. Samuels, **Dickensian**, 74 (1978), 111–13.

816.  Voss, A.E.  "A Note on Theme and Structure in **Hard Times**." **Theoria**, 23 (1964), 35–42.

Analyzes the novel mainly in terms of its major themes, order and disorder and appearance and reality. The apparent order of Coketown hides a real disorder, Voss states, and the apparent chaos of the circus people masks an organic, human order, the ambiguities in the presentation of Sleary's notwithstanding (the dependence on money, the dissoluteness). Voss argues that while Blackpool's marriage appears to be an image of disorder and Bounderby sees him as a threat to the industrial order, Stephen represents a deep spiritual order and he sees society for the "muddle" it is. The tragic significance of the novel is limited only by its moral explicitness, Voss concludes.

817.  Wagenknecht, Edward. **The Man Charles Dickens**. Boston and New York: Houghton Mifflin, 1929, passim. Rev. ed. Norman: Univ. of Oklahoma Press, 1966.

Remarks upon various aspects of the novel: its Carlylean nature, Sissy's role as the redeemer of the soulless utilitarianism of the Gradgrinds, Stephen as the martyr of the union and the vehicle of Dickens's message of the common interests of employers and workers, etc. Wagenknecht suggests that Dickens's telling Cunningham that Preston was not the original of

Coketown (131) is an instance of Dickens's not always having told the truth. Compare Shusterman (743).

818.   Waldock, A.J.A.   "The Status of **Hard Times**."   **Southerly**, 9 (1948), 33-39.

A careful response to Leavis (553). Waldock argues that "significance" is important but so is "life," that the moral fable is too insistent, that Gradgrind does not develop but rather changes from one caricature to another, and that what Leavis calls flexibility is really only a confusion of modes between irony and realism. Dickens is ostensibly writing a novel, but his heart is really set on a pamphlet, Waldock believes. He suggests that Leavis re-read **David Copperfield** or the Gamp sequences.

819.   Walsky, Joan Ross.   "Thespians and Theater: Performance in the Novels of Charles Dickens."   **DAI**, 33 (1972), 1747A   (Rutgers Univ., 1972).   244 pp.

Studies the friction between the two antithetical narrators in Dickens's novels, one theatrical and dramatic, the other didactic and moral. The contention between narrators may take place within certain characters who are sometimes pure and sometimes performers, Walsky states, and offers Tom and Louise Gradgrind as instances.

820.   Walters, John C.   **Phases of Dickens: The Man, His Message and His Mission**.   London: Chapman & Hall, 1911, passim.   Rpt. New York: Haskell, 1971.

Bounderby is cited with admiration and quotation in "His Gallery of Hypocrites" and Dickens's anti-Gradgrindism is noted as part of "His Plea for Justice."

821.   Ward, A.C.   **Foundations of English Prose**.   London: Bell, 1931, p. 111.

**Hard Times** is included with a half-dozen other books in a list of social and industrial novels of the period which have passed into literature.

822.   Ward, Sir Adolphus William. **Dickens**. London and New York: Macmillan, 1882. Rpt. in English Men of Letters series. Ed. John Morley. New York: Harper, 1902, pp. 126-30.

Finds the novel to suffer from narrowness of space and excess of didactic purpose, particularly in the exaggeration of character. Nonetheless the moral is forceful, Ward asserts, and both the love-story of Louisa and the circus are scenes well done.

823.   -------. "Introduction." **North and South**. By Elizabeth Gaskell. New York: Putnam; London: Smith, Elder, 1906, pp. xi-xxvii.

Suggests that **Hard Times** must suffer the disadvantage of Dickens's ignorance of the North. Ward accords the novel respect in the comparison with **North and South**, but finds the latter superior because Gaskell knows her material.

824.   -------. "Introduction." **Ruth**. By Elizabeth Gaskell. New York: Putnam; London: Smith, Elder, 1906, pp. ix-xxxii.

Considers that the "moderation" of the portrait of Mr. Bradshaw in **Ruth** "becomes apparent if it is compared with that of Mr. Bounderby in **Hard Times**, of whom, especially in his relation to his daughter, Mrs. Gaskell's earlier creation may fairly be held to have suggested the first outline."

825.   Ward, H. Snowden, and Catherine Weed Barnes. **The Real Dickens Land**. London: Chapman & Hall, 1904, pp. 178, 188.

States that Coketown cannot be localized but that its general atmosphere was meant to suggest Manchester.

826.   Warner, Rex. "On Reading Dickens." **The Cult of Power**. London: John Lane; Philadelphia: Lippincott, 1947, pp. 29-50.

States that **Hard Times** "shows that the tyranny of modern 'efficiency' is just as disgusting to him [Dickens] as are the tyrannies of feudal pride, of inhuman religion, or of stupid parliamentarianism."

827.   Watson, George. **The English Ideology: Studies in the Language of Victorian Politics**. London: Allen Lane, 1973, passim.

Argues that the satire in **Hard Times** is a majority belief, part of a consensus, and that it does not imply criticism of the society as a whole. Watson appears to think that Gradgrind is shown as a mercenary or miserly person and dates the novel 1853. He offers it as an instance of the failure of the critics of political economy to understand the theory's explicit limits.

828.   Watson, Thomas L. "The Ethics of Feasting: Dickens' Dramatic Use of **Agape**." In **Essays in Honor of Esmond Linworth Marilla**. Ed. Thomas Austin Kirby and William John Olive. Louisiana State Univ. Studies in the Humanities, ser. 19. Baton Rouge: Louisiana State Univ. Press, 1970, pp. 243-52.

Investigates four significant feasts, one of which is Bounderby's wedding breakfast, in four different novels, that are related to the broader social and ethical concerns of the novels. The pure form is Christmas at Dingley Dell; in **Hard Times** the wedding breakfast is ironic, satiric, demonstrating the distortion of the Christian values of **agape**.

829.   Watt, William W. "Introduction." In the Rinehart edition, 1068 (40), pp. vii-xxxiii.

Reviews the social issues, set within the times, and the careful planning for the novel (in defense of Dickens's artistry). Watt indicates that Dickens failed to find a consistent style in this mixture of art and propaganda, literal realism and symbolism, but that Dickens's approach had always been partly allegorical, especially in the Christmas stories. He wonders how Louisa developed her taste for the fustian she displays in the breakdown scene, arguing that if her education denied her good poetry it should also have kept her free from bad. He concludes in praise of the "taut structure, the dramatic pace, the symbolic economy, and the single-minded dedication to a serious purpose." Review: Anne Smith, **DSN**, 4 (1973), 115-22.

830.   Watts, Richard J. **The Pragmalinguistic Analysis of Narrative Texts: Narrative Cooperation in Charles Dickens's Hard Times**. Tubingen: Gunter Narr, 1981. 240 pp.

Invokes speech act theory (J.L. Austin, John Searle, Mary Louise Pratt), discourse analysis (William Labov) and the Gricean cooperative principles to create a system that, by following **ad absurdum** Lodge's (577) and Sonstroem's (761) criticism of the narrator's lack of sympathy for Mrs. Blackpool and Tom and Watts's own view of inconsistency in Gradgrind, finally proves that the narrator of the novel "is meant to appear as a hypocrite." Thus the narrator is implicated by Dickens to be an example of blind failure of compassion, and Dickens shows us that Stephen's decision to join the union was wrong (if the hypocritical blind narrator endorses it, it must be wrong). Other conclusions are less remarkable. This reading of the novel is offered as part of an intention "to account more adequately for self-contradictory critical interpretation" of the novel.

831.    Waugh, Arthur. "Hard Times" (Introduction). In the Biographical edition, 1903 (33), pp. xviii–xxi.

Repeats the information from Forster concerning the circumstances of publication, the titles, the cramping of the weekly format, and the failure of the visit to Preston. Waugh quotes Ruskin's "sound and discriminating criticism" (150).

832.    Webb, Igor. **From Custom to Capital: The English Novel and the Industrial Revolution.** Ithaca and London: Cornell Univ. Press, 1981, pp. 86–100 and passim.

Examines **Hard Times** in the context of an assumption that all the novels of the period record the transformation of England from custom to capital. Webb sees the novel as overtly ideological and the ideological aspects as giving meaning to the characters. Dickens sets out to find what will and will not make life liveable in Coketown; that is, he accepts Coketown and tries to find solace within it. The circus is not a solution because it goes away, Webb points out. He notes ideological contradictions in Stephen (his marital problem is not a condition of Coketown) and in Bounderby (the revelation of his true background contradicts the argument concerning the evils of Gradgrind's unloving system). He finds that it is the energy of the prose that "defines the human impulse that abominates Coketown as a system" and is not wholly content that the energy should be so much there and so little in the vision and structure of the novels. On the prose, compare Sonstroem (761) and Stewart (776). Reviews: R. Brown, **TLS,** 18 June 1982, p. 660; Peter Christmas, **MP,** 80 (1982), 214–17; Michael Cotsell, **Dickensian,** 78 (1982), 116–18.

833.    Welsh, Alexander. **The City of Dickens.** Oxford: Clarendon, 1971, passim.

Treats the city in Dickens "both as an historical reality and as a metaphor that provides a context for values and purposes expressed by the English novel." Welsh looks at satire, at the nineteenth-century city, and at the Christian idea of the city of destruction. **Hard Times** is not subject to extended analysis, but occurs at several points in the argument. Reviews: Barbara Hardy, **Encounter**, 36 (1971), 48-54; Sylvere Monod, **EA**, 25 (1972), 165-66; Martin Price, **YR**, 61 (1972), 271-79; Michael Slater, **NCF**, 26 (1972), 492-94; Raymond Williams, **Dickensian**, 68 (1972), 53-54.

834.   -------. "Satire and History: The City of Dickens." **VS**, 11 (1968), 379-400.

Does not deal with Coketown, but brings up **Hard Times** in connection with the issue of statistics. Welsh asserts that on the whole Dickens admired the tabulated investigations of the condition of England and attacked only "the fallacious application of aggregate figures to individual cases."

835.   Welsh, Alfred H. **Development of English Literature and Language**. Chicago: Griggs, 1882, pp. 448-51.

An impressionistic commentary on the novel, emphasizing the highlights: Stephen at his death, the children in school, etc.

836.   West, Anthony. "The Customer Comes First." **New Yorker**, 28 (10 January 1953), 81-88. Rpt. in **Principles and Persuasions: The Literary Essays of Anthony West**. New York: Harcourt, Brace, 1957.

A review of Johnson (500) leads to an alternative evaluation of Dickens. Louisa's speech to her father is offered as an instance of dreadful sentimental rhetoric in the manner of Balzac. **Hard Times** as a whole West finds merely derivative from Gaskell and Disraeli, Dickens as usual seizing on the majority view to create his best-seller. Dickens was totally ignorant of both business and industry, West states, and all he could offer in the face of brutal conflict was a gospel of good cheer.

837.   West, E.G. **Education and the Industrial Revolution**. New York: Barnes & Noble, 1975, p. 54.

A brief reference to M'Choakumchild is interesting as another example of the way in which, in some quarters, the character has become an accepted type. See Reed (698); compare Tropp (809).

838.    Weygandt, Cornelius. **A Century of the English Novel.** New York: Century, 1925, pp. 8, 77-8.

Considers **Hard Times** both the least Cockney and the least effective of Dickens's novels. Weygandt suggests that either the provincial background or Dickens's illness at the time of writing may account for the lessened power. He speculates that the characters Hoggard and Prabble in **Saints and Sinners** (1884) by Henry Arthur Jones may have come from **Hard Times** (or **The Alchemist**).

839.    Wheeler, Burton Maynard. "Charles Dickens: In Service of Two Masters. A Study of the Novel of Social Protest." Ph.D. Dissertation. Harvard Univ., 1961. 338 pp.

Focusses on **Hard Times** as social criticism. Concludes that Dickens saw himself in the role of a Jeremiah warning mercantile and industrial England of impending destruction.

840.    Wheeler, Michael. "Apocalypse in a Mechanical Age: **Hard Times.**" **The Art of Allusion in Victorian Fiction.** London and Basingstoke: Macmillan; New York: Barnes & Noble, 1979, pp. 61-77.

Examines eight novels and seven novelists, with Dickens represented by **Hard Times**, for their use of literary and biblical allusion. In Dickens Wheeler finds the allusion and symbolism as wooden or as viable as the characters; Stephen and Rachael are instances of the former sort, Harthouse and Mrs. Sparsit of the latter. Louisa, whom Wheeler sees as the emotional and thematic center of the novel, "is handled with a sustained sureness of touch." Wheeler examines in particular the allusions to the Four Last Things. An extended comparison with **Mary Barton** demonstrates how Dickens (uniquely) subsumed his allusions into his own rhetoric. Review: C. Perri, **Style**, 15 (1981/82), 463-64.

841.    Whiteford, Robert Naylor. **Motives in English Fiction.** New York and London: Putnam's, 1918, pp. 324, 363.

Offers no extended discussion of particular novels. **Hard Times** is cited as an example of novels that study the manufacturer, and is asserted to have given orthodox political economy "a good pounding." Sissy figures in a list of children between 1838 and 1865 whose conditions are treated with some optimism.

842.  Whitfield, A. Stanton. **Mrs. Gaskell, Her Life and Work.** London: Routledge, 1929, pp. 103, 105.

States that Dickens was greater in characterization than in political insight, and that therefore the didactic side of **Hard Times** "fell flat."

843.  Whitlock, Roger Dennis. "Charles Dickens and George Eliot: Moral Art in the 'Age of Equipoise.'" **DAI**, 35 (1974), 484A (Univ. of Washington, 1973). 158 pp.

Argues for similarity of purpose and technique in Dickens and Eliot through an examination of three pairs of novels, including **Hard Times** and **Silas Marner**, both moral fables that attack utilitarianism.

844.  Whitlow, Roger. "Animal and Human Personalities in Dickens' Novels." **CLA Journal**, 19 (1975), 65–74.

Examines how dimensions of personality may accrue to characters through their associations with animals with striking personalities. Among the instances offered is Merrylegs, who Whitlow believes softens the impression we get of the child-deserter Jupe.

845.  Wiener, Martin J. "Middle-Class Intellectuals and Gentry Values." **English Culture and the Decline of the Industrial Spirit, 1850–1980.** Cambridge and New York: Cambridge Univ. Press, 1981, pp. 30–40.

Traces the growth of the seed of dissatisfaction in Dickens's early devotion to the steam-whistle party. In **Hard Times** Dickens associated with industrialism everything hateful, Wiener asserts; the seed had become full-blown alienation. But when Dickens turned away from the values of industrial capitalism it was "not to take up some protosocialist stance, but to join in the renovation of older gentry values."

846.    Wierstra, F.D.    **Smollett and Dickens.**    Den Helder: De Boer,
        1928, p. 85.

        Noting that both Smollett and Dickens use names sugges-
        tive of appearance, character, or occupation, instances Bound-
        erby and M'Choakumchild.


847.    Williams, Ioan.    **The Realist Novel in England: A Study in De-
        velopment.**    London: Macmillan, 1974, p. 148.

        Argues that although Dickens's social criticism develops as
        his art advances, it never supersedes his analysis of human
        character and of the general condition of mankind. Williams
        asserts that Dickens's recognition of the importance of social
        factors includes the power of machinery (**Hard Times**) and also
        of forces such as rationalism and political economy, which do
        not allow for the actual nature of man.


848.    Williams, Raymond.    "Dickens and Social Ideas."    In **Dickens
        1970.**    Ed. Michael Slater.    London: Chapman & Hall; New York:
        Stein & Day, 1970, pp. 77-97. Rpt. in **Sociology of Literature
        and Drama: Selected Readings.**    Ed. Elizabeth and Tom Burns.
        Harmondsworth and Baltimore: Penguin, 1973.

        Uses **Hard Times** to illustrate two of the seven kinds of
        relation between fiction and ideas defined by this study: works
        in which ideas are propagated and works in which ideas are
        embodied.    In further discussion of Dickens's relations with
        major ideas of his time, **Hard Times** and utilitarianism form the
        "key case." Williams examines the apparent contradiction be-
        tween Dickens's sympathy with the main tenets of utilitarianism
        and his creation of Gradgrind and offers this resolution: "At a
        certain point in the real history of England during the industrial
        revolution, the teachings of utilitarianism and of philosophical
        radicalism became inextricably entwined with the teachings of
        classical economics and of restraint of the poor .... What can
        readily be separated as contradictory ideas were in fact com-
        bined ... by ... the interests of a class .... Dickens penetrated the
        contradiction, not analytically, but in an act of emotional and
        substantial recoil and revulsion." Dickens judged an idea by its
        alliances, Williams states, and so rejected a "whole social for-
        mation."

849.    ———————. "The Industrial Novels." **Culture and Society,**
        **1780–1850.** London: Chatto & Windus, 1958, pp. 87–109. Rpt.
        as "The Industrial Novels: **Mary Barton** and **North and South,**
        Mrs. Gaskell; **Hard Times,** Dickens; **Sybil,** Disraeli; **Alton Locke,**
        Kingsley; **Felix Holt,** George Eliot." In **The Victorian Novel:**
        **Modern Essays in Criticism.** Ed. Ian Watt. London, Oxford,
        and New York: Oxford Univ. Press, 1971.

   Studies the "structure of feeling" that complements the
"facts of the new society" in six novels, including **Hard Times.**
Williams argues that the novel offers analysis rather than experience of industrialism, and hence a greater understanding of
the system than Mrs. Gaskell's, but a lesser understanding of
the working people. Dickens blurs Bounderby's aggressive ec
onomic behavior with his personal lack of charm, so that we do
not notice how one set of feelings affects the other. Dickens's
vision of reform and exploitation as two sides of the same coin
leads to his construction of an alternative set of values, in the
circus, that are based in individual experience, according to
Williams. He argues that Carlyle's influence on Dickens's social
position was largely negative, since Dickens offered no Heroes.
Dickens's innocence sees through society and rejects it; this is
"the retained position of an adolescent." All told, Williams con
cludes, the novel is more a symptom of the confusion of the
industrial society than an understanding of it. Reviews: Seymour Betsky, **VS,** 3 (1960), 298–301; Madeline L. Cazamian, **EA,** 13
(1960), 491; Richard Chase, **ParR,** 27 (1960), 148–54; Richard
Hoggart, **EC,** 9 (1960), 171–79, with rejoinders by Ian Gregor,
425–30, and Malcolm Pittock, 430–32, and reply by Williams,
432–27; Irving Howe, **NewR,** 5 February 1959, pp. 17–19, and 9
February 1959, pp. 23–24.

850.    ———————. "Introduction." **Hard Times.** In the Fawcett edition,
        1966 (46), pp. 9–24.

   Looks briefly at the circumstances of writing and publication and at utilitarianism, noting Dickens's affinities with it and
explaining his revulsion at it through the historical intertwining
of philosophical radicalism with classical economics. Williams
finds the literary method of the novel very like that of all Dickens's later fiction but with an added concentration that yields a
"worked morality." He relates the work to Bunyan and Fielding
but also to Dostoevsky and Kafka in its creation of a world cast
in a dominant image——with Dickens's authorial presence signifying his intention to change that world, not just to present it.
He also reviews briefly the critical history of the novel. Review:
Anne Smith, **DSN,** 4 (1973), 115–22.

851.    –––––––. "People of the City." **The Country and the City**.
        London: Chatto & Windus; New York: Oxford Univ. Press, 1973,
        pp. 153–64.

        This discussion of Dickens's London opens with a compari-
        son to Coketown, where Dickens can offer "a simpler, more
        rhetorical approach." Williams remarks the contradiction be-
        tween Dickens's statement that Coketown and its people are
        uniform and his characteristic way of showing them; in fact,
        their differences are "the decisive organisation of the novel."
        He also points out the confusion between the idea of the city
        and the idea of industry. Reviews: Malcolm Andrews, **Dicken-
        sian**, 70 (1974), 56–57; C.C. Barfoot, **ES**, 55 (1974), 380; R.L.
        Brett, **RES**, 25 (1974), 366–69; M. Byrd, **ParR**, 41 (1974), 132–37;
        Louis James, **VS**, 18 (1974), 113–14.

852.    –––––––. "Social Criticism in Dickens: Some Problems of
        Method and Approach." **CritQ**, 6 (1964), 214–27. Rpt. in **Der
        englische soziale Roman im 19.Jahrhundert**. Ed. Konrad
        Gross. Wege der Forschung, 466. Darmstadt: Wissenschaft-
        liche Buchgesellschaft, 1977.

        A careful definition of Dickens's social criticism, includes
        this rebuttal to Ruskin's criticism (150) of Bounderby and Ste-
        phen: "The force of Dickens's social criticism is radically relat-
        ed, first, to his capacity to typify rather than to individualise;
        and, second, to his capacity to typify in a dramatic rather than
        in a representative mode." Dickens dramatizes the experience
        of a society, not its isolatable facts.

853.    Wilson, Angus. "Charles Dickens: A Haunting." **CritQ**, 2 (1960),
        101–08. Rpt. in **Dickens: Modern Judgements**. Ed. A.E. Dyson.
        London: Macmillan, 1968. Also in **The Dickens Critics**. Ed.
        George Ford and Lauriat Lane, Jr. Ithaca: Cornell Univ. Press,
        1961.

        Asserts that **Hard Times** is "equally shaped and impover-
        ished by discipline." Wilson disagrees with Leavis (553): the
        novel is a skeleton, a menu-card, and not a true Dickensian
        feast.

854.    ———. "The Heroes and Heroines of Dickens." **REL**, 2 (1961),
        9–18. Rpt. in **Dickens and the Twentieth Century**. Ed. John
        Gross and Gabriel Pearson. London: Routledge & Kegan Paul,
        1962. Also in **Dickens: A Collection of Critical Essays**. Ed.
        Martin Price. Englewood Cliffs, N.J.: Prentice Hall, 1967. Also in
        **British Victorian Literature: Recent Revaluations**. Ed. Shiv K.
        Kumar. New York: New York Univ. Press, 1969.

        Describes Edith Dombey and Louisa as suffering the bore-
        dom and self-distaste of women in a loveless marriage. They
        are proud cold beauties who do not respond to sexual advanc-
        es.

855.    ———. **The World of Charles Dickens**. London: Secker &
        Warburg, 1970, pp. 235–41 and passim.

        Notes that the social theme that is new in **Hard Times** is
        the idea of self-help, which had been the essence of Dickens's
        career but was increasingly at odds with his social views. Wil-
        son argues that the differences between Dickens's views of the
        unions here and in **Household Words** can be accounted for as
        artistic heightening, but disagrees with Leavis and his followers
        over the achievement of the novel as a whole, finding it suffer-
        ing from want of elbow room. The major loss is in Louisa, a
        character worthy of George Eliot who remains a sketch. Re-
        views: John Bayley, **NYRB**, 8 October 1970, p. 8; K.J. Fielding,
        **Dickensian**, 66 (1970), 248; John Holloway, **Encounter**, 34
        (1970), 63–68; V.S. Pritchett, **NS**, 79 (1970), 807–08.

\*       ———.

        See A.E. Dyson and Angus Wilson (356).

856.    Wilson, Arthur. "The Great Theme in Charles Dickens." **Sus-
        quehanna University Studies**, 6 (1959), 422–57.

        Quotes a summary of **Hard Times** from Helen Rex Keller,
        **The Reader's Digest of Books** (New York: Macmillan, 1924, p.
        377). Wilson treats the novel, briefly, as Dickens's "heaviest
        blow," quoting Johnson (500) and Shaw (738).

857.    Wilson, Edmund. "Dickens: The Two Scrooges." **New Republic,**
        102 (March 1940), 297-300, 339-42. Rev. and enl. in **The**
        **Wound and the Bow.** Boston: Houghton Mifflin, 1941. Also in
        **Eight Essays.** New York: Doubleday, 1954. Rev. ed. New York:
        Oxford Univ. Press, 1947. Rpt. London: Methuen, 1961.

        Does not treat **Hard Times** as extensively as the other late
        novels. Wilson sees Dickens balancing between sympathy with
        the workers and criticism of the unions by the "rather implau-
        sible device" of Stephen's promise and identifies this ambiva-
        lence with Dickens's attitude toward the mob. The novel is the
        first, Wilson believes, in which Dickens traces "with any degree
        of plausibility the process by which people become what they
        are." Wilson looks also at the symbolism of the Old Hell Shaft
        and the coherence that the industrial town gives the novel.

858.    Wing, George. **Dickens.** Edinburgh: Oliver & Boyd, 1969, pp.
        57-62.

        Finds that theoretical exposition inhibits Dickens's great
        powers. **Hard Times** is best, Wing states, where the theories
        of economics are absent or only minimally present, as in the
        stories of Tom and Louisa.

859.    Winterich, John T. "How This Book Came to Be" (Introduction).
        In the Heritage edition, 1966 (47), pp. ix-xiv.

        Calls **Hard Times** the only instance in Dickens in which
        "the propaganda element was heavily dominant." Winterich re-
        views the circumstances of publication and Dickens's difficulties
        with the confined space.

860.    Winters, Warrington. "Dickens and the Psychology of Dreams."
        **PMLA,** 63 (1948), 984-1006.

        Offers useful background to Stephen's dream through a
        study of Dickens's theory of dreams, illustrated at points by
        Stephen's dream.

861.    -------. "Dickens' **Hard Times:** The Lost Childhood." **DSA,** 2
        (1972), 217-36.

Explains all the problems of the novel as the results of the intrusion of Dickens's own life into the novel, a life that did not document the thesis of the novel. (The lost childhood is Dickens's own.) Thus Bounderby's pretended origins are Dickens's real ones, and, according to Winters, the novel cannot endure the revelation of utterly different origins. Dickens miscalculates because he is too closely involved. The novel's revulsion at Tom Winters sees as arising from the fact that Tom is Charley (compare Sonstroem [761] and Stoehr [778]). Louisa's victimization is exactly like what Dickens's was, and here the author, character, and theme are in perfect accord. Again, Dickens's personal feelings intrude in his portrayal of Mrs. Gradgrind (Mrs. Dickens), Winters states, and Rachael has something of his feelings for Georgina. Winters interprets Stephen's dream, finding him and Rachael entirely successful characters. He uncovers a host of ambiguities surrounding the circus, however, because Dickens knew that an entertaining father was not reliable and not conducive to a happy childhood.

862. Wolfe, Charles Keith. "Charles Dickens and the **Theatrum Mundi.**" **DAI**, 31 (1970), 6076A-77A (Univ. of Kansas, 1970). 279 pp.

Sleary's horse riding is an instance of the pervasion of the stage metaphor throughout Dickens's career. For Dickens, the theater was a symbol or an image of writing.

863. Woodfield, Kate. "Fancy **versus** Fact." **Dickensian**, 5 (1929), 96-98.

An appreciation of the "most delightful and appealing thoughts" that the reader with eyes to see will find in **Hard Times**, focussing on childhood.

864. Worth, George J. **Dickensian Melodrama: A Reading of the Novels.** Lawrence: Univ. of Kansas Press, 1978, pp. 129-32.

Defines Dickensian melodrama and notes its increased subtlety in the later novels. There are melodramatic elements in Louisa's situation, Worth states, but they never lead to a melodramatic scene since she meets only the various silences of her father and Tom. Worth concludes that the hard soil of Coketown is not conducive to melodrama. Reviews: C. Herbert, **NCF**, 34 (1979), 448-52; Grahame Smith, **Dickensian**, 75 (1979), 75-76; J. Sudrann, **DSN**, 11 (1980), 56-58.

865.    Wright, Edgar.  **Mrs. Gaskell: The Basis for Reassessment.**
        London and New York: Oxford Univ. Press, 1965, pp. 29, 52–53,
        57.

        Suggests that Dickens drew on the episode of Bradshaw
        and his son in **Ruth** for Mr. Gradgrind and Tom and extends the
        comparison, noting as a significant difference Gaskell's more
        optimistic ending.  Dickens may also have used the elder Brad-
        shaw as a model for Bounderby, Wright adds.

866.    Wright, Thomas.  **The Life of Charles Dickens.**  New York:
        Scribner's, 1936, p. 227.

        Finds **Hard Times** unattractive and boring, Dickens's first
        failure, and hints at "affinities" with Gaskell's **Mary Barton.**

867.    Young, G.M.  "Mr. and Mrs. Dickens."  **Daylight and Champaign.**
        London: Jonathan Cape, 1937, pp. 26–30.  Rpt. in **Victorian Es-
        says.**  London: Oxford Univ. Press, 1962.

        A review–essay of Walter Dexter's edition of Dickens's let-
        ters to his wife.  Young asserts that after **David Copperfield**
        Dickens's genius was depleted, the nadir being reached by **Hard
        Times**, and sees a revival with **Great Expectations**, which he
        attributes to the separation from Catherine.

868.    –––––––.  **Victorian England: Portrait of an Age.**  London: Ox-
        ford Univ. Press, 1936.  2nd ed. 1953, pp. 101–02.

        In regard to the excitement of the fifties, remarks that
        "Tennyson in **Maud**, Dickens in **Hard Times** turned savagely on
        the age that had bred them."

869.    Yowell, Phyllis K.  "The Techniques of Characterization in the
        Novels of Charles Dickens."  Ph.D. Dissertation.  Univ. of Wash-
        ington, 1946.  385 pp.

        Accords relatively little attention to **Hard Times.**  Yowell
        notes its similarities to **Ruth** and **Mary Barton** and suggests
        that the lack of humor in Stephen and Rachael may be due to
        Mrs. Gaskell's influence.  She declares this the one novel of
        Dickens in which the characters are largely types, finds Slack-
        bridge among the "unquestionably bad thesis-characters," but

offers praise for E.W.B. Childers and Kidderminster. She concludes that the novel suffers from its compression, which leaves the symbolism broad and obvious but unenriched by detail.

# XII

## HANDBOOKS; TEXTS, GUIDES, AND
## COMMENTARY FOR SCHOOLS

870. Albert, Edward. **A History of English Literature**: **A Practical Text-Book**. New York: Crowell, 1924, p. 475.

Asserts that **Hard Times**, like all the later novels, suffers from the decline following **David Copperfield**.

871. Atkinson, F.G. "'Hard Times'--Motifs and Meanings." **Use of English**, 4 (1963), 165-69.

Argues that the themes and motifs of the novel make it good for school study and a better introduction to Dickens than many of his more characteristic works. Atkinson suggests the themes of the challenge to Gradgrindian philosophy and the assertion of the worth of human relations, outlining an analysis of the novel according to these themes. The analysis is traditional, except perhaps in its finding Rachael obstinate and smug and offering Sissy as a positive contrast. For Atkinson, however, the principal contrast to Sissy is Bitzer; he believes that they become in effect protagonist and antagonist in a battle for a humane outlook upon life.

872. Baker, Isadore L. **Charles Dickens: Hard Times**. Notes on Chosen English Texts. London: James Brodie, 1961. 70 pp.

Summarizes the plot and reviews the history of the novel in **Household Words**, Dickens's letters on its purpose, and the social background. Baker sees the novel as one in which the theme is developed by character, not action. She also reviews the characters, comments generally on the style, and offers chapter summaries, textual notes, and "revision questions." The notes are keyed to the Chesterton edition (35).

873.   Brown, Terence. **Hard Times.** Dublin: Educational Co. of Ire-
       land, 1974. 36 pp.

       A guide for children in Irish post-primary schools, includes
       the following sections: Introduction, Dickens and His Age, The
       Occasion of **Hard Times**, Characters, Plot and the Victorian Di-
       lemma, Dickens and Carlyle, Imagery, Techniques, The Meaning
       of the Novel, Projects, Guide to Reading, Some Essay Topics.
       The Introduction views the novel as a moral fable or allegory.

\*      Carnell, Hilary.

       See Dorothy Eagle and Hilary Carnell (882).

874.   Coles Editorial Board. **Dickens. Hard Times. Notes.** Toronto:
       Coles, 1982. 94 pp.

       Offers background for Dickens's life and works, Dickens's
       England, and **Hard Times** itself (the conditions of publication,
       the influence of Carlyle, industrialism as a target of satire, the
       divorce laws, education and the Department of Practical Art).
       The volume includes a brief plot summary, a descriptive list of
       characters, a chapter-by-chapter summary, character sketches,
       a review of the critical history, and a critical appraisal that
       notes the usual blemishes but concludes that the novel is a
       work of genius.  Selections are reprinted from Johnson (500),
       Stevenson (774), Ruskin (150), Gissing (418), Chesterton (265),
       Shaw (738), Orwell (650), Hobsbaum (468), and Cockshut (284).
       The work concludes with study topics and a brief bibliography.

875.   Crothers, George D., ed. **Invitation to Learning: English and
       American Novels.** New York: Basic Books, 1966, p. 102.

       A series of radio talks about great books.  In one talk Edgar
       Johonson mentions Dickens's point in **Hard Times** about the
       irrelevance of education based on pure facts, compared to one
       based on human nature.

876.   Davies, Hugh Sykes. "Hard Times." In **Charles Dickens: Notes
       on Literature.** Ed. Kenneth Allott **et al.** The British Council and
       Eichosha Publishing Co., 1977, pp. 15–25.

A basic introduction, reviews the social history in regard to education and industrialism. Sykes discusses Dickens's use of names and of repetition and asserts that the novel is "poetry." He translates Stephen and Sleary for our readier edification.

877.    Dickens, Charles. **Hard Times**. Abridged by G.T. Johns. London: Oxford Univ. Press, 1959. viii, 184 pp.

Illustrated by Lynton Lamb (107). Johns abridges the text and normalizes all dialect. The notes on "difficult words and phrases," pp. 181–84, include words such as "graminivorous" and "Gorgon." The novel is presented in thirty chapters, without book divisions.

878.    –––––––. **Hard Times**. Ed. N.L. Clay. The Guide Novels. London: Heinemann, 1960. 312 pp.

Various school materials follow the text. The "Assessment" calls the novel "an underrated success, a concentrated moral fable," but not as good as other Dickens novels.

879.    –––––––. **Hard Times**. Abridged and simplified by Roland John. Longman Structural Readers: Fiction, Stage 5. London: Longman, 1975. 107 pp.

The text is reduced to twenty-one chapters in 101 pages. The exercises that follow are mainly in sentence construction; some address comprehension of plot.

880.    –––––––. **Hard Times**, Adapted by Rosemary Border. Alpha Classics. Oxford: Oxford Univ. Press, 1979. 96 pp.

For non-native speakers of English, defined as "1500 headword level." Glossary includes words such as "innocent" and "rob." Stephen's speech is normalized. With six illustrations by Martin Cottam (96).

881.    –––––––. **Hard Times**. Abridged and simplified by Viola Huggins. London and Glasgow: Collins, 1979. 127 pp.

For non-native speakers of English and "reluctant" native readers, defined as for a 1500-word basic vocabulary. No apparatus except a "word puzzle" at the end. With twelve illustrations by Scoular Anderson (94).


882.    Eagle, Dorothy, and Hilary Carnell, eds. **The Oxford Literary Guide to the British Isles**. Oxford: Clarendon, 1977, p. 236.

   Claims that Manchester is the setting for **Hard Times**.


883.    Easson, Angus. **Hard Times: Critical Commentary and Notes**. London: Univ. of London Press, 1973. 71 pp.

   This booklet is divided into four sections: "Critical Commentary," pp. 7-48, "Biographical Note," pp. 49-50; "Further Reading," p. 51; "Notes," pp. 52-71. Easson offers the novel as a deliberate social tract occasioned by the need to bolster the sales of **Household Words**. He reviews the background and offers a close but basic analysis of chapters 1 and 2. The other sections of this introduction, brief and also basic, are: Education, Its Effects, Fancy, Fancy and Wonder, Fancy and Desire, Fancy and the Feelings, Fancy and Christianity, Dickens's Satire of the Men of Fact, Dickens's Christian Ideal of Society, The 'System' and People: Tom, James Harthouse, Coketown, Bounderby, Slackbridge, Stephen Blackpool, Gradgrind, Sissy Jupe, Sleary, Theme and Structure, Imagery, and Conclusion--The Place of **Hard Times** in Dickens's Work. Though "among Dickens's lesser works," this novel is "perhaps the greatest moral fable in English," Easson asserts. The notes are keyed to lines or phrases in the text and include much reference to secondary materials (criticism and social history). They also offer very good and thorough explications of allusions and obsolete terms such as "chandler's shop." Reviews: Ivan Melada, **DSN**, 6 (1975), 64-66; Anne Smith, **Dickensian**, 70 (1974), 62-63.


884.    Fisher, Lois H. **A Literary Gazeteer of England**. London and New York: McGraw Hill, 1980, pp. 482, 574.

   Locates Coketown as Preston or Rochdale or Oldham or Manchester, with the last seen as the most likely.


885.    Fyfe, Thomas Alexander. **Who's Who In Dickens. A Complete Dickens Repertory in Dickens' Own Words**. London, New York, etc.: Hodder & Stoughton, [1913], passim. Rpt. New York: Haskell, 1971; Detroit: Gryphon, 1971; Folcroft, Pa.: Folcroft, 1971; Norwood, Pa.: Norwood, 1975; Philadelphia: R. West, 1977.

Presents the characters in dictionary form, described by quotations from Dickens. Includes **Hard Times**.

\*      Gadd, W. Lawrence.

See Alex J. Philip and W. Lawrence Gadd (905).

886.   Gerber, Helmut E. "**Hard Times**: An Experience in Teaching." **College English**, 15 (1954), 351–53.

Asserts that the brevity and heterogeneity of the subject matter make **Hard Times** an excellent freshman text. Gerber suggests a variety of approaches for the instructor, including biographical detail, social history, theme and characterization, and bearing upon contemporary society.

887.   Greaves, John. **Who's Who in Dickens**. London: Elm Tree, 1972; New York: Taplinger, 1973, passim.

An alphabetical index; includes **Hard Times**. Review: George Worth, **CEA**, 37 (1974), 32–35.

888.   Handley, Graham. **Hard Times**. Oxford: Blackwell, 1969. 102 pp.

Part of the series "Notes on English Literature" designed for school, college, and university students. The "Introduction" begins with a brief critical history of the novel and a judicious review of Leavis (553), as well as a look at other modern critics. The section "The Uses of Character" emphasizes the variousness of purpose and portrayal in the characters and notes patterns of contrast: Bounderby and Stephen, Mrs. Sparsit and Sissy (Sissy is a sentimentalized "failure in imaginative projection"; Mrs. Sparsit is "grotesquely worth living with"). "Style and Structure" is divided into "Image and Symbol" and "Satire and Irony." Handley notes the parallel between the staircase and Stephen's fall into the pit and the wider opposition between natural images and the man-created. A central image is Louisa's fire. Handley analyzes in detail the various "voices of irony" and notes patterns of contrast. The next section, "Analysis of Chapter XV: Father and Daughter" is a close analysis with regard to the issues set forth hitherto. Finally, in the "Revaluation," Handley argues that the novel is in two modes, "a realistic mode or presentation and a Christian–cum–mythical one." Except for a few passages (Sissy with Louisa and some of Stephen's speeches), he finds this novel "singularly free from blemishes against truth."

889.   Hardwick, Michael, and Mollie Hardwick. **The Charles Dickens Companion.** London: John Murray, 1965, pp. xiii, 144–45, 247.

Places **Hard Times** within the chronology of Dickens's work, offers a plot summary, and notes how the unfamiliar locale lessens the effect of the book.

890.             , compilers. "Hard Times." **The Charles Dickens Encyclopedia.** Reading: Osprey; New York: Scribner's, 1973, pp. 20–21.

Finds the novel a tract rather than a story told for its own sake; blames the failure on the cramped space and Dickens's poor ear for dialect. The Hardwicks also summarize the plot.

891    Hardy, Barbara, and Michael Slater. **Dickens: Hard Times and Social Criticism; Great Expectations and Dickens's Art.** Recording. Audio Learning 11. Tape or cassette; supp. booklet by John Sutherland and Keith Walker.

Moves from a general discussion of the differences in Dickens's writings between his novels and his journalism to the particular instances in **Hard Times.** Notes the role of Merrylegs in upsetting Gradgrind's notions of human motivation and Dickens's belief in "original virtue." The supplementary booklet summarizes the discussion and offers background information on Dickens and recent Dickens criticism. Review: A[lan] S. W[atts], **Dickensian,** 73 (1977), 174–75.

892.   Harting, Emilie C. **A Literary Guide to England and Scotland.** New York: Morrow, 1976, p. 150.

Points out that Dickens wrote **Hard Times** during the period of his residence at Tavistock House.

893.    Hayward, Arthur L.    **The Dickens Encyclopedia: An Alphabeti-
cal Dictionary of Reference to Every Character and Place
Mentioned in the Works of Fiction, with Explanatory Notes
on Obscure Allusions and Phrases.** London: Routledge; New
York: Dutton, 1924, passim. Rpt. London: Routledge & Kegan
Paul, 1969.

> **Hard Times** is entered as are the other novels.  Coketown
> is identified as Manchester with "very little doubt."

894.    Hirschfield, Claire.    "**Hard Times** and the Teacher of History: An
Interdisciplinary Approach." **DSN**, 13 (1982), 33–38.

> Describes her experience of making **Hard Times** the center
> of a history course on the transition from agrarian to industrial
> production. The method is to discuss Coketown, "its problems,
> and its people, as if they existed in fact."

895.    Hogan, Emma.    **Charles Dickens' Hard Times: A Critical Introduction.** Cork and Dublin: Mercier Educational, 1973.  48 pp.

> Includes a brief biography, an outline of the plot, a section
> on Dickens's style in general illustrated from **Hard Times** (on
> apostrophe, emotionalism, the mock-heroic, dramatic imagery,
> humor, and details of characterization), a section on the techni-
> que of **Hard Times** (**Hard Times** as moral fable, the effects of
> weekly serialization; symbolism, pathos, imagery, satire, narra-
> tive, characterization), a section on the major characters, "Pro-
> jects and Questions," and a bibliography of five books.

896.    Jennings, John.    "**Hard Times**." Helicon Student Guides.  Dublin: Helicon, 1977.  56 pp.

> Contains a brief biography; short discussions of plot,
> themes, historical background, irony and moral fable, and im-
> agery; a chapter-by-chapter study with questions and some
> close questions on passages of text; a very brief bibliography.

897.    Johnson, Norman Croom.    **The Life-Story of Charles Dickens.**
London: Stead's, 1921, p. 37.

> This is Stead's Great Men Series, "FOR THE HOMES and
> SCHOOLS of the EMPIRE." Finds **Hard Times** a serious story
> about the poor, but not one of Dickens's happiest efforts.

898.    Johnson, William C. "Dickens and Demons: A Comparative Approach." **English Record**, 22, iii (1972), 33-40.

Argues that the teacher who assigns Dickens must make connections that will justify the assignment. Among the suggestions explored here are the evil character seen as monster or ogre, of which line Gradgrind is a member; Sissy as a good character compared to Jack the Giant-Killer; and Mrs. Sparsit as Bank Fairy/Bank Dragon similarly related to fairy-tale.

899.    Lincks, J.F. "The Close Reading of **Hard Times**." **English Journal**, 58 (1969), 212-18.

A description of procedures and methods in teaching **Hard Times** to eleventh-grade students.

900.    Locker, Kitty O. "Social Criticism as Theme: A Strategy for Teaching **Hard Times** and **Great Expectations**." **Illinois English Bulletin**, 67 (Fall 1979), 35-43.

Suggests a carefully limited study of social criticism as theme as the best approach to Victorian novels for American high school students. The limit can be derived from an emphasis on the contrast between a novel "whose social protest is straightforward" (**Hard Times**) and one that makes its points "less directly and more artistically" (**Great Expectations**). Further contrast can be provided by a sample of non-fictional social criticism, such as the Report on the Employment of Children in Coal Mines of 1842 (suitably abridged), Locker points out, demonstrating stylistic differences.

901.    McSpadden, J. Walker. **Synopses of Dickens' Novels**. New York: Crowell, 1904, 1909, pp. xii, 129-39. Rpt. Folcroft, Pa.: Folcroft, 1971; Norwood, Pa.: Norwood, 1975; Philadelphia: R. West, 1978.

Offers a cast of characters and a plot synopsis.

902.    Martin, Augustine. **Charles Dickens: Hard Times**. Study-guide Series. Dublin: Gill & Macmillan, 1974. 37 pp.

Includes a list of "Significant Dates," a section on Dickens's life and works, a section on the "Publishing History and Genre" and one on the "Themes and Their Background" of the novel, a chapter-by-chapter series of questions and occasional "verbal analysis," a series of general study questions, and a short reading list.

903.   Maxwell-Mahon, W.D.   "Charles Dickens: 'Hard Times.'" **Crux**, 5 (1971), 20-24.

Appearing in the section "For High Schools," reviews the story first as a tale of the proponents of Fact, then more briefly as Stephen's story, which is seen as properly overstated from the perspective of achieving reform, but as spoiling the novel somewhat.   Maxwell-Mahon concludes that this novel is significant for any period "in which people are treated as percentages, census increases, identity numbers, anything but human beings."

904.   Page, Norman, ed.   **Dickens: Hard Times, Great Expectations, Our Mutual Friend: A Casebook.**   London, Macmillan, 1979. 211 pp.

The "Introduction" reviews the genesis of the novel in the sales of **Household Words**; Dickens on the weekly serial; the reception of the novel, its later neglect, Leavis's discovery of it, and the anti-Leavis reaction.   Reprints selections from "Frauds on the Fairies" (14) and the letters; reviews in the **Athenaeum** (113), **Examiner** (115), **Rambler** (119), and **Westminster Review** (120); and excerpts from Taine (153), Ruskin (150), Whipple (155), Gissing (418), Shaw (738), House (475), Butt and Tillotson (240), and Lodge (577).

905.   Philip, Alex J., and W. Lawrence Gadd.   **A Dickens Dictionary**. London: Routledge; New York: Dutton, 1909.   2nd ed. Gravesend: "The Librarian"; London: Simpkin Marshall; Leipzig: Hedeler, 1928, passim. Rpt. New York: B. Franklin, 1970.

The authors' synopsis of the plot of **Hard Times** emphasizes the "futility of eliminating love and kindness from human life and intercourse."   The characters are included in the dictionary portion.

906.   Pierce, Gilbert A. **The Dickens Dictionary**. With additions by
       William A. Wheeler. Boston: Houghton Mifflin, [1872]. Rev. ed.,
       1914, pp. 360-70. Rpt. New York: Kraus, 1965; New York: Has-
       kell, 1972.

       As for all the novels, presents a brief introduction, a list of
       characters with quotations, and a plot summary for **Hard
       Times**.

*      Slater, Michael.

       See Barbara Hardy and Michael Slater (891).

907.   Stapleton, Peter T. "**Hard Times**: Dickens' Counter Cultures."
       **Clearing House**, 47 (1973), 380-81.

       On how to approach **Hard Times** with high school stu-
       dents. Stapleton emphasizes picking up the relevance of the
       schoolroom theme and the conflict of cultures (utilitarianism as
       opposed to "romantic individualism").

908.   Stones, Sandi Brinkman. "Pollution and the Relevance of the
       Nineteenth Century." **English Journal**, 62 (1973), 1177-79.

       Suggests that the issue of pollution can be a way to make
       nineteenth-century literature relevant to contemporary secon-
       dary school children, and offers Coketown and **Hard Times**
       among other instances.

909.   Williams, Mary. **The Dickens Concordance**. London: Francis
       Griffiths, 1907, pp. 37-38 and passim. Rpt. Folcroft, Pa.: Fol-
       croft; New York: Haskell, 1970; Folcroft, Pa.: Folcroft, 1974; Nor-
       wood, Pa.: Norwood, 1978.

       Includes a list of characters and places for **Hard Times** as
       for all the novels. The characters are also included in the al-
       phabetical index. Review: Joseph Gold, **DSN**, 3 (1972), 14-16.

910.   Zeiss, Cecilia. "Hard Times." **Crux**, 7 (1973), 19-23.

       Appears in the section "For High Schools." Starting from
       an exposition of laissez-faire economic theory, Zeiss reviews
       the background and then the characters of the novel. This

novel is exceptional to the rule that Dickens satirizes by
exaggeration and presents double-dyed villains, she claims.
Gradgrind and Bounderby are "more multifaceted and credible
than most Dickensian malefactors, and Louisa Gradgrind is relatively free of the insipid sentimentality that mars many of his
heroines." Zeiss believes that in this novel Bitzer and Mrs.
Sparsit are the only two Dickensian caricatures. Beyond these
remarks, this analysis proceeds along conventional lines to the
usual conclusions.

# XIII

# SELECTED BIBLIOGRAPHY

911. Carr, Sister Lucile. **A Catalogue of the VanderPoel Dickens Collection at the University of Texas**. Austin: Univ. of Texas, Austin, pp. 115, 124.

Lists two copies of the Bradbury & Evans first edition, one copy each of the Harper and McElrath 1854 editions, two other early editions, one translation, and various sets of **Household Words**.

912. Churchill, R.C. "**Hard Times**." **A Bibliography of Dickensian Criticism, 1836-1975**. New York: Garland; London: Macmillan, 1975, pp. 93-98.

Within the sections, devoted to the individual works and then to various topics, works are arranged chronologically. The preface asserts a certain emphasis on criticism of the early twentieth century, and the entries for **Hard Times** bear out this principle, but no other that is apparent. There are forty-eight items, ranging from the obvious and essential to the obscure, but there are also great omissions. Substantial quotations for several of the citations, particularly the earlier ones, make the bibliography more readable, a sort of miniature anthology (as intended). The cross-referencing is not systematic and there is no index. Reviews: Alan M. Cohn, **DSN**, 7 (1976), 120-22; K.J. Fielding, **MLR**, 72 (1977), 924-25; G.W. Kennedy, **VS**, 20 (1977), 343-45.

913. Cohn, Alan M., and K.K. Collins. **The Cumulated Dickens Checklist; 1970-1979**. Troy, New York: Whitston, 1982, passim.

An invaluable listing of secondary materials and recent editions, including items in obscure journals and some work in foreign languages. Annotations are occasional and very brief, but often very helpful. Reviews for books are also included.

The index is full and cross-referenced. This collection subsumes the quarterly checklists published in the **Dickens Studies Newsletter** (914), but also goes beyond them. Because the entries are merged, the cumulation is much easier to use than the quarterly lists.

914.    Cohn, Alan M.. et al. "The Dickens Checklist." **DSN**, 1,ii (September 1970)--.

A timely list in every quarterly issue of the newsletter. Includes reviews, adaptations, editions.

*       Collins, K.K.

See Alan M. Cohn and K.K. Collins (913).

915.    Collins, Philip. "Charles Dickens." In **Victorian Fiction: A Second Guide to Research**. ed. George H. Ford. New York: Modern Language Association, 1978, pp. 34-113.

Treats **Hard Times** both under the topical sections (on Industrialism in particular) and in the studies of individual novels. Collins's essay, like the others in this volume, covers the period 1963 through 1974; it is a sequel to Nisbet (926). Collins is deliberately very selective, offering a remarkable perspective in very short space. A few errors in the citations notwithstanding, this is the best overview of Dickensian criticism, including criticism of **Hard Times**, for the duodecade under examination.

916.    **A Dickens Library: Exhibition Catalogue of the Sawyer Collection**. [Letchworth, England], privately printed, 1936.

The catalogue includes a first edition of **Hard Times**, inserted in which is the letter from Dickens to the Rev. W. Harness (19 August 1854) concerning a copy of the novel that he had sent him and including the remark, "A great misgiving is upon me that in many things (this thing among the rest) too many are martyrs to our complaisancy and satisfaction, and that we must give up something thereof for their poor sakes." The letter is included in **Letters**, 2, 580 (1).

917.    Dunn, Frank T. **A Cumulative Analytical Index to the Dickensian, 1905-1974**. Hassocks: Harvester, 1976, passim.

Of great assistance, although the index does miss occasional items.

918.  Eckel, John C. **The First Editions of the Writings of Charles
Dickens.** New York: Inman; London: Maggs, 1913 p. 131.  2nd
ed. 1932. Rpt. Folcroft, Pa.: Folcroft, 1973; Havertown, Pa.: R.
West, 1976; Norwood, Pa.: Norwood, 1976.

Mainly for collectors.  Eckel omits **Hard Times** from the
first section, "The Important Novels," but includes it in the second, "The Secondary Books."

919.  Fenstermaker, John J. "Hard Times." **Charles Dickens,
1940-1975: An Analytical Subject Index to Periodical Criticism
of the Novels and Christmas Books.** Boston: G.K. Hall, 1979.
Pp. 165-74.

Selectively covers the period 1940-75.  Fenstermaker includes sixty-eight items on **Hard Times** listed alphabetically in
the "Bibliography for **Hard Times**" and deeply cross-references
in the subject index under fourteen major headings and several
dozen sub-headings.  The major headings are characterization;
characters; composition; critical assessment; explanatory notes,
historical background, and sources; influences; language and
style; literary parallels; point of view; setting; structure/unity;
various techniques; text; themes.

920.  Fridlender, IU., and I. Katarsky. **Charl'z Dikkens, bibliografia
russkih perevodov i kriticheskoi literatury na russkom iazyke,
1838-1960.** Moscow, 1962, pp. 92-93, 201-02.

Includes a table of contents in English.  Lists nine articles
in Russian on **Hard Times** between 1854 and 1952 and two
translations, 1855-1954.

921.  Gold, Joseph. **The Stature of Dickens: A Centenary Bibliography.** Toronto: Univ. of Toronto Press, 1971, pp. 157-61 and
passim.

**Hard Times** is covered pp. 157-61. See also the minimally
annotated section "Books, essays,  and articles primarily on
Dickens," pp. 3-114, which is not cross-referenced to the section on individual novels but does inevitably include work rele-

vant to them. Dissertations are listed in a separate section.
This bibliography covers 1870–1968, with some listings for
1969. It omits most "peripheral, occasional, and ephemeral
items." Reviews: Richard D. Altick, **NCF**, 17 (1972), 107–10;
Duane DeVries, **Dickensian**, 68 (1972), 188–91; K.J. Fielding,
**RES**, 24 (1973), 100–02; Robert Partlow, **DSN**, 2 (1971), 103–05.

922.    Gummer, Ellis N. **Dickens' Works In Germany 1837–1937**. Ox-
        ford: Clarendon, 1940, passim. Rpt. New York: Octagon, 1976.

        Surveys Dickens's reputation and influence in Germany
        1837–1937 and includes a list of German critical works on
        Dickens 1870–1937 as well as articles in German periodicals
        1837–77. Gummer suggests both the declining German interest
        in foreign literature after the revolutionary years and the dislike
        for **Bleak House** and **Hard Times** as causes for the diminished
        attention to Dickens in that period. On **Hard Times** he cites
        Julian Schmidt, Hermann Margraff, Otto Ludwig, A. Banning, P.
        Aronstein, W. Stumpf (783), Dibelius (337), Anselm Schlosser,
        and a number of unsigned contemporary reviews.

923.    Kitton, Fred[eric G.]. **Dickensiana: A Bibliography of the Lit-
        erature Relating to Charles Dickens and His Writings**. Lon-
        don: George Redway, 1886, passim. Rpt. New York: Haskell,
        1971.

        The sections of particular interest for **Hard Times** are Divi-
        sions I and II of the second part, "Critical," which survey essays
        and reviews criticizing Dickens and his works in general and
        essays and reviews criticizing particular works. The surveys
        are far from complete, but have the attraction of frequent
        lengthy quotation from the items discussed. The scrapbooks
        that collect much of the material in this book are at the Dick-
        ens House, London.

924.    Miller, William. **The Dickens Student and Collector: A List of
        Writings Relating to Charles Dickens and His Works,
        1836–1945**. Cambridge, Mass.: Harvard Univ. Press, 1946, pas-
        sim.

        Includes a few items for **Hard Times**. For a thoroughly
        critical review, see Philo Calhoun and Howell J. Heaney, "Dick-
        ensiana in the Rough," **Papers of the Bibliographical Society
        of America**, 41 (1947), 293–320. Another review: Ralph Straus,
        **Dickensian**, 43 (1947), 150–51.

925.    ———. "The Value of First Editions." **Dickensian**, 33 (1936),
        38–39.

        Gives 1936 values, for collectors, of first editions of the
        novels, including **Hard Times**, in the original cloth (30 to 50
        shillings) and rebound in leather (10 to 20 shillings).


926.    Nisbet, Ada. "Charles Dickens." In **Victorian Fiction: A Guide
        to Research**. ed. Lionel Stevenson. Cambridge, Mass.: Harvard
        Univ. Press, 1964, pp. 44–153.

        A magisterial and widely acclaimed selective review of
        Dickens criticism through 1962, refers directly to **Hard Times** at
        a variety of points but is most valuable for the critical context
        it offers.


927.    Podeschi, John B. **Dickens and Dickensiana: A Catalogue of
        the Richard Gimbel Collection in the Yale University Library**.
        New Haven: Yale Univ. Library, 1980, passim.

        Includes all four 1854 editions of **Hard Times**, a number of
        later editions, a number of translations, and a variety of adap-
        tations. Podeschi offers full bibliographical information for all
        items listed.


928.    Shepherd, Richard Herne. **A Bibliography of Dickens**. No im-
        print, [1880], p. 31.

        Lists the 1854 edition of **Hard Times**.

# INDEX OF PROPER NAMES
## (Authors, Historical Figures, Places)

Arabic numbers refer to numbered entries, small Roman numbers to pages in the Introduction. Numbers in bold indicate main entries. Works by authors other than Dickens are not named in the index, but references to them are included under the authors' names. References to authors that occur in a title but do not pertain to the commentary on **Hard Times** are not listed. Cross-references in the annotations are not listed. Charles Dickens is not listed.

Adams, Mabel Ellery  xv.
Abbs, Peter  xvi.
Addison, William  **156**.
Adrian, Arthur A.  **157**, **158**.
Aeschylus  791.
Alain [Emile Chartier]  **159**.
Albert, Edward  870.
Alexander, Edward  **160**.
Allbut, Robert  xiv.
Allen, Patrick  69.
Allen, Walter  44, **161**, **162**, **163**.
Allott, Kenneth  876.
Allott, Miriam  **164**.
Altick, Richard  787, 921.
Amalric, Jean-Claude  717.
Ames, Winslow  **165**.
Anderson, Scoular  **94**, 881.
Anderson, Warren D.  502.
Andrews, Malcolm  **166**, 851.
Andrews, Michael  **167**.
Angus, Ian  650, 651.
apRoberts, Ruth  **168**.
Armstrong, Nancy  xx, **169**, **170**.
Arneson, Richard J.  **171**.
Arnold, Matthew  643.
Aronstein, P.  922.
Atkinson, F.G.  **871**.
Augburn, Gerald Richard  **172**.

Austin, J.L. 830.
Axson, Stockton **173**.
Axton, Marie 192.
Axton, William **174, 175**, 247.
Aydelotte, William O. **176**.

Bacon, H. **95**.
Baily, F.E. **177**.
Baird, John D. xx, **178**.
Baker, Ernest **179**.
Baker, Isadore L. **872**.
Baker, William J. **180, 181**.
Ballflower, Robert 363.
Balzac, Honore de 199.
Banerjee, N.K. **182**.
Bank, Sylvia. **See** Sylvia B. Manning.
Banning, A. 922.
Barfoot, C.C. 546, 760, 803, 851.
Barish, Jonas **184**.
Barlow, George **185**.
Barnard, Robert **xviii, 186**.
Barnes, Catherine Weed **825**.
Barnes, Samuel G. **187**.
Bartrip, Peter W.J. xx, **6**.
Basch, Francoise **188**.
Bastable, Adolphus **70**.
Baugh, Albert C. 268.
Bayley, John **189, 190**, 449, 855.
Beadle, Gordon **191**.
Becker, May L. xiv.
Beer, Gillian **192**.
Beer, Max **193**, 394.
Belcher, Margaret E. **194**.
Bell, Quentin **195**.
Benn, J. Miriam **196**.
Bennett, Arnold **197**.
Bennett, Rachel 420.
Bentham, Jeremy 171, 191, 217, 338, 367, 368, 424, 432, 458, 499, 544,
    601, 737.
Bentley, Eric 272.
Bentley, Thomas 67.
Bentzon, Jorgen **89**, 91.
Bergmann, Helena **198**.
Bergonzi, Bernard 730.
Berman, Ronald **199**.
Bernard, Catherine Adelaide **200**.
Betsky, Seymour 849.
Bidder, George Parker 747.

Bilan, R.P. **201**.
Birmingham  1, 16, 63, 289, 334.
Bishop, Charles William  **202**.
Blackburn  336, 398.
Blake, William  189.
Blom, J.M. **203**.
Boarman, Joseph C. **204**.
Boarman, Martin Hollie  204.
Bodelsen, C.A. **205, 206**.
Boege, Fred W. **207**.
Bony, Alain  **208**, 756.
Border, Rosemary  **880**.
Bornstein, George  **209**.
Booth, Meyrick  **210**.
Boulogne  1.
Boulton, J.T. **211**.
Boulton, Marjorie  xvi, **212**.
Bracher, Peter Scholl  **213, 214**.
Bracken, Thomas  705.
Bradford  339.
Brantlinger, Patrick  **xx**, **215, 216, 217**, 289.
Brereton, Frederick  38, **218**.
Brett, R.L.  851.
Brice, Alec W.  378.
Briggs, Asa  52, **219**, **220**, 391, 680.
Bronte, Charlotte  319, 363, 674.
Brook, George L. **221**.
Brooker, Arlin Ihro  **222**.
Brooker, Peter  xvi, **223**.
Brough, Robert B. **90, 91**, 141, 293.
Brown, A.M.C.  363.
Brown, Arthur Washburn  **224, 225**.
Brown, Derek  235.
Brown, Ivor  **226, 227**.
Brown, James M. **228**.
Brown, Hannah Meredith  2.
Brown, Richard  832.
Brown, Robert Edwards  **229**.
Brown, T.H.  xiv.
Brown, Terence  **873**.
Browne, Gerald Duane  **230**.
Buchan, John  **231, 232**.
Buchen, Irving  **233**.
Buckler, William E.  xiii, **234**.
Buckley, Jerome H.  438.
Bulwer, Edward Lytton  194, 363.
Bunyan, John  763, 850.
Burdett-Coutts, Angela  1, 2, 294, 295, 379, 604.

Burgan, William   401.
Burke, Alan   363.
Burns, Elizabeth   848.
Burns, Tom   848.
Burton, Anthony   69, **71**.
Burton, H.M.   **235**.
Burton, Richard   **236**.
Bush, Douglas   **237**.
Butt, John   **238, 239, 240**, 299, 367, 414, 500, 904.
Butwin, Joseph C.   **241, 242**.
Byrd, Max   851.
Byron, George Gordon Lord   454, 780.

Cahill, Patricia Ann Ellen   **243**.
Calder, Jenni   **244**.
Calhoun, Philo   924.
Camerer, Rudi   **245**.
Canning, Albert   xiv.
Cannon, Susan Faye   **246**.
Carey, John   221, **247**, 554.
Carlisle, Janice Margaret   **248, 249**.
Carlton, W.J.   500.
Carlyle, Jane   390.
Carlyle, Thomas   1, 21, 22, 36, 162, 187, 223, 231, 256, 269, 288, 294,
    297, 326, 342, 350, 351, 362, 390, 421, 424, 452, 476, 489, 512, 522,
    529, 560, 570, 571, 587, 609, 613, 631, 644, 681, 738, 775, 784, 795,
    796, 810, 817, 849, 873, 874.
Carmichael, Thomas Arthur   **250**.
Carnall, Geoffrey   **251**.
Carnell, Hilary   **882**.
Carpenter, Mary   130.
Carr, Sister Lucile   **912**.
Carre, Jacques   **252**.
Carter, John Archer   **253**.
Cassid, Donna   **254**.
Caudwell, Christopher [Christopher St. John Sprigg]   **255**.
Cazamian, Louis Francois   203, **256**, 296, **558**.
Cazamian, Madeline L.   849.
Cecil, David   **257**.
Chadwick, Esther Alice [Mrs. Ellis H.]   **258**.
Chancellor, Edwin Beresford   **259**.
Chapman, Raymond   **260**.
Chapple, J.A.V.   135.
Charles, Edwin   **261**.
Chartier, Emile.   **See** Alain.
Chase, Richard   849.
Cheek, Edwin Rives   **262, 263**.
Chesterton, G.K.   35, **264, 265, 266**, 374, 422, 484, 529, 546, 874.

Chevalley, Abel **267**.
Chew, Samuel C. **268**.
Christian, Mildred G. **269**.
Christie, Octavius F. **270**.
Christmas, Peter 832.
Church, Michael 69.
Churchill, R.C. **271, 272, 273, 274, 275, 913**.
Clark, Charles xiii.
Clark, Cumberland **276, 277, 278**.
Clark, Harold Frank, Jr. **279**.
Clark, Mary Cowden xiii.
Clarke, I.F. 414.
Clarke, Jack 459, 635.
Clarke, Joseph Clayton. **See** Kyd.
Clay, N.L. **878**
Clay, Walter Lowe **130**.
Clayborough, Arthur **280**.
Clipper, Lawrence Jon **281**, 543.
Clutton-Brock, Arthur **282**.
Cockshut, A.O.J. 43, **283, 284, 285**, 815, 874.
Cohn, Alan M. 912, **914, 915**.
Colby, Vineta 787.
Cole, Henry 1, 165, 195, 376.
Coleridge, Samuel Taylor 643.
Coles Editorial Board **874**.
Coles, Nicholas Joe Howard **286**.
Collier, John 359.
Collin, Dorothy **287**.
Collins, K.K. **914, 915**.
Collins, Philip xvi, xx, 35, 45, 134, 139, 140, 149, 152, 260, **288, 289,**
    **290, 291, 292, 293, 294, 295, 296**, 500, 603, 605, 664, **916**.
Collins, R.G. 452.
Collins, Wilkie xvi, 326, 327.
Colmer, John **297**.
Colwell, C. Carter **298**.
Conrad, Joseph 519, 656.
Cook, E.T. 151.
Cook, Eliza 373.
Cooke, Michael 515.
Coolidge, Archibald C., Jr. **299, 300, 301**, 326.
Cooper, F. Renad 59, **72**.
Cooper, Frederick Fox **54**, 59, 72, 74, 76, 82, 84, 85, 141, 339.
Cooper, Lettice **302**.
Cooperman, Stanley **303**.
Coppieters, Rudy 659.
Cotsell, Michael 832.
Cottam, Martin **96**, 880.
Coustillas, Pierre 419, 482.

Coutts, Angela Burdett. **See** Angela Burdett-Coutts.
Coveney, Peter **304**, 343.
Cowden, David **305**.
Cowell, George 251.
Cowell, William **56**, 82.
Cox, C.B. **306**.
Craig, David 48, **307**, **308**.
Craig, G. Armour 766.
Crane, R.S. 505.
Crane, Walter **97**.
Cribb, T.J. 174, 778.
Crockett, Judith **309**.
Cross, Wilbur L. **310**.
Crotch, W. Walter **311**, **312**, **313**, **314**, **315**, **316**.
Crothers, George D. **875**.
Crothers, Samuel McChord **317**.
Cruikshank, George 14.
Cruse, Amy **318**.
Cunliffe, John W. **319**.
Cunningham, Peter 1, **131**, 681, 743, 817.
Cunningham, Valentine **320**.

Daiches, David **321**, 561.
Dark, Sidney **322**.
Darley, F.O.C. 28, **98**.
Darwin, Bernard **323**.
Darwin, Charles 45.
Daumier, Honore 593.
Davey, Samuel J. **324**.
David, Deirdre 464, 546.
Davies, Hugh Sykes **876**.
Davis, Earle **325**, **326**.
Davis, Nuell Pharr **327**.
Davis, Robert Con **328**.
Dean, F.R. **329**.
DeBacco, Ronald Eugene **330**.
DeCerjat, W.F. 1.
Defoe, Daniel 773.
DeMille, Barbara Munn **331**.
Deneau, Daniel P. 45, **332**.
Dennis, Carl **333**,
Dent, Harold C. **334**.
de Vooys, Sijna **335**.
DeVries, Duane 606, 921.
Dexter, Walter xv, 1, **8**, **336**, **522**, 867.
Dibelius, Wilhelm **337**, 922.
Dicey, A.V. **338**, 368.
Dickens, Catherine 861.

Dickens, Charles, the Younger  34, **339**, 861.
Dickens Fellowship  xv, **340**.
Dickens, Henry Fielding  1.
Dickens, Monica  50, **341**.
Dickins, Louis G.  **342**.
Dilnot, Alan  **343**.
Disraeli, Benjamin  xix, 176, 203, 525, 661, 678, 755, 836.
Dobie, Alan  69.
Dodsworth, Martin  225.
Dolby, George Charles  **344**.
Donovan, Frank  **345**.
Doran, W.J.  **346**.
Dostoevsky, Fyodor  284, 551, 588, 595, 607, 850.
Drew, Philip  **347**.
Duckworth, Alistair  780.
Dudai, Eleanor Joan  **348**.
Duncan, Robert W.  **349**.
Dunn, Frank T.  **917**.
Dunn, Richard J.  **350**, **351**, **352**, **353**, 390, 421, 803, 815.
Dyson, A.E.  **354**, **355**, **356**, 475, 853.

Eagle, Dorothy  **882**.
Eagleton, Mary  **357**.
Eagleton, Terence  **358**.
Easson, Angus  **359**, **360**, 361, 420, 500, 664, **883**.
Eckel, John C.  xiv, **918**.
Edge, Charles  187.
Edwards, Osman  **362**.
Eigner, Edwin M.  **363**, 511.
Eliot, George  xvii, 534, 536, 694, 843, 855.
Eliot, T.S.  607.
"Eliza"  **132**.
Ellison, Eugenia Adams  **364**.
Ellison, Owen  xiv.
Elloway, D.R.  49, **365**.
Elton, Oliver  **366**.
Engel, Monroe  43, 45, **367**, **368**.
Engels, Friedrich  489.
Evans, Mabel  **369**.
Ewing, Barbara  69.
Ewing, Majl  232.
Eytinge, Solomon, Jr.  26, **99**.

Fadiman, Clifton  **370**.
Farrah, Mary  **61**.
Faulkner, William  513, 514, 535.
Favorsky, V.  **100**.
Fawcett, Frank D.  60, **74**.

Fawkner, Harald William  **371**.
Fechter, Charles  1.
Fenstermaker, John J.  **919**.
Fido, Martin  256, **372**.
Fielding, Henry  164, 239, 850.
Fielding, K.J.  xvi, xx, **16**, 43, 45, 115, 165, 195, 247, 288, 308, **373**, **374**, **375**, **376**, **377**, **378**, **379**, **380**, **381**, **382**, 390, 421, 583, 622, 644, 776, 778, 784, 855, 912, 921.
Fields, James T.  146.
Finlay, Ian F.  **75**.
Fisher, B.F., IV  **383**.
Fisher, Lois H.  **884**.
Fisher, M.  30, **101**.
Fitzgerald, Edward  1, 571.
Fitzgerald, Percy  **384**.
Fitz-Gerald, S.J. Adair  59, 60, **76**.
Fleishman, Avrom  472, 730.
Fleissner, Robert E.  **385**.
Foot, Dingle  39, 53, **386**.
Ford, Boris  271, 525, 534.
Ford, George  xvi, xviii, **45**, 150, 249, 299, 340, 343, **387**, **388**, **389**, **390**, **391**, **392**, 401, 554, 738, 811, 853, 915.
Forster, John  xiii, 1, **115**, **133**, 135, 140, 234, 292, 293, 314, 378, 466, 530, 533, 831.
Forsyth, William  **134**, 293.
Fowler, Roger  **393**.
Fraser, Claud Lovat  **102**.
French, H.  **103**.
Freud, Sigmund  506, 579, 735, 778.
Frewer, Louis B.  **384**.
Fridlender, IU.  **920**.
Friedman, Alan W.  437.
Froude, J.A.  694.
Frye, Northrop  170, **395**, **396**, 402, 579.
Fulkerson, Richard P.  **77**.
Furness, Edna L.  **397**.
Fyfe, Thomas Alexander  **885**.

Gadd, W. Lawrence  **398**, **905**.
Gallagher, Catherine  **399**.
Ganz, Margaret  **400**.
Garis, Robert D.  **401**.
Garland, Barbara Carolyn  **402**.
Garnett, Richard  31, **403**, **404**.
Garrett, Peter K.  543.
Gaskell, Elizabeth  xiv, xvi, xix, 1, 123, 124, 125, 126, **135**, 176, 203, 251, 258, 287, 319, 357, 360, 373, 399, 450, 479, 509, 515, 525, 549, 585,

658, 659, 677, 678, 689, 723, 751, 758, 762, 774, 823, 824, 836, 840,
    849, 865, 866, 869.
Gaskell, William   359, 658.
Gattegno, Jean   **405**, **406**.
Gelfert, Hans-Dieter   **407**.
Gerber, Helmut E.   **886**.
Gerould, Gordon Hall   **408**.
Gerson, Stanley   **409**, **410**.
Gibson, Frank A.   **411**.
Gibson, John W.   **412**.
Giddings, Robert   247, 603.
Gifford, James Allen   **413**.
Gill, Stephen   420, 449.
Gilmour, Robin   xvi, xx, **414**, **415**, **416**, **417**, 803.
Gissing, George   216, **418** 419 874, 904.
Glancy, Ruth   730.
Gold, Joseph   **420**, 472, 909, **921**.
Goldberg, Michael   247, **421**, **422**, **423**, **424**.
Goldfarb, Russel M.   **425**.
Goldknopf, David   **xvi**, **426**.
Goldsmith, Oliver   773.
Gomme, A.H.   **427**.
Gooch, Bryan N.S.   89, **92**, 93.
Goode, John   584, 585.
Gordon, Elizabeth H.   **428**.
Gosse, Edmund   xiv, 404, 788.
Gourdault, Jules   **136**.
Graham, Eleanor   xv.
Gray, Donald   664.
Gray Paul E.   240, 264, 284, 288, 326, 373, 380, 418, **429**, 475, 500, 577,
    626, 631, 650, 775.
Greaves, John   **887**.
Green, Frank   **430**.
Green, Robert   **431**.
Greenwood, Edward   **432**.
Grego, Joseph   141.
Gregor, Ian   166, 379, 849.
Greiffenhagen, Maurice   39, 53.
Greimas, A.J.   169, 170, 491.
Grice, H. Paul   830.
Grimshaw, Mortimer   156, 193, 373.
Groom, Bernard   **433**.
Groome, W.H.C.   **104**.
Gross, John   190, 283, **434**, 471, 854.
Gross, Konrad   524, 852.
Grubb, Gerald Giles   **435**, 573.
Grylls, David   **436**.
Guerard, Albert   **437**.

Gummer, Ellis N.  922.

Haberman, Melvyn  438.
Haley, Bruce  439.
Halperin, John  440.
Hammond, R.A.  xiii.
Handley, Graham  888.
Hanley  341.
Hanworth, S.  60, 74, 76, 82, 84.
Harbage, Alfred B.  441.
Harder, Kelsie B.  442.
Hardwick, Michael  443, 889, 890.
Hardwick, Mollie  68, 443, 889, 890.
Hardy, Barbara  186, 247, 437, 444, 445, 446, 447, 448, 449, 554, 778,
    833, 891.
Harness, Rev. W.  916.
Harper, Howard M., Jr.  187.
Harris, Adrian  66.
Harris, Jack T.  450.
Harris, Stephen Leroy  451.
Harris, Wendell V.  452.
Harrison, Lewis  453.
Harte, James L.  204.
Harting, Emilie C.  892.
Harvey, W.J.  326, 577.
Harvey, William R.  454.
Hass, Robert  455.
Hawthorne, Nathaniel  363, 627.
Hayman, Ronald  456.
Hayward, Arthur L.  893.
Hazama, Jiro  457.
Hazen, Lynn Shuford  458.
Heany, Howell J.  924.
Hearn, Arthur S.  459.
Heck, Edwin J.  460.
Henderson, James P.  461.
Henkle, Roger B.  462.
Herbert, Christopher  864.
Hewitt, Douglas  659.
Hibbert, Christopher  463.
Hill, A.G.  401.
Hill, Nancy K.  464, 465.
Hill, Octavia  137.
Hill, Thomas W.  9, 93, 466, 790.
Hirsch, David M.  45, 467, 761.
Hirschfield, Claire  894.
Hobsbaum, Philip A.  468, 874.
Hodge, Jan Douglas  469.

Hodgson, W.B.   116, **138**.
Hoey, Mrs. Frances Cashel   **139, 140**.
Hogan, Emma   **895**.
Hogarth, Georgina   529, 560, 861.
Hoggart, Richard   849.
Holdsworth, William S.   **470**.
Holloway, John   xv, 45, 216, 221, 289, 297, 379, 415, 467, **471**, 554, 585, 761, 855.
Hopcraft, Arthur   69.
Hoppe, A.J.   113.
Hornback, Bert G.   **472, 473**.
Horne, Lewis B.   **474**.
Horton, Susan   225.
Hotten, John C.   54, **141**.
Houghton, Arthur Boyd   **105**.
House, Humphrey   215, **475**, 904.
Houtchens, Lawrence Huston   **476**.
Howard, David   **477**, 584, 585.
Howe, Irving   849.
Howells, William Dean   **478**.
Hudson, Samuel, Jr.   **479**.
Hudson, Virginia O'Rear   56, **78**.
Huggins, Viola   **881**.
Hughes, Helen S.   **581**.
Hughes, James Laughlin   **480**.
Hughes, William Richard   **481**.
Hulin, Jean-Paul   **482**.
Humphrey, Harold E.   **483**.
Hunt, Peter R.   **484**.
Hurley, Edward   **485**.
Huxley, Aldous   xvii, 618, 619, 698.
Hynes, Samuel   255.

Ibe, Marcellinus Ukanwata   **486**.
Inglis, Fred   **487**.
Irwin, John   69.
Irwin, Michael   69, **79**.

Jackson, Holbrook   **488**.
Jackson, Thomas A.   **489**.
Jacox, Francis   **142**.
Jain, S.P.   **799**.
James, Henry   189, **490**, 517, 643, 769, 779, 803.
James, Louis   515, 851.
Jameson, Fredric   xvi, 170, **491**.
Jan, Isabelle   **406**.
Janowitz, Katherine E.   **492**.
Jansonius, Herman   **493**.

Jarmuth, Sylvia L. **494**, **495**.
Jaspers, Karl  467.
Jeans, Samuel  **496**.
Jeffreys, Stephen  **66**.
Jennings, John  **896**.
Jerrold, Walter  30, **497**.
Jerrold, William Blanchard  **143**.
John, Roland  **879**.
Johns, G.T.  **877**.
Johnson, Alan P.  **498**.
Johnson, E.D.H.  **499**.
Johnson, Edgar  1, **2**, 340, 367, 387, 401, 449, **500**, **501**, **502**, **503**, 595, 680, 836, 856, 874, 875.
Johnson, Norman Croom  **897**.
Johnson, Samuel  164.
Johnson, Wendell Stacy  **504**.
Johnson, William C.  **898**.
Jones, Elizabeth Falk  **505**.
Jones, Ernest  **506**.
Jones, Florence  **507**.
Jones, Henry Arthur  838.
Jonson, Ben  838.
Joubert, Andre  **508**.
Joyce, Patrick  **509**.
Jump, J.D.  **510**.

Kafka, Franz  535, 765, 850.
Kaplan, Fred  **511**.
Karl, Frederick R.  **512**.
Karlin, David  546.
Katarsky, I.  **920**.
Kauffman, Linda  **513**, **514**.
Kay–Shuttleworth, Sir James  2.
Keating, P.J.  xix, **515**.
Keim, Albert  **516**.
Keller, Helen Rex  856.
Kellogg, Robert  **728**.
Kelly, Thomas  **517**.
Kelty, Jean McClure  **518**.
Kennard, Jean E.  **519**.
Kennedy, Alan  **520**.
Kennedy, G.W.  **521**, 912.
Kennethe, L.A.  **See** Walter Dexter.
Kent, William R.G.  **523**, **524**.
Kettle, Arnold  203, **525**, **526**, 535.
Killham, John  **527**.
Kincaid, James R.  320, 343, 468, **528**.
Kingsley, Charles  xix, 176, 203, 755, 774.

Kingsmill, Hugh [Hugh Kingsmill Lunn]   529.
Kirby, Thomas Austen   828.
Kirkby, Joan   515.
Kitton, Frederic G.   xiv, 32, **530**, **531**, **532**, **533**, **923**.
Klingopulos, G.D.   **534**.
Knapp, Bettina   535.
Knight, Charles   1, 133, 141, **144**, 211, 379, 471, 497, 655.
Knight, Everett   **535**.
Knoepflmacher, U.C.   **536**.
Kogan, Bernard   **537**.
Korg, Jacob   515
Kotzin, Michael   **538**, **539**.
Kovacevic, Ivanka   **540**, **541**.
Kreutz, Irving W.   **542**.
Kroeber, Karl   780, 787.
Kucich, John   **543**.
Kumar, Shiv K.   854.
Kyd [Joseph Clarke Clayton]   **106**.

Labov, William   830.
Laird, John   **544**.
Lamb, Cedric   **545**.
Lamb, Lynton   **107**, 877.
Lambert, Mark   **546**.
Lane, Lauriat, Jr.   150, 174, 449, 606, 738, 811, 853.
Lang, Andrew   29, **547**.
Lang, Cecil Y.   780.
Langer, Suzanne   402.
Langland, William   507.
Langton, Robert   **548**.
Lansbury, Coral   **549**.
Larson, Janet Karsten   **550**.
Lary, N.M.   **551**.
Lawrence, D.H.   xvi, xviii, 190, 434, 595, 617, 619, 675, 702, 785.
Layard, Henry   681, 685.
Lazenby, Walter Sylvester, Jr.   56, **80**.
Leacock, Stephen   **552**.
Leavis, F.R.   xv, xvii, xviii, xix, xx, 45, 162, 168, 170, 189, 201, 203, 223,
       271, 274, 284, 288, 289, 297, 302, 325, 326, 367, 375, 380, 401, 412,
       427, 432, 437, 456, 467, 471, 527, **553**, **554**, 583, 585, 590, 595, 632,
       643, 647, 678, 686, 703, 713, 714, 732, 749, 761, 764, 766, 769, 818,
       853, 855, 888, 904.
Leavis, Q.D.   **554**, 703.
Leech, Geoffrey N.   **555**.
Leffman, Henry   **556**, **557**.
Legouis, Emile   **558**.
Leigh, Percival   154.
Leimberg, Ingeborg   **559**.

Lemmonier, Leon  **560**.
Lemon, Mark  1, 659.
Lerner, Laurence  **561**, **562**, **563**, 577.
Levine, George  51, **564**, **565**.
Levine, Richard A.  175, 363, **566**.
Levy, Herman Mittle  **567**.
Ley, J.W.T.  133, **568**, **569**, **570**, **571**.
Lewis, Leslie L.  326.
Lightwood, James T.  **572**.
Lincks, J.F.  **899**
Lindsay, Jack  **573**.
Linehan, Thomas M.  **574**, **575**.
Lion, Leon M.  67.
Liverpool  336, 368.
Locker, Kitty O.  **900**.
Lodge, David  xvi, 520, **576**, **577**, 830, 904.
Lohrli, Anne  14.
London  405, 730.
Long, William J.  xiv.
Lopez, Toni Ann  **578**.
Lord, William Frewen  xiv.
Lougy, Robert E.  **579**.
Love, Theresa R.  **580**.
Lovett, Robert M.  **581**.
Lowe, James  **14**.
Lucas, Audrey  **582**.
Lucas, John  203, 477, **583**, **584**, **585**.
Ludwig, Otto  801, 922.
Lukacs, Georg  769.
Lumet, Louis  **516**.
Lundgren, Bruce Raymond  **586**.
Lunn, Hugh Kingsmill.  **See** Hugh Kingsmill.
Lupton, Edward B.  **587**.
Lynn, Eliza  **14**.

McCarthy, Mary  **588**.
McCormick, I.C.  **589**.
McCormick, John  **590**.
M'Culloch, J.M.  45, 429, 471.
McGillis, Roderick F.  **591**.
MacInnes, W.D.  558.
McKenzie, Charles H.  **592**.
McKenzie, Gordon  **593**.
McKenzie, Jeanne  **594**.
McKenzie, Norman  **594**.
MacKenzie, R. Shelton  **145**.
McMaster, R.D.  288, 326, 472, 539, **595**.
McMurtry, Jo  **596**.

McNulty, J.H. **597**.
McSpadden, J. Walker **901**.
McVeagh, John **598**.
Macaulay, Thomas B. xx, **146**, 155, 264, 612, 668, 695.
Macey, Samuel L. **599**.
Mack, Maynard 379.
Maddox, James 780.
Magnuson, Gordon Arnold **600**.
Maine, Sir Henry James Sumner 368, **601**.
Manchester 1, 289, 329, 336, 398, 443, 530, 531, 548, 571, 608, 758, 825, 882, 884, 893.
Manheim, Leonard F. **602**.
Mankowitz, Wolf **603**.
Manning, John **604**, **605**.
Manning, Sylvia B. **606**.
Marcus, Steven 284, **391**, **607**, **608**.
Marcuse, Herbert 579.
Margraff, Herman 922.
Marriott, Sir John **609**.
Marshall, Percy **610**.
Marshall, William H. **611**.
Martin, Augustine **902**.
Martin, Robert Bernard **663**.
Martineau, Harriet 14, 17, 45, **147**, **148**, 293, 382, 540.
Marx, Karl xvi, 176, 489, 616.
Marzials, Frank T. **612**.
Mason, Tom **62**, 82.
Masson, David xiii.
Matz, B.W. **81**, **613**, **614**, 655.
Maurois, Andre **615**.
Maxwell-Mahon, W.D. **903**.
Meakin, David **616**.
Meckier, Jerome 584, 585, **617**, **618**, **619**.
Meers, Geneva Mae **620**.
Meier, Stefanie **621**.
Meisel, Martin 174.
Melada, Ivan **622**, 882.
Melville, Herman 363, 385.
Meredith, George xvi, 233, 702, 762, 780.
Michasiw, Barbara Lorene **623**.
Middendorf, John H. 41, **624**.
Middlebro', Thomas Galbraith **625**.
Miles, Hamish 615.
Mill, John Stuart xx, 45, 155, 160, 162, 171, 176, 180, 285, 342, 365, 380, 415, 458, 512, 654, 713, 808.
Miller, J. Hillis 284, 340, **626**.
Miller, William **9**, 93, **924**, **925**.
Mills, Nicolaus C. **627**.

Miyazaki, Koichi  **629**.
Moers, Ellen  **630**.
Moliere [Jean Baptiste Poquelin]  788.
Monod, Sylvere  xvi, **10**, **45**, 247, **340**, 343, **392**, 421, 546, 594, **631**, **632**, **633**, **634**, 664, 730, 776, 780, 784, 803, 833.
Montague, Charles W.  459, **635**.
Morley, Henry  **14**, 17, 43, 241, 368, 376, 415, 417.
Morley, John  822.
Morley, Malcolm  55, 56, 57, 58, 59, 60, 62, **82**.
Morris, William  376.
Moses, Belle  **636**.
Mudrick, Marvin  554.
Muller, Charles H.  **637**.
Mumford, Louis  xvi.
Murray, Isobel  xvii.
Murry, John Middleton  **638**.

Nadel, Ira Bruce  **639**.
Naslund, Sena Jeter  **640**.
Nation, W.H.C.  **59**, 72, 74, 76, 82, 84, 141, 533.
Nelson, Harland S.  **641**, **642**.
Nevius, Blake  382.
Newman, John Henry  431.
Newman, S.J.  **643**.
Nicoll, Allardyce  55, 57, 58.
Nisbet, Ada  367, 382, 915, **926**.
Northrop, F.S.C.  578.
Norton, Charles Eliot  151.

O'Connor, Feargus  193.
Oddie, Walter  **644**.
O'Faolain, Sean  **645**.
O'Flinn, Paul  **646**.
O'Kell, R.  217.
Oldham  220, 716, 884.
Oliphant, Margaret  **xiii**, **122**, **124**, 530.
Olive, William John  828.
Olney, James  500.
Olsen, Stein Haugom  **647**.
Olson, Elder  505.
O'Mealy, Joseph Howard  **648**.
Organ, Dennis  **649**.
Orr, William Somerville  181.
Orwell, George  xvii, 191, 535, 585, **650**, **651**, 698, 764, 874.
Orwell, Sonia  650, 651.
Osborne, Esther Euraleen  **652**.
Ousby, Ian  **653**.

Packe, M. St. John  **654**.
Page, John T.  **655**.
Page, Norman  221, 577, **656**, **657**, **658**, **659**, 738, **904**.
Palmer, William J.  **660**.
Panitz, Esther  **661**.
Parnell, Nancy Stewart  **662**.
Parrott, Thomas Marc  **663**.
Parssinen, T.M.  511.
Partlow, Robert B., Jr.  292, 921.
Parton, Jeff  64, 91.
Patten, Robert L.  xiii, 372, **664**, 730.
Paulson, Ronald  577.
Payne, Clyde Ladell, Jr.  **665**.
Peacock, W.F.  **666**.
Pearce, Roy Harvey  377, 395.
Pears, Charles  36, **108**.
Pearson, Ann Bowling  **667**.
Pearson, Gabriel  190, 283, 434, 471, 854.
Pearson, Hesketh  **668**.
Pechey, R.F.  **669**.
Pendered, Mary L.  **670**.
Perkins, Donald  **671**.
Perri, Carmela  840.
Perrins, Tony  **64**, 70.
Petersen, Barry Thorvald  **672**.
Petlewski, Paul John  **673**.
Peyrouton, Noel C.  340, 367.
Phelps, William Lyon  xiv.
Philip, Alex J.  **905**.
Pickering, Sam  247.
Pierce, David  **357**.
Pierce, Dorothy  **84**.
Pierce, Gilbert A.  **906**.
Pinion, F.B.  **674**, **675**.
Pitt, George Dibden  **55**, 82.
Pittock, Malcolm  849.
Pocock, D.C.D.  **676**.
Podeschi, John B.  24, **927**.
Pollard, Arthur.  xix, 135, 285, **677**, **678**.
Pook, John  **679**.
Pope, Norris  **680**.
Pope-Hennessy, Una  **681**.
Pothet, Lucien  xx, **682**.
Potter, Robert  791.
Pratt, Branwen Elizabeth Bailey  603, **683**, 815.
Pratt, Mary Louise  830.

Preston   1,  14,  118,  131,  133,  148,  156,  235,  251,  302,  336,  373,  375,
    443, 493, 497, 531, 560, 603, 613, 681, 716, 743, 775, 817, 831, 884.
Preston, Edward A.  **684**.
Price, Martin   401, 444, 449, 606, 778, 833, 854.
Priestley, J.B.  **685, 686**.
Pritchett, V.S.   766, 855.
Procter, William C.  **687**.
Propp, V.  170.
Pugh, Edwin   524, **688**.

Quiller-Couch, Sir Arthur   xiv, **689**.
Quirk, Eugene Francis   **690**.
Quirk, Randolph D.  **691, 692, 748**.

Raleigh, John H.  **693**.
Rance, Nicholas   **694**.
Rantavaara, Irma   **695**.
Rathburn, Robert Charles   237, 389, **696**.
Ray, Gordon N.   154, 500.
Ray, Laura Krugman   **697**.
Raymond, Charles   47, **109**.
Reade, Charles   126, 203, 581.
Reed, John P.  **698**.
Reed, John R.   xvii, **699**.
Reynolds, Margaret   464.
Ricardo, David   155.
Richardson, Joanna M.   35, **700**.
Roberts, David   **701**.
Roberts, Thomas J.   xvi, **702**.
Robertson, P.J.M.  **703**.
Robertson, T.W.  **57**.
Robison, Rosalee Irene   **704**.
Robson, W.W.   446, 554.
Rochdale   398, 884.
Rodd, Walter B.  **705**.
Roe, Frank G.  **706**.
Rogers, Hudson   387.
Rolfe, Franklin P.   387.
Romanofsky, Barbara Ruth   **707**.
Rooke, Eleanor   **708**.
Rosenberg, Edgar   **709**.
Rounds, Stephen R.   550, **710**.
Routh, Harold Victor   **711**.
Rudolf, Anthony   188.
Ruskin, John   xv, xx, xxi, 43, 45, 133, **150**, **151**, 155, 195, 216, 223, 246,
    256, 293, 294, 376, 378, 401, 496, 497, 524, 530, 569, 585, 597, 612,
    622, 655, 688, 695, 738, 788, 831, 852, 874, 904.
Russell, Frances Theresa   **712**.

Russell, Percy  xiv.
Ryals, Claude de L.  503.
Ryan, Alan  **713**.

Sacks, Sheldon  505.
Sadock, Geoffrey Johnson  **714**.
Sadrin, Anny  **406, 715, 716, 717**.
Saintsbury, George  **718, 719, 720**.
Sala, George Augustus  539.
Sampson, George  **721**.
Samuels, Allen  815.
Sanders, Andrew  594, **722**.
Sanders, George DeWitt  **723**.
Sawchuck, Mariette Timmins  **724**.
Schachterle, Lance Edward  **725**.
Schelly, Judith May  **726**.
Schilling, Bernard N.  **727**.
Schlosser, Anselm  922.
Schmidt, Julian  922.
Scholes, Robert  **728**.
Schramm, David Eugene  **729**.
Schwarzbach, F.S.  **730**.
Schuster, C.I.  776.
Schwob, Marcel  197.
Scollins, Richard  50, **110**.
Scudder, Vida D.  **731**.
Searle, John  830.
Sedgely, Anne  **732**.
Seehase, Georg  **733**.
Seiple, Jo Ann Massie  **734, 735**.
Senelick, Lawrence  225, 778.
Shaftesbury, Lord  571.
Shakespeare, William  xvi, 159, 284, 617, 702.
Shapiro, Charles  42, **736**.
Sharma, Basudeo  **737**.
Shatto, Susan  546.
Shaw, George Bernard  xv, xx, xxi, 36, 45, 325, 422, 463, 501, 529, 569, 633, 685, 709, **738, 739**, 856, 874, 904.
Sheff, Pamela H.  **740**.
Shelden, Michael Carl  **741**.
Shelley, Percy Bysshe  579.
Shelston, Alan  **742**.
Shepherd, Richard Herne  **928**.
Short, Michael H.  **555**.
Shusterman, David  **743**.
Shuttleworth, Sir James Kay.  **See** Sir James Kay-Shuttleworth.
Simon, Irene  766.
Simons, Victor  **63**.

Simpson, David  **744**.
Simpson, Richard  **119**, 293.
Sinnett, Jane  **120**, 293.
Skilton, David  **745**.
Slater, Judith Fairbank  **746**.
Slater, Michael  65, **85**, 447, 594, 644, 833, 848, **891**.
Sloane, David E.E.  **747**.
Smiles, Samuel  760.
Smith, A.H.  **748**.
Smith, Adam  155.
Smith, Anne  35, 40, 42, 45, 46, 48, 308, **382**, 700, 736, **749**, **750**, 829, 850, 882.
Smith, David  **751**.
Smith, Frank  **752**.
Smith, George W.  **753**.
Smith, Grahame  299, **754**, 864.
Smith, Mabelle S.C.  612.
Smith, Sheila M.  203, 515, **755**, **756**, **757**, **758**.
Smithers, David Waldron  **759**.
Smollett, Tobias  846.
Solomon, Pearl Chesler  **760**.
Sonstroem, David  **761**, 830.
Spanberg, Sven–Johan  **762**.
Speare, Morris Edward  **763**.
Spector, Robert Donald  43, **764**.
Sperry, Stuart  780.
Spilka, Mark  **765**.
Sprigg, Christopher St. John.  **See** Christopher Caudwell.
Stacey, W.S.  **111**.
Stang, Richard  **766**, 784.
Stansky, Peter  217.
Staples, Leslie  63, 386.
Stapleton, Peter T.  **907**.
Stark, Myra Carol  **767**.
Steedman, Amy  xiv.
Steig, Michael  326.
Stein, Sondra Gayle  **768**.
Steiner, George  **769**.
Steinmann, Martin, Jr.  237, 389, **770**.
Stephen, Fitzjames  **126**.
Stern, J.P.  **771**.
Sterne, Lawrence  xvi, 702.
Stevens, James S.  **772**, **773**.
Stevenson, Lionel  xvi, 573, **774**, **775**, 874.
Stewart, Garrett  **776**, **777**.
Stoddard, Francis  xiv, xvii.
Stoehr, Taylor  **778**.
Stone, Donald David  **779**, **780**

Stone, Harry  14, **16**, 539, 594.
Stonehouse, Roy  69.
Stones, Sandi Brinkman  **908**.
Stott, George  **152**, 293.
Straus, Ralph  **781**, **782**, 924.
Stumpf, Willy  **783**, 922.
Sucksmith, Harvey Peter  664, **784**.
Sudrann, Jean  864.
Sullivan, Mary Rose  **785**.
Supple, Barry  **563**, **786**.
Sussman, Herbert L.  **787**.
Sutherland, J.A.  299.
Sutherland, James  664.
Sutherland, John  891.
Swift, Jonathan  **593**.
Swinburne, Algernon Charles  313, 419, **788**, **789**.
Symons, Julian  **790**.
Szirotny, J.S.  **791**.

Taine, Hippolyte A.  45, 133, **153**, 293, 303, 533, 904.
Tanabe, Masami  **792**.
Taplin, Kim  **793**.
Tarantelli, Carole Beebe  **794**.
Tarr, Rodger I  350, 390, **795**, **796**.
Taverner, H.T.  141.
Tassone, Frank Allen  **797**.
Tennyson, Alfred Lord  868
Tennyson, G.B.  606, 644.
Ternan, Ellen  446.
Tewari, R.P.  **798**, **799**.
Thackeray, William Makepeace  xiii, 19, 141, **154**, 239.
Thatcher, David S.  **92**.
Theimer, Robert Hugo  **800**.
Thomas, Deborah  664.
Thomas, Gilbert  288.
Thomas, Hugh  **65**, 73, 85.
Thomas, L.H.C.  **801**.
Thomas, W.M.  141.
Thompson, A. Hamilton  **802**.
Thomson, Patricia  784.
Thorlby, Anthony  561.
Thurley, Geoffrey  **xix**, **803**.
Tick, Stanley  **804**.
Tillotson, Kathleen  **240**, 299, 766.
Timmerman, John Hager  **805**.
Tindall, William York  **806**.
Tomlin, E.W.F.  226.
Tong, Jacqueline  69.

Torchiana, Donald T. 766.
Torgovnick, Marianna **807**.
Trilling, Lionel **808**.
Tropp, Asher xvii, **809**.
Turow, J. **383**.

Ueki, Kensuke **810**

Van Ghent, Dorothy **811**.
Van Hall, Sharon K. **812**.
Van Heyningen, C. **813**.
Van Laun, H. 153.
Venturi, Emilie 789.
Vicinus, Martha 515.
Vincent, John **814**.
Vogel, Jane **815**.
Vos, Nelvin 402.
Voss, A.E. **816**.

W., A. **125**.
W., C. 91, **93**.
Wagenknecht, Edward **817**.
Waldock, A.J.A. **818**.
Walker, Frederick 25, 27, 28, 29, 31, 33, 39, 53, **112**.
Walker, Keith 891.
Wall, Stephen 583, 784.
Waller, A.R. 719.
Walsky, Joan Ross **819**.
Walters, John C. **820**.
Ward, A.C. **821**.
Ward, Sir Adolphus William 719, **822**, **823**, **824**.
Ward, H. Snowden **825**.
Warner, Rex **826**.
Warren, William 78, 80.
Watson, George 814, **827**.
Watson, Mrs. Richard 1.
Watson, Thomas L. **828**.
Watt, Ian 395, 554, 849.
Watt, James C. xiv.
Watt, William W. 40, 764, **829**.
Watts, A.S. 680, 891.
Watts, Cedric 356, 563.
Watts, Richard J. **830**.
Waugh, Arthur 33, **831**.
Webb, Igor **xx**, **832**.
Wedderburn, Alexander 151.
Weintraub, Stanley 738.
Wells, H.G. 619.

Welsh, Alexander   420, 776, 778, **833**, **834**.
Welsh, Alfred H.   **835**.
West, Anthony   500, **836**.
West, E.G.   xvii, **837**.
Weygandt, Cornelius   **838**.
Wheeler, Burton Maynard   **839**.
Wheeler, Michael   **840**.
Wheeler, William A.   906.
Whipple, Edwin P.   xiii, 28, 43, 45, **155**, 293, 904.
Whiteford, Robert Naylor   **841**.
Whitfield, A. Stanton   **842**.
Whitlock, Roger Dennis   **843**.
Whitlow, Roger   **844**.
Widdowson, Peter   223.
Wioner, Martin J.   **045**.
Wierstra, F.D.   **846**.
Wilde, Oscar   xvii.
Wilkins, William Glyde   xiv.
Williams, Bransby   67.
Williams, Ioan   **847**.
Williams, Mary   **909**.
Williams, Raymond   46, 192, 203, 585, 833, **848**, **849**, **850**, **851**, **852**.
Wills, W.H.   1, **14**, 17.
Wilson, Angus   **350**, **440**, **053**, **054**, **855**.
Wilson, Arthur   **856**.
Wilson, Edmund   551, **857**.
Wilt, Judith   680.
Wimsatt, William K.   395.
Wing, George   **858**.
Winterich, John T.   47, **859**.
Winters, Warrington   **860**, **861**.
Wise, T.J.   788.
Wolfe, Charles Keith   **862**.
Woodfield, Kate   **863**.
Woodings, R.B.   **11**.
Wordsworth, William   xvi, 162, 246, 702, 780.
Worth, George J.   420, 421, 546, 733, **864**, 887.
Worth, Katherine J.   174.
Wright, Edgar   **865**.
Wright, Thomas   **866**.

Yates, Edmund H.   91.
Young, G.M.   **867**, **868**.
Yowell, Phyllis K.   **869**.

Zambrano, Ana Laura   **87**, **88**.
Zeiss, Cecilia   **910**.

# SUBJECT INDEX

This index does not cover the Introduction to this volume. Works by Dickens other than **Hard Times** are listed below, under his name. Works by other authors are not listed (see index of proper names for references by authors' names). Characters in **Hard Times** are listed by name. References to characters in other novels by Dickens are subsumed under the references to the novels.

Action. **See** Plot, etc.
Aesthetics and art   14, 160, 165, 195, 288, 290, 294, 325, 337, 376, 379, 471, 472, 874.
Alienation   392, 460, 576, 616 (**see also** Disorder **and related entries**).
**All the Year Round**   368, 766, 802.
Allegory   196, 199, 229, 500, 517, 524, 549, 559, 565, 624, 628, 679, 740, 751, 770, 815, 829, 873.
Allusion   539, 772, 773, 791, 840, 882.
Autobiographical issues   157, 176, 178, 225, 310, 374, 392, 529, 548, 560, 564, 672, 708, 782, 790, 861.

Bible. **See** Religion, Christianity, and the Bible.
Bibliography   43, 45, 51, 84, 874, 895, 896, 911–928.
Bitzer   61, 106, 196, 223, 311, 315, 357, 365, 409, 427, 436, 444, 491, 553, 604, 621, 682, 706, 747, 752, 761, 870, 910.
Blackpool, Stephen   1, 6, 10, 11, 14, 54, 55, 66, 69, 70, 71, 79, 83, 90, 91, 98, 99, 100, 106, 112, 113, 118, 120, 122, 129, 136, 153, 162, 171, 178, 179, 196, 200, 201, 208, 218, 221, 226, 241, 252, 256, 260, 268, 271, 276, 284, 294, 308, 310, 320, 322, 337, 346, 349, 363, 365, 382, 385, 386, 405, 407, 409, 410, 416, 418, 420, 424, 427, 428, 429, 443, 450, 457, 468, 474, 475, 485, 489, 500, 507, 508, 511, 517, 524, 535, 539, 540, 546, 547, 548, 553, 561, 572, 573, 574, 579, 589, 615, 624, 629, 631, 634, 644, 646, 666, 669, 674, 682, 692, 699, 701, 705, 706, 711, 714, 719, 731, 732, 738, 745, 750, 752, 757, 778, 779, 782, 787, 794, 811, 813, 815, 816, 817, 830, 832, 835, 840, 852, 857, 860, 861, 869, 876, 880, 882, 888, 903.
Blackpool, Mrs.   55, 98, 106, 752, 761, 830.
Blue Books. **See** Parliament and Blue Books.

Bounderby, Josiah   15, 17, 19, 54, 55, 70, 78, 80, 90, 99, 102, 106, 112,
    117, 120, 128, 133, 136, 150, 153, 155, 171, 178, 192, 194, 196, 204,
    205, 212, 214, 215, 217, 225, 252, 260, 268, 283, 284, 315, 322, 334,
    340, 347, 349, 357, 369, 372, 373, 382, 385, 386, 392, 400, 405, 407,
    409, 420, 426, 427, 428, 429, 442, 448, 450, 468, 474, 493, 496, 507,
    510, 511, 516, 517, 524, 529, 534, 540, 547, 548, 550, 552, 561, 564,
    572, 574, 579, 585, 588, 598, 615, 622, 624, 644, 650, 653, 657, 661,
    663, 666, 669, 682, 688, 710, 715, 716, 732, 750, 752, 757, 760, 761,
    765, 788, 790, 792, 816, 820, 824, 828, 832, 846, 849, 852, 861, 865,
    882, 888, 910.
Brother/sister relationship   551, 573, 726 (see also Incest).

Capitalism   226, 326, 335, 337, 358, 375, 433, 440, 455, 468, 488, 646,
    674, 733, 832 (see also Industrialism and related entries).
Caricature and exaggeration   114, 117, 121, 123, 134, 195, 270, 326,
    372, 379, 493, 512, 529, 663, 719, 733, 774, 782, 818, 822, 910.
Characterization   80, 113, 120, 125, 141, 150, 155, 169, 196, 218, 235,
    255, 260, 294, 299, 314, 315, 341, 352, 353, 354, 365, 372, 386, 400,
    403, 408, 449, 467, 483, 517, 533, 569, 589, 596, 688, 742, 752, 774,
    775, 780, 785, 840, 842, 869, 888, 895, 919 (see also Caricature
    and exaggeration).
Characters.   See individual names.
Childers, E.W.B.   106, 409, 869.
Children and childhood   1, 13, 14, 157, 167, 208, 210, 214, 279, 289,
    302, 304, 327, 333, 345, 369, 377, 405, 406, 409, 436, 448, 480, 485,
    504, 574, 580, 621, 662, 672, 697, 707, 767, 805, 841, 863 (see also
    Education).
Christianity.   See Religion, Christianity, and the Bible.
Circus (clowns)   1, 91, 122, 127, 133, 136, 146, 159, 162, 171, 174, 179,
    184, 192, 199, 242, 247, 252, 280, 288, 290, 297, 303, 311, 323, 326,
    327, 334, 344, 360, 365, 400, 409, 415, 420, 426, 431, 434, 438, 452,
    462, 468, 471, 484, 500, 513, 528, 535, 539, 545, 548, 553, 556, 560,
    573, 574, 577, 579, 584, 585, 599, 615, 621, 626, 637, 659, 692, 694,
    714, 719, 745, 751, 752, 782, 787, 803, 810, 816, 822, 832, 861, 862
    (see also Horses).
City   482, 642, 682, 833, 851 (see also Coketown).
Clocks   206, 599.
Coketown   15, 79, 119, 120, 127, 128, 156, 158, 159, 173, 177, 199, 208,
    214, 235, 242, 252, 354, 360, 365, 368, 391, 392, 401, 405, 407, 464,
    467, 468, 482, 502, 539, 559, 561, 571, 574, 580, 585, 599, 608, 616,
    623, 637, 640, 641, 676, 678, 693, 730, 744, 751, 756, 757, 758, 784,
    790, 811, 816, 832, 851, 864, 882, 894, 907 (see also Setting) loca-
    tion of   1, 220, 336, 341, 375, 398, 443, 530, 531, 548, 608, 613,
    716, 825, 882, 884, 893.
Comedy   235, 271, 462, 593, 732 (see also Humor).
Compression (restriction of space, crowding, condensation)   1, 10, 115,
    118, 133, 162, 196, 227, 294, 302, 319, 326, 355, 367, 375, 401, 533,

553, 564, 631, 632, 668, 742, 831, 859, 869, 890 (**see also** Economy).

Condition-of-England novel 164, 176, 203, 236, 286, 297, 525, 566, 576, 581, 723, 821 (**see also** Industrialism **and related entries**).

Creativity 643 (**see also** Fancy **and related entries**).

Crime and criminals 281, 332, 491.

Critical history 162, 170, 293, 341, 387, 401, 405, 420, 429, 466, 483, 537, 564, 597, 624, 632, 695, 700, 830, 874, 888, 904, 915, 926.

"Dark" novel 175, 261, 266, 326, 460, 499, 667, 774.

Death 172, 543, 579, 643.

Dialect 10, 49, 221, 252, 294, 359, 410, 443, 463, 548, 658, 659, 666, 691, 748, 877, 880, 890.

Dickens, Charles, other works by:

**American Notes** 532;

**Barnaby Rudge** 25, 26, 28, 213, 558;

**Bleak House** 2, 31, 152, 161, 174, 175, 185, 188, 200, 213, 222, 230, 263, 267, 295, 330, 353, 377, 387, 389, 405, 412, 446, 451, 468, 478, 489, 490, 495, 537, 630, 664, 665, 720, 724, 730, 734, 757, 769, 790, 799, 807;

**A Child's History of England** 664;

**The Chimes** 12, 187, 457, 493, 670;

Christmas Books 33, 532, 829;

**A Christmas Carol** 16, 255;

**David Copperfield** 187, 253, 352, 377, 388, 524, 542, 629, 648, 664, 818, 867;

**Dombey and Son** 136, 152, 161, 167, 174, 188, 244, 250, 253, 288, 300, 348, 407, 427, 440, 446, 449, 451, 463, 566, 572, 580, 584, 598, 611, 642, 656, 664, 679, 750, 854;

"Frauds on the Fairies" 1, 14, 579, 904;

"Full Report of the ... Mudfog Association" 13, 45, 174;

"George Silverman's Explanation" 29, 53, 112;

**Great Expectations** 34, 112, 128, 161, 175, 243, 270, 300, 324, 388, 427, 440, 449, 566, 567, 623, 630, 651, 719, 769, 799, 867, 900;

"Holiday Romance" 29, 53, 112;

"Hunted Down" 29, 53, 112;

Letters **1**, **2**, 43, 45, 368, 374, 766, 867, 872, 916;

**Little Dorrit** 126, 149, 161, 217, 230, 249, 293, 387, 405, 427, 440, 451, 489, 490, 495, 508, 515, 517, 561, 566, 583, 630, 665, 690, 720, 724, 730;

**Martin Chuzzlewit** 152, 200, 213, 353, 400, 517, 551, 651, 818;

**Master Humphrey's Clock** 111;

**The Mystery of Edwin Drood** **282**, 383, 673;

**Nicholas Nickleby** 146, 167, 253, 330, 343, 400, 410;

"No Thoroughfare" 36, 108;

The Old Curiosity Shop    128, 337, 341, 343, 354, 355, 372, 528,
        734, 757, 800;
Oliver Twist    190, 191, 229, 281, 343, 372, 388, 451, 503;
"On Strike"    14, 43, 561;
Our Mutual Friend    15, 175, 229, 243, 263, 288, 291, 315, 348, 440,
        449, 451, 455, 536, 542, 545, 630, 684, 800;
Pickwick Papers    119, 172, 383, 684;
Pictures from Italy    27, 532;
Reprinted Pieces    112;
Sketches by Boz    32, 242, 532;
A Tale of Two Cities    207, 213, 230, 313, 315, 324, 388, 558, 630,
        670, 673, 722, 746, 788;
"To Working Men"    14, 43.
Didacticism   See Novel of purpose, etc.
Discontinuity   175, 543 (see also Disorder and related entries).
Disguise   517.
Disorder   673, 816 (see also Alienation, Discontinuity, Disruption).
Disruption   765 (see also Disorder and related entries).
Divorce   14, 83, 114, 118, 119, 178, 250, 294, 338, 403, 470, 631, 644,
        738, 768, 799, 874 (see also Marriage).
Dogs   1, 97, 128, 277, 411, 556, 682, 780 (see also Merrylegs).
Dream   200, 485, 778, 860, 861.
Dystopia   395, 420, 618, 619.

Economy of the novel   537 (see also Compression).
Editions   8, 10, 45, 911, 916, 925, 927, 928.
Education and schools   1, 2, 13, 14, 16, 79, 86, 114, 120, 122, 127, 128,
        132, 139, 142, 160, 167, 174, 180, 208, 209, 210, 233, 236, 253, 260,
        288, 291, 294, 300, 304, 308, 311, 312, 332, 345, 358, 364, 365, 369,
        371, 374, 379, 392, 397, 405, 406, 415, 417, 421, 424, 426, 429, 430,
        438, 439, 447, 449, 464, 476, 480, 483, 484, 486, 501, 534, 540, 564,
        596. 597, 604. 605, 606, 620, 623, 637, 662, 668, 671, 675, 695, 696,
        698, 713, 715, 737, 751, 762, 775, 783, 797, 809, 815, 829, 835, 874,
        875, 876, 882, 907 (see also Children and childhood).
Ending   447, 521, 573, 735.
Exaggeration.   See Caricature and exaggeration.

Fable.   See Moral fable.
Factory accidents   6, 10, 14, 147, 382.
Facts and figures (statistics)   12, 13, 114, 119, 128, 130, 137, 138, 142,
        144, 148, 162, 174, 186, 206, 322, 364, 369, 395, 421, 430, 467, 467,
        469, 471, 474, 487, 491, 550, 574, 588, 604, 636, 637, 671, 694, 713,
        717, 744, 755, 761, 766, 769, 780, 797, 800, 803, 804, 806, 834, 875,
        882.
Fairy-tale (nursery tale), Hard Times as   208, 386, 463, 577, 628, 756,
        780, 800.

Fairy-tale, in **Hard Times**   13, 14, 192, 249, 284, 538, 539, 591, 898 (see also Fancy **and related entries).**
Family   348, 399, 489, 491, 504, 672, 682, 807 (see also Brother/sister relationships, Father/daughter relationships, Father/son relationships, Marriage).
Fancy and imagination   1, 13, 14, 83, 114, 115, 120, 130, 138, 142, 171, 186, 202, 208, 217, 219, 247, 249, 279, 288, 294, 296, 318, 321, 331, 340, 354, 363, 367, 370, 389, 395, 415, 417, 421, 437, 452, 472, 474, 486, 491, 500, 560, 561, 574, 577, 618, 623, 624, 625, 639, 640, 641, 649, 668, 714, 717, 761, 764, 776, 779, 780, 797, 805, 810, 815, 882 (see also Creativity, Fairy-tale, Feelings and affection, Poetry).
Father/daughter relationships   458, 708, 732.
Father, figure of the   328, 560, 580, 861 (see also Father/daughter relationships **and** Father/son relationships).
Father/son relationships   708, 732.
Feasts   828.
Feelings and affection   704, 707, 784 (see also Fancy **and related entries).**
Figure (imagery, metaphor, motif, symbolism)   182, 185, 206, 209, 215, 225, 228, 280, 288, 299, 304, 309, 365, 383, 392, 401, 412, 413, 431, 436, 467, 471, 492, 495, 498, 517, 518, 520, 545, 553, 573, 615, 649, 653, 660, 682, 692, 714, 716, 722, 730, 737, 740, 744, 746, 754, 761, 771, 785, 791, 804, 829, 840, 857, 862, 869, 870, 873, 882, 888, 895, 896.
Fire   202, 383, 498, 517, 660, 776, 888.

Genre   208, 363, 429 (see also **various genres).**
Gradgrind, Louisa   4, 11, 69, 70, 71, 91, 99, 100, 106, 122, 159, 162, 171, 174, 178, 181, 185, 188, 196, 202, 207, 208, 214, 218, 225, 243, 244, 247, 254, 260, 262, 270, 332, 335, 347, 348, 364, 369, 400, 407, 425, 426, 427, 429, 436, 444, 446, 448, 449, 453, 458, 471, 474, 478, 489, 491, 511, 513, 517, 545, 547, 549, 564, 582, 615, 617, 623, 628, 636, 657, 682, 701, 708, 719, 731, 732, 734, 735, 752, 754, 776, 780, 808, 815, 819, 822, 829, 836, 840, 854, 855, 858, 861, 864, 888, 910.
Gradgrind, Mrs.   106, 254, 367, 369, 513, 656, 682, 691, 752, 759, 761, 861.
Gradgrind, Thomas   1, 12, 55, 59, 61, 69, 79, 99, 100, 106, 114, 117, 120, 127, 128, 134, 136, 139, 142, 152, 153, 165, 167, 174, 180, 181, 194, 196, 204, 210, 214, 218, 233, 236, 246, 255, 259, 276, 280, 281, 284, 288, 300, 304, 311, 315, 317, 334, 340, 342, 348, 363, 367, 369, 379, 380, 382, 392, 397, 405, 406, 407, 408, 420, 426, 427, 429, 430, 431, 436, 442, 444, 446, 448, 457, 458, 467, 475, 487, 491, 493, 511, 513, 516, 534, 536, 549, 550, 552, 560, 561, 574, 577, 580, 585, 588, 598, 599, 601, 609, 610, 611, 617, 621, 628, 629, 637, 644, 650, 657, 660, 661, 662, 666, 669, 671, 677, 682, 708, 710, 713, 715, 716, 717, 732, 737, 750, 752, 754, 755, 759, 761, 764, 766, 769, 792, 798, 807, 810, 815, 817, 818, 820, 827, 830, 848, 864, 865, 870, 882, 891, 898, 910.

Gradgrind, Tom (Thomas Jr.)   54, 55, 91, 95, 99, 100, 106, 112, 122,
     171, 181, 184, 218, 242, 260, 332, 347, 348, 364, 425, 426, 427, 436,
     444, 453, 458, 507, 513, 545, 574, 577, 615, 624, 630, 682, 708, 710,
     715, 716, 732, 752, 761, 778, 815, 819, 830, 858, 861, 864, 865, 882.
Grotesque   280, 353, 360, 372, 464, 752, 756.
Guilt   245, 778.

Harthouse, James   91, 99, 112, 114, 122, 153, 205, 238, 283, 284, 300,
     315, 347, 363, 409, 428, 446, 453, 467, 471, 474, 478, 507, 511, 542,
     628, 629, 630, 644, 661, 682, 706, 738, 812, 840, 882.
Horses   167, 246, 288, 556, 682 (**see also** Circus).
**Household Words**   1, 2, 4, 6, 11, **14**, **18**, 24, 43, 45, 123, 133, 147, 148,
     156, 166, 178, 234, 241, 279, 287, 292, 294, 334, 368, 373, 374, 376,
     379, 381, 415, 417, 529, 561, 573, 583, 664, 757, 766, 855, 872, 882,
     904, 911.
Humor   80, 114, 121, 128, 162, 247, 260, 313, 325, 326, 353, 400, 418,
     510, 516, 537, 569, 631, 632, 634, 688, 712, 738, 739, 757, 788, 869,
     895 (**see also** Comedy).

Ideology   191, 223, 228, 251, 358, 399, 421, 429, 447, 455, 551, 564,
     576, 685, 745, 751, 832 (**see also** Industrialism **and related en-
     tries**).
Idyllic, the   492.
Imagery. **See** Figure.
Imagination. **See** Fancy and imagination.
Incest   171, 332, 425, 453, 485, 545 (**see also** Brother/sister relation-
     ships **and** Sexuality).
Industrialism   2, 14, 79, 113, 118, 120, 122, 123, 125, 126, 147, 150, 156,
     188, 198, 199, 204, 216, 231, 252, 259, 260, 286, 289, 294, 302, 308,
     314, 316, 319, 330, 337, 341, 345, 347, 355, 357, 358, 366, 371, 375,
     392, 414, 418, 429, 433, 438, 446, 450, 461, 471, 475, 493, 500, 502,
     503, 509, 512, 529, 535, 541, 547, 558, 561, 562, 563, 573, 585, 596,
     598, 603, 616, 617, 618, 619, 622, 625, 631, 642, 695, 712, 714, 727,
     732, 741, 745, 751, 757, 771, 774, 782, 786, 787, 794, 801, 816, 823,
     836, 841, 845, 848, 849, 851, 856, 874, 876, 894, 915 (**see also**
     Capitalism, Condition-of-England novel, Factory accidents, Ideolo-
     gy, Machinery, Paternalism, Politics, Social Criticsm, **and** Trade
     Unions).

Jupe, Cecelia (Sissy)   11, 55, 61, 91, 99, 106, 114, 120, 122, 127, 128,
     136, 137, 176, 185, 188, 191, 198, 223, 242, 243, 249, 254, 279, 323,
     327, 337, 347, 354, 363, 365, 369, 376, 401, 427, 444, 446, 458, 463,
     467, 469, 474, 477, 485, 511, 512, 513, 545, 553, 564, 599, 617, 621,
     623, 624, 628, 636, 641, 642, 657, 682, 706, 710, 714, 737, 738, 752,
     761, 780, 793, 803, 815, 817, 870, 882, 888, 898.
Jupe, Signor   55, 242, 844.

Kidderminster   106, 869.

Language  221, 520, 555, 591, 653, 657, 659, 691, 692, 776, 919.
Letters of Dickens.  **See** Dickens, Charles, other works by.
Love  186, 199, 218, 279, 332, 333, 420, 469, 472, 491, 511, 545, 623,
    624, 625, 626, 737, 905 (**see also** Incest **and** Sexuality).

Machinery  6, 156, 228, 241, 321, 405, 787 (**see also** Industrialism **and**
    **related entries**).
Manuscript  2, 6, 7, 9, 10, 45, 481, 659, 804.
Marriage  188, 244, 284, 332, 369, 392, 489, 661, 813, 854 (**see also**
    Divorce).
M'Choakumchild  2, 61, 106, 132, 205, 270, 276, 288, 291, 312, 340, 345,
    382, 397, 428, 429, 430, 442, 463, 572, 604, 605, 666, 698, 737, 770,
    809, 837, 846.
Melodrama  119, 174, 222, 271, 325, 334, 364, 386, 537, 643, 814, 004.
Merrylegs  97, 411, 666, 844, 891.
Mesmerism  511.
Metaphor.  **See** Figure.
Metaphysical novel  363.
Money  715, 799, 816.
Montage  391.
Moral fable or drama  2, 162, 164, 219, 284, 321, 375, 471, 472, 500,
    507, 526, 553, 660, 678, 736, 745, 751,, 764, 818, 843, 873, 878, 882,
    895, 896.
Motif.  **See** Figure.
Music  64, 65, 572.
Myth  420, 472, 482, 573, 611, 682, 888.

Names  205, 409, 428, 442, 550, 552, 555, 666, 706, 710, 770, 846, 876.
Narrator  249, 349, 546, 600, 653, 761, 776, 819, 830 (**see also** Point of
    view, narration).
Narration.  **See** Point of view, narration.
Narrative structure.  **See** Plot, etc.
Nature  482, 535, 641, 682, 752, 793, 888.
New Comedy  395.
Novel of purpose, didacticism, pamphlet fiction, propaganda  179, 190,
    268, 325, 326, 355, 366, 433, 505, 512, 515, 558, 559, 574, 575, 583,
    587, 589, 624, 686, 720, 763, 764, 770, 774, 818, 822, 829, 858, 859,
    882, 890.
Number plans  2, 45, 238, 240, 300, 381, 691, 753, 842.

Pantomime  576.
Parable.  **See** Sermon, parable.
Parliament and Blue Books  14, 126, 173, 424, 520, 547, 612, 755, 798.
Paternalism  701.
Pathos.  **See** Sentimentality, etc.
Pegler, Mrs.  106, 428, 760.
Philosophic materialism  172.

Plot, narrative structure, action   114, 141, 226, 235, 299, 305, 325, 326, 367, 399, 400, 426, 533, 537, 589, 629, 719, 729, 752, 774, 778, 816, 829, 872, 873, 882, 888, 895, 919.
Poetry, as theme   119, 138, 621 (**see also** Fancy **and related entries**).
Poetry or imaginative structure, **Hard Times** as   118, 216, 219, 228, 247, 354, 370, 427, 553, 590, 876.
Point of view, narration   207, 212, 349, 392, 919.
Political economy.   **See** Utilitarianism, political economy.
Politics   37, 128, 265, 339, 362, 368, 370, 612 (**see also** Industrialism **and related entries**).
Powler   706.
Proof copy   4, 5, 6, 10, 11, 45, 381, 659.
Propaganda.   **See** Novel of purpose, etc.
Purpose.   **See** Novel of purpose, etc.

Rachael   4, 6, 10, 11, 54, 69, 70, 71, 91, 99, 106, 112, 120, 122, 136, 179, 185, 188, 198, 218, 221, 241, 242, 271, 515, 529, 545, 546, 560, 573, 589, 629, 631, 634, 669, 719, 731, 750, 782, 787, 793, 840, 861, 869, 870.
Realism, probability   79, 196, 228, 308, 337, 472, 500, 540, 586, 615, 628, 660, 711, 733, 745, 751, 756, 769, 771, 774, 818, 829, 888.
Reification and mechanization of people   228, 371, 606, 811.
Religion, Christianity, and the Bible   117, 129, 158, 171, 186, 199, 209, 249, 256, 279, 290, 320, 358, 363, 386, 464, 469, 523, 574, 592, 669, 671, 680, 682, 687, 699, 713, 714, 772, 773, 776, 815, 828, 833, 840, 882, 888.
Rhetoric in **Hard Times**   468, 471, 836.
Rhetoric and style of **Hard Times**   113, 114, 118, 120, 222, 303, 326, 427, 431, 441, 452, 473, 476, 510, 546, 574, 577, 585, 631, 632, 720, 732, 784, 810, 832, 851, 872, 888, 895, 900, 919.
Romance   170, 579, 586, 781.

Sales (cost)   8, 123, 133, 234, 334, 388, 529, 613, 664, 882, 904.
Satire (sarcasm)   71, 79, 153, 155, 162, 191, 204, 207, 218, 242, 254, 288, 303, 308, 316, 338, 372, 376, 380, 403, 404, 427, 464, 471, 475, 484, 499, 540, 541, 575, 593, 606, 622, 670, 712, 728, 739, 745, 782, 788, 827, 828, 833, 874, 882, 888, 895, 910.
Scadgers, Lady   811.
Schools.   **See** Education and schools.
Science   246, 487, 606, 668.
Self-help, self-made man   414, 540, 622, 760, 855.
Sentimentality, mawkishness, pathos   70, 91, 166, 179, 207, 249, 271, 272, 280, 313, 320, 350, 365, 409, 427, 452, 467, 537, 631, 632, 688, 745, 788, 836, 895, 910.
Serialization   18, 20, 43, 166, 237, 240, 241, 275, 297, 341, 381, 435, 567, 631, 724, 725, 753, 895, 904.
Sermon, parable   472, 473, 512, 559, 803.
Setting   329, 391, 413, 667, 919 (**see also** Coketown).

Sexuality 199, 225, 332, 446, 455, 682, 778, 854 (see also Incest).
Sissy Jupe. See Jupe, Cecelia.
Slackbridge 106, 156, 193, 205, 214, 260, 271, 326, 337, 373, 374, 405, 409, 427, 468, 471, 500, 540, 561, 564, 577, 624, 631, 666, 688, 738, 750, 761, 764, 794, 869.
Sleary 1, 10, 106, 120, 128, 137, 219, 221, 276, 278, 284, 294, 304, 311, 426, 427, 428, 459, 462, 472, 635, 639, 640, 657, 659, 682, 691, 706, 737, 765, 876, 882.
Sleary's horse-riding. See Circus.
Social criticism (social reform, social thought) 15, 115, 124, 157, 162, 189, 209, 217, 226, 247, 250, 256, 272, 273, 297, 302, 311, 396, 399, 400, 407, 441, 447, 499, 500, 520, 537, 540, 569, 595, 610, 612, 632, 634, 652, 670, 681, 685, 690, 724, 749, 758, 774, 778, 783, 790, 802, 805, 826, 827, 829, 839, 847, 848, 852, 872, 900 (see also Industrialism and related entries).
Socialism 80, 145, 226, 264, 345, 508, 524, 530, 650, 668, 688, 781 (see also Industrialism and related entries).
Sparsit, Mr. 789.
Sparsit, Mrs. 91, 99, 106, 120, 188, 214, 225, 261, 276, 311, 347, 372, 386, 400, 405, 428, 471, 507, 513, 550, 560, 596, 643, 682, 710, 732, 751, 752, 761, 788, 840, 888, 898, 910.
Statistics. See Facts and figures.
Strikes. See Trade unions, strikes.
Style. See Rhetoric and style.
Symbolism. See Figure.

Theme 170, 186, 196, 219, 222, 259, 271, 288, 305, 309, 413, 444, 455, 468, 492, 541, 564, 579, 623, 660, 665, 684, 714, 730, 816, 870, 872, 882, 919.
Time 230, 377, 474.
Titles, for Hard Times 1, 133, 497, 530, 533, 700, 784, 831.
Trade unions, strikes 1, 135, 176, 186, 215, 227, 251, 284, 322, 365, 368, 370, 373, 427, 457, 489, 515, 534, 541, 553, 564, 574, 581, 606, 678, 679, 694, 731, 738, 749, 751, 758, 764, 790, 803, 817, 855, 857. (see also Industrialism and related entries).

United States of America, the 76, 80, 213, 664, 803, 900.
Utilitarianism, political economy 2, 14, 86, 115, 118, 128, 138, 139, 144, 155, 160, 171, 176, 177, 191, 207, 211, 217, 223, 231, 252, 257, 285, 297, 305, 338, 343, 347, 365, 395, 401, 404, 414, 415, 421, 429, 438, 452, 486, 493, 512, 525, 534, 540, 541, 547, 565, 609, 621, 625, 631, 653, 661, 694, 713, 715, 732, 737, 742, 745, 751, 758, 765, 775, 817, 841, 843, 847, 848, 850, 907, 910. (see also Bentham and Mill in index of proper names).

Visual effects 391, 464.

Women   185, 188, 198, 243, 244, 254, 262, 263, 270, 478, 495, 582, 589,
   606, 731, 854.